THE PLAN DE SAN DIEGO

Charles H. Harris III and Louis R. Sadler
University of Nebraska Press | Lincoln and London

The Mexican Experience | William H. Beezley, series editor

THE PLAN DE SAN DIEGO

Tejano Rebellion, Mexican Intrigue

Manufactured in the United States of America

♾

Library of Congress Cataloging-in-Publication Data
Harris, Charles H. (Charles Houston)
The Plan de San Diego: Tejano rebellion, Mexican intrigue / Charles H. Harris III and Louis R. Sadler.
pages cm. — (The Mexican experience)
Includes bibliographical references and index.
ISBN 978-0-8032-6477-9 (pbk.: alk. paper)
1. Plan de San Diego. 2. Insurrections—Texas—History—20th century. 3. Subversive activities—Texas—History—20th century. 4. Mexico—History—Revolution, 1910–1920—Diplomatic history.
5. Mexico—History—Revolution, 1910–1920—Social aspects. 6. Mexican Americans—Texas—History—20th century. 7. Texas—Relations—Mexico. 8. Mexico—Relations—Texas. 9. Texas—History, 1846–1950.
I. Sadler, Louis R. II. Title.
F391.H278 2013
976.4'063—dc23 2012046476

Set in Minion Pro by Laura Wellington.
Designed by Jesse Vadnais.

To William H. Beezley

Contents

Illustrations

Preface

There appeared in South Texas in January 1915 a most remarkable document—the Plan de San Diego. Ostensibly written in the small town of San Diego in Duval County, it called for nothing less than a Hispanic uprising designed to achieve the independence of the Southwest as a Hispanic republic. The Plan proclaimed a genocidal war without quarter against Anglos. The most striking feature of this revolutionary manifesto was a call to kill all Anglo males over the age of sixteen. Predictably, attempts to implement the Plan produced a massive Anglo backlash, and during 1915–16 conditions in the lower Rio Grande valley of Texas deteriorated to the point that a race war seemed imminent. The Plan de San Diego of course had no chance of succeeding, but it left a legacy of racial animosity that endures to the present day.

The Plan and its subsequent modifications remain controversial, both because of their racial aspects and because some events are still obscure. In discussing the Plan, the first question to be addressed is whether the manifesto should even be taken seriously. Especially among Hispanics, the answer is yes, focusing on the oppression endured by Hispanics in Texas. Second, was the insurrection in fact a homegrown Tejano liberation movement? Third, was there substantial involvement from Mexico, guiding, supplying, and manipulating the insurgents? If so, were revolutionary factions or the Mexican government involved? In this connection, some historians have attributed the Plan to the followers of the anarchist Ricardo Flores Magón, others to the followers of the exiled strongman General Victoriano Huerta, still others to the regime of President Venustiano Carranza. There is particular disagreement over whether Carranza himself was involved.[1] The main things in dispute about the Plan de San Diego are who wrote it and when, where, and why it was written. Thus, the definitive study of the Plan has yet to appear.

As far as Anglos and the authorities were concerned, the *sediciosos* (those engaged in sedition) were bandits. Hence, the troubles have been referred to as the "Bandit War." Hispanics quickly point out that many of those involved in the Plan weren't bandits. True, but then many of them weren't freedom fighters either. The Plan de San Diego affair defies simplistic treatment, especially when some of the violence had nothing to do with the Plan. The manifesto provided a splendid umbrella for paying off old scores and seizing new opportunities.

There has developed a considerable literature concerning the Plan de San Diego. However, some of it has been ideologically driven, with disregard for inconvenient facts, or characterized by superficial research and glittering generalities. For instance, there has been no effort made even to determine whether the Plan was actually written in San Diego. In addition, the literature has focused on a few of the *sediciosos*' leaders, with little or no attention to the rank and file. Heretofore, writers have emphasized the background—that is, the conditions that produced the Plan. A number of works have exhaustively addressed these conditions—oppression of and discrimination against Tejanos, loss of their land, abuse by peace officers, especially the Texas Rangers, and so forth.[2]

Our approach is significantly different. From our perspective, what is important isn't who wrote the Plan or when it was written but the use to which it was put and who benefited by that use.[3] What hasn't been investigated is the Mexican connection, and that is our emphasis. As the United States has learned in Afghanistan, when the enemy can operate from a privileged sanctuary, in this case Pakistan, the enemy is much harder to defeat. Regarding the Plan de San Diego, had the *sediciosos* not enjoyed a base of operations in Mexico, the Plan would have been merely a curiosity. But those Mexicans supporting the Plan had their own agendas, and sometimes they differed considerably from the aims of the *sediciosos*. Unfortunately, most of those who have written about the Plan de San Diego do not understand the complexities of the Mexican Revolution. This understanding is crucial to understanding the course of the Plan conspiracy.

Our thesis is that the Plan de San Diego became an instrument of Mexican government policy. In a brilliant covert operation, President

Venustiano Carranza manipulated the *sedicioso* insurgents as pawns in order to gain desperately needed diplomatic recognition in 1915 of his regime by the United States. That objective achieved, Carranza immediately suppressed the Plan and stopped financing it. In an unexpected development, when in 1916 Pancho Villa's raid on Columbus, New Mexico, resulted in the dispatch into Chihuahua of General John J. Pershing's Punitive Expedition, plunging the United States and Mexico into a confrontation, Carranza revived the Plan de San Diego in an effort to force the withdrawal of the Punitive Expedition. The result was the crisis of June 1916, in which the two countries literally came to the brink of outright war. Happily, the war crisis was defused by diplomacy; Carranza promptly shut down the Plan de San Diego once again. The *sedicioso* leadership hiding in Mexico had little alternative but to dance to Carranza's tune. These refugee Tejanos could only watch their movement disintegrate.

We propose to treat not only the insurrection itself but also aspects such as the subsequent careers of some of the protagonists, the continuing controversy over the number of casualties, and some of the more interesting interpretations of the Plan.

The principal United States source we utilize is the archive of the Federal Bureau of Investigation (at the time named the Bureau of Investigation), the agency most directly involved in investigating the Plan. The key files are those available since 1977 on microfilm in what's called "Old Mex 232,"[4] supplemented by files the bureau has recently made available on the Web as "232-84." The bureau's archive provides almost a day-to-day picture of the troubles in South Texas. Like any other law enforcement agency, the bureau relied heavily on informants. An extremely useful source is the affidavit in the Department of State's Office of the Counselor by one Juan K. Forseck, an important Carranza agent who had intimate knowledge of the conspiracy. Supplementing these sources are federal court cases, the Texas Ranger archive, the State Department's Matamoros post records, and the U.S. Army's reports.

As for Mexican sources, there is the multivolume *Documentos Históricos de la Revolución Mexicana* and the papers of General Pablo González. Whereas Forseck's affidavit provides an invaluable window into the conspiracy, by far the most significant Mexican source is the archive of Agustín de la Garza Solís, the leader of the Plan de San Diego and the tragic hero of this affair. The Museum of South Texas History, in Edinburg, recently acquired the Agustín Garza Collection, and this archive lays to rest much of the conjecture and speculation that characterize what has been written about the Plan de San Diego.

In short, the Plan de San Diego affair has significance far beyond just the events in South Texas. It is a striking example of Venustiano Carranza, the leader of a country wracked by revolution, outmaneuvering the Wilson administration. The Plan thus has a direct bearing on the history of U.S.-Mexican relations. Moreover, it had an important impact on the preparedness of the United States for World War I. Whereas we do not presume to have written the definitive account of the Plan, the present work does illuminate heretofore unknown aspects of this fascinating conspiracy.

Acknowledgments

We owe a considerable debt of gratitude to our colleague Jeff Brown, who informed us that the Museum of South Texas History had recently acquired the papers of the Plan de San Diego leader, which was the impetus for writing this book.

Thirty-five years ago (in January 1977 to be precise) one of the authors (Charles Harris) was plowing his way through dozens of reels of microfilm of the Pablo González archive at the Nettie Lee Benson Latin American Collection at the University of Texas at Austin. Buried in the reels was a letter to González from one of his officers with an extraordinary handwritten postscript explaining that he had sent dozens of cavalry disguised as vaqueros across the Rio Grande into Texas to penetrate the interior of the state with plans to attack after midnight on June 10, 1916. A few months later one of the authors (Louis Sadler), after digging through thousands of telegrams in the Carranza archive in Mexico City, found two key telegrams that tied the invasion to the Carranza administration.

Since that time we have persistently pursued the Plan de San Diego, which was what the invasion was about. A number of institutions and individuals have greatly assisted our endeavors. The Weatherhead Foundation, New York City, provided generous financial support for our early research. The Arts and Sciences Research Center at New Mexico State University supported our initial investigation and assisted us in obtaining funding. As indicated above, our earliest work was at the Nettie Lee Benson Collection, arguably the finest collection on Mexico in the United States. We had the great good fortune to both know and consult with the late Dr. Benson. Her staff, including Laura Gutiérrez Witt, Jane Garner, Wanda Turnley, and Carmen Sacomani, was of great assistance over an extended length of time.

Most recently the staff of the Museum of South Texas History were of exceptional help. We thank Shan Rankin, the executive director, Barbara Stokes, the senior curator of archives, and Esteban Lomas, the IT specialist and archives assistant.

At the Lorenzo de Zavala Texas State Library, senior archivist Donaly Brice has for decades patiently answered queries and found documents for us. Photo archivist John Anderson has combed their extensive photo collections on our behalf. The staff of the Texas National Guard at their headquarters at Camp Mabry in Austin allowed us access to their Texas Ranger holdings.

At the Texas Ranger Hall of Fame and Museum in Waco, director Byron Johnson has been more than helpful. His assistant director and archivist Christina Stopka and librarian Christy Smith handled dozens of requests for photographs and documents with unfailing good grace. The staff of the Centro de Estudios Históricos Carso (formerly Condumex) in Mexico City guided us in our research in the huge Venustiano Carranza archive.

At the National Archives (I and II) a number of archivists, including Timothy Nenninger, Sue Falb (before she became FBI historian), Rick Cox (now retired), the late John Taylor, George Chalou, Rebecca Livingston (now retired), Trudy Peterson (now retired), and Mitchell Yokelson, were extraordinarily helpful over a period of decades. The archivists at four Federal Records Centers were most helpful. At Fort Worth the late George Youngkin was extraordinarily helpful; more recently Barbara Rust and Rodney Krajca went out of their way to find court records for us. At the Federal Records Center, Denver, archivist Marene Sweeney Baker helped locate documents for us, as did archivists at the Federal Records Center Laguna Nigel, California, and the Federal Records Center, East Point, Georgia.

We thank the archivists at the British National Archive, Kew (formerly the Public Record Office), for their courtesy to a non-British historian. In Austin, Texas, Paul Harris obtained for us an extremely important and virtually unobtainable document some years ago. We are extraordinarily indebted to him for his assistance. In addition, he intervened in our behalf to enable us to copy key court documents in Brownsville and Laredo.

This manuscript required some unique assistance. Our friend David

Kahn, the historian of American cryptanalysis, was consulted regarding how we might attack the coded messages in the Garza archive. We took David's advice and had the good fortune to obtain the assistance of Colonel John Smith, U.S. Army, Retired. Colonel Smith, as we noted in our footnotes, was an Army Security Agency cryptanalyst during his army career, and he cryptanalyzed a key coded telegram in the Garza papers.

We thank the courteous and highly competent staff of the Manuscript Division of the Library of Congress, who made several weeks of recent research both productive and pleasant.

For a number of years we compiled lists of documents relating directly and indirectly to the Plan de San Diego found in the name indexes in the Mexican Foreign Relations Archive (Archivo de Relaciones Exteriores de México). Elena Albarrán, who took her PhD at the University of Arizona under Professor William Beezley, copied these documents for us while she was doing her dissertation research. She has graduated and is now teaching Mexican history at Ohio University. We thank her for her assistance. A former graduate student, Bill Boehm, whose thesis Ray Sadler directed, was of considerable help in locating documents in various Washington archives. Bill is now a National Guard historian in Arlington, Virginia.

We benefited from discussions with colleagues Colin MacLaughlin, Friedrich Schuler, Lawrence Taylor, Jeff Pilcher, Daniel Newcomer, José Garcia, Tim Kraft, Jim Hurst, Theo Crevenna, Frank Rafalko, Floyd Geery, and Jack Wilson. We miss our friends Michael Meyer, Ricardo Aguilar-Melantzon, Bill Timmons, Thomas F. McGann, and Jack McGrew, all of whom assisted us over a period of decades; we mourn their absence.

A decade ago David Holtby, who edited our first two books before he retired, talked to us about this one. At the Department of History at New Mexico State, department head Jon Hunner tolerated with good grace two emeritus historians whose office was slightly overgrown with documents.

History Department secretary Mary Herrera was a constant help clearing paper jams on departmental printers, among other things. We thank her. Finally, our former student and now colleague Mark

Milliorn, a computer genius and historian par excellence, pulled us out of more computer jams than either of us is willing to admit. What we will admit is that this manuscript would not be going off to the press without his extraordinary assistance.

We end these acknowledgments by thanking our friend and colleague William Beezley of the University of Arizona, who encouraged us to write the book years ago and invited us to place it in the Latin American series he edits for the University of Nebraska Press.

MAP 1. South Texas and northeastern Mexico. Created by Alma D. Pacheco, 2012.

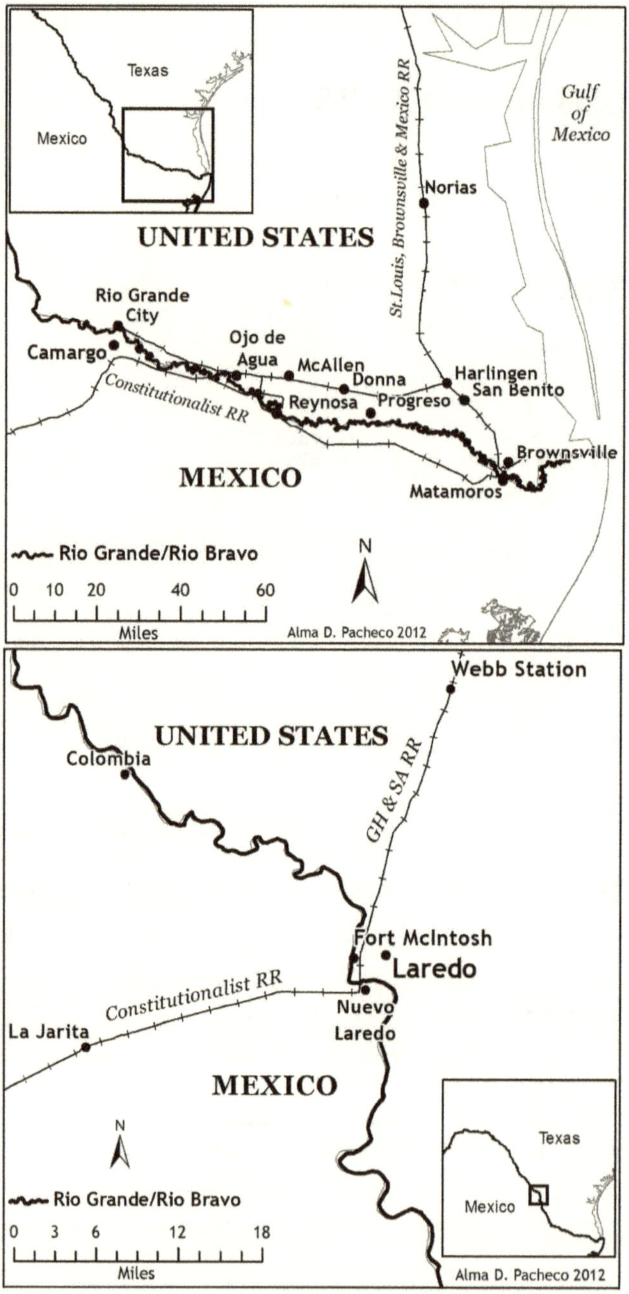

MAP 2. Lower Rio Grande, Texas side (*above*) and Mexican side (*below*). Created by Alma D. Pacheco, 2012.

THE PLAN DE SAN DIEGO

1 The Plan de San Diego

The most extraordinary indictment ever handed down in an American court was issued in Laredo, Texas, on May 13, 1915, charging nine individuals with conspiring "to steal certain property of the United States of America, contrary to the authority thereof, to wit, the states of Texas, Oklahoma, New Mexico, Arizona, Colorado, and California."[1] Their offense was being the signers of the Plan de San Diego, a manifesto allegedly promulgated in the South Texas town of San Diego (population approximately 2,500 and 75 percent Hispanic), on January 6, 1915. The manifesto called for nothing less than a Hispanic insurrection and the creation of an independent Hispanic republic in the Southwest:

TRANSLATION[2]

PROVISIONAL DIRECTORATE

OF THE

PLAN OF SAN DIEGO, TEX.

PLAN (PLOT) OF SAN DIEGO, STATE OF TEXAS,

JANUARY 6TH, 1915

We who in turn sign our names, assembled in the REVOLUTIONARY PLOT OF SAN DIEGO, TEXAS, solemnly promise each other, on our word of honor, that we will fulfill, and cause to be fulfilled and complied with, all the clauses and provisions stipulated in this document, and execute the orders and the wishes emanating from the PROVISIONAL DIRECTORATE of this movement, and recognize as military Chief of the same, MR. AGUSTIN S. GARZA, guaranteeing with our lives the faithful accomplishment of what is here agreed upon.

1. On the 20th day of February, 1915, at two o'clock in the morning, we will arise in arms against the Government and Country of the United States of North America, ONE AS ALL AND ALL AS ONE, proclaiming the liberty of the individuals of the black race and its independence of Yankee tyranny which has held us in iniquitous slavery since remote times; and at the same time and in the same manner we will proclaim the independence and segregation of the states bordering upon the Mexican Nation, which are: TEXAS, NEW MEXICO, ARIZONA, COLORADO, and UPPER CALIFORNIA, of which states the REPUBLIC OF MEXICO was robbed in a most perfidious manner by North American imperialism.
2. In order to render the foregoing clause effective, the necessary army corps will be formed, under the immediate command of military leaders named by the SUPREME REVOLUTIONARY CONGRESS OF SAN DIEGO, TEXAS, which shall have full power to designate a SUPREME CHIEF, who shall be at the head of said army. The banner which shall guide us in this enterprise shall be red, with a white diagonal fringe, and bearing the following inscription: "EQUALITY AND INDEPENDENCE," and none of the subordinate leaders or subalterns shall use any other flag (except only the white flag for signals). The aforesaid army shall be known by the name of: "LIBERATING ARMY FOR RACES AND PEOPLES."
3. Each one of the chiefs will do his utmost, by whatever means possible to get possession of the arms and funds of the cities which he has beforehand been designated to capture, in order that our cause may be provided with resources to continue the fight with better success, the said leaders each being required to render an account of everything to his superiors, in order that the latter may dispose of it in the proper manner.
4. The leader who may take a city must immediately name and appoint municipal authorities, in order that they may preserve order and assist

in every way possible the revolutionary movement. In case the Capital of any State which we are endeavoring to liberate be captured, there will be named in the same manner superior municipal authorities, for the same purpose.

5. It is strictly forbidden to hold prisoners, either special prisoners (civilians) or soldiers; and the only time that should be spent in dealing with them is that which is absolutely necessary to demand funds (loans) of them; and whether these demands be successful or not, they shall be shot immediately, without any pretext.
6. Every stranger who shall be found armed and who cannot prove his right to carry arms, shall be summarily executed, regardless of his race or nationality.
7. Every North American over sixteen years of age shall be put to death; and only the aged men, the women, and the children shall be respected; and on no account shall the traitors to our race be spared or respected.
8. The APACHES of Arizona, as well as the INDIANS (Redskins) of the territory, shall be given every guarantee; and their lands which have been taken from them shall be returned to them, to the end that they may assist us in the cause which we defend.
9. All appointments and grades in our army which are exercised by subordinate officers (subalterns) shall be examined (recognized) by the superior officers. There shall likewise be recognized the grades of leaders of other complots which may not be connected with this, and who may wish to co-operate with us; also those who may affiliate with us later.
10. The movement having gathered force, and once having possessed ourselves of the States above alluded to, we shall proclaim them an INDEPENDENT REPUBLIC, later requesting (if it be thought expedient) annexation to MEXICO, without concerning ourselves at that time about the form of government which may control the destinies of the common mother country.
11. When we shall have obtained independence for the negroes, we shall grant them a banner, which they themselves shall be permitted to select, and we shall aid them in obtaining six States of the American union, which states border upon those already mentioned, and they may form

from these six States a republic, and they may be, therefore, independent.

12. None of the leaders shall have power to make terms with the enemy without first communicating with the superior officers of the army, bearing in mind that this is a war without quarter; nor shall any leader enroll in his ranks any stranger, unless said stranger belong to the Latin, the Negro, or the Japanese race.
13. It is understood that none of the members of this COMPLOT (or any one who may come in later), shall, upon the definite triumph of the cause which we defend, fail to recognize their superiors, nor shall they aid others who, with bastard designs, may endeavor to destroy what has been accomplished by such great work.
14. As soon as possible, each local society (junta) shall nominate delegates who shall meet at a time and place beforehand designated, for the purpose of nominating a PERMANENT DIRECTORATE OF THE REVOLUTIONARY MOVEMENT. At this meeting shall be determined and worked out in detail the powers and duties of the PERMANENT DIRECTORATE, and this REVOLUTIONARY PLAN may be revised or amended.
15. It is understood among those who may follow this movement that we will carry as a singing voice the independence of the negroes, placing obligations upon both races; and that, on no account will we accept aid either moral or pecuniary, from the Government of Mexico; and it need not consider itself under any obligations in this, our movement.

"EQUALITY AND INDEPENDENCE"
San Diego, Texas, Jan. 6, 1915

President. [Signed] L. Ferrigno.
Secretary. [Signed] A. González.

[Signed] A. S. Garza
[Signed] Manuel Flores
[Signed] B. Ramos, Jr.
[Signed] A. A. Saenz
[Signed] F. Cisneros
[Signed] Porfirio Santos
[Signed] A. G. Almaraz

This visionary Plan is interesting in several respects. First is the matter of whose ox is being gored. Hispanic militants were outraged that Americans stole Texas from the Mexicans—"who stole it from the Spaniards, who stole it from the Indians, who stole it from each other."

Second, the social justice envisioned virtually ignored Indian claims. Aside from a nod toward Arizona Apaches, there was no reference to other tribes whose claims to land presumably had equal merit. Third, the future of blacks lay not in a Southwest ruled by Hispanics but in an independent South. However, blacks would be permitted to select a flag of their very own. Last, and most intriguing, was the reference to Japanese. The Plan embodied no concern for Asians in general, for it mentioned only Japanese.[3]

2 The Plan Surfaces

The Plan de San Diego came to light on January 23, 1915, at the town of McAllen in Hidalgo County, Texas, with the arrest of one Basilio Ramos Jr. He was a Mexican citizen, single, twenty-four years old, five feet eleven inches tall, with dark hair and black eyes, weighing about 140 pounds, and having a mole on the upper left corner of his mouth and a small one on his nose. He had two suitcases filled with expensive clothing and about twenty-five dollars in cash. An immigration inspector described him as having an "intelligent-looking face."[1] Ramos was one of the signers of the Plan and was in town trying to persuade Dr. Andrés Villarreal to support the manifesto.

Villarreal was a wealthy physician who had been Pancho Villa's chief medical officer and was currently the principal *villista* representative in the lower Rio Grande valley. Villarreal was busy organizing filibustering expeditions of *villistas* to cross the Rio Grande and strike at the *carrancistas* in northeastern Mexico.[2] According to Bureau of Investigation agent Frank McDevitt, certain Mexicans, assisted by some Anglo local and county officers, were busily recruiting *villistas* in Brownsville, Mercedes, Donna, McAllen, Mission, Sam Fordyce, and Rio Grande City for military service in Mexico. Their problem was that Carranza forces controlled the border across the Rio Grande from these towns.

Those allegedly the most active were:

Dr. Villarreal, McAllen, Texas
Deodoro Guerra, McAllen, Texas
Ysidro Valli [Ballí?], Deputy Sheriff, Donna, Texas
A. Y. Baker, Hidalgo County Sheriff
José Castillo, residing between Mission and Sam Fordyce, Texas
Everett Anglin, former Customs officer, now city marshal at McAllen[3]

These people played rough. The bureau agent emphasized that "They have an active and efficient secret service system and do not hesitate to kill to preserve their organization and their 'concentration camps.'" Recently one Eloy, a Carranza operative masquerading as a U.S. agent, was held up and searched on the main street of McAllen by City Marshal Everett Anglin, who released Eloy when an army patrol approached. But Anglin warned Eloy that "We will get you yet." Since then Eloy had mysteriously disappeared and it was suspected that he'd met with foul play at the hands of the *villistas*.[4]

The bureau agent also reported that "The telegraph and telephone system of this whole section seems to be at the service of this organization. The Texas State Rangers and Military authorities find that all their orders given in that manner 'leak' and find their way to these people, making their efforts abortive." The term "concentration camps" referred to the *villista* technique whereby a sympathizer obtained a contract to clear a section of land of brush for farming. The workers, supposedly Mexican refugees, were actually recruits, and when a sufficient number had assembled they were slipped across the river at night.[5]

The bureau managed to insert an informant into this *villista* network. And the *carrancista* consul in Brownsville, José Z. Garza, of course also had secret agents operating against the *villistas*.[6]

On occasion Villa sympathizers made no effort to conceal their activities. According to the army, during the *villista* siege of Matamoros in the spring of 1915, "the banking and business arrangements for their supply through Hidalgo has been reported as made at Pharr and McAllen by D. Guerra and city Marshal Anglin of McAllen and the Villista Generals entertained by them by a banquet given yesterday [March 26] at Pharr."[7]

Commenting on the general situation, Agent McDevitt observed that this section of the border had historically been a lawless area infested with desperados, of whom there was still an excessive number. Filibustering expeditions, traffic in stolen cattle, and the marketing of loot from Mexico constituted the order of the day. "Most of the support of Americans is bought and paid for in cash."[8] His colleague Charles E. Breniman characterized the locals as "a suspicious and curious lot, and among them many dangerous and vicious men."[9]

With regard to Basilio Ramos's arrest, Dr. Villarreal was staying at the Rio Grande hotel in McAllen and went by night to inform Everett Anglin that Basilio Ramos had been to see him and had shown him the Plan de San Diego. Ramos said he'd been sent by unspecified parties to confer with Villarreal, whom Ramos wanted to join the Plan. Anglin arranged with Villarreal to meet Ramos the next morning at 9:00 and take him to Deodoro Guerra's store in McAllen. In the meantime, Villarreal had informed Guerra, who was not only a merchant and saloon keeper in McAllen but the political boss of Hidalgo County and a strong *villista* sympathizer, about Ramos and his mission.[10] Guerra in turn notified the Hidalgo County sheriff, A. Y. Baker, who instructed Deputy Sheriff Tom Mayfield that Ramos be arrested and held until Baker could arrive on the scene. When Ramos appeared for the meeting the next day, January 23, Mayfield, who also held a Special Ranger commission, duly arrested him.[11] Guerra searched Ramos and kept all the documents Ramos had on his person. Mayfield and Guerra were stunned by what they'd discovered. Sheriff Baker transported Ramos to jail in Edinburg, the county seat, while Guerra secured the papers in the safe in his store.[12]

As was the case with a surprising number of Mexican revolutionists arrested in the United States, Ramos's pocket litter included a number of incriminating documents. The papers included a carbon copy of the Plan de San Diego and a copy of a memorandum dated at Monterrey on January 6, 1915, recording the election of the Provisional Directorate of the Plan, with L. Ferrigno as president and Agustín S. Garza as supreme leader of the movement. Signing the memorandum were A. S. Garza, L. Ferrigno, B. Ramos Jr., D. A. Peña, A. Durán, Raymundo Ferrigno, E. Cisneros, A. Garza Almaraz, Lic. Amado González,[13]

Manuel Flores, Porfirio Santos, and A. A. Saenz. A notation on the memorandum stated that the original copy was in Monterrey in the archives of the secretary of the Provisional Directorate, Amado González. Moreover, there was Ramos's commission from the Provisional Directorate as organizer in Arizona, New Mexico, Colorado, California, Texas, and along the northern border of Mexico, also dated at Monterrey on January 6 and signed by L. Ferrigno, A. González, and A. G. Almaraz. And there was a letter of introduction for Ramos to one Ignacio Ríos in Eagle Pass signed by A. S. Garza, who assured Ríos that "I am convinced that his testicles are in the proper place." Another letter of recommendation was to Serafín Benavides in San Pedro, Zapata County, Texas, signed by Arturo A. Saenz, both dated at Monterrey on January 7. Ramos also had a letter of introduction to Ignacio Rodríguez, the head of a fraternal organization known as the "Mexican Knights of Honor," in Brownsville. Lastly, Ramos carried a small code book and a coded letter.[14]

Realizing that this was something important, Sheriff Baker became anxious to be rid of Ramos, who was being held incommunicado in the Edinburg jail, fearing an attempt to rescue him. Accordingly, Baker telephoned Captain T. B. Bishop, a deputy U.S. marshal for the Southern District of Texas at Brownsville, urging him to come to Edinburg to interrogate Ramos and take charge of him and the documents.[15] Bishop arrived three days later, on January 27, accompanied by federal Bureau of Investigation special agent Frank McDevitt. After questioning Ramos and reviewing the documents, the officers immediately transported the prisoner to Brownsville. They held him secretly in Marshal Bishop's office in the federal building rather than in the jail because all the jailers were Hispanics, and Bishop and McDevitt feared they would warn others involved in the Plan de San Diego. Uncertain of how to charge him, Agent McDevitt hesitated to swear out a complaint against Ramos.[16] Instead, Bishop dumped Ramos on the Immigration Service, delivering him to E. P. Reynolds, the immigration inspector in charge, for possible deportation proceedings.

At Brownsville on January 28, immigration inspectors informed Ramos that he could make a voluntary statement but warned that it could be used against him. Ramos made a sworn and signed statement about his activities and was interrogated by E. P. Reynolds, the inspector in charge of the Brownsville immigration station. Inspector S. B. Hopkins acted as interpreter, for Ramos spoke in Spanish, and Inspector J. R. Harold functioned as stenographer. Also present was Agent McDevitt.[17] Ramos gave his complete name as Basilio Ramos Jr., stating that sometimes he'd used Basilio Ramos García to differentiate himself from his father. Moreover, he'd called himself B. R. García in Mexico because he'd been jailed in Nuevo Laredo and had been freed on the condition that he never return to Mexico. He had, however, entered that country through Piedras Negras, and to avoid arrest had used the name B. R. García. Ramos said he was a native of Nuevo Laredo, was twenty-four years old, was a Mexican citizen, was single, and had never been married.

Ramos claimed he had last entered the United States sometime between January 13 and 15, 1915, via the international bridge at Brownsville. Asked if the immigration inspector at the bridge had registered him, Ramos said that when the inspector on duty asked him where he was from, he answered that he lived in San Diego, Texas, and was en route there, planning to leave that night for Laredo, where some of his relatives lived. Asked why he'd gone to Mexico, Ramos told the inspector that he had planned to travel to Tampico but hadn't been able to get there. The inspector had allowed Ramos to pass without further ado. Ramos's interrogator asked if he had told the inspector that he'd been born in San Diego; Ramos responded that he had told the inspector that he'd been born in Nuevo Laredo but had lived in San Diego for four to five months.

Ramos stated that after having been arrested in Nuevo Laredo, he had been arrested in Monterrey while on his trip to Tampico for the same reason as in Nuevo Laredo—because he was a *huertista*, a follower of the conservative General Victoriano Huerta, who had seized power in Mexico in 1913 but had been defeated and driven into European exile in 1914. Ramos claimed to have been a secretary in the Nuevo Laredo customhouse during the administrations of General Porfirio Díaz and of Huerta and to have lived in the United States since May 20, 1914, the date when he was expelled from Mexico. He was in Laredo about a month without a job. Later he worked in San Diego, Texas, as an agent of the Royal Brewing Company of Kansas City, which had an agency in Laredo. On December 28, 1914, he left his job with the company to travel to Tampico via San Antonio, Piedras Negras, and Monterrey. He got as far as Monterrey, where he was arrested as a *huertista*. From Monterrey he came to Matamoros and Brownsville.

Reynolds showed Ramos his copy of the Plan de San Diego. Ramos admitted that his signature was on the document. Asked if he'd been in San Diego on January 6, Ramos said no, he'd been in jail in Monterrey on that date. According to Ramos, the Plan de San Diego was prepared by "a friend of ours." When pressed on that point Ramos said that a friend of the signers, from Monterrey, had prepared the document; the friend had also previously been arrested, but Ramos declared that he didn't know the man's identity. The Plan de San Diego was brought into the jail by the servant who delivered the meals, and it was there that he and the other eight *huertistas* signed it. Ramos said that on January 7 or 8 he was freed, along with A. S. Garza, another of the document's signers. Ramos didn't know if the rest of the signers were still in prison.

Asked who among the signers were from Monterrey, Ramos named A. L. Ferrigno, A. G. Almaraz, and A. S. Garza, a Mexican citizen who operated a commission business in Monterrey. The other signers were also Mexican citizens. Ramos didn't know if they had been born in Monterrey, but they'd lived there a long time. The rest of the signers, like Ramos, were natives of Nuevo Laredo. Ramos stated that two copies of the Plan had been smuggled into the Monterrey jail and that he and the other signers had read the Plan secretly in jail after signing it. When the interrogator asked if the document marked "Exhibit 1" was the original, Ramos replied that it was a carbon copy but was identical to the original; both were typed at the same time. All nine men had signed both the original and the copy. When asked where the original was, Ramos said he didn't know. "They gave me this carbon copy when I was freed, and I suppose they still have the original." Asked who gave Ramos the carbon copy when he was freed, he replied that it was A. L. Ferrigno, the president. "He had the two documents, and when I was freed he gave me one."

Asked if any of the other signers were now in the United States, Ramos said he didn't know. A. S. Garza had been freed the same day as Ramos, and there was no reason for Garza not to return to the United States via Laredo. Ramos couldn't take the same route, because he'd previously been arrested in Nuevo Laredo. He traveled by way of Matamoros and Brownsville, while Garza remained in Monterrey awaiting the first train from Monterrey to Laredo. Ramos didn't know the current whereabouts of Garza.

Ramos stated that he'd been named an organizer for the Plan and was the only one so designated until now. Asked if he'd assembled any recruits or signers for the movement in the vicinity of Brownsville, Ramos lied, stating that he'd made no effort to interest anyone in that connection.[18] (It would be interesting to learn how Agustín Garza acquired both the English and Spanish versions of Ramos's statement, which are in Garza's personal papers.)

Some writers have accepted that the Plan was promulgated at San Diego, Texas, but to our knowledge there has been no effort to determine whether this was indeed the case.[19] There is evidence that the Plan was in fact written in San Diego. A Mexican revolutionary manifesto, or plan, was generally named for the place where it was promulgated. (An exception was Francisco Madero's Plan de San Luis Potosí, which touched off the Mexican Revolution on November 20, 1910. That Plan was actually written in San Antonio, Texas.)

One B. H. Hall of Sabinal, Texas, claimed in June 1916 that Agustín Garza, while in San Diego "about two years ago, was preparing what is said to be known as the 'Plan of San Diego.'"[20]

Bureau agent Robert Barnes wrote in November 1916 that the agency's investigation revealed that in early 1915 several Mexicans arrived in San Diego and rented a saloon, using it as cover while they organized Tejanos in support of the Plan de San Diego. "Sufficient witnesses can be provided to show their operations in San Diego."[21]

Another bureau agent reported in January 1917 that he'd interviewed one Evaristo Barrera in San Diego. Barrera denied any contact with Basilio Ramos and his associates Daniel Vela and Marcial Rodríguez; the three had formed a partnership, D. Vela and Co., in the beer business. The enterprise had failed because it was only a front for their nefarious activities—formulating the Plan de San Diego.[22] If in fact the Plan de San Diego was written in that town, it was done at the Casa

Blanca building, a one-story stone structure built in the 1850s that served as the headquarters for the Royal Brewing Company.[23]

However, evidence is still inconclusive. What writers about the Plan de San Diego have failed to consider is the context in which the Plan supposedly appeared. Duval County was run with an iron hand by the Democrat political boss Archie Parr from 1912 until his death in 1942. His son, George, continued as political boss until he committed suicide in 1975.[24] As an example of Archie Parr's techniques, in 1914, when his political enemies demanded an audit of the county's books, the courthouse mysteriously burned down, destroying all kinds of official records. And when his Republican and Independent enemies demanded an audit of the county's finances and announced that they were prepared to take Parr to court, Parr and the sheriff forcibly seized the account books from the grand jury. For this egregious offense, a judge sentenced Parr to a hundred-dollar fine and a whole hour of jail time.[25] Archie Parr was supremely confident of his control over the majority Hispanic population, who duly voted as they were told in blatantly fraudulent elections.[26] Were Ramos and company clever enough to plot figuratively under Archie Parr's nose? Or did Parr consider their plotting too preposterous to be of concern?[27] Besides the D. Vela and Co. beer business, the only recent connection to San Diego was Ramos's stint representing the Royal Brewing Company there.

Previous writers have overlooked the Royal Brewing Company connection. This Kansas City, Missouri, brewery maintained an agency in Laredo, Texas, and employed Ramos in San Diego for four or five months until December 28, 1914, when he said he left for Tampico. The Royal Brewing Company was owned by a certain Jack Danciger and his brothers, prominent Kansas City businessmen. Their principal market was Mexico. The exclusive distributor along the Texas border from Val Verde through Dimmit Counties (roughly from Langtry to Carrizo Springs) and in the entire state of Coahuila was J. K. Forseck & Company, a partnership consisting of John Kvake Forseck, who will feature prominently in the Plan de San Diego affair, and Colonel Sebastián Carranza Jr., one of First Chief Venustiano Carranza's nephews.[28]

Danciger and Sebastián Carranza met in Laredo in July 1915.[29] According to Danciger's sympathetic biographer, Sebastián Carranza inquired whether the Royal Brewery could provide at least one hundred boxcar-loads of beer for sale through Veracruz. Danciger replied that he could, and he suggested that they charter a ship instead. Sebastián traveled to Kansas City to conclude the deal, and he formed a close friendship with the Danciger brothers. Jack Danciger and Sebastián left New Orleans with the beer on August 3, 1915, aboard the Wolvin Line *City of Mexico*, traveling via Tampico to Veracruz, where they arrived ten days later. Veracruz was at the time Sebastián's base of operations as well as the temporary capital of Venustiano Carranza, the first chief of the Constitutionalist Army, who was fighting for the survival of his regime against the forces of Pancho Villa. A transaction involving one hundred boxcar-loads of beer required the payment of serious money, and it would be interesting to know whether Carranza subsidized his nephew's enterprise in order to supply Constitutionalist soldiers with a beer ration. Through Sebastián, Danciger was soon introduced to the first chief, whom he greatly admired. Venustiano Carranza proved friendly, and in short order Danciger was one of Carranza's most enthusiastic supporters in the United States.[30]

Among his various enterprises, Jack Danciger acquired a Spanish-language weekly in Kansas City, *El Cosmopólita*, which became a principal organ of Carranza propaganda in the United States, frequently receiving exclusive information.[31] And Carranza was keenly aware of the value of good publicity in the United States, employing one George Weeks as his publicity chief[32] as well as utilizing the talents of the prominent journalist Lincoln Steffens. Through his political contacts Danciger even secured an audience with President Woodrow Wilson to sing Carranza's praises.[33] In recognition of his considerable efforts, Carranza appointed Danciger as honorary Mexican consul in Kansas City, on September 23, 1915.[34] However, many members of the Mexican colony in Kansas City bitterly resented the appointment of Danciger, an American Jew, instead of a deserving Mexican national.[35]

The connection between Basilio Ramos, the Royal Brewing Company, Jack Danciger, John Forseck, Sebastián Carranza Jr., and Venustiano Carranza is suggestive. Why, for example, is the contract and agreement between J. K. Forseck & Co. and the Royal Brewing Company in the personal papers of Agustín S. Garza?

Ramos's examining trial was held in Brownsville on February 4, 1915, before U.S. commissioner E. K. Goodrich.[36] Ramos announced that he had nothing to say, except that the documents found on his person were made and executed in Monterrey; everything else he'd said in his statement on January 28. Immigration inspectors E. P. Reynolds and S. B. Hopkins, Deputy U.S. Marshal T. P. Bishop, Sheriff A. Y. Baker, and Deodoro Guerra testified at the examining trial. Bureau agent Charles E. Breniman asked Ramos whether it was his and his associates' intention to carry out the Plan. Ramos replied that it wasn't his intention but he didn't know what the others would do.[37]

Bureau agent Breniman, accompanied by city marshal of McAllen Everett Anglin, interviewed Deodoro Guerra, who recounted the events leading up to Ramos's apprehension. Guerra also speculated that A. A. Saenz, one of the Plan's signatories, lived in San Diego, as possibly did Porfirio Santos, another of the signers. Guerra added that he was acquainted with Benacio Salinas, who had signed one of the documents found in Ramos's possession, and that Salinas lived in San Diego and was connected with many revolutionary movements in Mexico. Among Ramos's papers was a letter from "A. S. or Agustín S." Garza to one Risa in El Paso.[38] Guerra stated that Risa was notorious and had been mixed up in many criminal acts in Mexico. Guerra also claimed that a certain Joaquín Herrera of Mission, Texas, was associated with Ramos and allegedly told Ramos not to mention his plans to any of the Mexicans in McAllen.[39] The Bureau of Investigation developed information that one R. S. Herrera, 404 South Alamo Street in San Antonio, had corresponded with Ramos, and that Eufrasio Pérez, of Brownsville, had probably assisted him. Pérez had been a consul during Porfirio Díaz's administration, and his name appeared in a little notebook taken from Ramos, with whom he was apparently corresponding.[40]

After investigating the whole matter, immigration inspector E. P. Reynolds informed his superiors that the Ramos case was a criminal matter—conspiracy to commit treason—rather than a deportation case. Were Ramos to be convicted, deportation could be considered after he'd served his sentence. Accordingly, on January 29, Agent Breniman filed a complaint before the U.S. commissioner charging Ramos and the other signatories. Ramos was the only one apprehended so far, and he was arraigned the same day. His bond was set at five thousand dollars, which he was unable to post, and he was remanded to the Cameron County jail, to await trial at the May term of the federal court, his maintenance expense to be charged to the Department of Justice. There was even some doubt as to Ramos's sanity. Federal Judge Waller T. Burns declared that Ramos needed "a hospital rather than a jail."[41]

As it turned out, immigration wasn't through with Ramos. Inspector Reynolds conducted a hearing in his office on March 20, 1915, with Inspector Harold again serving as interpreter. Reynolds informed Ramos that he could be released on bail if he could furnish a thousand-dollar bond. Ramos couldn't. When advised that he had a right to counsel, Ramos declined on the ground that he had no money for a lawyer. The object of the hearing was to determine whether in fact Ramos had entered Brownsville via the international bridge or had crossed illegally by a skiff several miles above the town. The immigration inspector on duty at the bridge at the time testified, but he was unable to resolve the matter.

When interrogated about his activities, Ramos proceeded under oath to furnish some personal information. He recapitulated his January 28 statement, including having been a secretary and clerk in the Nuevo Laredo customhouse for about two years. Ramos said he'd stayed at the San Carlos Hotel in Brownsville for one day, then rented a room at the home of a Mrs. Rodríguez, on Adams Street, for the rest of his stay in Brownsville. Asked whether he had carried a letter of recommendation to Ignacio R. Rodríguez, P.O. Box number 5 in Brownsville, relative to his mission in the United States, Ramos admitted having the letter but claimed he'd not been able to meet with Rodríguez. As to why he'd been in McAllen, Ramos claimed that he'd gone to Mission because he had a letter of recommendation to a man in Mission and had stopped in McAllen on his way back. Ramos claimed he didn't remember the name of his contact in Mission but had his name written down in a little memorandum book. When asked who was financing his mission, Ramos stated that he had about fifty dollars of his own money and had written to Agustín S. Garza for additional funds.

As to his imprisonment in Monterrey, he had been incarcerated for about five days. General Felipe Angeles, Pancho Villa's brilliant subordinate, was conducting the military campaign against the *carrancistas* in northeastern Mexico. He was driving on the strategic city of Monterrey, third largest in the country and a major industrial center. To halt Angeles's advance, the *carrancistas* concentrated their forces at the town of Ramos Arizpe, ten miles from Saltillo. Angeles won a ferocious battle at Ramos Arizpe on January 8, 1915.[42] On January 15 the *villistas* occupied Monterrey. Carranza troops began massing to retake the city, which they finally did on May 22.[43]

In his statement Ramos alleged that he and his *huertista* companions in prison signed the Plan de San Diego on January 6—while the city was still under *carrancista* control. And Deodoro Guerra testified at Ramos's examining trial that "after his arrest, he told me that he was a prisoner at Monterrey, and that when he was a prisoner there some parties, friends of some other prisoners then in jail, had taken them these papers for them to sign, and that on account of these papers the authorities let him out of jail."[44] How very odd—*carrancista* authorities freeing supposed *huertistas* immediately after the latter signed the Plan de San Diego.

Ramos said his education consisted of having completed primary public school in Nuevo Laredo and then having attended a Catholic school in Norman, Oklahoma, for several months. He said he'd learned to speak a little English while at the Catholic school and from his work along the border as a clerk. He also gave the names of his parents, Basilio Ramos Sr. and Refugia García, and of four brothers, Eduardo, Juan, Ernesto, and Alfonso, all of whom lived at 905 Zaragoza Street in Laredo, Texas. Another brother, Antonio, lived in Tampico, Mexico, and an uncle, Epignacio Cuéllar, lived in Piedras Negras.[45] Inspector Reynolds recommended that Ramos be deported, deportation being deferred pending the outcome of the criminal charge against him. The hearing transcript concluded with a note: "This alien is rather stubborn and evasive in his answers, and gives the impression of not desiring to tell all that he knows in reference to the charges against him."

At the hearing, Ramos had been particularly reticent when questioned about the letters seized from his person. Besides not remembering the name of the man in Mission or having contacted Rodríguez in Brownsville, for both of whom he had letters of recommendation, he flatly refused to explain a letter to him from "F. H. U." addressed from 575 Zaragoza Street, Laredo, on February 2, 1915, and apparently referring obliquely to the acquisition of weapons.[46] The letter was mailed from Laredo on February 4. It was delivered to the jailer in Brownsville, who opened it on February 16 and turned it over to a deputy U.S. marshal. A bureau agent in Laredo made several unsuccessful efforts to learn who F. H. U. was and found that there was no 575 Zaragoza Street address.[47]

While Ramos languished in the Cameron County jail, the authorities were busily searching for the other signatories of the Plan de San Diego. They particularly wanted to apprehend Agustín S. Garza, whom they suspected was using the alias "León Caballo." That worthy had evidently been released from prison in Monterrey the same day as had Ramos and had traveled to Laredo by train. He wrote to Ramos from there on January 15, answering the letter Ramos had written to him from Brownsville the previous day and expressing his chagrin at not being able to send Ramos any money, explaining that he'd had to pawn his watch to pay for his room and meals, but promising to send funds immediately if he received any. However, "since my arrival I have been at work, and it appears that everyone accepts the idea in the highest degree, and therefore I think that much may be done in a short time. Before such a cloud on the horizon, pregnant with the crimes of the damned big-footed creatures against our poor race, to be quiet is a crime against one's country, because it is the homesick hour of the weak, and it ought to be announced to them. Therefore I wish you happiness on the arid rocky road which we shall traverse. Equality and Independence. Your friend [signed] A. S. Garza."[48]

The next day, January 16, Garza again wrote to Ramos, this time a letter in cipher, which the authorities broke and translated. Addressing the letter to Ramos as Garza's "Esteemed Companion and Friend," Garza requested that in any documents Ramos was producing, after they had been signed, aliases be used to ensure security. Further, "When you write to me, use my assumed name, and I will sign the name 'León Caballo.' We will continue working. I trust that today everything will be finished in this city, in order to leave soon. Equality and Independence. [signed] León Caballo."[49] Garza emerges as the key figure in the Plan de San Diego.[50]

While the American authorities tried to determine whether the Plan represented a real threat and, if so, which agency should deal with it, they kept Ramos's arrest secret in hopes of apprehending his fellow conspirators. They especially wanted to track down Garza, the signer of the Plan who was also commander of the "Liberating Army of Races and Peoples." Garza was described as being slender, weighing 110 pounds, being five feet six inches tall with a beak nose and a fair complexion. He had a glass eye, wore glasses, was clean shaven, a neat dresser who carried a cane. Garza spoke very little English and had a family living at or near San Diego.[51]

The manhunt centered on Laredo, but it proved fruitless. The authorities also searched for A. A. Saenz, another signer of the Plan, whom Sheriff A. Y. Baker and Deodoro Guerra thought might be in San Diego. Warrants were issued for the arrest of Saenz and Garza, but there was no definite information as to their whereabouts, although Garza was allegedly spotted in San Diego on January 25. In early March, U.S. Marshal J. A. Herring suggested that he be searched for in San Antonio and Waco. In early May, Garza was reportedly in Corpus Christi. In short, the authorities hadn't a clue where he might be.[52]

To the authorities' dismay, the Associated Press broke the Plan de San Diego story on February 2, and Texas newspapers began carrying it. On February 4 the *Brownsville Daily Herald* had a front-page banner headline, ATROCIOUS PLOT UNEARTHED, and a lengthy article described developments stemming from Ramos's arrest.[53] General Emiliano Nafarrate, the *carrancista* commander of the garrison in Matamoros, stormed into the American consulate and indignantly denied a newspaper account that he knew of the Plan de San Diego and supported it. In fact, Nafarrate claimed that it was he who'd furnished the U.S. consul in Matamoros, Jesse H. Johnson, the information that led to the uncovering of the conspiracy. The consul issued a statement that "It is my personal opinion that General Nafarrate never heard of the San Diego, Texas, junta until he saw it in the newspaper, and further, do not believe that he could be induced to do or say anything on behalf of said diabolical plot. In all my dealings with him I have seen no evidence of his hostility toward Americans."[54] As we'll see, Nafarrate was a consummate liar, and Johnson was pathetically naive.

The manhunt continued. On February 10 federal officers arrested in San Diego a Manuel Flores, who published a Spanish-language newspaper there. Flores was charged with seditious conspiracy, as was Antonio González, also of San Diego.[55] They were charged jointly with Ramos for the alleged violation of section 6 of the Federal Penal Code on February 4, 1915, at Brownsville. González was placed under a five-hundred-dollar bond, while Flores's case was still before the U.S. commissioner.[56] But this apparent triumph proved disappointing. After investigation it was determined that there was absolutely nothing to indicate that either man had any connection with the conspiracy, and they were released.[57]

Some people have accepted that the Plan de San Diego was a Huerta operation just because Ramos said it was. However, captured secret agents have been known to lie. Ramos's account was an elaborate cover story.

3 The Magonistas

Magonistas wrote the Plan de San Diego, as is readily apparent from the Plan itself and especially from the "Manifesto to the Oppressed Peoples of America." General Victoriano Huerta and his followers never showed much interest in social justice issues or in the plight of Hispanics in the United States, much less that of American blacks. The *magonistas* did. An immigration inspector described Ramos as being "a fanatic of anarchical tendencies and dangerous."[1] Furthermore, one of the signers of the revised and expanded Plan of San Diego was León Cárdenas Martínez, a militant *magonista*.

The *magonistas* were so called because they were the followers of Ricardo Flores Magón (Mexican political factions tended to be named after their leader). Flores Magón, a native of the state of Oaxaca, had embarked on a study of the law but instead became a student activist, protesting against the dictatorship of General Porfirio Díaz. In 1900, Flores Magón began publishing an opposition newspaper, *Regeneración*, which the authorities suppressed. Determined to continue his crusade, Flores Magón, and his brother Enrique, went into exile in the United States, first in Texas, then in St. Louis, Missouri, and continued their campaign. The American authorities took action against them, and Flores Magón fled to Canada for a time. He eventually made Los

Angeles his headquarters, being harassed by agents of the Mexican and U.S. governments and on occasion jailed for violation of the American neutrality laws. In 1906 he was instrumental in forming the Partido Liberal Mexicano (PLM), on the grounds that the traditional Liberal party in Mexico was now indistinguishable from the Conservatives in its support of Díaz. The PLM announced a sweeping program of fundamental reforms. But Flores Magón kept moving to the political left, becoming an avowed anarchist, a position that cost him the support of moderate Mexicans.

Flores Magón's goals were to overthrow the Díaz regime and to abolish the capitalist system in Mexico, and he failed on both counts. The *magonistas* were thoroughly penetrated by agents of the two governments and were habitually broke, the faithful being largely laborers who could contribute little to the revolutionary treasury, and Flores Magón lost credibility by remaining safely in Los Angeles while urging his followers to take up arms against Díaz. Flores Magón was a thinker, not a fighter. The one area where the *magonistas* excelled was propaganda.

The Plan de San Diego has the same grandiose unreality as some other *magonista* schemes, and given that faction's impressive record of military incompetence, it had absolutely no chance of success. To illustrate the *magonistas*' military ineptitude one need only refer to their 1906 attempt to overthrow the dictatorial regime of Porfirio Díaz. Flores Magón himself went to El Paso to direct operations. Their junta in that city devised a plan of campaign. First, two hundred armed militants would assemble in El Paso, cross the river to Ciudad Juárez, blow up the barracks, police station, and city hall, and seize the customhouse, the banks, and the house of the richest citizen. A contingent would then take the train and go capture the state capital, the city of Chihuahua. The El Paso junta would continue to supply war materiel. The victorious *magonistas* would name one of their colleagues as governor of Chihuahua, the rest of that state would rally to their cause, and there would occur a domino effect as state after state rebelled against Díaz's rule. The Díaz authorities soon learned of the plan, and two army officers were assigned to function as agents provocateur, claiming that they could induce the Juárez garrison to defect to the *magonista* cause. When the militants tried to implement their plan, scheduled for October 21, it never happened. On the night of October 19–20, instead of two hundred armed fighters, a small group of idealistic young militants undertook to capture Juárez. They were quickly arrested. Flores Magón, prizing discretion over valor, fled El Paso as quickly as he could.[2]

The *magonistas* had mounted their major military campaign in 1911 from California. A force of several hundred, many of them foreign mercenaries, managed to seize several towns in what was then the territory of Baja California. They planned to use the peninsula as a base from which to overthrow the Mexican government. However, within less than six months that government crushed the invasion, and the survivors fled back to California. After this latest fiasco the *magonistas* as a faction in the Mexican Revolution became increasingly marginalized.

The only hope they had in 1915 for implementing the Plan de San Diego was by securing support from Mexico, and this was the crucial factor in the whole affair. A "liberation movement" conducted solely within Texas had absolutely no chance of success. The *magonistas* had to secure the support of some Mexican revolutionary faction in order to establish a base of operations in Mexico. The dominant faction was that headed by the first chief of the Constitutionalist Army, Venustiano Carranza, whose forces controlled the Mexican side of the lower Rio Grande valley. From the beginning the *magonistas* were willing to be used by the *carrancistas*, who had their own agenda. Basilio Ramos's approach to Dr. Villarreal was in hopes of getting the *villistas* on board and persuading them to end their raids across the Rio Grande against the *carrancistas*.

On February 12 the bureau's San Antonio office learned that an armed body of Mexicans, probably *carrancistas*, had crossed into Texas, cutting telephone lines and seizing horses. Several raiders had been captured and were in jail in Rio Grande City.[3] The cutting of telephone lines seemed a bit odd but was not a major cause for concern. Nevertheless, the chief of the bureau notified the State and War Departments of the incursion.[4]

This raid increased Anglo tension with the approach of February 20, the announced date for the Hispanic rising. There were probably a lot of Plan de San Diego sympathizers, such as Andrés Roma, who held mass meetings at Rio Grande City and other locations,[5] but very few of them actually picked up a rifle and prepared to take on the Texas Rangers, the U.S. Army, and vigilantes.[6] The only thing that happened was the appearance of a revised Plan, a "Manifesto to the Oppressed Peoples of America," dated February 20. In the manifesto the "Revolutionary Congress" reaffirmed the original Plan but also proclaimed a social revolution and the establishment of the "Social Republic of Texas." With Texas as a base, the revolution would encompass New Mexico, Arizona, California, Colorado, Utah, and Nevada.

To the relief of the Anglo population at least, the next few months were generally peaceful, although in June a band of twenty to thirty Mexicans was spotted near the village of Sebastian, thirty-five miles north of Brownsville. Thirty deputy sheriffs and a number of citizens joined the chase but failed to make contact. Thereafter Anglo and Tejano ranchers and farmers frequently reported the loss of cattle, but this could be attributed to garden-variety rustling. It seemed that the Plan de San Diego had been nothing more than a curiosity.

Viewed in isolation, the Plan de San Diego was ridiculous. Its visionary program of action, which included seizing state capitals and conducting a war without quarter, was risible. The "Revolutionary Congress"—a handful of men whom nobody had elected to anything—purported to have met on February 21, 1915, at San Diego to review "the military and civil qualifications of the various military commanders at its disposal" and unanimously commissioned León Caballo (Agustín S. Garza) with the grandiose titles of "General of the Army Corps" and "General in Chief of the Liberating Army of Races and Peoples of America." As far as can be determined, he had absolutely no military experience, which did not bode well for the movement.[7]

Agustín S. Garza Solís, the key figure among the plotters, was born on June 11, 1881.[8] He grew up in San Diego, Texas, where his father was a schoolteacher. He lost an eye when he was eight years old and wore a glass eye.[9] Garza was living in San Diego as of 1910, but that year he went to work for the Monterrey, Mexico, clothing firm of M. Cirilo and Company.[10] As of 1913 he was the firm's representative in Torreón, Coahuila. And he was a patriot. In August and September 1913, as relations between the United States and the Mexican strongman General Victoriano Huerta worsened, Garza organized protest meetings in Torreón.[11] When the United States bombarded and occupied the key Mexican port of Veracruz on April 21, 1914, to hasten Huerta's downfall, Garza telegraphed to Huerta from Saltillo offering his services in repelling the American aggression. Huerta replied, congratulating Garza and ordering General Joaquín Maas to provide him with the necessary armament. Garza secured an interview with Maas, who informed him that no money, ammunition, or weapons were available for the volunteer corps Garza was organizing. Garza implored him to supply only arms and ammunition; he would gather the necessary supplies himself. Maas refused, and Garza reluctantly disbanded the two hundred volunteers he'd organized in Saltillo.[12] Now, in 1915, under the aegis of the Plan of San Diego, he assumed military command of the movement under the nom de guerre "León Caballo."

4 The Mexican Connection

As George Crile noted in his extraordinary book on the war against the Russians in Afghanistan, an insurgent movement simply can't survive unless it has a sanctuary for its fighters.[1] Despite some historians' assertions that the Plan was a liberation movement led by Tejano chieftains Luis de la Rosa and Aniceto Pizaña and was entirely a homegrown product of Hispanic outrage at generations of prejudice and oppression, it is obvious that if the *sediciosos* had to operate strictly within Texas their chances of success were nil. They needed a privileged sanctuary as a base, and that sanctuary was across the Rio Grande. Civil war was raging in Mexico between Carranza, backed by Generals Alvaro Obregón and Pablo González, against the Convention, supported by Generals Pancho Villa and Emiliano Zapata. The Convention's military muscle came from Villa and his formidable Division of the North. In this struggle Carranza desperately needed U.S. diplomatic recognition, for otherwise the United States retained the option of recognizing his enemies. With diplomatic recognition came the privilege of importing munitions into Mexico while the United States curtailed the arms traffic among those factions lacking formal recognition.

Historian Robert Mendoza has succinctly stated Carranza's strategy, one that at first glance seems counterintuitive: Carranza, whose forces controlled the Gulf of Mexico ports and the state of Tamaulipas bordering South Texas, devised a plan to secure both diplomatic recognition and the arms he needed to defeat the Convention. The plan consisted of four steps: (1) Carranza armed and funded "bandits" who would raid Texas border communities; (2) The U.S. State Department would demand that Carranza subdue the "bandits"; (3) Carranza would reply that the "bandits" were able to operate only because Carranza lacked U.S. recognition and sufficient arms to combat them; and (4) having received recognition and arms, Carranza "arrests" the raiders. Mendoza asserted that Carranza's scheme to obtain diplomatic recognition and munitions was disguised as a Tejano uprising.[2]

Necah S. Furman seconds this interpretation, writing that Carranza's ploy was to force recognition by a planned program of depredations along the border under the Plan de San Diego. *Vida Nueva* (the *villista* publication) charged that the *carrancistas* were responsible for the movement and that the border raids were being conducted in hopes of provoking a war with the United States.[3]

Interestingly, Sherburne G. Hopkins, the prominent Washington attorney who had represented Francisco Madero and subsequently Venustiano Carranza, stated that while he was at Carranza's headquarters in July 1914 he had heard the generals discussing a scheme to invade Texas south of the Nueces River.[4]

Besides matters of policy, there is a tantalizing allegation regarding Carranza's personal motives for supporting a rebellion in Texas. According to Adolfo de la Huerta, interim president of Mexico in 1920 and unsuccessful rebel in 1923–24, Carranza always harbored a profound resentment against the United States, a resentment that made him dream of avenging the Mexican War and regaining the territory lost to the Americans in that conflict. Moreover, he believed in the possibility of a race war in the United States, pitting whites against blacks. Mexico might support the blacks in hopes of thus regaining its lost territories. Lastly, Carranza thought it possible that there might erupt class warfare in the United States—workers against capitalists. Again, Mexico might support the workers and thus regain its territories. Of these scenarios, Carranza felt that supporting a rebellion in

Texas was the most feasible, but he'd have to proceed cautiously and shrewdly. It would be necessary to sound out the blacks, and the best way was to invite them to settle in certain parts of Mexico. To that end, a black representative went to Piedras Negras in 1913 and discussed with Carranza the matter of black colonization in Mexico. For whatever reason, nothing came of these negotiations.[5]

The Mexican connection was the crucial element in the Plan de San Diego movement. Without Mexican support, the Plan de San Diego would have had the same impact as a precursor manifesto signed by one Francisco Alvarez Tostado on November 26, 1914. It called on "The Sons of Cuauhtémoc, Hidalgo, and Juárez in Texas" to rise in rebellion and establish a republic, thereafter requesting annexation to Mexico. The proclamation ended with the ringing slogan "Restauration or Death."[6] Nothing happened.

Benjamin Johnson asserts that Ramos's claim that he and other *huertistas* drafted the Plan de San Diego while imprisoned in Monterrey "convinced nobody."[7] He is wrong on two counts. First, Ramos never claimed that he and his companions drafted the Plan—only that they signed it. Second, Ramos indeed convinced somebody—several American historians accepted his *huertista* story at face value.

Michael C. Meyer, for instance, wrote that some Mexican Americans with *huertista* sympathies promulgated the Plan, and he asserted that Mexican exiles visited General Huerta in New York to brief him on the progress of the San Diego movement. Meyer further recounted Allen Gerlach's erroneous description of Basilio Ramos, his father, and his brothers organizing raiding bands.[8] In writing about the Huerta-Orozco movement, Gerlach stated that the principal extension of that movement was the Plan de San Diego, a *huertista* operation that began in early 1915 and had significant German involvement.[9] James Sandos concluded that the Plan began with Huerta's followers and was taken over by the Germans, who subsequently shared control with Carranza.[10] Mario D. Longoria also subscribes to the Huerta interpretation.[11] And so does Thomas A. Bruscino.[12] However, historians George J. Rausch Jr. and Kenneth J. Grieb did not ascribe the Plan to Victoriano Huerta.[13]

The federal Bureau of Investigation's archive on the Mexican Revolution contains hundreds of telegrams from the San Antonio Western

Union office acquired by a subpoena *duces tecum*. Among them are translated telegrams from a ranking *huertista* operative in San Antonio, "Rogelio" (no last name given) to Severino Herrera Moreno, a member of Huerta's staff in New York. On April 25, 1915, "Rogelio" wired to Herrera Moreno: "Be tranquil. Keep absolutely secret. Carranzistas [*sic*] agitating with secrecy Negroes and Texans in their favor." On April 29, 1915, "Rogelio" telegraphed that "I spoke personally with Carranzista [*sic*] J. S. Pedroza who is agitating negroes and Mexico-Texans favor Venustiano. He offered to pay me well to aid him. . . . He continues agitation has agents various towns. . . . Answer wire of yesterday."[14] This is further evidence of *carrancista* sponsorship of the Plan de San Diego.

And there were strange doings involving Basilio Ramos. Deodoro Guerra testified that not only had Ramos told him he'd been released from prison in Monterrey as soon as he had signed the Plan, but that Ramos stated in his and Sheriff Baker's presence "to be careful that the Carrancistas did not know that he was arrested." Why would the *carrancistas* care? Perhaps because at the time of his arrest Ramos carried a safe-conduct pass issued by *carrancista* Brigadier General Emiliano Próspero Nafarrate Ceceña, commander of the Matamoros garrison.

Nafarrate, who was a major player in the Plan de San Diego affair, was born in Yecorato, Sinaloa, on July 29, 1882. Before the Mexican Revolution he had been a carpenter at the Ojuela Mines, in the state of Durango.[15] He later became a merchant in the town of San José de Gracia. When Francisco Madero initiated the Mexican Revolution in 1910, Nafarrate immediately became a *maderista*, fighting in Durango and Chihuahua. During the Orozco rebellion in 1912 against Madero, Nafarrate remained loyal to Madero. When Madero was overthrown and murdered in 1913, Nafarrate joined the Constitutionalist movement led by the governor of Coahuila, Venustiano Carranza.[16]

Regarding Ramos's story, what we have here is something analogous to a man purporting to be a Jewish escapee from Auschwitz but who was carrying a safe-conduct pass signed by Heinrich Himmler. General Nafarrate issued the pass on January 12, 1915, permitting Ramos to travel at will between Brownsville and Matamoros. That same day Nafarrate issued another document, which was also seized on Ramos's person: "The bearer of this letter, Senor Basilio Ramos, Jr., is authorized by me to find the whereabouts of my brother Manuel M. Nafarrate, for which reason I desire that my friends give him such information for this purpose as he may need."[17]

That Nafarrate was involved from the beginning is shown by Agustín Garza's letter to Ramos on January 15, in which he stated:

> With pain and with pleasure I read your letter, for it was very much to be regretted that individuals who, like General Nafarrate, bathe in the inexhaustible fountains of wisdom, should not accept with fervor, abnegation, and respect, an idea so sublime, and which, if not one of the grandest of America, it is not less than the challenge unto death of all the peoples of decapitated Latin America to the white-faced hogs of Pennsylvania. Therefore, my dear Basilio, I think that General Nafarrate is one of those Mexicans of pure blood, descended from Cuauhtémoc and Juárez, and it would please me that individuals of this stature should co-operate in an indirect manner with those of us who are pledged to the fulfillment of our word. Please express to General Nafarrate my sincere admiration and respect; for, in spite of the fact that I am not acquainted with him, I believe he will accept your idea.[18]

As the months passed without any noticeable Plan de San Diego activity, the Plan began to be regarded as a joke. As an indication of how lightly the Plan was now regarded, when Ramos was indicted on May 13 his bond was reduced from five thousand to one hundred dollars. The bond was posted by José Webb and José Martínez.[19] Ramos then jumped bond and fled across the river to Matamoros, where he was lavishly entertained by the *carrancista* authorities.[20] Strange goings-on indeed for someone purporting to be a *huertista*.

A commentary on the Plan came from an unusual source. That intellectual revolutionary, José Vasconcelos, was secretary of education in the cabinet of General Eulalio Gutiérrez, the titular head of the Convention that Villa and Zapata dominated and which opposed Carranza. Gutiérrez and his entourage were driven out of Mexico City in January, heading for the American border while being harassed by enemy forces. Gutiérrez had designated Vasconcelos with the grandiloquent title of "General Representative of the Government of Mexico Before the Government of the United States of America," with special and extraordinary powers.[21] Running for their lives, a bedraggled Vasconcelos and sixteen companions splashed across the Rio Grande on March 6, 1915, at Rio Grande City in Starr County and were promptly arrested. They were released four days later because no charges were pending against them in the United States. Vasconcelos made the interesting reference to "an absurd plan fomented by the *carrancistas* for the reconquest of Texas."[22] Vasconcelos, incidentally, was comfortably ensconced by March 24 in the Shoreham Hotel in Washington DC.

Nothing much happened in the spring of 1915, probably because the *villistas* and *carrancistas* were still battling for control of the lower border region. However, on March 31 a southbound St. Louis, Brownsville, & Mexico passenger train transporting troops to Brownsville was derailed near Calallen by a sabotaged switch. Whether Plan de San Diego militants were involved is unknown.[23] On several occasions Hispanic peace officers were killed or wounded at *bailes*, or open-air public dances. Whether these incidents were related to Plan de San Diego militants is unclear, because *bailes* had a long history of violence.[24] The Carranza forces were desperately trying to hold Nuevo Laredo, where General Maclovio Herrera and subordinates such as General Alfredo Ricaut were digging in, and Matamoros, where General Emiliano Nafarrate was in command. Nafarrate constructed a defensive perimeter incorporating sixteen machine guns and gasoline-filled trenches and awaited a major *villista* assault. It came on March 27, and failed, in part because Nafarrate set fire to the gasoline-filled trenches. Nafarrate distinguished himself by riding horseback along the line rallying his troops. They responded by smashing three fierce *villista* cavalry charges. The siege of Matamoros lasted until April 13, when Nafarrate launched a surprise attack that routed the *villistas*, who fell back toward Monterrey destroying the railroad track as they retreated.[25] The U.S. Army had reinforced its Brownsville garrison with three batteries of artillery, and an infantry regiment had been on standby.[26]

Many people now understandably dismissed the Plan de San Diego. For instance, army intelligence's weekly report on February 27 had stated that around Harlingen "Conditions have remained normal in this section during the week. The much talked of 'Plan of San Diego,' the provisions of which, it was reported, were to be put into effect on certain days of the past week, resulted in nothing more than to create a certain amount of interest among a few of the people of this district."[27] But matters were just simmering.

These machinations were of course initially unknown to people such as the staunchly Republican Hispanic district attorney of the Forty-Ninth Judicial District of Texas, based in Laredo, Webb County, since 1902, John A. Valls. He testified that "in February, 1915, I first heard of the plan of San Diego. . . . To me it appeared so visionary and ridiculous that I paid no attention to it."[28] But on April 10, Valls learned that a *sedicioso* cell existed in Laredo. He notified an unidentified local lawman and asked for his help, but the officer indiscreetly let it be known that the organization was being investigated, which of course spooked the plotters, who were all strangers to Laredo. They immediately fled. After that Valls kept a careful watch on matters along the border.[29]

So did the federal Bureau of Investigation. Robert L. Barnes, the special agent in charge of the San Antonio Division, encompassing Texas, New Mexico, and Arizona, went to Brownsville and spent about a month personally investigating the Plan's ramifications.[30] In November 1915 he reported: "While it was not known at the time that Ramos was arrested, that the movement was so well organized, later developments along the border clearly showed that there were two or three hundred Mexicans in that vicinity organized for an uprising against the authority of the United States. . . . They were materially aided by Governor Luis Caballero of Tamaulipas, General Emilio [*sic*] Nafarrate and Col. Policarpio Elizondo, first and second in command of the De Facto Government troops in the district of Matamoros."[31]

5 The "Bandit War" Begins

What is important about the Plan de San Diego is how it was used, and this is what some writers who subscribe to the "liberation struggle" interpretation fail to address. Since the *magonistas* wrote the Plan it was foredoomed to failure. And Huerta's attempt to regain power in Mexico collapsed with his arrest in El Paso on June 27, 1915. Whether Ramos and his companions were really *huertistas* or *magonistas* is not the point. It would seem that they were the willing tools of the Carranza faction. Factional loyalty during the Mexican Revolution was often fragile. On various occasions the *magonistas* had entered into cynical alliances of convenience with conservative factions to provide the cannon fodder if the conservatives provided the money.[1] What the Plan de San Diego conspiracy desperately needed was a base of operations, and only the *carrancistas* were in a position to provide such a base. To his credit, Nafarrate was a competent commander who had repulsed a major *villista* attack and siege of Matamoros in March and April, inflicting such heavy losses on the attackers that they ultimately retreated back to Monterrey, subsequently evacuating the territory all the way to Piedras Negras. The *carrrancistas*, and only the *carrancistas*, now controlled the territory across the Rio Grande from South Texas. It was from this Mexican sanctuary that a series of raids would plunge South Texas into such turmoil that a race war became a real possibility.

The troubles in the lower valley jeopardized the booming economy of the "Magic Valley," built largely on irrigated citrus crops. The influx of homeseekers, mainly from the Midwest, helped greatly to inflate land values, and members of the establishment were financially overextended. As an example of the boom, in July a new company was formed in Saint Louis, the John T. Beamer Company, which bought the entire holdings of the American Rio Grande Land & Irrigation Company of Mercedes, consisting of one hundred thousand acres of land, the town site and hotel of Mercedes, and the Mercedes canal system—for $3.5 million. This was the largest financial transaction yet in the valley.[2]

The key figure in the lower border was General Emiliano Nafarrate, the commander at Matamoros. As time passed it became increasingly apparent that he was at least protecting, if not actively aiding, abetting, and directing, the raiders. Sheriff W. T. Vann of Cameron County, for one, was convinced. Vann crossed to Matamoros to speak personally with Nafarrate, who not only denied any involvement but promised faithfully to assist the American authorities. When Vann informed Nafarrate that two raiders in Carranza uniforms had been killed in Texas, Nafarrate disingenuously stated that they'd probably stolen the uniforms.[3]

In June 1915 a band of Mexicans was spotted in the vicinity of the Rancho de los Indios west of Sebastian and north of Brownsville. Sheriff Vann formed a large posse and searched through the thick brush for days without result. According to a witness, Lon Hill, "They found out afterwards why they could not overtake them. . . . Well, every Mexican in the country was in sympathy with them, for them; and Mexicans that we would get to guide of course, they would just take you around somewhere else, and they never did catch anybody until we let the Mexicans alone, and then we got to catching them."[4]

In June, Cameron County judge H. L. Yates warned Secretary of War Lindley Garrison that bands of marauders had crossed the Rio Grande and had penetrated Cameron County as far as fifteen to twenty miles from the river. He requested additional troops to protect the area.[5]

Complacency regarding the Plan was shattered in July by a series of raids into Texas that convulsed the lower Rio Grande valley. On July 6, Sheriff Vann led a thirty-five-man posse, including five Texas Rangers, through the chaparral thickets forty miles north of Brownsville. He hoped to bring to bay a gang of Mexican bandits, reported to be twenty to thirty strong, who had been terrorizing the northern part of the county for the last four days. They hadn't killed anybody, but from several ranches they'd stolen four horses, several goats, a saddle, and a number of livestock. Vann stated that he didn't know who these miscreants were—they might be rustlers, filibusters, or raiders from across the Rio Grande. The posse soon swelled to fifty, including Sheriff A. Y. Baker of adjoining Hidalgo County, and divided into several groups. Two alleged bandits were killed west of Raymondville, but eleven marauders robbed a store near Lyford of food and ammunition and kidnapped a Hispanic man, forcing him to be their unwilling guide. The *Brownsville Daily Herald* pointed out that "The country for miles around the scene of the robbery is covered with brush impassable for man or horse except along the trails beaten by cattle and goats." The bandits managed to dodge cavalry patrols and escape across the Rio Grande. General Nafarrate announced that he'd ordered his troops to keep a lookout to capture any of the gang operating on the Mexican side of the river.[6]

The *Lyford Courant* stated skeptically that "we do not believe there were as many men in the gang as reported."[7] The *Brownsville Herald* reported these incidents but implied that they were isolated cases. The newspaper injected a bit of humor by describing an "invasion" at the northern edge of Brownsville by three hundred Mexican parrots who raided a cornfield. "Here at last is a certified case of an invasion of Texas by a band of native Mexicans bent on pillage. Border raiding, according to popular rumor, is as regular as bull-fighting used to be with our neighbors across the way. Now comes the first actual proof that raids are made."[8]

Sheriff Vann was not amused, and he doggedly continued to search for the bandits, even employing an unusual method: "A human bloodhound, in the person of an aged Mexican Indian, of pure aboriginal stock, is on the trail of the Mexican bandits in the north of Cameron county who last Sunday at daylight robbed the store of Nils Peterson, four miles southeast of Lyford. No luck." On July 19, Sheriff Vann reluctantly announced that he was withdrawing his men from the fruitless three-week bandit hunt.[9]

His deputy, C. A. Monahan, offered a realistic view of the situation, stating that no posse could run down the marauders and suggesting that only men working alone or in pairs, quietly, and secretly might get some of the gang. "Officers in numbers might as well carry a brass band with them." Monahan's experience and observation convinced him that seemingly innocent residents could be alerting the thieves, who might be close friends. The result was that the approach of peace officers in force was advertised hours before the officers arrived. Monahan had been constantly on the trail of the supposed bandit gang for three weeks, and he was certain that a network of sympathizers existed. Moreover, the brush in that section was so thick that it afforded an ideal hiding place.[10]

Sporadic incidents of violence occurred. On July 17 an Anglo was shot on the San Francisco ranch east of Raymondville.[11] And on July 23, deputy sheriffs killed two Hispanic brothers who allegedly resisted arrest.[12] These deaths weren't conclusively connected with the Plan de San Diego.

But on July 25, raiders burned a bridge on the St. Louis, Brownsville & Mexico Railroad just south of Sebastian. This occurred in the morning just as a train approached; fortunately the engineer was able to back away from the blazing structure. Investigation uncovered numerous footprints and tracks of some thirty to forty horses. An attempt to trail them ended in failure. Railroad bridges were evidently a favorite target, for on three occasions bridges in the vicinity were set on fire. What was significant about this incident, though, was that the bandits not only set fire to the bridge but also cut the telephone and telegraph wires. "Railroad officials can assign no reason for the act, except downright malicious mischief."[13] But this seemed like the things guerrillas, not bandits, would do.

The level of racial animosity, creating more potential *sedicioso* recruits, increased because of an incident in the town of San Benito. On July 28, Deputy Sheriffs Frank Carr and Daniel Hinojosa took one

Adolfo Muñiz from the jail at 10 p.m. and started for Brownsville, the county seat, to place Muñiz in jail. Muñiz had allegedly tried to rape a young girl and was under indictment for theft. The deputies claimed they were stopped two miles south of San Benito and their prisoner was taken from them by masked men in another automobile. The next morning Muñiz was found hanged and shot at the scene. The knot around Muñiz's neck was a "hangman's knot," indicating that the man who tied it "knew his business."[14] There was suspicion that Carr and Hinojosa had killed Muñiz.

By early August, bandit activity was being reported in southern Cameron County. A party of surveyors driving to Point Isabel was fired on repeatedly about fourteen miles from their destination by a group of armed men camped beside the road. And north of Brownsville there were three reports of armed gangs seizing horses, saddles, and guns from ranches. On one occasion bandits forced two farm laborers to accompany them as guides. The raiders were bold, seven of them striking a ranch only seven miles north of Brownsville.[15]

The ostensible leaders of the raids were both from Cameron County. Luis de la Rosa was a former deputy sheriff at Rio Hondo described as being age fifty, weighing 150 pounds, with black hair and mustache streaked with gray and having one or two fingers off his left hand.[16] Ex-Texas Ranger Joe Taylor testified that years earlier he'd arrested de la Rosa for rustling but for lack of evidence had to release him.[17] Federal Bureau of Investigation agent Robert Barnes said that "If I recall correctly, de la Rosa was a butcher at a little town there on this side of the border—or grocery keeper, I don't know which—I think he was a butcher, though; Pizaña, I think, had a little ranch."[18]

The other *sedicioso* leader, Aniceto Pizaña Dávila, was born on March 2, 1877, at the Sombrerito Rancho into a respected ranching family. He moved to Los Tulitos ranch, eighteen miles north of Brownsville. Interestingly enough, Lon C. Hill stated that "That ranch is one of my ranches" and Pizaña "was living there on this ranch of mine about 12 or 15 years." Unlike most other ranchers, Pizaña was a poet.[19] In 1904 he met Ricardo Flores Magón and became a fervent *magonista*, helping to form in Brownsville a branch of that movement. As a *sedicioso* chieftain in 1915 he rarely led a raid himself but directed operations from the safety of Mexico, which must have had an effect on the morale of his followers.[20]

Bureau agent Louis Mennet went to Rio Hondo, the former residence of Luis de la Rosa, to elicit information. He spoke with the merchant and postmaster N. B. Maynard, who stated that prior to the Plan de San Diego, de la Rosa had operated a small grocery store and was a man of some prominence among the Hispanic population. A Mexican had told Maynard that Aniceto Pizaña had often visited de la Rosa at Rio Hondo and that they would have long conferences. The postmaster produced a large amount of mail that had accumulated for de la Rosa, but it contained nothing of a *magonista* nature.[21]

A Hispanic informant, Amaro Rodríguez, told Mennet that he, Rodríguez, had been an itinerant peddler, traveling around ranches, and had often seen Aniceto Pizaña sitting with a bunch of his friends reading to them the newspaper *Regeneración* and telling them that everything contained in the paper was true.[22] Pizaña was a fervent *magonista* and remained in contact with Flores Magón, who on February 11, 1915, wrote to him from Los Angeles replying to Pizaña's letter of January 29, addressing him as "Dear Brother" and expressing his condolences on the death of Pizaña's nine-day-old son, Praxedis (probably named for Praxedis Guerrero, a famous *magonista* militant).[23]

Despite the Tejano facade to the movement, the strings continued to be pulled from across the Rio Grande. Accompanying the raids was an intensive propaganda campaign. Not only did the official Carranza newspapers in Mexico City, Monterrey, Matamoros, Tampico, Veracruz, and elsewhere publish the Plan de San Diego Manifesto verbatim, but the Constitutionalist newspaper *El Demócrata* of Monterrey published on August 26 the latest *sedicioso* manifesto, which read in translation:

> ENOUGH!
>
> The Mexicans in arms in the southern part of the United States issue a statement to our compatriots, the Mexicans of Texas. A cry of real indignation and wrath has arisen from the depths of our souls at the sight of the crimes and outrages which are daily being committed on defenseless old women and children of our race by the bandits and miserable rangers who

guard the banks of the Rio Grande. Just and righteous indignation which causes our blood to boil and impels us, orders us to punish with all the energy of which we are capable, that crowd of savages that would put to shame a hungry tiger or a loathsome hyena. How can we remain indifferent and calm in the face of such crimes? How can we permit such offenses inflicted on our race? Is it possible that our feelings of humanity and of patriotism have ceased to exist? No! They may be asleep but it will be easy to arouse them. Enough of tolerance, enough of suffering insults and contempt. We are men conscious of our acts, who know how to think as well as the "Gringo"; who can and will be free; who are intelligent enough and strong enough to choose our authorities; and who will do it. The moment has arrived. It is necessary for all good Mexicans, the patriots, and those in whom there remains a sense of shame and pride, it is necessary to repeat, for us to repair to arms, and at the cry, "Viva the independence of the States of Texas, New Mexico, California, Arizona, part of Mississippi, and Oklahoma!," which from today shall be called the Republic of Texas, to unite with our companions in arms who have already begun the conflict, giving proof of courage and patriotism.

Viva independence, land, and liberty!

General Headquarters in San Antonio, Texas
First Chief of Operations, LUIS DE LA ROSA
Chief of the General Staff ANICETO PIZANA[24]

The manifesto's proclamation of a "General Headquarters in San Antonio, Texas" was an exercise in wildly wishful thinking, since it implied that the rebels had captured that city. They might as well have claimed that revolutionary headquarters were in Milwaukee.

The propaganda campaign became even more imaginative. Reporting on the triumphant progress of the Texas revolution, the official Carranza organ in Monterrey trumpeted on August 26 that eighty American soldiers had been killed in an engagement with the *sediciosos*. Furthermore, *El Demócrata* of Monterrey announced on August 28 that the *sediciosos*, who numbered five thousand heavily armed fighters, had not only captured Brownsville but had the American army fleeing in headlong retreat. In a further piece of creative writing, *El Dictamen* of Veracruz announced that the Indians of the Southwest had risen in arms to support the revolution and were committing all manner of depredations. The American postal authorities finally banned these newspapers. If nothing else, the *carrancista* propaganda campaign proved that the pen is indeed mightier than the sword.[25]

Propaganda was also being cranked out on the American side of the Rio Grande. In Laredo the Carranza-subsidized newspaper *El Progreso* published similar articles. In fact, George Carothers, special agent of the State Department, said that "the Editor of El Progreso at Laredo had been secretly instructed by General [*sic*] Carranza to, through the use of his paper, incite the Mexicans along the border against the United States."[26] The editor, Leo D. Walker, attacked the American authorities and censured Hispanics who sympathized with Anglos. Some Anglos finally had enough of Walker. Texas Ranger captain John Sanders arrested him on May 15, 1916. Walker posted a five-thousand-dollar bond, underwritten by three wealthy Laredoans—A. M. Bruni, Eusebio García, and L. R. Ortiz. Walker promised not to publish anything outrageous for a year.[27] But people didn't believe him, and a group of thirty Anglos seized Walker on June 15, marched him down to the Rio Grande, dispatched him to Mexico, and informed him that if he returned to Laredo he was a dead man. That night many Anglos slept with their weapons in case Walker's Mexican friends might carry out some kind of attack against Laredo. In June 1918, Walker was the editor of the *carrancista* newspaper *El Progreso* in Monterrey.[28]

In the papers of Agustín Garza is an undated and typed article in English titled "The Revolution in California." Although in English, it was obviously written by someone whose native language was Spanish: "The most important news received by the General Quarter of the Army Liberator [*sic*] of Races and Countries in America. . . ." The article advised that the entire state of California was burning in the face of the revolutionary hurricane. In a town called "Stock" (Stockton) intense fighting occurred as a revolutionary division commanded by "the German General Von Kagwer," commander in chief of operations in California, captured the town and established its headquarters there. The soldiers of the republic captured "800 'gringos' in the action, all soldiers, having the mayority [*sic*] been executed and hung in the streets and public squares. The booty was an excellent one, as they could get [*sic*] 6 pieces of artillery and 9 machine guns." General Von Kagwer was preparing to march to encircle Sacramento. In a dispatch, the good general announced the occupation by his troops of Beaumont, Banning, San Jacinto, Murrieta, and Riverside, with an attack on San Bernardino impending.[29] Obviously the writer had a rich fantasy life.

Whatever efforts were made to foment rebellion in Arizona apparently had scant effect.[30] And the *Laredo Weekly Times* reported that on August 14 one Rudolph Herler, "an emissary from Mexico," was arrested in Pueblo, Colorado, "after inciting 500 Mexicans to prepare to join the insurrection of Mexicans in South Texas. The police claim to have papers proving that Herler came here to enlist Mexicans in the revolution. Many workers in the smelters and steel works have 'enlisted.'"[31] The newspaper account was considerably overblown. The Pueblo police investigated and learned that Herler was a forty-three-year-old Mexican. He had previously been arrested for vagrancy, and on August 14 he had been arrested for drunkenness in a local saloon. According to the bureau, "The impression among the officers at the police station seemed to be that Herler was simply a drunken bum who talked too freely when drunk."[32]

Although the effort to spread the Plan de San Diego throughout the Southwest generated little traction, an undated handwritten list of names in the Garza papers is apparently one of Plan operatives, or at least sympathizers, eight each in Arizona, Colorado, and California, and six in New Mexico.[33]

One potential organizer was a man by the name of José Isabel Abarca, a former lieutenant colonel in the federal army under General Ignacio Morales Zaragoza, who was living in El Paso. Abarca, now a captain in the Constitutionalist Army, went to El Paso to ask his old commanding officer's advice. Abarca showed the general a document signed by León Caballo and others in Mexico City appointing him a propagandist for the Plan de San Diego; he later brought three propaganda circulars to show to Morales Zaragoza. The general observed that "these people are of the Flores Magón–type Socialists" and advised Abarca to have nothing to do with them, adding that "I do not think that anybody of any intelligence could be mixed up in this movement, as the plan itself was not intelligent and had many defects." The general added:

"I naturally suppose that Carranza did know of it, because this Agent had been a regular Federal Officer and had become a Carranza Officer and had been on this mission to Monterrey, Torreón, Matamoros, and Brownsville, therefore Carranza must have known of it, as this man was going about with the knowledge and approval of many of Carranza's Chiefs." Abarca, incidentally, died a few months later from complications after surgery.[34]

The focus of activity remained in South Texas, where propaganda continued. On August 28 the collector of customs at Eagle Pass reported that a Plan de San Diego organizer, one Domingo Peña, was having secret meetings and attempting to recruit men in Eagle Pass and Piedras Negras for the movement.[35] Of greater concern for the authorities was that on August 30 one José Angel Hernández, a thirty-two-year-old resident of San Antonio born in Tepic, Mexico, addressed a mass meeting in San Antonio. Hernández was a member of the radical Industrial Workers of the World, having joined in Chicago two years earlier, and was a fervent *magonista*. He had returned to San Antonio on February 2, 1915, and was currently unemployed. From his home at 908 Durango Street he had written six articles for the socialist publication *Lucha de Clases*, which had produced three issues.[36] Hernández organized a meeting at the marketplace to distribute copies of *Lucha de Clases* and recruit militants for the Plan de San Diego. He and two other speakers, Lucio Luna and Donacio Hernández, delivered flowery speeches to about a thousand listeners, stressing the oppression of Hispanics and urging their listeners to take up arms against the United States. The police, led by Chief F. H. Lancaster, an ex-bureau agent, charged the crowd and arrested Hernández, whose bond was fixed at one thousand dollars. Lucio Luna made a short speech censuring the police for arresting Hernández. Twenty-six men were arrested. As matters developed, only Hernández was charged with inciting rebellion. And he and a co-defendant, Lucio Luna, were fined two hundred dollars for unlawful assembly. The rest of the defendants were charged with vagrancy and received a ten-dollar fine. Their sentences were subsequently revoked on their promise not to participate in similar meetings. Flores Magón in his newspaper *Regeneración* championed the cause of Hernández. When his case was submitted to the grand jury, it returned "no bill." Hernández was later said to be in Waco spreading socialist propaganda. The bureau promptly sought to locate him and had the postmaster place a cover on his mail.[37]

At San Marcos, one Matías Rocha was arrested for having written a seditious letter. The bureau investigated, using informant Manuel Sorola. A grand jury in San Antonio returned "no bill."[38]

Along with the propaganda offensive, the *sediciosos* continued waging guerrilla warfare. The authorities had been hearing of suspicious activity at Los Tulitos ranch, the home of Aniceto Pizaña. A party of lawmen had located a band close to the ranch house on the evening of August 1. Before sunup on August 2, a detachment of sixteen men of Troop A, Twelfth Cavalry, under a Lieutenant Lutz, accompanied by Deputy Sheriffs Mike Monahan and José Longoria, mounted customs inspector Joe Taylor, and rancher Jess W. Scribner, rode up to the ranch house, whereupon several Mexicans with rifles in their hands ran into the dwelling. They fired from the house, while others opened fire from the stock pens and from the brush, killing Private G. W. McGuire and wounding Deputy Sheriffs Monahan and Longoria and a civilian. The Anglos retreated hurriedly in considerable disarray.[39] A young son of Pizaña's had been shot in the right leg, which had to be amputated. Monahan recalled that "I saw Pizaña hiding behind a tree. I also saw a number of horses with saddles on them hitched in the brush near the house. We exchanged several shots with them and I was wounded in the leg. It appeared that there were others in the party than those who took refuge in the house and we thought we were surrounded and retreated. I was brought to Brownsville for treatment but I think Lt. Lutz returned to the vicinity of the Pizaña residence."

The next day Sheriff Vann and a party went to the Pizaña ranch, where they arrested Ramón Pizaña, Aniceto's brother, who was found hiding under a blanket. They also seized eleven horses and saddles, and searched the house, where they found letters, papers, circulars, and poems, which they turned over to the bureau.[40] Further searching turned up some small red books titled "Libertad y Tierra de Texas," some circular letters exhorting Mexicans to join the revolution for the recovery of Texas, a great many letters from different parts of the United States, and a handful of celluloid buttons bearing a similar legend to that of the red books. The roster of *sediciosos* found at Los Tulitos after the fight was turned over either to Sam Robertson, president of the San Benito & Rio Grande Valley Railroad, or to Jeff W. Scribner, whose ranch adjoined Los Tulitos, both of whom were prominent in combating the bandits. The roster may well have become a "hit list."[41]

Ominously, the *Brownsville Herald* editorialized:

> As a result of this clash between soldiers and citizens and officers with bandits the entire lower part of the Cameron county is in arms. No fewer than fifty automobiles loaded with citizens armed to the teeth have departed from San Benito for the scene of the fighting which is about fourteen miles from San Benito and about eighteen miles due north of Brownsville. . . . Automobiles have also poured north from Brownsville, loaded with citizen and various state, county and federal officers. . . . Fears that similar gangs may spring up about the city has resulted today in an active demand for rifles and other weapons of warfare, and if any attempts are made to reach any of the communities, including San Benito or Brownsville, a warm reception is awaiting the adventurers.[42]

This marked the beginning of what became a massive Anglo backlash. Sam Robertson and Lon Hill, a prominent landowner, called a closed-door meeting on August 5 in San Benito to discuss the bandit raids. Attending the meeting were peace officers from Cameron and Hidalgo Counties and prominent citizens of the valley. The press was barred and the deliberations remained secret. The next day the adjutant general of Texas, Henry Hutchings, and Texas Ranger captain Henry Lee Ransom arrived in Brownsville to confer with Sheriff Vann about the situation.[43]

Some idea of the immediate object of this backlash came from one Abraham Ybarra, who was forced to accompany bandits who raided his home. He was taken to a point near Rio Hondo "where he declares he saw a large number of Mexicans—he did not know how many—all armed and wearing cartridge belts over both shoulders and around their waists. He said also that they wore leggings and appeared to him to be soldiers. He said the crowd appeared to be in command of a young Spaniard. Ybarra says the Spaniard told him he was from a point below Matamoros."[44]

On August 4 raiders struck again, burning a railroad trestle thirty-three miles north of Brownsville and cutting telegraph and telephone wires, effectively isolating the valley for some nine hours. Not surprisingly, there were calls for substantial numbers of troops to be stationed permanently in the valley rather than be dispatched from Fort Sam Houston in San Antonio along a vulnerable railroad line. This time the bandits added a refinement—stringing wires across the road paralleling the railroad at a height calculated to decapitate anyone driving along the road. And the next day they fired some twenty shots at a work train engaged in repairing the burned trestle.[45]

On August 6 a posse of Rangers and deputies attacked a ranch at the Paso Real crossing of the Arroyo Colorado, about thirty-two miles north of Brownsville. Adjutant General Hutchings led the posse, which included Sheriff Vann and Captain Ransom. The posse's members included Ranger Joe Anders and former Texas National Guard captain George J. Head. The newspaper account of this incident stated that on the night of August 6, officers opened fire on three alleged bandits. The officers fired as soon as they recognized the men, who were on a list of twenty-one *sedicioso* residents of Cameron County. Allegedly the band had planned to meet at the Armendáriz ranch and kill the foreman. The posse went to the ranch house after learning that one of the men they sought was there.[46] As soon as the posse sighted Desiderio Flores and his two sons, they opened fire. According to Sheriff Vann, Flores and one of the sons, who weren't armed, were shot to death in the backyard. The other Flores son was wounded in the leg and hid under a bed. When Ranger Anders started to look under it, the son shot at him with a pistol. He missed, but not by much—powder burns scarred Anders's nose. Another member of the posse jerked the mattress off the bed, and Flores was riddled.[47]

A prominent Republican politician in the valley, R. B. Creager, shed some light on incidents such as this. He estimated that "conservatively 100, maybe 200, Mexicans were killed due to the bandit troubles. In my judgment 90% of those killed were as innocent as you or I of complicity in those Bandit outrages. They had a practice of making 'black lists.'"[48]

In a related development, the authorities arrested two men near

Sebastian and one near San Benito, all believed to be *sediciosos*. Two prisoners were taken to San Benito by Sam Robertson and Deputy Constable Frank Carr and lodged in jail. The third suspect, thought to have been involved in the Los Tulitos fight, was "held in a business house where officers are said to be trying to persuade him to tell what he knew concerning the members of the gang."[49]

Francisco Alvarez Tostado, who had signed the 1914 manifesto exhorting "The Sons of Cuauhtémoc, Hidalgo, and Juárez in Texas" to rise in rebellion,[50] was charged with sedition for being implicated in a raid at Sebastian on August 6, 1915.[51] He was charged with organizing a number of men there and in the vicinity of Laredo, and he was identified as participating in one of the raids. Agent Barnes described him as being slender, about five feet eight inches tall, thirty-six years old, having a sickly appearance, and sometimes sporting a mustache. He was said to speak Spanish, English, and German. Alvarez Tostado generally used various disguises and aliases. When living in a town, he didn't remain more than one or two nights at the same place.[52]

Mrs. Adolfo Magnón and Miss María Villarreal, who knew Alvarez Tostado personally and had corresponded with him, provided the bureau with a copy of his 1914 proclamation and supplied a great deal of background information about his revolutionary activities.[53]

Informant Viviano Saldívar Cervantes didn't think much of Alvarez Tostado, whom he'd known for seven years, and who used to spend a good deal of time at Nogales, Arizona. "Tostado is always talking about revolutionary matters and trying to start revolutions but he has never shot a gun. Informant says Tostado is crazy and a dangerous man."[54]

A party of bureau agents, city detectives, and a deputy sheriff arrested Alvarez Tostado on May 27, 1916, in San Antonio and searched his room, confiscating several papers. The officers took him to the police station, where he was photographed and measured. He was then taken to the bureau office to be interviewed. Alvarez Tostado said his home was in Tepic, Mexico, but he had come to the United States in 1900 and had lived in San Antonio for seven or eight years. He was a journalist by profession. "Tostado denied any knowledge except that obtained by him from the newspapers with reference to bandit raids,

Mexican uprisings, and similar disturbances." He was taken to the county jail pending further investigation.[55]

Although the U.S. attorney regarded the evidence against Alvarez Tostado as "rather unsatisfactory," he left it up to the bureau whether to file a complaint against the Mexican. Agent Barnes instructed Agent Rogers in Brownsville to file such a complaint before the U.S. commissioner charging Alvarez Tostado with violating section six of the Federal Penal Code—an "overt act consisting of organizing about fifteen Mexicans for Brownsville raids and participating in attacking wherein [the] Austins [father and son] were killed." Alvarez Tostado, who couldn't post his thousand-dollar bond, waived his examining trial and remained in the San Antonio jail at government expense. He was bound over to await the action of the Brownsville grand jury that met on December 4, 1916.[56] The grand jury returned "no bill," and Alvarez Tostado was released.[57] He must have been both relieved and mortified, relieved because he was freed, but mortified because the grand jury didn't take him seriously as a dangerous revolutionist.

Yet the bureau kept its eye on him. Informant Manuel Sorola was assigned to ingratiate himself with Alvarez Tostado,[58] who informed Sorola that they could make money by going from town to town and living off the generosity of gullible *magonista* sympathizers. He boasted that he'd worked 394 towns and cities in Texas in 1914 and part of 1915.[59] In March 1917, Alvarez Tostado and Sorola indeed set out on such a trip. In San Antonio, Alvarez Tostado ran into trouble. He called at the home of Hipólito Villa, Pancho Villa's refugee brother, asking Villa to finance a train ticket to El Paso, where Alvarez Tostado claimed to have urgent business. Villa not only refused but pulled a gun and ordered Alvarez Tostado out of his house.[60]

Perhaps the most intriguing part of the journey was when, according to Sorola, they met with Catarino Garza, the man who had tried in the 1890s to mount a revolution from Texas against Porfirio Díaz and who was supposed to have died in exile in Panama, and who on March 27, 1917, wrote a letter to Sorola.[61] According to Sorola, Catarino Garza was living under the alias "Librado Garza González" at 602 Bridge Street in Victoria, Texas. Sorola hoped to learn the location of a supposed *magonista* arms cache buried in 1914.[62] Again according to Sorola, Garza had been approached in 1916 by Plan de San Diego types who "wanted him to take the lead and start burning railroad bridges, but that he did not want to do this, stating that they were not well armed and equipped for the expedition and that he refused to go and told them that it was not the proper time; that he did not want to start anything unless he could make a success of it."[63]

Regarding Alvarez Tostado, informant Sorola concluded that he was more a con man than revolutionist, preying on credulous *magonistas* for hospitality and financial support.[64] Alvarez Tostado illustrates how some people cynically used the Plan de San Diego for personal gain.

6 The "Bandit War" Intensifies

On August 6, 1915, a band of fourteen heavily armed Mexicans (Lon Hill claimed there were twenty-five or thirty) appeared at the village of Sebastian. They robbed a saloon, crossed the railroad track to Alexander's store, which contained the post office, and looted that establishment. Some of the raiders then proceeded to the granary near the railroad track where several people were repairing a corn sheller. They seized A. L. Austin and his son, Charles, respectively president and secretary of the local Law and Order League, recently organized to assist the peace officers in preserving order. After taking them to the Austin home, they transported the Austins in a wagon, driven by a lad named Elmer Millard, whom they had also taken prisoner. A short distance from the house the raiders made the two Austins get out of the wagon and shot them to death. Millard was released. According to Lon Hill, several of the raiders were identified, and most of them were thought to have come from Texas.[1] The *Brownsville Herald* editorialized that the time had come for citizens to take "energetic measures" against the bandits.[2]

Marauders continued to steal horses from area ranches. Fifteen armed men appeared at the Yturria ranch, sixty miles north of Brownsville. They held several cowboys at gunpoint while they made off with five horses, two saddles, two Winchesters, and a pistol. Los Tulianos ranch near Brownsville lost eight horses, six saddles, and a mule to raiders, but a detachment of the Twelfth Cavalry recovered the loot after a brisk firefight.[3]

Also on August 6, a band of Mexicans shot at an automobile near Los Fresnos, twelve miles from Brownsville, wounding one Sonny Huff.

The Mexican consul and intelligence chief in San Antonio, Teódulo R. Beltrán, issued a public statement categorically denying that the bandits operating near Brownsville belonged to any Mexican faction and suggested that they were American citizens. Thus their depredations were a local affair "and do not threaten international complications." He stressed that the Mexican military at Matamoros had taken precautions to prevent raids into Texas from Mexico. Furthermore, Beltrán declared that the radical labor organization the Industrial Workers of the World was responsible for the raids.[4]

On August 7 a circular printed in Matamoros appeared in Brownsville urging Mexicans to join the Texas revolution, which would constitute a "vindication of right and justice lost to us for so long a time."[5]

A band of Mexicans shot and wounded Charles Jensen, night watchman at the gin at Lyford, on August 8.

The same day, Caesar Kleberg, manager of the Norias Division of the enormous King ranch, learned that a band of raiders had been sighted on the Sauz ranch, one of the five divisions of the ranching empire. Kleberg happened to be in Brownsville at the time, and he immediately asked the army and the Texas Rangers for assistance. Corporal Allen Mercer and seven privates from Troop C, Twelfth Cavalry, were detailed to Las Norias. Joining them were the adjutant general of Texas, Henry Hutchings, who had come to the lower Rio Grande valley to direct counterinsurgency operations, and Texas Ranger captains Henry Ransom and Monroe Fox and the men of their two companies. The soldiers and Rangers traveled on a special train the seventy miles north to Norias, whose two-story wooden ranch house was also a flag station on the St. Louis, Brownsville & Mexico Railroad.

Meanwhile, the *sediciosos*, estimated to be about fifty and led by Luis de la Rosa, captured an elderly King ranch employee, Manuel Rincones, and forced him to serve as a guide, which of course meant that they weren't locals. Rincones stated that at their nearby encampment there were about fifty officers and soldiers.[6] Rincones related that "The band consisted of a chief, a major, a captain, and 25 soldiers from Mexico; the rest were picked up on this side of the Rio Grande. At Nopal the major took a paper from his pocket and directed the first sergeant to read it. It stated that the object of the expedition was to reclaim the land that had been taken by the United States from Mexico. It was ordered in the name of Carranza, and the officer stated it emanated from him. . . . The chief was called Luis; the major, Miguel; the captain, Gabriel. There was also a commander named Ricardo Gómez Pizaña, from Rancho Viejo, which is south of the Arroyo Colorado, but near Paso Real." (In 1917, Felipe Sandoval, a participant, corroborated Rincones's account and identified Luis de la Rosa, chief; Miguel Guevara, major; Evaristo Ramos, Gabriel Tijerina, and José Benavides, captains.)[7]

At Norias the Rangers and some King ranch employees rode into the brush in hopes of intercepting the raiders. Ironically, they rode right past the *sediciosos* hidden in the chaparral. The latter had no intention of taking on the Rangers, for their object was the soft target of the two-story ranch house at Norias, which they expected to be lightly guarded and full of loot. According to Rincones, the "attack on Norias was for the purpose of securing tools from the section house, with which to remove a rail and wreck a train. This was the scheme of Ricardo Gómez Pizaña." Only two Anglos lived at Norias: Frank Martin, an ex-Ranger and currently ranch foreman, and George Forbes, the ranch carpenter.[8] The Mexicans were unaware that the squad of cavalrymen had arrived, as had Cameron County deputy sheriff Gordon Hill, two customs inspectors (ex-Ranger Joe Taylor[9] and ex-Ranger sergeant Marcus Hines),[10] and immigration inspector David Portus Gay Jr. The trio had also come up by train in hopes of participating in any clash with the raiders.

About 6 p.m., Hines noticed a large group of riders coming in from the east. At first he thought they were the Rangers returning, but soon realized from their big hats that they were Mexicans, and they were coming at a dead run carrying a white flag and a red one, presumably the red for "no quarter" and the white for a parlay leading to the surrender of Norias. Hines gave the alarm, and the scratch force prepared to fight for their lives. The guerrillas halted their charge about 250 yards from the ranch house, dismounted, and began firing. Two soldiers as well as Frank Martin and George Forbes were wounded in the initial exchange of gunfire.

Nonplussed by the unexpected resistance, the guerillas blundered by failing to cut the telephone line. The defenders put in a frantic call for help to Caesar Kleberg, who was at Kingsville, requesting ammunition and reinforcements. To no avail. Kleberg later explained that no locomotive engineer was willing to make the run to Norias, but as far as the defenders were concerned they'd been abandoned to their fate, and this remained a sore point for years.

The firefight at Norias raged for two and a half hours. Forbes and Martin were seriously wounded but recovered.[11] The cavalrymen, three of whom suffered minor wounds, demonstrated admirable fire discipline, using their ninety rounds apiece judiciously, but eventually they and the other defenders were nearly out of ammunition. The climax of the engagement came at 8:30 p.m., when the raiders mounted a determined charge against the ranch house. They got within forty yards before breaking and retreating. As Manuel Rincones recalled, "The leaders were gallant, but the soldiers failed to respond and a withdrawal was ordered. The men scattered, but soon reassembled and the first sergeant called the roll." At the roll call after the fight at Norias there were three missing in addition to the four men killed. The missing were thereafter carried on the rolls as deserters. One of the missing was Ricardo Gómez Pizaña, a nephew of Aniceto Pizaña, who was allegedly de la Rosa's lieutenant in the raid.[12]

The dejected raiders fled into the night, leaving four of their comrades dead on the field. One was later identified as a Tejano—a Jesús García who lived on the Cortillo ranch near San Benito. Two more raiders died of their wounds on the retreat. One of them, named Ricardo, from the town of Sebastian, was badly wounded, was unable to continue, and was killed by Major Miguel Guevara. Another Sebastian resident, Evaristo Ramos, was also a member of the Norias raiders, as were "José Benavides, from the Bonita Ranch, near Cañitas . . . Juan Romero, who has recently been employed at Los Lipanes, Darío

Mercado who worked as a laborer at the Pie Ranch near Sebastian, Antonio Rocha, an old employee of the King Ranch [Rocha was wanted in Cameron County for several murders], Teodoro de la Fuente, who furnished supplies and tobacco at the Jesús María Ranch, fifty-five miles north of Edinburg, and who guided the band through the dense brush about the place."[13]

The only Norias fatality was a Hispanic woman whose husband was a section hand on the railroad. The raiders had seized her, and Antonio Rocha demanded that she tell him how many gringos were at Norias. According to her son, she defiantly called Rocha a coward and told him to go find out for himself. He shot her in the mouth. (Rocha got his just deserts in 1919—he was killed by Mexican soldiers as, handcuffed, he attempted to escape just as he was being delivered together with Pedro Paz to the sheriff of Cameron County on an extradition warrant.)[14]

Finally, at 10 p.m. a relief train arrived from Kingsville loaded with armed and angry men. A railroad surgeon attended to the five men wounded in the engagement. An hour later, a relief train from Brownsville arrived.[15]

Fearing an ambush in the dark, the Rangers decided to wait until daylight before pursuing the Norias raiders. By the time they began following the trail the raiders were long gone. Guiding the raiders in their retreat to the Rio Grande was Teodoro de la Fuente. According to Rincones, "the object in heading for the Rio Grande was to secure reinforcements and a new supply of ammunition when the operations were to be continued." This didn't happen. The raiders released Manuel Rincones and crossed the river. For fear of retribution, Rincones had to go into hiding on one of the Kleberg ranches near Kingsville.[16]

Everett Anglin testified that "Mr. Baker [sheriff of Hidalgo County] phoned me the day following the raid, asked me if I would meet him out at Mr. Sprague's ranch; that he was going to try to get this bunch of bandits that raided the Las Norias ranch. So we went out there in cars—there were ten of us in the party—and got some horses there and went to the Jesús María ranch, owned by Amado Cavazos, who is deputy sheriff. These bandits had been there and had just left. They had butchered a cow there and ate, and Cavazos told us who was in the party and gave us some literature—some circulars—that they had left there." Anglin said the literature consisted of *sedicioso* propaganda: "there was going to be a general uprising; they were going to kill all the Americans, especially the rangers, soldiers, and [peace] officers; said it was an order from Carranza. They had left several of those circulars and he gave them to us. He also knew some of the people that were in the party."[17]

By striking at the King ranch the *sediciosos* had hoped to win a symbolic victory, since the ranch epitomized Anglo domination in South Texas. And by striking seventy miles inland from the Rio Grande they had hoped to cause terror throughout a wide swath of South Texas. But their tactics had been amateurish, notably the failure to reconnoiter and determine how many defenders were at Norias and the failure to cut the telephone line. They had mounted what proved to be their major military operation, outnumbering their opponents by four to one, and it had been a complete failure, defeated by a scratch force of a squad of cavalrymen and a handful of civilians.

One might try to spin the *sediciosos*' defeat at Norias into a moral victory by stressing that the clash terrified Anglos in the region. If so, it was a pyrrhic moral victory. Anglo fear manifested itself by a quantum leap in the backlash against the militants. Not only were the Rangers increased, and a company stationed at Norias, but army reinforcements poured into the valley. Most ominously, it became open season on "bad Meskins." It's hard to see how these developments were good news for the *sediciosos*.

It should be stressed that both sides tended to exaggerate the enemy's casualties. As an example of exaggerated claims, on September 2, 1915, General Alfredo Ricaut at Nuevo Laredo wrote to General Pablo González in Mexico City enclosing six postcards made from photos allegedly taken at Norias. One showed the ranch house, "where a fierce combat took place, with *more than thirty American soldiers killed* [italics added]"; another showed American troops who survived the encounter; the rest were of dead revolutionaries, "many of them innocents taken from their homes to be hanged."

Significantly, Ricaut also enclosed a report from "Major Manuel Amarante, the agent whom I had in Texas in compliance with your orders and who arrived here [Nuevo Laredo] yesterday." Amarante was a member of Ricaut's staff. So at least one Mexican officer had been in Texas observing, if not participating in, the raids.[18]

The Norias raid did have significant consequences. For one thing, it panicked the citizens of Kingsville, who feared a similar attack. The sheriff asked the state to lend fifty rifles with which to arm the citizenry against Mexican bandits, and the Anglo citizens organized a home guard.[19] The *Brownsville Herald* reported that the Rangers were now said to be working under special orders from General Hutchings, receiving "certain instructions." The newspaper speculated that these "special instructions" ordered them "to shoot to disable suspicious characters on sight." There were now thirty-eight Rangers in Cameron County, practically the entire force. And the Rangers were being increased to fifty men.[20]

The key Ranger figure was Captain Henry Lee Ransom, arguably the most controversial captain in the history of the Texas State Ranger Force. Ransom was a piece of work. Frank Hamer, the most famous Ranger of his generation and a pretty tough customer himself, described Ransom as being as "cold-blooded as a rattlesnake," and one of the most dangerous men Hamer had ever known.[21] Ransom had been a Fort Bend County deputy sheriff from 1902 to 1905. He served in the Rangers in 1905, resigning to become city marshal of Colorado City, and resigning that office in 1907 to become a ranch manager. He reenlisted in the Rangers in 1909, resigning to become a Waller County deputy sheriff.

In 1910, Ransom became a special officer in Houston, one of several ex-Rangers, including Hamer, that Mayor Rice hired to clean up the city. Ransom certainly did his part, shooting dead the most prominent criminal defense attorney in town—and being acquitted on a plea of self-defense. In 1912, Mayor Rice appointed Ransom as Houston police chief. His tenure was marked by controversy and charges of excessive use of force. Ransom then became manager of a Texas prison farm.

On July 20, 1915, Governor Ferguson commissioned Ransom as captain of a new Ranger company, Company D, and gave him the assignment of cleaning up the lower valley. The governor ordered Ransom to do whatever it took, assuring him that he had the pardoning power.[22]

Ransom evidently felt that he was an instrument of justice in carrying out Ferguson's orders. The Ranger captain soon became notorious because of his ruthless approach to counterinsurgency—when in doubt, shoot.[23]

Conventional wisdom has generally accepted Special Ranger Pat Haley's dictum that "The soldiers did the guarding and the Rangers did the hunting."[24] Captain Ransom was the most prominent of the hunters. One reporter's comments shed light on the situation: "One injustice which is done to the Mexicans, it seems to me, is to assume that guilt runs in consanguinity. When a certain man is discovered to have taken part in a bandits' raid, his brothers, half-brothers, and brothers-in-law are assumed to be guilty and are immediately arrested or killed. Cousins are not proven guilty by such kinship, but are placed under strong suspicion."[25] Articles about the troubles on the border appeared in national magazines.[26]

A photograph of "Texas Rangers" (on the left was Ranger captain Monroe Fox, in the middle future Special Ranger E. B. Scarborough, and on the right Tom Tate, ex-Ranger and current King ranch employee) on horseback at Norias lassoing the bodies of dead Mexican raiders in order to drag them to a common grave caused considerable attention. Some were outraged, decrying the triumphalism and callousness of the Rangers. Others viewed the photograph as a metaphor for the Plan de San Diego—try to mount a rebellion in Texas and you end up as dead meat being dragged off to a common grave. The photograph has exercised some present-day historians who evidently feel that the Rangers didn't display sufficient reverence toward their fallen enemies.[27] These writers condemn the Rangers' callousness, but significantly, they are silent regarding the case of an American soldier captured by Mexicans, taken across the Rio Grande, shot to death, his ears cut off as souvenirs, decapitated, his head displayed on a pole for the benefit of his comrades across the river, and the body thrown into the Rio Grande, from where his remains were later recovered. This would appear to be a much greater atrocity than lassoing a few corpses. Selective moral outrage is wonderful to behold.

On the night of August 8, twelve armed Mexicans boldly rode up to the municipal slaughterhouse on the northern outskirts of Brownsville.

They were riding good horses, and each man sported a new rifle and pistol and crossed cartridge shoulder belts. They asked the night watchmen whether there were any cows in the corral awaiting slaughter. When he showed them the empty corral they rode away into the night.[28]

After dark on August 9, Mexicans fired on a cavalry patrol at the Mercedes pump. One Mexican was killed. On August 10, Mexicans fired on a three-man cavalry detachment stationed at Palm Garden crossroads, just west of Mercedes, killing Private L. C. Waterfield. Army reinforcements and a civilian posse failed to locate the Mexicans. After the engagement American soldiers found several documents, including a vaccination certificate issued at Matamoros on March 25, 1915, to José Angel Elizondo, a printed proclamation, and a letter to Elizondo from Lorenzo Juárez, chief of immigration at Matamoros, long suspected of supporting the *sediciosos*. These papers were abandoned together with twenty-eight horses, five hundred cartridges, and some other personal effects, the bandits taking to the brush. The cavalrymen also captured a large flag bearing the inscription "El Ejército Libertador de los México-Texanos."[29]

And at the scene of the fight City Marshal Everett Anglin found a Mexican officer's blouse. The blouse had some red on the inside, indicating that the owner's underwear had faded on the blouse. Several hours after the fight at Palm Garden, a tall Mexican named Cantú was drinking in a saloon at Donna only a few miles from the scene of the clash. Cantú wore trousers matching the blouse found by Anglin. He was arrested on suspicion, and it developed that he wore red underclothing and that the underclothing had faded on the trousers as well as on the blouse. Sheriff Baker released Cantú, but army officers believed that he'd participated in the Palm Garden fight.[30]

Everett Anglin stated that Amado Cavazos, owner of and a deputy sheriff at the Jesús María ranch, was visited by a party of sixty-eight guerrillas, among them Teodoro de la Fuente and Evaristo Ramos. They roughed up Cavazos and gave him a circular signed by Pizaña and de la Rosa calling on Mexicans to unite in an uprising to regain Texas. After this incident Cavazos resigned his commission as deputy sheriff and moved to Laredo. On another occasion, George Burton, foreman on Young's ranch, was approached by a group of twenty bandits and made to furnish three horses. He recognized José Regalado and several others.

On August 9 the *Brownsville Herald* reported that "Three alleged stock thieves were reported Saturday night to have been killed by a posse in western Hidalgo county, in the vicinity of Monte Christo."[31]

Snipers shot at an army truck carrying supplies to a detachment near Los Tulitos ranch. On its next run the truck was guarded by a strong force of cavalry.[32] And the reports continued to pour in. Six cavalrymen patrolling the Rio Grande between Mercedes and Donna were attacked during the night by a band of supposed bandits. After a brief firefight the troopers dispersed their antagonists, killing one, and captured three horses and a mule loaded with ammunition. When news reached the nearby towns, civilians quickly formed posses and began searching for the outlaws.[33]

On August 13 a press report from Brownsville read: "One Mexican was killed today near Lyford by soldiers and peace officers. The Mexican was arrested near dawn suspected of wounding Night Watchman Fritz Georgie at Lyford and while being taken in an automobile to Lyford made a break for liberty and was shot. Rangers and troopers guard a wide section of the state here and seemingly have the bandit situation in control."[34]

On the night of August 15, Mexicans on their bank of the Rio Grande fired on a cavalry patrol near Progreso, about one mile north of the river. No one was hurt. But the next night Mexicans again fired across the river at a twenty-man cavalry detachment of Troop C, Twelfth Cavalry, guarding the crossing. Although the detachment had changed its location several times, a Mexican force estimated at seventy-five to one hundred men managed to locate them. At nightfall a surprise volley by the Mexicans killed a cavalryman and wounded two others. The cavalrymen withdrew from the river and called for reinforcements from Mercedes. A company of the Twenty-Sixth Infantry rushed to the scene in automobiles, followed by the balance of Troop C of the Twelfth Cavalry and six Texas Rangers. In pitch darkness the two sides fired at each other's rifle flashes. The intense firefight lasted about twenty minutes.[35]

A Brownsville newspaper reported that in response to the deteriorating situation, "Rangers and peace officers are disarming all Mexicans outside of the larger towns throughout this section. Firearms in the possession of Mexicans in the rural sections who are unknown to the officers mean serious consequences."[36] Moreover, a battalion of the Ninth Infantry was rushed by special train from Fort McIntosh at Laredo to Kingsville to be deployed in small detachments to protect towns in the vicinity of Brownsville. Two days later, a second battalion of the regiment was rushed to the area by special train. Immediately, the people of Laredo asked the federal government for additional troops to protect Laredo. They were reassured when the two battalions of the Ninth Infantry returned within a week, being replaced near Brownsville by the Twenty-Sixth Infantry from Texas City and two batteries of artillery and an airplane from Fort Sill, Oklahoma. The lower valley was thus protected by some twenty-five hundred soldiers.[37]

Major General Frederick Funston, commander of the Southern Department with headquarters at Fort Sam Houston in San Antonio, initially had dismissed the troubles as being merely an enhanced version of the rough politics endemic in South Texas or as just garden-variety crime. As a newspaper reported, John Nance Garner, the congressman from South Texas, "is of the opinion that constituted authorities in Mexico are responsible for the trouble, a statement in which Gen. Funston does not seem to agree. But it must be remembered that Mr. Garner is familiar with conditions along the border, while Gen. Funston is not."[38] But as evidence mounted about the true nature of the raids, the general finally became convinced that they were supported from Mexico. He ordered the above reinforcements in response to urgent requests from Congressman Garner and a delegation of Brownsville citizens. Laredoans were further reassured when the Fourteenth Cavalry at Fort McIntosh was reinforced, enabling it to patrol the river more effectively.[39]

The *sediciosos* continued their propaganda. On the night of August 22, one Miguel (later referred to as Manuel) Saiz was at a *baile* at the Placeres dance ground near Brownsville. Late at night when only a few men were left, Saiz harangued them for over an hour, saying things such as "now is the time to rise up and arm ourselves and retake all of the land the Americans have stolen from us." Deputy Constable Bonifacio González arrested Saiz, who was charged with "inciting a rebellion against the authority of the United States." Saiz claimed that he'd been drunk and didn't remember what he'd said. However, in his suitcase the authorities found a "red flag." He was committed to the Cameron County jail in default of a two-thousand-dollar bond. Saiz was indicted by the grand jury.[40]

The *sediciosos*' main triumphs were in the imagination of propagandists. For example, the August 19 edition of the Carranza newspaper *El Demócrata* in Monterrey triumphantly reported the capture of Mercedes after a fierce fight, witnessed by many innocent spectators who later joined the rebels, swelling their numbers to three hundred well-armed and -equipped men. Unfortunately, the *sediciosos* later had to abandon Mercedes.[41] Stories such as these caused considerable merriment in Brownsville. Hilarity increased when *El Demócrata* published an article on "The Revolution in Texas" which announced that *sediciosos* had captured Brownsville and were advancing on Rio Grande City. "The revolution has taken on great force having become of such serious proportions that the Americans are now unable to suppress the trouble; that the uprising is not confined to the Mexican revolutionists, but that many other Mexicans have joined the cause and fully 5000 men are now armed and equipped." The article added that "all railroad and telegraph communications from the Rio Grande to the north has been cut and that American women and children are fleeing to the interior as the Americans have given up all hope of suppressing the uprising."[42]

But Anglo newspapers sometimes didn't help to reassure the citizenry. On August 15 an Associated Press story was published under the headline "Over Thousand Carrancistas Have Invaded Texas and Started Uprising." The subhead read: "Troops from Nafarrete's Command at Matamoros and under Command of [Juan] Santos, [Vicente] Dávila and [Carlos] García Said to Have Crossed Rio Grande and Scattered with Purpose of Inciting Mexicans to Armed Revolt."[43] The report proved untrue. General Nafarrate emphatically refuted the story, pointing out that he had only five hundred soldiers in Matamoros; hence the report that a thousand *carrancistas* had invaded was patently false.[44] As one newspaper observed, "A whole lot of these alleged bandit attacks on certain places are a huge hoax" to justify requesting the stationing of troops in certain towns, to the delight of the business community.[45] The commanding officer at Fort Brown warned newspapers against printing lurid and sometimes false reports about conditions on the border.[46]

Sometimes apprehensive people saw raiders where there weren't any. On June 24, 1916, for instance, Company K of the Fourth Infantry was rushed to the Piper plantation near Brownsville because a band of bandits was massed across the river. The American troops spent the weekend camped in full view of the Mexicans, who made no menacing moves of any kind. The reason was because they weren't bandits after all—they were civilians guarding an extensive crop of corn ready for harvest.[47]

But vigilance was the watchword. As the *Alice News* reported, there were no bandits in Jim Wells County, but peace officers remained on alert: "While owing to sickness Sheriff Osborn has not been 'in the saddle' much of late, he has been keeping vigilant watch on the Mexican situation, and his deputies don't let anything suspicious get by them. For instance, a strange Mexican rode into town Monday and he had hardly gotten out of his saddle when Deputy Bob Rizer was at his side. The result was that Mr. Mexican was relieved of a big husky six-shooter, failed to give an accurate account of himself, and is now comfortably reclining in the County Bastille."[48]

On the other hand, ethnic relations in Kingsville seemed rather cordial, according to the local newspaper: "Next week the Mexicans of this city will start a ten or fifteen day celebration. It is headed by reputable citizens of this county who have homes here, jobs in town and have lived in this part of the state for generations. We fully expect, when the news goes abroad, to have the papers over the country—the excitable sort—herald the fact? [*sic*] in box car letters, that Kingsville is enjoying the novelty of a Mexican uprising. For the benefit of the timid in other sections of Texas where these papers circulate, we state that the Mexicans here have had such a fiesta ever since the town was and will continue to celebrate their independence day just as we will continue to celebrate the Fourth of July."[49]

Conditions in the valley varied. At San Diego there was quiet, and business as usual was the order of the day, although as a precaution many ranchers had sent their families to Corpus Christi for safety.[50] On August 25, Texas Ranger captain John J. Sanders reported that "the citizens of San Diego are very much alarmed and I am told Americans [Anglos] have all sent their families away." Yet that same day the Duval County officials complained about the presence of a six-man army detachment stationed in San Diego to protect the town and requested that the soldiers be removed immediately because they weren't needed and their presence was objectionable. This when many towns in South Texas were clamoring for more troops. Political boss Archie Parr had the situation well in hand.[51]

Precautions were also taken at the Santa Gertrudis ranch, located three miles west of Kingsville and owned by Mrs. H. M. King. The Anglo employees were instructed to sleep on the roof of the main building, where an ample supply of cots and firearms had been provided. Several antique smooth-bore cannon, used to protect the ranch in the nineteenth century, were refurbished and were ready in case of necessity.[52]

Summary justice was reportedly being meted out in places such as Mercedes. An Anglo woman coming from Mercedes told the *Brownsville Herald* that home guard vigilantes had hanged a Mexican, and that night another Mexican sought medical help for a crudely bandaged hand, explaining to the doctor that it was a "bad sore." Upon examination, it proved to be a bullet wound. The doctor notified the vigilantes, who promptly executed the Mexican. Before being shot he confessed that two of his associates were in town. They too were captured, and before being shot confessed that they'd come into town to purchase supplies for a band of *sediciosos* camped in the brush. As the newspaper put it, "The story cannot be proved or disproved, but if it be true it will serve to throw light on the situation through which up-Valley towns have passed coincident with the recent outlaw raids in Cameron and Hidalgo counties."[53]

A few days later, two Mexicans who had allegedly participated in killing the Austin father and son were taken from the jail in San Benito; their bodies were found the next day alongside the railroad track. And near Raymondville, an alleged participant in the Norias raid was killed.

"According to officers, this man's name was among those given by the member of the band who made a deathbed statement. . . . Officers were watching for him. He attempted to resist arrest, and was shot and killed."[54]

But despite the raids there were hopeful developments. It was reported that Mexican troops fired on Mexicans trying to cross the river into Mexico near Mercedes, presumably *sediciosos* fleeing from a posse. General Nafarrate notified the American authorities that he was doing everything he could to stop bandit raids.

The American consul in Matamoros reported on August 20 that ten deserters from the Carranza army had crossed to the Texas side above Hidalgo. Cavalry units, the sheriff and deputies of Hidalgo County, and Texas Rangers gave chase. The Rangers managed to capture one man who allegedly had papers on him implicating several residents of Hidalgo County. But after a pursuit lasting four days the authorities failed to catch up with the rest of the band, who crossed back into Mexico about sixty-two miles west of Brownsville.[55]

On August 25 late in the afternoon at Progreso, some fifteen to twenty Mexican troops on the Mexican side of the Rio Grande fired on an American patrol on the Texas side. The Americans were caught out in the open, whereas the Mexicans were concealed in the thick brush. The Americans took cover and fired back at the rifle flashes. Two American horses were killed. The Mexicans had dug trenches at night and fired from them. Five Mexicans were reportedly wounded.[56]

American consul Jesse Johnson remained convinced that General Nafarrate had nothing to do with the raids. "Referring again to Gen. Nafarrate, I have found him a man of his word and if he has any great prejudice against Americans, I have not been able to discover it. He has especially been considerate with me and has granted me many favors."[57]

A disquieting development occurred at Corpus Christi in late August, when the authorities arrested one Andrés Esquivel on a charge of seditious conspiracy for complicity in the "Plan de Calallen," so named for the little South Texas town of Calallen. It urged the Mexicans of Nueces County to rise in rebellion on the night of September 5. The authorities claimed to have found a letter written by Esquivel to a confederate in Laredo. As the newspaper related, "It is such plots as this that cause the Americans to wonder if the plotters are possessed of good sense." Not surprisingly, nothing resulted from this affair. Esquivel was deported to Mexico as an undesirable alien and the charges were dismissed.[58] Nevertheless, such incidents served to keep the Anglo citizenry on edge.

No one traveled on the roads at night.[59] On August 26 it was reported that twenty heavily armed Mexicans had crossed into Texas a short distance west of Progreso. Immediately a chase began, but the Mexicans succeeded in recrossing. On this occasion Nafarrate took action, arresting several men at Reynosa, for which Colonel Bullard of the Twenty-Sixth Infantry expressed his appreciation.[60]

But the level of violence was decreasing. As of August 30, "With the exception of the killing of one alleged participant in the Sebastian raid and the shooting and wounding of a Mexican prowling about the ranger camp at Norias Saturday night, Saturday night, Sunday, Sunday night and today passed without any reported disorders in the section affected the past three weeks by bandits or raiders," the Brownsville press reported. As far upriver as Starr County, there were no reports of raids. Doubtless contributing to this desirable state of affairs was the fact that the Rio Grande was at a near-historic high, making raids considerably more difficult.[61]

The respite proved short lived. On the night of August 30 a band of some twenty-five Mexicans burned a fifteen-foot-long trestle on the St. Louis, Brownsville, & Mexico Railroad near Barreda, only fourteen miles from Brownsville. The lawmen and soldiers who rushed to the scene found a dynamite bomb, daggers, machetes, an old rifle, and two pistols, as well as some wire, leading the officers to speculate that the raiders were frightened off before they could complete all the damage they planned. Although marauders cut the telephone line on both sides of San Benito, they left the telegraph line intact.[62]

At about 9 a.m. on September 1, this same band boldly emerged from the chaparral surrounding the pumping plant of the Fresnos Canal Company, eight miles from the Rio Grande. They burned the buildings and seized Stanley S. Dodds, who had the contract to build the pumping station; a certain J. T. Smith; and two Mexican employees. One of the employees, the carpenter Ventura Rodríguez, subsequently stated that the *sediciosos* made him carry some of their equipment, including bombs, an electric firer, and a bag of cartridges. Juan Simo allegedly acted as interpreter between Dodds and Aniceto Pizaña, who led this band.[63] Dodds testified that their personal possessions were stolen, and they were lined up to be shot. However, one of the gang had previously worked for Dodds, and he and the two Mexican prisoners successfully pleaded that the Anglos be spared. The raiders and their prisoners started toward the little village of Los Fresnos, where a few American farmers had settled. En route they encountered Henry Donaldson, a newcomer to the region who was driving a wagon going to town for a load of lumber. The raiders seized him too and hustled their prisoners down the canal right-of-way for several miles. Then around noon four of the raiders took Smith and Donaldson out in the brush, asked them if they were Germans, and when the prisoners just shook their heads they shot them to death. One account alleges that Smith and Donaldson were tortured and mutilated before they were shot.[64]

The Mexicans then took their surviving prisoners to the end of one of the lateral canals, fed them lunch, and treated them considerately. After several hours the party started in the general direction of the coast but were intercepted by armed civilians from San Benito and Brownsville together with several detachments of cavalry who had rushed to the scene. Just east of Los Fresnos as the raiders and their prisoners were crossing a clearing they were sighted, and a firefight ensued in the heavy chaparral. Dodds seized the opportunity to escape. He said later he had heard that one Mexican had been killed in the fight, the others having escaped. Dodds also claimed that Aniceto Pizaña, dressed in a Mexican Army uniform, had led the raiders, half of whom were armed with new Mauser rifles and the rest with .30-.30s and sporting rifles. He also mentioned that raiders carried bombs made of a one-and-a-half-inch-diameter piece of iron pipe with a stick of dynamite inside.[65] Soldiers of the Twenty-Sixth Infantry subsequently found in the brush a box containing thirty-six sticks of dynamite, which they exploded harmlessly.[66]

The bodies of Smith and Donaldson were taken to Brownsville, where hundreds of irate townspeople filed through the funeral parlor to view them. The murders of the two men caused the *Brownsville Herald* to editorialize that "The Time Has Come!" The editorial stated, among other things, that "The murders at the Fresnos plant yesterday are the signal for action by every self-respecting, loyal citizen of Texas, living on this border. The time has come when every law-abiding citizen must do his part to protect the people who are living on this border. A heinous crime was committed by the band of desperados who killed those men. That crime must be punished. The blood of those innocent men must be avenged. This outlawry must cease. . . . There can be no middle ground. Every man who is on the side of law and order here must show himself as such." The army at Fort Brown appealed to the public for any information about bandit activities.[67]

On the night of September 2, bandits robbed the post office at the hamlet of Abram, near the Rio Grande southwest of Mission. According to Postmaster J. L. Longoria, the bandits were Vicente Cantú, Francisco Sánchez, Manuel Medina, Guadalupe Cantú, and Pancho Hernández.[68]

On September 3 the *Lyford Courant* commented on the Plan de San Diego and the resulting troubles in the lower valley, emphasizing that only a few Hispanics had joined the insurgents and that what had saved the situation was not the actions of the army and peace officers but the fact that the great majority of Hispanics had remained loyal. "We were absolutely at the mercy of such an uprising had it really been successful."[69]

On September 3–4, at Cavazos Crossing, just south of Mission, a party of Mexicans looted the village of Ojo de Agua. Captain (and future major general) Frank R. McCoy, commanding the Mission Sub-District of the Brownsville Cavalry Patrol District, with detachments of Troops H and G, Third Cavalry, and Sheriff A. Y. Baker and deputies, struck the trail and followed the Mexicans to the crossing. The raiders made it back to Mexico, but their leader had been wounded and had lost his diary and company roster. The names were sent to the Mexican consul in the vain hope that the Mexican authorities would take action. The diary showed that the raiders had been at de la Rosa's camp at Corrales, near Reynosa, about a week previously. Captain

McCoy also had information that some Japanese were with de la Rosa at Corrales, making bombs.[70] (Japanese involvement in the Plan de San Diego affair is a topic requiring further research. It may be speculated that Carranza sought Japanese support for his regime.)

McCoy had several sources of intelligence about the bandits. He received detailed information from a volunteer, Miss E. Bliss Baldridge, the schoolmarm at Peñitas, a hamlet in Hidalgo County on the Rio Grande west of Mission. She had been teaching there for the past five years and informed McCoy that "I know many of the bandits in person and I know most of them are Carranzista [*sic*] soldiers." She added that "I have the children of the bandits, outlaws, gamblers, smugglers etc. all in my school" and from them she obtained considerable information. She had ostensibly to remain neutral, but in addition to writing to McCoy she met with him on the weekends in Mission.[71] Miss Baldridge, incidentally, wasn't motivated entirely by civic duty; she was sweet on McCoy, who unfortunately for her was a confirmed bachelor.

Besides what he learned from Miss Baldridge, McCoy between March 1 and December 1, 1915, used one L. M. Kirkes as a secret agent. Kirkes, a notorious smuggler of cattle into Texas, was particularly valuable because of his unsavory connections across the river. He assured McCoy that he was a reformed smuggler, influenced in part by McCoy's success in combating smuggling. As McCoy later reported, "During the whole period of the raiding times of last summer and fall [of 1915] he assisted me in many ways, accompanying my scouts along the river. He showed himself brave and manful and a sought [sort?] of American that would be extremely used in trying times especially in Mexico." However, because of his criminal antecedents, Texas Rangers and deputy sheriffs wanted to serve a warrant on Kirkes, who feared being shot out of hand. His wife appealed to McCoy, who arranged for Kirkes to deliver his weapons to the captain and surrender to face the charges. McCoy notified the Rangers and deputies and saw to it that Kirkes was released on bond. Unfortunately, the bad blood that existed between Kirkes and customs inspector Sam McKenzie led to a shooting affray on the main street of Mission in which both men were shot.[72]

On September 4, Mexicans fired from their side of the Rio Grande at American troops on the Texas side. In the battle that ensued, one

American soldier was wounded and reportedly eleven Mexicans were killed and forty wounded.

On September 6, Sheriff Baker and six deputies were scouting along the river near Mission, at Cavazos Crossing. They sighted Carranza cavalry on the opposite bank. Everett Anglin recalled that "We stood under cover there quite a while to see what we could see, and Mr. Baker, the sheriff of the county, walked out upon a levee that had been thrown up, and they saw him, and when they did they commenced shooting at him." The Mexicans hated Baker, and he became the target for several rifles from across the river about a hundred yards away. The sheriff counted on Mexicans habitually shooting high, and he gave a convincing performance of being shot. The Mexicans erupted in jubilant cheers and tossed their hats in the air. Baker's deputies immediately opened fire when the Mexicans thus showed their position. Anglin continued: "We returned the fire and we fought there about an hour, I guess, and finally we ran them off; and so there was a kind of horseshoe in the bend of the river there, and they would get around and kind of cross-fire on us; and we thought it was about time to move, and we went out to Mission and got two troops of Cavalry. Capt. Frank McCoy was stationed there, and Capt. Wells. We got back there and reported to them what we had run into, and they returned to the river with us. As soon as we reached—got back to where we had to fight, there had been some Mexicans killed; we didn't any of us get hurt. . . . There was one soldier wounded; he didn't die. . . . [T]hey started the fight about 9 o'clock and it lasted until 4:30 that afternoon, when they withdrew."[73]

In a significant development, on September 8 the army assumed exclusive control over the bank of the Rio Grande in the Brownsville vicinity to handle situations arising from firing across the river. This was done partly because on occasion citizens and deputies had provoked the Mexicans by opening fire. Henceforth, peace officers were to police only the interior.[74] Furthermore, General Funston persuaded Governor Ferguson to order that no males capable of bearing arms be allowed into Texas from Mexico unless they could explain their reason for seeking admission.[75]

On September 9 one Francisco Guerra was attacked and killed near

Lyford by a gang of five Mexicans. The *Brownsville Herald*'s account stated that "The killing of Guerra, a Mexican who spoke English well, by Mexicans, is the first incident of the kind reported since the beginning of the troubles in this section. The attacks of the bandits have in every case of violence been directed against Americans although it is known that many Mexicans peaceably inclined have been forced to join the bandit gangs."[76]

At about 3 a.m. on September 9, Sam Robertson, president of the San Benito & Rio Grande Valley Railroad, was ambushed. He'd played a leading role in combating the *sediciosos*. Robertson was driving about ten miles south of San Benito after spending the day collecting arms and ammunition that the Hispanic community had "voluntarily" turned in. San Benito's mayor had issued a proclamation requiring every male resident between twenty-one and sixty years of age to be subject to special police duty. As Robertson accelerated through a hail of gunfire, one bullet knocked his hat off, another pierced the passenger seat, and still another hit the gas tank, but Robertson was unscathed. He attributed his survival to bad marksmanship.[77]

In early September it was reported that General Pablo González was contemplating removing General Nafarrate from command of the Matamoros garrison because he was widely believed to be implicated in the raids into Texas. Further, González ordered subordinate commanders along the border to refrain from such activity and threatened them with severe punishment for violations. General Alfredo Ricaut, who happened to be another of Carranza's nephews, commander of the Nuevo Laredo garrison and the riverfront from Hidalgo to San Ignacio, received such an order.[78]

Nafarrate had become the bane of the U.S. Army's existence in the valley. When Colonel Blocksom, commanding the Brownsville District, demanded that Aniceto Pizaña, Luis de la Rosa, and their companions be arrested and turned over to American authorities, Nafarrate assured Blocksom that he would send his soldiers out to search for them and try to determine whether they had been involved in the revolutionary troubles in Texas. He promised to arrest them if found. That shouldn't have been too difficult, as it was public knowledge that Pizaña was seen in the main plaza of Matamoros receiving the congratulations of his friends over the recent attack by raiders against a cavalry patrol near Brownsville. De la Rosa was also repeatedly sighted in Matamoros and Reynosa.[79]

As to Nafarrate's involvement with the raids, Colonel Bullard had no doubts whatsoever. Bullard said that he arrived in Brownsville on August 17, 1915, and that immediately thereafter Nafarrate began to send him notices through the Mexican consul that some of his troops were deserting and joining the bandits. Bullard believed this was done to create the impression that Nafarrate wasn't assisting the bandits as some of these "deserters" rejoined the Carranza troops after participating in raids and being driven back across the Rio Grande. The colonel also resented that although he notified Nafarrate that U.S. Army airplanes would make flights they were fired on from Matamoros when they made their second and third flights.[80]

On September 13, just before daylight, Mexicans surrounded the house at Josiah Turner's Galveston ranch near San Benito. They fired on the nine sleeping soldiers, killing Private Anthony Kraft, Third Cavalry, and wounding two others.[81] After a firefight lasting half an hour the Americans managed to drive their assailants off. The residents of San Benito fully expected to be raided by bandits, but strong cavalry and infantry patrols around the town ensured that there would be no trouble. Colonel Blocksom ordered that with the assistance of the sheriff, soldiers search all Hispanic homes in the vicinity, seize weapons, and arrest every Mexican suspected of being implicated in the Galveston ranch shooting.

The Brownsville newspaper reported that "No trace has been obtained of the Mexican prisoner captured Monday in the search of houses for arms in the neighborhood of the fight Monday where the Mexicans attacked an army camp. Sheriff W. T. Vann said he feared that some mishap had occurred to the prisoner before he reached jail. Mr. Vann has given renewed instructions to his deputies to protect their prisoners at the risk of their own lives if necessary."[82]

During that day the soldiers and Rangers arrested five Mexicans living at the ranch. "Colonel Blocksom cautioned Major Edward Anderson to be sure that sheriff's posses and rangers do not kill any of these men." The five prisoners were taken to San Benito, turned over to a deputy sheriff, and placed in jail.[83] That night at about 9:30 deputy sheriffs took three of them out of jail, placed them in an automobile, and started down the Harlingen road. Next morning these three Mexicans were found dead some distance from the road. They had been executed. The peace officers claimed the prisoners had jumped out of the auto and had tried to escape into the brush. However, Josiah Turner, owner of the Galveston ranch, indignantly asserted that the three were innocent.[84]

Authorities kept a wary eye all along the Texas border to ensure that no Plan de San Diego disturbances accompanied the Mexicans' celebration of September 16, Mexican Independence Day.[85] None did.

While patrolling the river bank on September 17 within a mile of the western city limit of Brownsville with his troop of the Third Cavalry, Lieutenant E. L. N. Glass was fired upon by *carrancistas* from the Mexican side of the river. No casualties.[86]

On September 17 near Donna, at the Red House crossing of the Rio Grande, Mexicans fired on an army patrol. A Sergeant Llewellyn maintained his ground until Lieutenant Milton G. Holliday arrived with reinforcements. Quite a battle ensued, with the army claiming that seventeen Mexicans were killed or wounded.[87]

Despite these incidents, conditions seemed to be improving. Residents of the ranches and small towns around Harlingen requested that the army withdraw the detachments protecting them, there being no recent reports of raids. And the correspondents, including Floyd Gibbons of the *Chicago Tribune*, his colleagues of the *Chicago News*, the Associated Press, and the International News Service, all of whom had been in Brownsville for the last three weeks covering the border warfare, packed up and left town, believing the troubles were no longer newsworthy. Furthermore, a special train carrying 150 eager prospective homeseekers arrived in San Benito.[88] But the apparent peace proved to be only an interlude. The "Bandit War" would continue.

7 The "Bandit War" Peaks

Twelve mounted and armed Mexicans rode into La Palpa ranch, about twenty miles north of Mission, on September 23, 1915, at about 8 a.m. They remained about an hour and departed with a considerable amount of ranch property, including horses, mules, rifles, and ammunition. The ranch manager, Francisco Guerra, promptly notified the army at Mission. A large force of cavalry was deployed to search for the robbers, but they managed to escape.[1]

On September 23 an outpost of Troop M, Sixth Cavalry, was fired upon near the La Feria pumping plant, twenty-eight miles west of Brownsville. No casualties.

On September 24, Lieutenant W. King of the Twenty-Sixth Infantry, arriving at the Florencio Saenz store at Progreso, Hidalgo County, at about 7:30 a.m. was shocked to find Private Henry Stubblefield dead and Private Cecil Kennedy wounded. The alarm was given and reinforcements rushed from the Mercedes Canal head gates. Lieutenant King with his nine men opened fire on a party of Mexicans who were discovered on the American side, estimated to be about seventy-five men. At about 8 a.m., Captain A. V. Anderson and a troop of cavalry appeared at Progreso. In the battle, which lasted from 8 a.m. to 10 a.m., Captain Anderson was wounded in the arm. Soldiers beating the brush found parts of Mexican Army uniforms, including hats, belts, and also several Mauser rifles. The cavalry pursued the Mexicans, killing two on the American side of the Rio Grande, two crossing in boats, and several more as they clambered up the Mexican bank. As the raiders retreated back across the Rio Grande, several hundred Carranza troops, firing from a half-mile of trenches along the river, provided intense covering fire. General Nafarrate forcefully denied that any of his men could have possibly participated in the engagement. He pointed out that those who protected the raiders' retreat wore uniforms similar to those of Carranza soldiers, but this did not prove that they were Carranza soldiers, as the same uniforms could be gotten anywhere.[2]

It turned out that Privates Stubblefield and Kennedy had arrived at the Saenz store simultaneously, and after Stubblefield was shot down, Kennedy, shielding himself behind a little monument in front of the church, alone and unaided fought desperately against the bandits until the first reinforcements arrived. His assailants numbered more than fifty men. It was afterwards learned that Stubblefield had unsuspectingly encountered the Mexicans as they were setting fire to the Saenz house. As he entered the door he was riddled.[3]

Hidalgo County deputy sheriff Tom Mayfield and his partner captured one Guadalupe Cuéllar, a Mexican who had resided on the American side of the Rio Grande for eight years and who had participated in the raid, and turned him over to Captain McCoy. The prisoner gave a sworn statement "and told the way the raid was planned on the Mexican side by the two Carrancista garrisons coming together and making this raid on this store, and some property was taken back as well as some Government horses." According to Cuéllar, the raiders crossed the river in three boats hidden there for that purpose. The prisoner then made a shocking statement: "one soldier was captured and taken across the river, was shot four or five times, and his ears were cut off as souvenirs for the officers, each commander getting one. His head was cut off, and they paraded back and forth with his head on a pole."[4] The unfortunate soldier was Private Richard J. Johnson, who had been one of the ten men on guard at Progreso Crossing. This atrocity so infuriated General Frederick Funston that he requested permission from the War Department to proclaim "no quarter" against the insurgents. The secretary of war himself quickly denied the request.[5]

One result of the Progreso fight was that the army deployed a battery of mountain guns that commanded the Mexican entrenchments across the river and presumably got the Mexicans' attention. It was dryly pointed out that employing this artillery wouldn't cause hostilities with Mexico because General Nafarrate had officially notified the American authorities that he'd removed his troops from the riverbank, concentrating them in barracks in the border towns. So, if the guns had to lay down a barrage, it would just be against bandits.[6]

Perhaps not coincidentally with the emplacement of American artillery, General Nafarrate announced that he'd arrested all the Mexicans he could find who had been participating in the Texas revolution. It turned out that this reportedly amounted to a grand total of five arrests, carried out by one of his subordinates at Camargo, a hundred miles upriver from Brownsville.[7] As for Pizaña and de la Rosa, Nafarrate stated that they were still at large, but he had ordered that they be arrested on sight and brought to his headquarters in Matamoros. Nafarrate later stated that he'd in fact tried to arrest de la Rosa and Pizaña but that they had gone "by the time information that they had been in Matamoros reached him." Moreover, he claimed that five Carranza soldiers and an officer had deserted and joined the *sediciosos*.[8]

On September 23, bureau agent J. H. Rogers went to Matamoros and called on General Nafarrate. In reply to Rogers's questions Nafarrate reiterated that he had tried to cooperate with the American authorities and adamantly denied that he or any of his soldiers had assisted the raiders. As for those raiders killed or captured in Texas armed with rifles and ammunition similar to that used by *carrancistas*, defeated *huertistas* and *villistas* by the hundred had fled to Texas taking their weapons with them. Nafarrate blamed the troubles on these refugees and complained that American officials were unfriendly. He vigorously denied that he was anti-American. In reporting this conversation, agent Rogers mentioned that "I knew General Nafarrate in Mexico. He was friendly to me."[9]

Colonel Pedro Chapa, a member of Nafarrate's staff, published an article excoriating the *Brownsville Herald* for its editorial alleging that

General Nafarrate was the person responsible for the raids. Adhering to the official line, Chapa charged that the *Herald's* allegations were criminal. The uprising in Texas resulted from the oppression of Tejanos. The Mexican authorities had remained neutral and had respected international law by permitting Texas revolutionaries to enter Mexican territory. He vigorously denounced the insolent American attitude that if *sediciosos* crossed into Mexico the Americans would pursue them. Ending his tirade with a burst of bravado, Chapa asserted that if Americans pursued revolutionaries into Mexico "we will go to Fort Bliss [in El Paso] to get Huerta, Raul Madero, and other traitors who have found refuge beyond the [Río] Bravo."[10]

On September 24, eight of the Progreso raiders decided to go for what they believed were easy pickings—the San Juanito ranch of elderly millionaire James B. McAllen near Monte Christo in Hidalgo County. Only McAllen and María de Agras, his Hispanic cook and housekeeper, were in the single-story ranch house. The marauders rode up to the house and demanded that the cook tell McAllen to come out.[11] Realizing that they meant to kill McAllen, she woke him from his afternoon nap, gave him a shot of whiskey, handed him a loaded shotgun, and informed him that he'd have to fight for his life. He did so. The front of the house had windows covered by wooden shutters; McAllen fired both barrels of buckshot through one of the shutters, killing not only the leader of the raiders but his horse as well. The shocked survivors took cover in the outbuildings and laid siege to the ranch house. McAllen kept firing from window to window while his housekeeper reloaded his weapons. To the bandits' dismay, he killed another one and wounded three more, two of whom later died. Since this was not at all what they had anticipated, after twenty minutes the chagrined bandits left. McAllen hid out in the brush for a time in case they returned.[12]

Something unprecedented occurred on the night of September 27—the first attack on an Anglo woman. Grace Carter, who resided near Harlingen, encountered two Mexicans while going for a bucket of water. One of the Mexicans fired at her, grazing her forearm; she was armed with a pistol, which she fired three times, putting her assailants to flight. The Brownsville press reported that "The attack on Miss Carter was traced to the policy of killing off the bad men in this section, and

Miss Carter was the innocent victim of an attempt at revenge. . . . The attack was attributed to the fact that relatives of Miss Carter were reported among Mexicans to have been in a party that recently killed a bad Mexican. . . . Following the attack on Miss Carter, Mexican houses in the vicinity were searched for freshly fired fire arms, but nothing was found."[13]

But despite incidents such as that involving Grace Carter, the perception was that the bandit troubles were finally ending. To celebrate, the McAllen business community sponsored the showing of a free movie, an event that drew a capacity crowd at the Columbia Theater.[14]

Between August 25 and September 25 the American Red Cross operated a railroad train from Piedras Negras full of foodstuffs for distribution to the starving population of Coahuila. The Red Cross official in charge of the train talked with *carrancista* General Elizondo and his staff in Monclova, and this unit of some twelve hundred men were quite anxious to learn of their compatriots' success in the Texas revolution. They were dumbfounded when the Red Cross official informed them that the rebellion was nearly over. The Mexicans were under the impression that the Carranza lines were within a few miles of San Antonio. They departed shouting "Adios, Gringo; we will see you in San Antonio." The official commented that "San Antonio seems to be these Mexicans' seventh heaven; and it is evident that the chiefs have been promising these men a *paseo* in San Antonio when they take it," adding that if Washington wasn't aware that the *carrancistas* were backing the Texas revolution it was high time the administration realized that.[15]

It is not beyond the realm of possibility that the Red Cross was also gathering intelligence, for "A general plan for relief of the northern part of Mexico was instituted with the assistance of the War Department. This plan contemplated the assembling of relief supplies at all railroad points of entry into Mexico from Brownsville, Tex., to the Pacific coast. A special agent of the Red Cross was appointed who distributed supplies from Eagle Pass as far south as Monclova. United States consular officers also rendered assistance, particularly at Monterey [*sic*], Laredo, and Eagle Pass."[16]

On October 1 there was a report from Mission that Luis de la Rosa had been ambushed and killed by deputy sheriffs. This welcome news was later discredited, although "it is known that American peace officers had arranged a trap to lure de la Rosa across the river somewhere between Brownsville and Mission and then to ambush him. The plan was to take him prisoner." And General Nafarrate announced, as he had done repeatedly, that he intended to eliminate bandits, this time those concentrated across from Progreso, that is, de la Rosa's band concentrated near Reynosa. This although de la Rosa appeared openly on the streets of Reynosa.[17]

Americans, who were understandably skeptical about Nafarrate's pronouncements, received some good news on October 2. General Nafarrate, whose recent promotion in rank had been celebrated by a grand ball in the Reforma Theater in Matamoros, announced that he was being transferred, his successor being General Eugenio López, who assumed command on October 4, bringing three hundred of his own troops with him. Nafarrate left for Ciudad Victoria on October 11.[18] Interestingly, one O. H. Hinojosa, a lumber dealer from Rio Grande City, said a friend of his had ridden on the same train with Nafarrate from Matamoros when the general was going to his new command at Ciudad Victoria. When the train reached Corrales, the friend had seen Nafarrate unload and deliver to Luis de la Rosa five hundred rifles or carbines and some ammunition.[19]

While it has been suggested that Carranza had no control over Nafarrate and the latter's involvement in the Texas revolution, the fact that Carranza didn't just transfer Nafarrate but promoted him in rank to general of brigade and gave him the new assignment of commanding in Tampico, the strategic port through which most of Mexico's petroleum was exported, suggests strongly that this was all a reward for a job well done.

The greatest single atrocity of the "Bandit War" came to light on October 2. As the *Brownsville Daily Herald* reported:

> Fourteen bodies of Mexicans who had been dead from a week to two or three days were found yesterday and this morning on and near the road between Donna and Ebenezer, in Hidalgo county, according to report reaching Brownsville today, both from official and private sources. First reports

> by the army, made last night, said that eleven bodies had been found. Three additional bodies were reported this morning. Most of the bodies were clad in ordinary farm hand clothes, some of them with blue overalls and soft felt hats. Four or five were identified as having been employed on farms in the Donna section of late, and are said to have gone away with the bandit gangs which operated in that section. The question of the burial of the bodies of the fourteen men lies between Mexican friends and the coroner. The Mexican friends, it is said, are afraid to go out and bury the bodies, and it was reported from Donna today that the coroner was skeptical about undertaking the job alone. Arrangements were under way for an escort to accompany the coroner to where the bodies were found, and after the usual formalities of inquest have been gone through, the bodies will be buried.[20]

The Mexicans had all been shot in the head, and the bodies aligned in a row; as an added insult, five of the corpses had empty beer bottles stuck in their mouths.[21] Although the perpetrators were never identified, many suspected the Rangers.

There continued to be incidents. On October 3 about half a dozen Mexicans tried to ambush a four-man cavalry patrol near the La Feria pumping plant, about thirty miles upriver from Brownville. The Mexicans opened fire as the patrol rounded a bend in the road, but the patrol charged them, driving the ambushers into the brush, where they disappeared.[22]

However, on the night of October 18 the southbound St. Louis, Brownsville & Mexico Railroad passenger train was derailed at Olmito, a mere six miles north of Brownsville.[23] The army had been guarding every bridge on the route for several months but had removed the guard from this bridge two days earlier because there hadn't been any trouble in the vicinity. But through the *sedicioso* grapevine the raiders quickly learned that the bridge was unguarded. The Mexicans, some sixty in number, had removed all the spikes and fish plates connecting rails. With a wire attached to the rail on the west side, just as the train went by at about thirty miles an hour they pulled the rail from under the engine, which plunged into a ditch, lying perpendicular to the track. The baggage and mail cars were turned on their sides.

In the smoker were seated several soldiers on leave; Dr. Eugene S.

McCain, state health officer stationed at Brownsville; Harry Wallis, formerly a Ranger; District Attorney John Kleiber; and several others. According to Kleiber, "Scattering shots and then irregular volleys broke out and increased in volume; and cries, 'Viva Carranza,' they cried. 'Viva Luis de la Rosa.' 'Viva Aniceto Pizaña.'" As soon as the train had come to a complete stop, four unmasked Mexicans entered and began shooting at the terrified passengers, and then, seeing the soldiers, turned their fire on Corporal McBee, Private Claud J. Brashear, and Corporal C. H. Laymond, all from the Third Cavalry. McBee, just as he was rising from the floor, was shot and instantly killed. Brashear was approached by the leader and after several words was shot in the face just to the right of the nose, the bullet coming out in the neck. He survived. Laymond was shot in the leg and neck. He also survived.

Dr. McCain and Wallis sought refuge in the toilet, but one of the bandits coerced a young Hispanic boy to tell him where they were, saying that "We are not looking for anybody but the Gringoes [*sic*], the Americans."[24] The bandit fired repeatedly through the toilet door, one of the shots striking McCain in the abdomen. He died next day. Wallis was hit five times: "They shot one finger off here, broke my arm up here, shot me across this finger here, just a little flesh wound here where the bullet went across. He shot me twice in the leg."[25]

The engineer, H. H. Kendall, was pinned beneath his cab and killed, his hand still on the throttle. R. Woodall, the fireman, was painfully burned by escaping steam. A great many shots were fired from the brush into the train, but other than those fired in the smoker none took effect.

By ten o'clock next morning seven suspects had been captured, and later that same day the Rangers executed four of them—Santiago Salas, Trinidad Ybarra, Jesús Ybarra, and Severo García—at the scene for alleged complicity in the wreck.[26] Sheriff Vann, who was there, described what happened. Captain Ransom informed Vann that he was going to execute the Mexicans and asked, "Are you with me?" Vann said no, whereupon Ransom stated that "If you haven't got guts enough to do it, I will go myself." Vann retorted: "It takes a whole lot of guts—four fellows with their hands tied behind them." The sheriff went up the road to arrest two men wearing shoes allegedly taken from passengers in the train. When Vann returned, Ransom and his men had taken the four prisoners about a mile from the road and killed them. Ransom also wanted to execute Vann's two prisoners, but Vann refused to turn them over and took them to jail. This was fortunate, because they were later found to be innocent.[27]

The relatives of the four executed men were afraid to bury the bodies without protection from officials. No inquest was held. "The justice of the peace said he would probably return no verdict, but that the only possible verdict in the cases would be that the four deceased met their deaths as the result of bullet wounds inflicted by parties unknown." The bodies were buried at county expense.[28]

In the aftermath of the wreck, work crews built cribbing around the destroyed 185-foot trestle, and regular train service resumed by October 20. Brownsville residents, estimated at over a thousand, flocked to the scene of the wreck; hundreds of them were women, many of whom had to be carried from the scene because of fainting spells.

Sheriff Vann felt that the only effective way to prevent future bandit attacks was to clear all the brush for a half mile back along the riverfront and along both sides of the railroad track from Brownsville to San Benito. Caesar Kleberg favored clearing a strip a mile wide along the river, pointing out that "The vegetation along this zone now is principally prickly pear, which spreads wonderfully and grows six to eight feet high; mesquite and innumerable other semitropical plants, which make the underbrush almost impenetrable for American soldiers." Not only that, but Kleberg advocated imposing martial law in the area involved in the Plan de San Diego and establishing concentration camps for all Mexicans who couldn't give a good account of themselves.[29]

District Attorney Kleiber testified that according to Harry Wallis, Luis de la Rosa, whom Wallis knew well, was among the train wreckers. Furthermore, one Santiago "Chano" Flores, arrested in connection with the attack, claimed he had been working near Matamoros and had practically been kidnapped by the raiders, who numbered some sixty, all but five from Matamoros; about half were *carrancista* soldiers. They crossed the Rio Grande the morning of October 18 and reached the scene of the wreck about sundown. There they were joined by four or five Tejanos. They made camp and prepared to attack the train. Immediately after the train wreck they disbanded, and all the Mexicans except Flores returned to Matamoros. Further, Flores claimed that de la Rosa and Pizaña had lived in Reynosa for several weeks and maintained their headquarters there. He claimed that the "revolutionary army" consisted of about five hundred men, divided into several companies, the one to which he belonged consisting of fifty or sixty men.[30]

One Guadalupe Ramos shed further light on the Olmito wreck. He stated to Deputy Sheriff Mike Monahan that "he formerly lived in the vicinity of the Werbiske Ranch and one day José Benavides came to his house and told him that Evaristo [Ramos, his brother] and the others wanted him to join them and he did so, the band at that time being in the brush at La Rosita Ranch. They remained in this vicinity for some time while men were being recruited for the train wreck. They were fed by Ponciano Guajardo of the San Pedro or Guajardo Ranch and by Toribio Ramos of the San José Ranch. De la Rosa was very active recruiting." Ramos said that ten picked men boarded the train while the others stood guard over the wreck. He also gave the deputy the names of those whom he admitted were in the wreck.[31] After the wreck, the band went toward the Arroyo Colorado, east of San Benito, then doubled on their tracks, returning the following day at noon to a point near the Rio Grande west of the wreck site.[32]

Rogerio Caballero was tried in Brownsville in the fall of 1916 for complicity in the train wreck and the murders of Dr. E. S. McCain and Corporal McBee. He was declared not guilty.[33] Harry Wallis sued the St. Louis, Brownsville & Mexico Railroad for twenty thousand dollars in actual damages and five thousand in exemplary damages, alleging that the railroad had failed properly to protect its passengers and that as a result of being shot his earning capacity was permanently reduced.[34]

Colonel A. P. Blocksom, acting through Consul Johnson, requested that General Eugenio López, commanding in Matamoros, do all in his power to apprehend Pizaña and especially de la Rosa, who had been recognized as having led the Olmito train wreckers.[35] López replied that he was surprised at the request, because from reliable reports he'd received neither of them was to be found in the area under his command. Nevertheless, should they, or any other suspicious persons, be captured, he firmly proposed to punish them—should they prove to be guilty.[36]

Also at Colonel Blocksom's request Consul Johnson informed López on October 21 that de la Rosa had crossed the river on the night of October 19 and "was seen on the streets yesterday morning in Reynosa and that your officers seemed to pay no attention to him, that he was now three miles East of Reynosa on the Corrales Ranch. He wants you to have him arrested at once—that no Mexican will be safe hereafter in the Valley so long as de la Rosa and his partner in crime Aniceto Pizaña are at large."[37] Blocksom also requested that López arrest José Benavides, and stated that Vicente Dávila, "one of the ringleaders in the Norias fight, is now living just across the river east of the Eastern Matamoros trench" and earnestly requested that he too be arrested.[38]

According to López, de la Rosa hadn't been in the area for some time, and thus the reports reaching Colonel Blocksom were false.[39] Blocksom also received reports that Japanese were making bombs at de la Rosa's camp.[40] López then demanded that Blocksom specify exactly where the *sediciosos*' camp was, so that he could send a detachment to deal with them.[41] López later informed the consul that he had sent special agents to the Reynosa area and they'd reported that there was no *sedicioso* encampment.[42] General López's successor, General Alfredo Ricaut, stated in December that he'd issued strict orders to suppress any movement aimed at causing trouble in Texas.[43]

Benjamin Johnson touts the *sediciosos*' military accomplishments in August and September 1915—thirty-plus raids in eight weeks—which Johnson finds to be most impressive.[44] But the *sediciosos*' offensive consisted largely of hit-and-run raids, and they proved much better at running than hitting.

Official U.S. figures for Anglo casualties in the "Bandit War" list eleven soldiers killed and seventeen wounded and six civilians killed and eight wounded[45] for the period July 1915–June 1916. Compare this with Pancho Villa's raid on Columbus, New Mexico, on March 9, 1916. Villa burned part of the town, which was the base camp for the Thirteenth Cavalry regiment, and killed eighteen soldiers and civilians. So, in one nighttime guerrilla attack Villa killed as many Anglos as did the *sediciosos* and their *carrancista* allies during the *entire* "Bandit War." This puts the *sediciosos'* military endeavors in some perspective. Their campaign did very little to achieve the stated goals of the Plan de San Diego but quite a lot to advance Carranza's strategy of creating crisis and chaos on the border so that the United States would recognize his regime in order to end this deplorable state of affairs.

The *sediciosos* were never in any danger of losing their amateur status. Their leaders, Agustín S. Garza, Luis de la Rosa, and Aniceto Pizaña, had no previous military experience, and their rebellion reflected this unpalatable fact.

8 The "Bandit War" Winds Down

Meanwhile, on the diplomatic front Carranza's strategy succeeded brilliantly. On October 19, 1915, the United States formally extended diplomatic recognition to First Chief Venustiano Carranza as the de facto president of Mexico. The immediate benefit to Carranza was securing permission to rush seven thousand troops on American railroads from Eagle Pass, Texas, to Douglas, Arizona, in order to repel Pancho Villa's offensive against Agua Prieta, Sonora.[1] And now only Carranza could legally import arms and ammunition from the United States, whereas his enemies would have to resort to smuggling. Carranza played Woodrow Wilson like a violin. Villa, who up to then had been the least anti-American of the Constitutionalist chieftains, was especially outraged at Carranza's recognition and began planning his revenge—the raid on Columbus.[2]

Leon Canova, head of the State Department's Division of Mexican Affairs, was of the opinion that "once before, when we increased our border forces, it had the effect of curbing the raids from the Mexican side. I might add, in this connection, that it has often been reported that the Mexican Government and many of the people believe that the continuous raids into United States territory in the summer and early fall of 1915 forced this Government to recognize Carranza."[3]

General Frederick Funston declared he was confident that Carranza was not averse to supporting the raids. But because Carranza's strategy had been counterintuitive, Funston couldn't follow Carranza's line of reasoning and couldn't understand how the raids hastened his diplomatic recognition. Funston did believe that as soon as Carranza was recognized he wanted the raids stopped and, knowing that Nafarrate would object, he replaced Nafarrate.[4]

Rodolfo Rocha maintains that whereas Carranza may have permitted the raids to continue as he attempted to obtain diplomatic recognition, he never "officially" endorsed the raids.[5] The reason, of course, why Carranza didn't "officially" endorse the raids was because he was not a fool. Governments rarely "officially" endorse their covert operations.

In discussing the Plan de San Diego's demise, Douglas Richmond ascribed the defeat of the movement primarily to "the ruthless response of local authorities," but he then stated that once Carranza had "achieved his diplomatic objective" he temporarily ended the fighting.[6] Richmond later clarified his position, writing that Carranza's boldest undertaking was supporting the Texas revolution, using this as leverage for securing diplomatic recognition "and as a means of staving off incursions by U.S. troops."[7]

Richmond thus supports the position of Charles C. Cumberland, who in 1954 wrote that since the last great raid virtually coincided with formal recognition of the Carranza regime and since the raids ended as soon as Carranza wanted them ended, quite clearly Carranza used the raids as an instrument of policy.[8] William M. Hager likewise believed in Carranza's intrigues, asserting that Carranza himself ended the raids into Texas and quite evidently used the border troubles to force recognition by Wilson. Once recognition came, the disturbances ceased and the Plan de San Diego faded.[9]

Texas Ranger captain W. M. Hanson declared that: "Thereafter [after Carranza's recognition] General Nafarrate was called to Monterey [*sic*] where he was wined and dined and made much of, and publicly given the credit of forcing Wilson to recognize Carranza."[10]

The fact remains that within a week of Carranza's diplomatic recognition the raids into Texas stopped. Mere coincidence?

The Wilson administration had persisted in believing that the situation in the lower valley was one for the state authorities to deal with, not the federal government. This attitude had frustrated the locals, who repeatedly wired their senators and congressmen pleading for governmental action, stressing that as long as the bandits had a sanctuary across the Rio Grande the outrages would continue. Some two hundred prominent citizens from Cameron, Hidalgo, Brooks, Willacy and Kleberg Counties met in Brownsville to discuss the situation. Texas adjutant general Henry Hutchings was among the speakers. The consensus was that the citizens' patience was about at an end and the situation was fraught with the gravest consequences. A delegation had gone to Austin, Fort Sam Houston, and Washington to present their grievances.[11]

Carranza telegraphed to Governor Ferguson on October 29 reiterating that he had ordered his commanders on the border to arrest de la Rosa, Pizaña, and any other Tejano rebels who entered Mexican territory. And Carranza's personal envoy, Roberto Pesqueira, conveyed to Ferguson Carranza's warm felicitations and assured the governor that the Carranza government was ready to cooperate with American authorities in suppressing lawlessness along the border.[12]

The troubles in the valley had included the complete collapse of an entire industry—the little-known business of rattlesnake catching. Impressively sized rattlesnakes abounded in the brush, and Mexicans ordinarily did the catching, pinning the reptiles with a forked stick, slipping a noose over their heads, and tying the snakes to a tree while hunting for more of them. Dealers sold the snakes all over the United States and in various foreign countries. Now, however, the snake catchers feared encountering bandits in the brush and were refusing to chase snakes, "even at the lucrative figure of 50 cents to $1 per snake."[13]

De la Rosa continued to be of great concern to the American authorities, and he was evidently invisible to the Mexican authorities, who seemed unable to locate him although his camp was at the Corrales ranch, three miles east of Reynosa, and he was frequently seen on the streets of Reynosa itself.[14] But it was Aniceto Pizaña who would strike the next blow for the Texas revolution.

On the night of October 21–22, 1915, Pizaña participated in an attack on an American outpost at the Ojo de Agua ranch, seventy-four miles west of Brownsville and about one mile north of the Rio Grande.[15] There were eight Signal Corps soldiers manning a wireless station and seven men of Troop G, Third Cavalry, at the ranch. They stupidly failed to post a sentry and, suspecting nothing, were all fast asleep in a little wooden shack. Had the raiders chosen to sneak up on them they could have massacred the lot. Instead, about 1 a.m. the Mexicans stupidly opened the engagement with a terrific volley from 150 yards away, enabling the shocked Americans to grab their weapons and mount a spirited defense. The Signal Corps men were armed only with pistols, while the cavalrymen did have rifles. The firing was heard at Mission, eight miles away, and Captain McCoy ordered all troops in the vicinity to the scene. He led a troop of the Third Cavalry to Ojo de Agua, arriving just as the firefight ended. Meanwhile, Captain W. J. Scott, in bivouac at Peñitas, two miles west of Ojo de Agua, with twelve recruits, had reached the scene and had attacked from the west. He was largely responsible for driving the raiders off.

At Ojo de Agua the raiders burned the residence of one George Dillard, a prominent local rancher, and robbed the post office and a store. American casualties were three killed—Sergeant Herbert R. Smith, Signal Corps, commanding the detachment, and Privates Joyce and McConnell of the Signal Corps—and eight wounded.[16] Sergeant Smith was mentioned in general orders of the Southern Department for "having distinguished himself in action." Although wounded four times, Smith directed the defense until he died.[17] The Mexicans lost five killed, whose bodies were found within fifty feet of the ranch house, and reportedly nine wounded, three of whom subsequently died in Reynosa.[18] Everett Anglin, who arrived a short time after the raid, stated that there were three dead soldiers and four wounded soldiers lying in and under the shack, which had at least five hundred bullet holes in it. There were also ten dead cavalry horses. Among the Mexican dead were one Japanese and two Carranza soldiers. Across the front of their hats was a ribbon bearing the words "Viva la Independencia de Texas."[19]

An American cattleman, Ed Oliver, who visited Reynosa frequently, witnessed the return of the raiders, who brought four wounded, one of whom was Japanese. One of the Mexican wounded, named Gallegos, died for lack of medical attention, allegedly withheld by the better class of residents of Reynosa who disapproved of de la Rosa and his associates.

De la Rosa frequently rode around the plaza in Matamoros in the only automobile in town. But as soon as Carranza was recognized diplomatically he sent telegraphic instructions to arrest de la Rosa. Oliver subsequently saw four Japanese that de la Rosa had in his entourage. Oliver was told they were leaving for Monterrey. "They were rather discouraged, stating that de la Rosa had made them very flattering promises but had not fulfilled them."[20]

Regarding the homemade hand grenades the raiders carried, Tom Mayfield testified that "I never saw any of the bombs, but when De la Rosa was camped opposite where I had some cattle pastured we sent a number of different Mexicans into his camp to get information, and he had four Japs there making hand grenades out of green cowhides for him. We had quite a few witnesses who told us about those hand grenades." The Japanese placed the explosives in the cowhide while it was green and then let the cowhide dry. Mayfield added that "they would put bolts or pieces of iron in the hand grenade with the explosive, and sew this green hide on." They would also make signals, *pitos*, whistles that sounded something like a turkey. "These four Japs were employed all the time they were in camp there making these hand grenades, or these 'pitos.'" Mayfield said that the Japanese were making these bombs at a place called Garania [Corrales?], about three miles east of Reynosa; it was de la Rosa's camp. De la Rosa himself was staying at the Carranza garrison in Reynosa each night.[21]

On October 24 a band of Mexicans attacked the entrenched camp of the small army detachment guarding the rebuilt railroad bridge at Olmito. The camp was located at an oil well, about three hundred yards from the scene of the train wreck. The raiders struck about dusk and fired into the camp, the engagement lasting all of five minutes. One soldier, Herman C. Moore, was shot and died from his wounds several days later. Report of the fighting was received at Fort Brown during a band concert, and two companies of infantry, transported in automobiles, were immediately dispatched to the scene. Two troops of cavalry soon followed. Although they were pursued, the attackers escaped.[22]

Sam Robertson, who'd played a leading role in combating the *sediciosos*, led a charmed life. As we've seen, he had survived an ambush in September, and now, on October 25, he was again ambushed, while driving alone near San Benito. Some packages dropped from his car, and when he went back to retrieve them, five Mexicans appeared between him and his vehicle. They opened fire. Fortunately for Robertson, he had two firearms with him, a Winchester and a pump shotgun. Taking cover behind a tree, he returned fire, apparently wounding one of his assailants. Abandoning his car, Robertson struck out through the brush toward a neighboring ranch. Encountering a fourteen-year-old Mexican goat herder, Robertson took him along as reinforcement, giving him the Winchester. They'd traveled only a short distance when the boy sighted bandits behind them. Robertson and the boy began firing and were able to drive them off. Making his way through the brush, Robertson finally reached a telephone and gave the alarm. Infantry detachments from San Benito rushed to the scene and began a search, but without results. The young goat herder, who had handled the Winchester expertly, not only received Robertson's fervent thanks but also impressed the troops, who made him their mascot. Robertson could count his blessings, for he'd received a bullet through his coat, and a heel had been shot from one of his shoes. Robertson said he recognized two of the bandits, which didn't bode at all well for them.[23]

Governor Ferguson on October 27 issued a proclamation offering a thousand-dollar reward for the arrest and detention of Pizaña and de la Rosa and their delivery, dead or alive, to any sheriff in Texas. Ferguson recalled that "When I offered a reward of a thousand dollars for Luis de la Rosa, the border bandit raider, he offered a thousand for my head. Every bum and thug that hit the town would come out and walk around the mansion. My wife became alarmed and asked General Hutchings for the guard."[24]

Some were eager to collect the reward. Deputy Sheriff Tom Mayfield of Hidalgo County, the man who had arrested Basilio Ramos, told bureau agent E. B. Stone that he had a Mexican informant who'd agreed to deliver de la Rosa's and Pizaña's heads in a sack on the Texas bank of the Rio Grande. The informant's plan was to suborn the bodyguards of the Tejano chieftains, who would kill them and split the reward with the informant. Mayfield felt that since the state of Texas had offered a thousand dollars for each man, he'd have to increase his offer to the informant for an equal amount to get the best results. The Mexican informant, one Ramón, also reported that there was great resentment at Reynosa against Carranza for having removed General Nafarrate. However, Ramón, who was to report to Mayfield on October 31 regarding the progress of the assassination plot, incurred the suspicion of Mexican soldiers and was afraid to undertake any more clandestine missions.[25]

Captain Frank McCoy, Third Cavalry, who had commanded the Mission subdistrict since the beginning of the troubles, had, as we've seen, established a system for obtaining information from the female Anglo schoolteachers. McCoy said that he'd gotten considerable information from this source. Agent Stone added that in accordance with General Funston's policy of cooperation with the Bureau of Investigation regarding the border troubles, Captain McCoy had supplied Stone with letters, books, and lists of names of those implicated in the raids.[26]

Agent Stone further stated that McCoy and his subordinate, Captain Scott, who had an informant in de la Rosa's camp, both suggested that the Department of Justice authorize a reward of one thousand dollars each for the delivery of the leaders, dead or alive, in Texas. Stone suggested that if the reward was authorized, it not be made known to the public but just communicated directly by a bureau agent "to those parties who will agree to cross over and undertake the capture and delivery of the bandits to our forces."[27]

Carefully covering himself with his masters, Stone stipulated that he'd entered into no agreement with the parties involved, nor had he given any sanction, official or otherwise, to their planned "capture and delivery" of de la Rosa and Pizaña. He'd only confided in the military, presumably Captain McCoy, under authorization from Agent in Charge Barnes.[28]

Stone believed that the reason Tom Mayfield and people like Deodoro Guerra, who was one of Captain McCoy's best informants, were speaking frankly to government agents was because "they are all sympathizers of the Villa cause in Mexico and strongly anti-Carranza in their feelings over this border trouble."

Deodoro Guerra gave Agent Stone a picture of a button that de la Rosa's followers were wearing. Around de la Rosa's picture was written "Luis de la Rosa, Supreme Chief of the Movement Mexican Texas." Guerra also informed Stone that he'd sent a friend, Medado González, across the river several times to gather intelligence about the *sediciosos*. The friend stated that de la Rosa's wife was living in Hidalgo and had sent a messenger across the river to her husband informing him of the thousand-dollar reward on his head and urging him to move to Matamoros for safety. In addition, the *sediciosos* originally had four Japanese with them, but one had been killed at the Ojo de Agua fight.[29]

Guerra's other informant was Francisco Ponce, whom he had enlisted in de la Rosa's band. Ponce talked with de la Rosa at the latter's camp near the Carranza garrison at Reynosa. At first the militants were quite friendly and asked Ponce to join them, but he made the mistake of telling them that he wasn't quite ready, as he'd come to the area to purchase hides. Becoming suspicious of his refusal to join them immediately, the *sediciosos* thereafter refused to have anything to do with him and refused to allow him back in their camp. Nevertheless, Ponce reported that he had counted eighty-seven men in the camp, with plenty of arms and ammunition; they also told him they had two machine guns (which he didn't see) but lacked the ammunition to operate them. Both González and Ponce told Guerra that they'd seen a great many people on the other side of the river wearing the "bandit buttons" and that the Carranza garrison didn't molest them in any way.

Guerra told Agent Barnes that his informants were at Barnes's disposal for debriefing, and for a suitable reward he believed these two men would undertake to deliver Pizaña's and de la Rosa's corpses to the Texas bank of the Rio Grande.[30] But nothing happened.

The American authorities relied very heavily on informants to learn about the *sediciosos*, especially about their activities across the Rio Grande. The bureau reinforced its agent in Brownsville with the agent in charge in San Antonio and an agent brought from Oklahoma.[31] They were busy, especially in the red-light district. Agent Rogers reported that he "Spent the day in an effort to get first hand information from the inhabitants of the sporting section of the town confirming rumors that Mexican leaders of the bandits frequented the district for the purpose of recruiting and fomenting trouble. No information was elicited as it was impossible to get these Mexicans to talk. I did not take the names of any of them."[32]

And the bureau was not averse to sending informants across the river in an effort to gather intelligence. The agent in Brownsville requested permission to send one M. M. Gallagher, at a salary of three hundred dollars a month, to ascertain the attitude of Carranza soldiers.[33] And "confidential agent" Kelley reported on the arrangements that Nafarrate's successor, General López, had made. López was more cooperative and much less anti-American than Nafarrate.[34]

Sometimes citizens voluntarily informed the bureau, as did one F. A. Elliott, a discharged soldier, who was in Matamoros in late October and was introduced to de la Rosa, whom he described as "a slim light Mexican, speaks good English and wore light shirt and striped pants and a very large hat."[35] And on October 22 the military noted that "a Mexican from about 8 miles east of here (Lyford) and who requested his name be not mentioned, came here and reported that Luis Gómez, Florentino Pérez, Refugio Domínguez, and Pancho García were all 'bad men' and should be taken in." The informant also told where they could be found. A deputy sheriff and an army detachment arrested the four, plus Rogerio Caballero, and delivered them to Brownsville. Subsequent investigation concluded that all but Caballero had been involved in the Olmito train wreck.[36]

It was reported to Agent Barnes that Sóstenes Saldaña "was in the back part of the county boasting that he was a big man among the bandits and allegedly urged all Mexicans to join the movement." Barnes in turn reported this to Ranger captain Ransom, who said he had investigated, but Saldaña had disappeared the night of the Olmito train wreck. Ransom and Barnes led a posse through the northern part of Cameron County and found a number of Hispanic homes vacant.

In late October, one of Sam Robertson's informants, "Mexican No. Three" (identified by number to safeguard his identity), came to the Texas side of the river and said the bandits planned to attack another train in the vicinity of Olmito. Agent Barnes wrote that certain persons were willing to be paid to send a fake telegram to induce the bandits to cross into Texas and attack a train purportedly carrying a large sum of money. The soldiers guarding the high bridge at Barreda would have to be withdrawn, as this was to be the point of attack. The informant would wear distinguishing dress and would inform the troops of the bandits' movements. Robertson offered to disguise himself and cross the river to conclude the negotiations (Robertson was either very brave or very foolhardy), but Barnes told him "that in view of the fact that the plan suggested involved the inducing of the bandits to commit an act which they might not otherwise commit and of the probable loss of life that would be involved in carrying out the plan that I did not think that the Department would approve the suggestion. I also suggested that the Department would pay a reasonable sum for information as to when the band crossed of their own accord."[37] Barnes added "that the feeling of many of the Mexicans is in favor of the bandits there can be no doubt. De la Rosa was in Reynosa for weeks and maintained his 'headquarters' there, according to reliable information from that town. Still, there was no attempt made to arrest him, and the people of Reynosa made no effort to have him driven from the town."[38]

The authorities tried to locate one of the circulars issued by Pizaña and de la Rosa. Deputy Sheriff C. A. Monahan, Sheriff W. T. Vann, José Longoria, Tomás Tijerina, and George Head could testify that large numbers of them were in Pizaña's house and were widely distributed. The circular called on Tejanos to take up arms and assist in retaking Texas for the Mexicans and to avenge their grievances against the Anglos.[39]

The better to stay abreast of Hispanic feelings, the San Antonio office of the bureau sent letters to the postmasters and sheriffs along the border requesting that they inform the bureau of the activities of Hispanics in their jurisdiction. These letters went to 136 towns and cities in Texas alone.[40] The postmaster at Santa Cruz, Texas, for instance, provided a list of "Socialists who are renters of post office boxes and who receive Socialist literature."[41] The Pearsall postmaster sent a list of seven men whom he believed might be in sympathy with the Plan de San Diego. The postmaster at Bay City had the sheriff check on the whereabouts of one Teófilo Flores, an agitator for the Plan de San Diego. His wife said he'd gone to Brownsville and joined the raiders and was killed in one of the firefights the previous summer. The postmaster at San Diego replied that he didn't know any of the parties mentioned, except "León Caballo alias Agustín Garza, who resided here at one time." Garza had a sister living in San Diego married to Florencio Barrera and another sister living in San Antonio.[42]

Agent Clifford G. Beckham went to Fort Sam Houston and obtained copies of documents sent there by the military authorities in Brownsville. In addition, Agent Barnes requested that anything appearing in the anarchist newspaper *Regeneración* that might bear on the Plan de San Diego be forwarded to him. The Brownsville postmaster provided a list of local subscribers to *Regeneración*.[43] And the postmaster in Los Angeles, where Ricardo Flores Magón had his headquarters, obligingly furnished a list of who from where was writing to which *magonista* in Los Angeles.[44]

In November, Agent Barkey interviewed a Colonel Flores, formerly of Carranza's secret service but now in the Carranza army in Monterrey. According to Flores, he had recently seen there Luis de la Rosa, who was occupying room 18 of the Hotel Independencia in Monterrey, as well as Aniceto Pizaña and Agustín S. Garza. "These men are actively recruiting men to take part in the raids along the border above Brownsville and such contemplated action on their part is well known in the city and talked about generally. The plan has the support of a large number of the Carranza forces. These men joined the army primarily for the purpose of obtaining spoils but since the recognition of Carranza the authorities have placed a ban on their actions. This has caused the soldiers to become dissatisfied and they are willing to join any expedition that will give them a free hand and for this reason the plan outlined by de la Rosa and the others appeals to them."[45]

Agent Barnes utilized a confidential informant, Mateo Gómez, with whom he corresponded in Spanish as "Juanita L.," one of Barnes's cover addresses in San Antonio. Barnes paid Gómez a dollar or so in advance each time to gather intelligence in Mexico. By January 1916, Gómez had made several intelligence-gathering trips across the Rio Grande. Barnes sent him three dollars at Brownsville for the expenses of his last trip and informed him that he wouldn't have to make another trip for the next two weeks. At that time Barnes would send him some expense money. Gómez wrote from Brownsville on January 26 that he had been to the ranch as ordered and had located the foreman, José Regalado, and promised to have more news in his next letter. He also enclosed a receipt for ten dollars that he had to pay from the money left to him for expenses. Gómez begged for some expense money, for he was very short of funds.[46]

Agent Rogers dispatched Gómez to verify rumors concerning Pizaña and de la Rosa. Rogers reported that "the information he gathered is only general, but it is the universal opinion of these Mexicans that they will succeed this time in capturing a part of Texas at least. To understand this matter and to realize how it is possible for them to entertain such a hope it is only necessary to realize the ignorance and the desperate straits of these poor Mexicans. From our standards and from our viewpoint such a scheme is preposterous, but if we could put ourselves in their place it would be different."[47] Gómez reported that he'd spoken with Pedro Villarreal, who had a brother killed at Sebastian, and learned that another brother, Doroteo Villarreal, was still with the *sediciosos* and that they had a camp located about seven miles south of the Rio Grande opposite Mercedes.[48]

Another paid bureau confidential informant was James Werbiske, a former Brownsville policeman, hired on November 5. He reported that at Matamoros he saw at the ferry on the Mexican side one Ricardo Gómez known to have been with the bandits. A certain Lázaro Guerra, one of four *villista* officers who had recently surrendered in Matamoros, was also a bandit. Guerra told Werbiske that Gómez was waiting at the ferry to identify some Tejanos whom the bandits had heard the Rangers were sending over to spy on them. Guerra also said that de la Rosa had gone to Ciudad Victoria to see General Nafarrate and learn whether he was going to assist the *sediciosos* further. They would then know just how they stood and whether they would carry out any more raids.[49]

Werbiske also shed some light on the fight at Tulitos on August 3, 1915. He claimed that at 2:30 a.m. the day of the clash, a number of bandits passed through Werbiske's ranch west of Brownsville. He knew a number of them personally and would report their names as he recalled them. Among them were Luis de la Rosa, Evaristo Ramos, Vicente Dávila, and José Yvars (Ibarra). Yvars was then and was still a soldier in Matamoros, and there were in that party many other soldiers from that garrison whom Werbiske knew personally. He alleged that de la Rosa told him he'd gone from Matamoros to Ciudad Victoria to meet with the governor, General Luis Caballero, who had assured de la Rosa of assistance in men and munitions. De la Rosa also told Werbiske that Deputy Sheriff Mike Monahan, José Longoria, and Marcelino Rodríguez were on the list to be killed first. Finally, Werbiske claimed that some of these men confided that they were planning the train wreck that subsequently occurred at Olmito.[50]

An informant working for Sam Robertson in the bandits' camp alleged that Pizaña and de la Rosa had gone to Ciudad Victoria because they feared being delivered to the Americans as a result of the reward on their heads. Lázaro Guerra also reported to Werbiske that Pizaña had gone to see General Alvaro Obregón. Agent Barnes placed little credence in this statement, thinking it probably was a ploy by Pizaña to keep his followers in good spirits. Guerra also said the bandits were collecting the names of all persons who had been with the various posses and adding their names to their list of persons to be killed when they came across the river again. The insurgents thus maintained "hit lists" of their own. Guerra added that a captain of the bandits told him that the Tejano spy had been located and that they were going to kill him. Agent Barnes hadn't heard of any such execution. Not surprisingly, Guerra stated that the bandits kept several men in Matamoros to secure information concerning conditions, activities, and persons on the American side of the Rio Grande.[51]

Customs inspector White was using a certain Basiliano Villarreal to infiltrate the *sediciosos*. He had Villarreal join a band across the Rio Grande to gather intelligence, the reward being that Villarreal was given immunity from prosecution and was permitted to return to Texas.[52]

Agent Barnes employed a paid confidential informant in Monterrey beginning in November. Juan C. Cisneros, who used the name "José García" in his reports, lived at General Espinoza number 104 in Monterrey and had been recommended by Vice Consul Randolph Robertson.[53] Ostensibly, Robertson had nothing to do with Cisneros although he employed him. The bureau paid Cisneros's salary of two dollars a day and expenses, and Barnes instructed Cisneros to report to Agent Rogers in Brownsville for debriefing. Cisneros said that José Estrada, as he was known in Monterrey, was Agustín Garza's private secretary. Estrada was"about 22 years old, tall and slender, a victim of venereal disease, brunette, pallid, eyes brown almost black." On December 11, Estrada took the train to Matamoros to consult with Garza. From Matamoros, Estrada would cross into Brownville and proceed to Laredo to confer with parties connected with the Plan de San Diego. Among them were General Santiago Mendoza, a former federal officer, who was in business in Laredo, and Colonel José Lara and Manuel Leiva.[54]

Barnes noted in a telegram that "the movement formerly supported by Carranza but since recognition Carranza endeavoring prevent movement but may not be able to control all subordinates, some of whom pledged to new movement." Colonel Maurilio Rodríguez was currently under arrest in Monterrey by order of Carranza and was under a fifteen-thousand-peso bond. Rodríguez had been recruiting in Texas for the Plan; a month earlier he'd been in El Paso conferring with some *villista* officers, who had agreed to support the Plan. Informant Cisneros believed that de la Rosa and Pizaña were merely secondary chieftains, for they were under the orders of Garza and Rodríguez.

While out on bond, Rodríguez stayed busy. On December 12, Cisneros reported that Rodríguez had returned the previous night from a trip to the border. He reportedly visited Laredo, then drove by car to San Ignacio, where he crossed to the Mexican side to review the guerrilla band he was gathering in that section, planning to use it as the insurgents' main rendezvous. Because they were uncertain as to what General Ricaut's attitude toward them would be, the insurgents thought it prudent to move farther away from Ricaut's present headquarters than Camargo, their former headquarters. The insurgents were said to have a number of men on the Texas side of the river, mainly at Laredo, working in the onion fields. In transmitting this report, Agent Barnes suggested that "The Department of Justice should, in my humble opinion, have a man on the job in Monterrey."[55]

The German consul in Monterrey, Pablo Burchard, owner of the firm of C. Holck & Co., "the largest concern in northern Mexico," offered the *sediciosos* money, arms, and ammunition, said Cisneros.[56] One of the more intriguing aspects of the Plan de San Diego affair is the extent, if any, of German involvement. Obviously, it was to Germany's interest in 1915–16 to have the United States embroiled in difficulties with Mexico rather than joining the Allies. Germany allegedly financed the abortive comeback attempt of the deposed strongman General Victoriano Huerta in 1915, and it has been suggested that Germans manipulated Pancho Villa into attacking Columbus, New Mexico, in 1916 in order to force U.S. intervention in Mexico.[57] It has been claimed that Lothar Witzke, a German agent, was involved in the Plan de San Diego, an assertion that has no basis in fact.[58]

Dr. Paul Bernardo Altendorf, an Austrian chiropodist who was an agent of U.S. military intelligence, was a double agent ostensibly working for the Germans in Mexico. He alleged on September 3, 1919, that in 1918 he'd spoken with Carranza, who had assured him of support for a Mexican-German plot to invade the United States from Sonora.[59] Moreover, Altendorf testified that Otto Paglash, a hotel proprietor who was the German safe-house keeper in Mexico City, introduced him to the Carranza director of telegraphs Mario Méndez, one of three brothers living in the hotel whose expenses the German government paid in addition to their six-hundred-dollar monthly salary from the German minister, Von Eckhardt. Altendorf said that Mario Méndez used to meet a man by the name of Kettenbach, whom Altendorf described as a criminal, and hand over to him the telegrams the American ambassador received, as well as other communications from the United States.[60] But the State Department's special representative in Mexico City in 1916 plaintively inquired of State: "Can you give me any confidential information as to German operations in Mexico? Believe it exists but find it very difficult to confirm."[61]

Specifically regarding the Plan de San Diego, Walter Prescott Webb speculated that the Germans wrote the Plan de San Diego to "bring on trouble in Mexico." And Tom Mayfield testified that the guns he had captured were mostly German Mausers, the infantry and carbine (cavalry) Mauser. He displayed several bandoliers of Mauser ammunition found on the corpse of a raider after the Ojo de Agua fight. The bandit also had a German Iron Cross on his body. After the attack on the McAllen ranch, a belt of Mauser ammunition was taken from the body of a dead bandit.[62] But since the Mauser was the standard rifle of the Mexican Army, it is hardly surprising that there were Mausers all over the place. As for the Iron Cross, who is to say whether it was conferred by the kaiser himself or purchased at some army surplus store? And according to information from Randolph Robertson, the vice consul at Monterrey, and Ayers Robertson, ex-vice consul, the German and Austrian consuls were furnishing money to the group of conspirators preparing another invasion of Texas.[63] Yet German involvement has been difficult to prove.

In order to verify informant Cisneros's information, on at least one occasion Barnes forwarded to the chief of the bureau a copy of one of Cisneros's reports and requested permission to send, unknown to Cisneros, another paid Spanish-speaking informant disguised as a peddler to cover the same ground.[64]

As another check on Cisneros's information, the bureau decided to send Agent J. B. Rogers into Mexico. The State Department was "absolutely against the suggestion that the State Department assign an accredited representative to the matter and asked that Rogers be detailed as an agent of this Department for the work." Agent in Charge Barnes, having received the approval of the chief of the bureau providing the mission was not too dangerous,[65] instructed Rogers to proceed to Monterrey under cover to investigate the reports of Plan de San Diego followers preparing to invade Texas, and to investigate the rumor that the German consul in Monterrey was supplying them with money and armament.

Agent Rogers arrived in Monterrey on Christmas Eve. The next day, having paid a courtesy visit to the American consulate, he met at the Continental Hotel with a couple of Carranza officers, Colonels Flores and Peña, a friend of Flores's. They talked quite freely about the Texas revolution and how leaders of the *carrancistas* were promoting it. Flores mentioned that many of these leaders knew little about the United States, imagining it to be like the towns they knew along the Rio Grande. Flores added that since the recognition of Carranza, revolutionary activity had gradually diminished and he thought it had pretty well ended. "But he added that the ignorant and more degenerate, having now been encouraged by their superiors, would undertake to plunder the border if an opportunity were given them. Col. Flores says that Carranza took away with him some of the leading spirits of this movement, and he named especially as one of these Colonel [Maurilio] Rodríguez."

Rogers interviewed the Spanish and Italian consuls and learned that members of their colonies had been approached by Carranza officers soliciting funds for this expedition, who told them that the German consul was assisting them with money and munitions. "These consuls both said they had positive evidence of these activities of the German Consul in the connection but that they could not with prudence give the evidence first hand."

Rogers also traveled to Ciudad Victoria on December 28 to verify reports that de la Rosa was in that city. At the hotel dining room he noticed a heavily armed Carranza captain making notes of all the Americans at the dining tables. Rogers introduced himself to the officer, who said his name was Alberto Carrera. It turned out that he was the man who'd been sentenced to the Texas penitentiary some years earlier for the 1906 murder of Judge Stanley Welch in Rio Grande City. He had escaped from a prison farm. Rogers chatted about the border troubles with Carrera, who expressed contempt "for the judgment of those Mexicans who had attempted the Plan of San Diego, saying 'the poor fools did not know what they were going up against. They had only seen a few towns along the Texan border and supposed the United States was a good deal like Mexico,' but that he knew Texas too well and had turned down all propositions to him to join any such fool undertaking." Carrera was currently "prominently identified with the administration of Affairs [*sic*] at Victoria, Mexico." Besides the bureau, Frank Carr, the city marshal of San Benito, employed an informant to go to Matamoros to secure intelligence. Carr delivered to the bureau his informant's report dated on November 15:

> List of some of the bandits who are in Matamoros—José Benavides from La Bonita Ranch, Julio Quintero from San Benito Ranch, Miguel Guevara from Marrones Ranch. Guevara and Rodolfo Muñoz are the ones that killed Mr. ______ [Austin] at Sebastian. Pedro Paz from San Benito is the fellow

that stole Joe Tatum's horse and joined the bandits. . . . Luis de la Rosa and Pizaña are away from Matamoros; they are in the interior of Tamaulipas, and the number of bandits in Matamoros is about fifty. Fifteen miles west of Matamoros, at Las Prietas Ranch, are seventy five to a hundred bandits; at Corrales station there are between forty and fifty. Reynosa is the bandits' headquarters, where there are 100–150 bandits. Of course all Carranza soldiers joined the bandits. . . . So now everything is quiet because they wait the coming of Carranza, this is the reason why Luis de la Rosa and Pizaña are out of town. In Matamoros in a building on block No. 27, Bravo St., No. 7, is the place where they have their meetings. [signed] Miguel Rodríguez, Jr.

Another report from Rodríguez said that Juan Mejía was one of the leaders of the bandits in the Sebastian raid. Also that Abel Sandoval, Lauro Escamilla, Tomás Escamilla, and Antonio Escamilla[66] are the ones who in October robbed him of two saddles and a sum of money. Agent Barnes commented that "while this information comes from an anti-Carranza source it is in a large measure corroborated by information secured from other sources believed to be reliable."[67] Through immigration inspector in charge in Brownsville, E. P. Reynolds, the bureau secured photographs of certain members of the *carrancista* garrison in Matamoros in the hope of having them recognized as raiders.[68]

American intelligence managed to stay abreast of the *sediciosos*' machinations across the river.

9 The Plan de San Diego Collapses

Once Carranza withdrew his support the Plan de San Diego movement collapsed. Benjamin Johnson observes that almost overnight the *sediciosos* "were too busy avoiding the Constitutionalist regulars to continue their campaign in Texas." But Johnson can't explain why Constitutionalist regulars, who had been supporting and participating in the raids, suddenly turned against the *sediciosos*. Some guerrillas were arrested and a few were shot, but Johnson states that attempts to arrest de la Rosa and Pizaña failed, in all probability because they enjoyed significant local support.[1] It would appear that they were arrested whenever Carranza wanted them arrested, and "significant local support" was a minor consideration. De la Rosa and Pizaña were in fact arrested several times. Unfortunately, Johnson does not understand the Mexican Revolution and is largely unaware of the Mexican component of the Plan de San Diego affair. Thus he fundamentally misinterprets the subject.

A newspaper dispatch from Brownsville on October 29 read: "News was received at Matamoros of a battle on Mexican soil between the Carranza troops of the Reynosa garrison and bandits said to belong to the de la Rosa band at the same time that Matamoros announced that Carranza had ordered his Matamoros forces to pursue the bandits until all were killed or captured."[2] And on February 12, 1916, American consul Silliman reported from Guadalajara that the first chief's private secretary had just received a telegram announcing the arrest in Monterrey a few days earlier of Aniceto Pizaña, Maurilio Rodríguez, and eight associates. Silliman added that "the Government of Nuevo León informed me this afternoon that the men arrested in Monterrey had arms, ammunition, etc. in their possession. . . . The men are said to be Texas Mexicans, American citizens." The U.S. commissioner in Brownsville inquired whether Pizaña could be extradited, which of course the Carranza administration had no intention of permitting.[3] De la Rosa would be arrested in Monterrey on January 11, 1917.[4]

Minor violence continued. On November 1 a patrol of Company L, Twenty-Eighth Infantry, was fired upon at McConnell's Crossing, sixty-eight miles west of Brownsville. One Mexican was killed. On November 4 a Sixth Cavalry patrol was fired upon from across the Rio Grande at the Mercedes canal head gates. No casualties were reported. On November 12 a Tejano scout in United States service fired on five Mexicans at the Pedernales ranch. No casualties.

A positive development occurred in Reynosa. The mayor organized a force of *rurales* (mounted constabulary) consisting of eighteen officers and ninety enlisted men and divided the region around Reynosa into eighteen districts, with an officer and five men per district. In five days, fourteen bandits who'd been operating in Texas were captured; two were shot, seven were sent to Matamoros for trial, and the rest were held in Reynosa pending trial. Their names corresponded to those on lists American authorities had compiled. Moreover, the military in Reynosa reported that they'd received an order from Carranza directing that de la Rosa and Pizaña were to be summarily executed if apprehended.[5] Americans were understandably skeptical about the order.

As for Carranza himself, he was now much more agreeable in his dealings with American officials. In November he visited Nuevo Laredo and conferred for two hours with Governor Ferguson about the border situation. They placed no blame on any military officials from either side for the troubles, and they arranged for mutual cooperation to apprehend criminals. "The entire meeting was characterized by the utmost cordiality."

Carranza also promoted General Alfredo Ricaut, who was not rabidly anti-American, and placed him in command from Matamoros to Hidalgo, more than three hundred miles of the border. General Reynaldo de la Garza, formerly commander at Lampazos, succeeded Ricaut as commander in Nuevo Laredo. Ricaut assumed command on December 4, 1915, and made a favorable impression on Consul Johnson, who wrote that "He said he was fully determined to put an end to the bandits on the border, and I believe he will do his best to accomplish it. He is a very determined man and honest. He is a nephew of the First Chief Carranza and stands well as an honorable and upright officer and gentleman."[6]

On November 30, bureau agent J. B. Rogers accepted Mexican consul Jose Z. Garza's invitation and accompanied him to Matamoros to meet with Carranza during the latter's visit to that city. Rogers had met Carranza several times previously in Mexico. The bureau agent stressed that he hoped for Carranza's cooperation in ending the raids into Texas and in bringing the raiders to justice. Carranza assured Rogers that "he would use every means in his power to bring the guilty to justice, prevent a recurrence of the troubles, and restore order and good feeling between the two races." Rogers was impressed by General Ricaut, who had "the appearance of a strong, deliberate, determined character. His statements may be summed up in his last statement: 'I am just now assuming command here; in one month there will be no bandits.'" Ricaut promised to deal summarily with all violators.[7]

During Carranza's visit to Matamoros, General Nafarrate caused a sensation at a banquet honoring the first chief, according to *La República*, published in Brownsville, in its edition of December 3. In giving a toast to Carranza, Nafarrate protested against the United States' efforts to get him removed from Matamoros, and he mentioned Carranza's having yielded to Washington. Carranza was seated next to Nafarrate, and he leaned over and said something to the general, who hesitated a moment then continued his toast in a much less confrontational manner.[8]

Nafarrate's views were well known. The American consul in Tampico wrote on March 18, 1916, that Nafarrate was a dangerous man to be in charge militarily of that strategic district. Not only had he been involved in the border troubles, but he was bitterly anti-American and had publicly remarked that he'd welcome the opportunity to fight the United States.[9]

The United States remained keenly interested in Mexican affairs. Agent Rogers traveled to Monterrey on December 26, 1915. He reported that the *sediciosos* had attempted much but with little success. Yet he strongly emphasized the necessity for watchfulness. Conditions in Monterrey were "desperate." Rogers sent his report through Consul Robertson and returned to Texas within a week. Rogers, incidentally, had trouble writing his reports because his arm was so sore from the obligatory vaccinations that he got when reentering the United States at Laredo. He explained to his superior that "it was not only impracticable to make my reports promptly while in Mexico, but it would have been exceedingly dangerous to even keep notes from which to make reports. My reports on this trip were therefore unsatisfactory even to myself. The man who tells the truth about Mexico now would better stay out of Mexico unless the truth he tells is kept secret."[10]

While in Monterrey, Rogers had spoken with several leading citizens, reporting that "The impression is that when the First Chief was recognized, he pulled off his generals who had been assigned to this particular work." Rogers also learned that de la Rosa had already gone to Tampico. He decided to follow him there.[11] In Tampico he interviewed several prominent Americans, including the oil man William Buckley. They confirmed that the Texas revolution was well known to the Carranza government. Rogers was told that Pizaña was busily recruiting men at Jiménez, thirty miles from the railroad. Rogers went there but Pizaña had already left. The American agent also learned during his stay in Tampico that Pizaña and de la Rosa had a "hit list" of the Rangers, sheriffs, and citizens who had taken part in the border troubles. By January 19 he was en route back to Brownsville via Ciudad Victoria, Monterrey, and Nuevo Laredo.[12]

In May, Rogers volunteered to undertake another mission into Mexico. His superior, Agent Barnes, replied that "I beg to state that I appreciate your offer to undertake such a trip for the Government, but at this time I do not believe that such a trip is practicable. I would be glad to keep your offer in mind and take the matter up with you further at a later date."[13]

Meanwhile, in Brownsville a number of insurgents had been indicted on state charges.[14] The number of indictments against these men ranged from one to fourteen each. In addition, Antonio Rocha, Cástulo Ramírez, and Pilar Rostro merited being added to the list, Rocha because he had killed a Hispanic man who was helping the authorities.[15] Agent Barnes later submitted to his chief a list of "Mexicans at large in Mexico implicated in the Plan of San Diego and who have not been brought to justice."[16]

The Bureau of Investigation received a rude jolt from federal judge Waller T. Burns, who was presiding in Brownsville. Burns instructed the grand jury that the federal government was without jurisdiction to prosecute the case against Pizaña et al. because federal law hadn't been violated, and the offense allegedly committed by Mexican bandits should be prosecuted under state law. This greatly disappointed the members of the grand jury, who were eager to indict Pizaña and de la Rosa. Judge Burns did sentence Manuel (also referred to as Miguel) Saiz to ninety days in the county jail for having pled guilty to a charge of inciting rebellion against the United States by making an incendiary speech. Saiz had been incarcerated on August 23, having failed to post a two-thousand-dollar bond. Since he'd already served more than ninety days in jail, he was released.[17]

Agent Barnes, for one, was not happy with Judge Burns's ruling. He wrote to the U.S. attorney that a number of defendants were under indictment on state charges, and their punishment would probably be more severe than under U.S. statutes. There were, however, three reasons for the federal courts to take action. First, the federal authorities had better facilities for gathering and preserving evidence. State authorities frequently failed to record evidence, which in time tended to be forgotten or lost. Second, because of the political climate on the border, some defendants might through favoritism escape punishment. Third, state authorities hadn't dealt with many conspirators against whom, Barnes believed, the feds could develop cases.

Barnes must have been pleased when in December the U.S. attorney prepared to present the indictments to a federal grand jury. Barnes sent him a lengthy report regarding the *magonista* background to the Plan de San Diego and the Plan itself, commenting that "This so-called

Plan of San Diego appears of Anarchistic origin" and adding, "I would respectfully invite your attention to the fact that there are a large number of persons implicated in this conspiracy who have not and will not be reached by the State authorities and whose operations are continual sources of annoyance to the Government." He then recapitulated the incidents in 1915.

Barnes ended by enclosing a list of potential witnesses, but he asked that no subpoena be issued for James Werbiske because he was working undercover and such a procedure would destroy his value as an informant. The U.S. attorney agreed to present the case of Pizaña et al. to the grand jury in Brownsville on December 7 provided Barnes was in attendance throughout the procedure.[18] Barnes sent him the complete Plan de San Diego file, supplemented by documents the army had seized.[19]

On December 12 the federal grand jury returned sixteen indictments[20] charging seditious conspiracy in violation of Section 6, Federal Criminal Code, 1010. The next day the grand jury issued twenty more indictments for the same offense.[21] And it kept raining indictments; another batch on December 13 totaled forty-nine.[22]

In December 1916, Agent Rogers prepared a report on the indictments of Plan de San Diego participants. Rogerio Caballero had eight indictments against him in the district court of Cameron County. Number 3655 charged him with murder in connection with the wrecking of the train at Olmito in October 1915 (he was tried and acquitted on this charge).[23] Docket numbers 3677, 3678, and 3684 likewise charged him with murder, and 3679 with robbery by firearms. Numbers 3685 and 3686 charged him with murder in connection with the Fresnos raid when Donaldson and Smith were killed. Number 3687 also charged him with murder.[24]

Caballero was tried in Brownsville in March 1917 for participating in the murders of Smith and Donaldson. Stanley Dodds, who was captured by the raiders and escaped, was the principal witness against Caballero. "He said he felt sure Caballero was one of the band, but he would not swear that he was." Caballero was found guilty and was sentenced to fifteen years in the state penitentiary. He also had two additional years to serve on an earlier sentence for rustling.[25]

De la Rosa was charged in indictments 3655 and 3656 with murder and assault to murder in connection with the Olmito train wreck. Numbers 3677, 3678, and 3684 charged him with murder and 3679 with robbery by firearms.

Evaristo Ramos had the distinction of having thirteen indictments for capital offenses against him. He was charged with participation in the Olmito wreck, in the Sebastian raid when the two Austins were killed, in the Fresnos raid when Donaldson and Smith were killed, and in the Turner (Galveston) ranch firefight when several soldiers were killed.

Santiago Santillana was charged in numbers 3655 and 3656 with murder in the Olmito train wreck. Number 3655 also charged him with assault with intent to murder.

Lorenzo López was charged in numbers 3656, 3677, 3678, and 3684 with murder. Number 3679 charged robbery by firearms. Indictments 3677, 3678, 3679, and 3684 were based on the fight at Turner's (Galveston) ranch.[26]

Ramón Pizaña, Aniceto Pizaña's brother, was tried in the Cameron County district court on a charge of murder committed in the Los Tulitos fight. He was found guilty and sentenced to fifteen years in the penitentiary. The verdict was the result of a compromise in which nine jurors were holding out for the death penalty. Aniceto Pizaña, Ricardo Gómez Pizaña, Felipe Campos, Jesús Treviño, Manuel Treviño, and Ricardo García were also indicted for the same offense. The two Treviños were acquitted.[27]

Aniceto Pizaña, in addition to the above case, was also charged in numbers 3685 and 3686 with the murder of Donaldson and Smith in the Fresnos raid.

Ricardo Gómez Pizaña was charged in number 3687 with murder in the Los Tulitos fight. He had fled to Mexico.

Melquiades Chapa, charged in numbers 3673, 3674, 3675, and 3676 with the murder of the Austins at Sebastian, was tried in Cameron County district court, was convicted, and was hanged.

José Buenrostro was also tried and executed on the same charge. The star witness against Chapa and Buenrostro was Elmore Millard, who'd been spared by the bandits who killed the Austins.[28]

Felipe Campos was charged in number 3655 with murder at the Los Tulitos ranch fight. Also charged with complicity in the fight were Jesús Treviño, Manuel Treviño, and Eduardo García. Manuel Treviño was also charged in numbers 3685 and 3686 with murder in the Fresnos raid when Donaldson and Smith were killed. García was in the Cameron County jail. Campos and the two Treviños had fled to Mexico.

The following were charged in numbers 3673, 3674, 3675, and 3676 with murder and robbery by firearms: Pablo Pérez, José Benavides, Alberto Mejía, Ricardo López, Ricardo Flores, Gaspar Cantú, Pablo Saenz, Pedro Cavazos, and Darío Morado. Of these only Pérez and Cavazos had been apprehended. The others were in Mexico. In addition to the above charges against José Benavides, he was charged with participating in the Fresnos and other raids; there were eleven indictments against him, all for capital offenses. He was a fugitive and had often been seen in Matamoros.

Refugio Domínguez, Santiago Flores, and Martín Castorena were charged with complicity in the Galveston Ranch fight. Their docket numbers were 3677, 3678, 3679, 3684, and 3687. Santiago Flores was acquitted in one case, and the others were dismissed. Refugio Domínguez was removed from the jail because of illness and died a few days later. The other two were still awaiting trial.[29]

The following were charged in cases 3683 and 3686 with the murder of Donaldson and Smith in the Fresnos raid: Quirino Guajardo, Sóstenes Saldaña Jr., Marcelino Hinojosa, Catarino Soto, Gerónimo Cruz, Trinidad Tovar, and Felipe Tovar. Quirino Guajardo was on trial, and Gerónimo Cruz had turned state's evidence. The others were fugitives.[30]

Agent Barnes wrote a confidential letter to the U.S. commissioner in Brownsville advising him that for the present the State Department was neither making nor receiving requests for extradition from Mexico, adding that "In this connection, I beg to suggest that the State authorities press their request for the extradition of the fugitive."[31] But requests for extradition would be an exercise in futility.

Ominously, an Associated Press article on December 14 datelined Monterrey stated that another invasion of Texas by some six hundred raiders was being organized there, although at present the organization lacked sufficient arms and ammunition for raids. "A Mexican from San Diego, Texas, who helped to originate the 'Plan of San Diego,' which started the last summer's border raids, is reputed to be the head of the Monterrey organization. Luis de la Rosa and Aniceto Pizaña, leaders in the activities on the lower American border during last summer and the past fall, are taking an active part in this Monterrey movement."[32]

On February 11, 1916, the *Brownsville Herald* ran a banner headline: ANICETO PIZANA IS A PRISONER. The article announced that Colonel J. R. Quintanilla, General Ricaut's subordinate, had notified Colonel Blocksom that Pizaña and from three to five of his men had been captured the day before south of Matamoros by Carranza soldiers. Quintanilla said Pizaña had been dividing his time between the American and Mexican sides of the Rio Grande below Matamoros and was captured while visiting his family. Pizaña offered no resistance and went quietly to Matamoros, where he was confined. The prisoners were being held incommunicado in the Matamoros jail. But there was considerable skepticism about this, for "Pizaña was reported at various times to have been seen in Matamoros, but the Mexican authorities claimed they were never able to capture him. . . . Colonel Quintanilla said the arrest of Pizaña was effected upon the instructions of General Venustiano Carranza who also instructed the arrest of Luis de la Rosa, Maurilio Rodríguez, Basilio Ramos Jr., Agustín Garza and Domingo Arredondo."

In April, on orders from Carranza, General Ricaut took Pizaña with him to Querétaro, Carranza's temporary capital, presumably for further investigation, although officials in Matamoros professed not to know the reason.[33]

Pizaña fared considerably better than several of his *sedicioso* colleagues who were captured and tried. As mentioned, Melquiades Chapa and Jose Buenrostro, charged with murder, robbery by firearms, and assault to murder, were tried and convicted in Brownsville for the murder of the Austins at Sebastian in 1915. At their trial a number of witnesses identified them as being the perpetrators. On April 14, 1916, they were found guilty and were condemned to death, the executions being scheduled for May 19. At the request of the sheriff, a strong guard of soldiers was posted around the jail to preclude a rumored rescue attempt: a public subscription was being taken up in Matamoros to bribe the night watchman to permit them to escape from jail, and failing that, there was a plan to dynamite the jail. Colonel Blocksom also placed a patrol at the river crossing below Brownsville where an informant reported that would-be jail deliverers might cross. The plot, if there ever was one, was abandoned.[34]

Their lawyers and the Mexican consul in Brownsville, J. Z. Garza, appealed to Governor Ferguson to spare the condemned men and commute their sentence to life in prison, to no avail. In order to prevent any trouble in connection with the execution, troops patrolled Brownsville to prevent any crowds from gathering.[35] On the day before their execution Chapa reiterated his innocence, requested a bottle of whiskey to calm his nerves, and asked that there be music at his funeral. He and Buenrostro requested that they be hanged together. The authorities were happy to oblige; two nooses were prepared on the gallows. On May 19 the men were hanged.

Agent Rogers informed his superiors that "Since the execution of Chapa and Buenrostro, there is an attitude of stoicism among the Mexicans. They are both afraid and angry. Very little talk is being done. They feel that a great injustice was done by the execution of these two men. The men maintained to the last that they were innocent and their countrymen believe them. The race feeling has been greatly intensified by the occurrence. The danger of an outbreak has been aggravated."[36]

10 Intelligence Gathering

Agent Louis Mennet had been assigned solely to investigating the Plan de San Diego,[1] but the bureau's meager resources were urgently needed to investigate other Mexican revolutionary movements such as the *felicistas*, the followers of Porfirio Díaz's nephew General Félix Díaz, who were busily plotting in Laredo and Brownsville. There were also problems with securing information and with federal judge Waller Burns.

As Agent Mennet ruefully observed, in his investigation of the Plan he'd found it impossible to persuade people to give crucial evidence because they feared the consequences. They considered Judge Burns entirely too sympathetic toward defendants and believed that even if a man were convicted his sentence would be so light that he would soon be free to take vengeance on those who had testified against him. "Leniency and sympathy on the part of the judge toward such people is sadly misplaced and is an almost insurmountable barrier to the administration of justice and the suppression of banditry and the revolutionary spirit so unquestionably present along the border."[2]

Judge Burns was indeed a most unusual jurist. He had presided in 1911 over the trials of those charged with participation in General Bernardo Reyes's abortive attempt to launch a revolution from Texas against President Francisco Madero. Burns not only declined to sentence any of the convicted defendants to the penitentiary but actually loaned one of them the money to pay his fine and invited him to visit him at his home in Houston.[3] The chief of the bureau resignedly observed that "Judge Burns' attitude has been quite well known for a long time, but no practical way has ever suggested itself whereby the situation might be remedied."[4]

There were other problems, such as maintaining security. Agent Mennet wrote: "The following bit of information obtained by employee during investigations made in connection with the Plan of San Diego, while in attendance on sessions of the Grand Jury, is interesting to say the least and will illustrate a condition which occasionally is found along this border and which makes it difficult to keep Court matters, which are desired to be kept within the limits of the Court and its officials." Mennet related that Fidel A. Hinojosa, deputy clerk of the Brownsville federal court, was a nephew of Espiridón Hinojosa, whom some suspected of being intimately connected with the *sediciosos*. He was also a second cousin of Abel Sandoval, one of the Norias raiders.

Mennet explained that "This information was given to me in confidence by a very reliable informant so as to warn me against this relationship, as a possible point for leakage of confidential data. . . . This young man Hinojosa appears to be a very decent young fellow but I very much fear that on account of the union generally found among Mexicans and their blood relations it is very likely that the fact of his relations being mixed up in this proposition, would cause him to let some little tip get by which will make it very much more difficult for us to catch any of these men."[5]

Still, the bureau would continue to receive a steady stream of information. Agent Barnes was informed that a young Mexican known in Monterrey by the name of José Estrada, allegedly Agustín Garza's private secretary, was a passenger on a train leaving Monterrey on the morning of December 11, 1916, for Matamoros, where he allegedly went to consult with Garza. From Matamoros, Estrada was expected to cross to Brownsville and proceed to Laredo to confer with parties connected with the Plan de San Diego. Among them was General Santiago Méndez, a former Federal officer, who was currently said to be a businessman, and two other former Federal colonels, whose names Barnes hadn't yet secured. Agent Barnes asked Allen Walker, deputy U.S. marshal in Laredo, to be on the lookout for Estrada, whose description he supplied, and to hold him until a bureau agent could arrive. "We do not as yet have sufficient evidence upon which to file a complaint against him, but we will arrange in some way to frustrate any attempt which he may be making to further the movement from this side of the border."[6]

Colonel Blocksom, commanding the Brownsville Cavalry Patrol District, had his own informants, one of whom claimed to have reliable information that there had existed since May 1915, and still existed, a conspiracy by officials in Tamaulipas, between Luis Caballero, military governor, and officials under him, including General Nafarrate, Luis de la Rosa, and an American black, Dr. Jesse H. Moseley, to foment rebellion in Texas, the uprising being carried out by their subordinates. The leaders made their plans in Ciudad Victoria, and General Nafarrate orchestrated the raids. This information was given to Blocksom's informant by soldiers who were present when orders were given.

The informant alleged that conspirator Jesse M. Moseley spent about three months in Texas and Oklahoma trying to recruit blacks, his expenses being defrayed by Luis Caballero. Blocksom's informant said that the conspirators claimed to have an organization in Texas, New Mexico, Arizona, and California and to be well funded and confident of enlisting Germans and Japanese. De la Rosa and Moseley had been sighted in Ciudad Victoria a few days earlier.[7]

A sighting of de la Rosa was conveyed by the chief of the bureau, Bruce Bielaski, to Leland Harrison, counselor of the State Department. A reliable informant just returned from Mexico reported that he had recently seen in the Continental Hotel in Mexico City Luis de la Rosa wearing the uniform of a brigadier general in the Carranza army and dining at that hotel with six other Carranza officers. Bielaski added: "I have thought it well to lay the statements of this informant before you, without revealing his name, but great care should be exercised in the manner in which even this information is used, in order to prevent the Mexican officials from being able to surmise the source from which it has been obtained."[8]

Another report from a confidential informant in Monterrey stated that de la Rosa and "León Caballo alias Agustín Garza" were in that city but were not active because "it seems that General Alfredo Ricaut had threatened to imprison them should they resume their former activities. I seen [*sic*] de la Rosa and Caballo November 8th at the Progreso Saloon; de la Rosa was wearing a military uniform with the insignia of Colonel, while Caballo was in civilian clothes."[9]

In Matamoros one Miguel Guevara asked informant Werbiske if there were soldiers at Point Isabel and how many. He said he had two hundred men and he thought there was a good deal of money at the Point which he could get away with. Werbiske also talked with a Julián Barbosa, who was wanted in Texas on several charges, among them that he had taken ammunition to Lyford for the *sediciosos* during the preceding summer.[10]

Consul General Philip Hanna at Monterrey produced a lengthy dispatch in December 1915, focusing on the reports he'd received in the last four months concerning the Plan de San Diego. De la Rosa, Pizaña, and Agustín Garza were of course the leaders in Monterrey of planned raids to recapture Texas for Mexico. Recently a Constitutionalist colonel had come to the consulate and told Hanna that he'd been approached by the *sedicioso* leaders and offered big money to go to Texas as an organizer. When the colonel inquired as to where the money was coming from they assured him they were being backed by two of the richest nations of Europe, Germany and Austria. Other Carranza officers were reportedly approached in a similar way. Hanna mentioned that the consul of a neutral European nation said he'd been approached by one of the *sedicioso* leaders and asked to influence his compatriots to support the insurgent cause.

Hanna continued: "I have been told that quite a large organization has existed in Monterrey for some time—and am informed that they have had ribbon badges printed at one of the printing offices in Monterrey to supply their members with. But I am told that they have been more quiet since General Carranza has been recognized and especially since he came into Northern Mexico and has been visiting points on the International boundary, and especially since General Ricaut has been placed in supreme command of the Constitutional forces on the border."[11]

In December, Venustiano Carranza, Generals Ricaut and Nafarrate with their staffs, Military Governor Luis Caballero of Tamaulipas, and prominent citizens from both Brownsville and Matamoros met on the international bridge with American officers. "General [*sic*] Carranza said he was doing all in his power to suppress the bandits and would continue to do so; that he hoped and believed a more cordial feeling between the people on both sides of the river would soon be resumed."[12]

Nevertheless, there were warnings in December that bandit gangs headquartered in Monterrey were planning new raids, and bureau chief Bielaski sent the intelligence his agency had collected to the army's adjutant general, who passed along the information to General Funston.[13]

The lower valley braced for another round of raids.

11 The Plan de San Diego, Phase Two

As the year 1916 opened, the secretary of war, Lindley Garrison, inquired of Secretary of State Robert Lansing whether "in view of the improved conditions in Mexico and on the border," it was feasible to withdraw "any or all of the troops now on the border from the duty on which they have been engaged and returning them to their permanent stations." Lansing replied that "in view of the disturbances in certain portions of Mexico, reported during the last twenty-four hours, I do not deem it advisable at this time to withdraw any of the American troops from the Mexican Border."[1]

Disquieting reports were coming in from the lower valley. The commanding officer of the Brownsville Cavalry Patrol District received information from what he considered a reliable source that de la Rosa and Pizaña were organizing in Matamoros a new raid, specifically to wreck and loot a train. So far they'd assembled between 100 and 150 men, the usual arms and ammunition, and 200 lead pipe hand grenades. The Mexican consul was informed so he could alert General Ricaut. The commanders of army units in the lower valley were also put on alert.

This might prove to be a false alarm, but similar disquieting reports were also coming in from several places in the valley. From Harlingen reliable sources warned that 150 to 200 Mexican bandits were gathering in Matamoros for a raid and that some had already infiltrated across the Rio Grande. The authorities warned the citizenry, and deputy sheriffs were requested to arrest all strange Mexicans and to "require them to prove their identity and worthiness." Similar reports from Mission warned of Pizaña and de la Rosa's followers gathering—about 150 in Matamoros and 300–400 in the vicinity of Camargo. Although there were a few occasions when Carranza troops tried to prevent small bands from crossing into Texas,[2] American authorities requested that Carranza take immediate steps to shut down de la Rosa and Pizaña's operation.[3]

Conspicuously not mentioned among the leaders of the planned incursions was Agustín S. Garza, for he was now ostensibly involved in private business. On January 26, 1916, a mercantile corporation was organized in Mexico City: Garza Hermanos y Compañía, whose dominant partner was one of the "boy generals" produced by the Mexican Revolution—twenty-five-year-old General Fortunato Zuazua, born in Lampazos de Naranjo, Nuevo León. He fought with distinction in the Constitutionalist Corps of the Northeast under General Pablo González. In February 1915 he was stationed in Tampico. As of June 16, 1915, he was promoted to general of brigade.[4] On September 7, 1915, he recaptured Piedras Negras from the forces of Pancho Villa.

The other partners were Francisco V. Garza, Agustín S. Garza, José María Zuazua, and Hermenegildo Rosas. The firm was to last for ten years and deal in a wide variety of activities: the buying and selling of seeds, general merchandise, stocks, and commercial paper as well as commissions and the purchase and sale of commercial property. Initial capital was fifty thousand pesos, which General Zuazua provided, the other partners providing their talents and services. Francisco V. Garza was to be the traveling salesman, Agustín S. Garza the office manager, assisted by José María Zuazua, and Hermenegildo Rosas would fill in wherever needed. Profits would be distributed annually as follows: Fortunato Zuazua—38 percent; Francisco V. Garza—20 percent; Agustín S. Garza—15 percent; Hermenegildo Rosas—15 percent; and José María Zuazua—12 percent. General Zuazua committed himself to providing whatever additional capital the corporation required as a loan—at a mere 50 percent annual interest. All the partners declared that they were Mexican citizens.[5] Agustín S. Garza managed the firm's office at 17 Avenida Independencia.

Garza also handled the affairs of another syndicate that General Zuazua formed in March 1916, with Juan Kvake Forseck (Sebastian Carranza's partner in the Royal Brewing Company's distribution concession in Coahuila), a syndicate whose object was to acquire oil properties, either by deed or by lease, and subdivide them; to sell lots, subdividing them; to organize all kinds of commercial societies, either corporations or any other kind; and to raise capital. Shares in the syndicate were fixed at a thousand pesos each.[6]

Agustín Garza might be a legitimate businessman by day, but by night he was once again León Caballo, fomenting revolution in Texas, an enterprise in which General Zuazua and Juan Forseck were also very much involved.

Forseck is an intriguing figure. In 1919 he gave a sworn affidavit that is an invaluable window into the Plan de San Diego conspiracy. He was careful to portray himself as just an interested observer, but in fact he was Carranza's agent whose principal assignment was to keep an eye on the conspirators. According to Forseck, he was of Austro-Hungarian origin. President Victoriano Huerta himself had issued Forseck a certificate of naturalization as a Mexican citizen on December 12, 1913. In 1914, Forseck was living in Monterrey.[7] On April 21, 1914, when the United States bombarded and occupied the port of Veracruz, the *huertista* governor of Nuevo León, Salomé Botello, had Forseck interpret for U.S. consul general Philip Hanna, who had been arrested by the Huerta authorities for telegraphing to General Pablo González, the commander of the Constitutionalist forces attacking Monterrey. Several days later, when the *huertistas* evacuated Monterrey, Forseck accompanied them, going to Mexico City, where Huerta was still in power. Through the recommendation of Governor Botello, Forseck was appointed as an official in the Mexico City police, his commission dated May 25, 1914.[8] When Huerta resigned and turned the government over to Francisco Carbajal, Forseck was reappointed as a police official, on July 27, 1914.

When the Constitutionalists under Venustiano Carranza occupied the capital, Forseck offered his services to the Constitutionalists. They promptly commissioned him as a police official. About a month later, the diplomat Eliseo Arredondo asked that Forseck be placed under his orders, and he remained on this detail for about two months. But he decided that Carranza couldn't impose order, so he asked Arredondo as a favor to furnish him railroad passes for himself and his family to Nuevo Laredo. His family received passes, but since Forseck didn't consider it safe to go through Monterrey, he went to Veracruz in September 1914, where he remained for a month and allegedly assisted the American occupying force. Forseck also said he accompanied Francisco Cuéllar, a member of the Coahuilan legislature in 1912 whom he'd known for years, to Veracruz. Cuéllar allegedly told Forseck that Carranza had intended to overthrow President Francisco Madero. Forseck, acting under orders, kept Cuéllar under surveillance. Forseck traveled to Galveston by steamer, then by rail to Laredo to join his family.

The Hungarian remained in Laredo until March 1915, when he moved to Eagle Pass with his family and established an agency—J. K. Forseck & Company—for Jack Danciger's Royal Brewing Company of Kansas City. Forseck's partner was Sebastián Carranza and, as we have seen, Danciger was an active Carranza propagandist. In 1915, when Carranza visited Piedras Negras, Eliseo Arredondo, the Mexican ambassador to the United States, came from Washington to join Carranza's entourage, and while there recruited Forseck's son Lisandro to work for him in Washington. Arredondo later wrote to Forseck at Piedras Negras, informing him that Jesús Acuña, secretary of interior (gobernación) in the Carranza cabinet, requested Forseck's services in Mexico City.[9] Forseck and his son Sandor arrived there in early June 1916, and for the next two weeks he tried unsuccessfully to arrange an interview with Acuña, who repeatedly put him off.

Forseck later said that when in Mexico City he lived with Rafael Zubarán Capmany, formerly secretary to Mexican ambassador Arredondo.[10] During this time he met several interesting people, among them Manuel Ochoa, an employee of the Treasury Department and father of Captain Manuel Ochoa of Carranza's staff,[11] who introduced him to Agustín S. Garza, alias León Caballo. Forseck accompanied Agustín Garza and Manuel Ochoa Sr. to Garza's office at 17 Avenida

Independencia, where he was introduced to General Zuazua. They invited Forseck to become an associate of Zuazua's in securing oil leases and organizing companies to promote the oil industry. "They also asked me to help them raise funds to carry on the Plan de San Diego or the Texas Revolution." Forseck said he asked whether Carranza knew of this plan, and they replied: "that part was all fixed and that any commission which they would issue to me in connection with the 'Plan of San Diego' or the Texas Revolution presented anywhere would secure me ample protection." Forseck said his reply to this proposition was that he was in Mexico City at Jesús Acuña's request and thus couldn't give them an answer until he had consulted with that official. When he did so, explaining in detail Garza's proposition, Acuña advised Forseck to accept it and assist in the Plan de San Diego.

Forseck then informed Garza that he was of the opinion that the Carranza government approved of the Plan de San Diego, but that since he was to work under Acuña it would be impossible for him to accept a commission under the Plan, as no man could serve two masters. However, he did become General Zuazua's associate in the oil business. After organizing the company with Zuazua, they opened an office in the same building with Garza, at 17 Avenida Independencia. Forseck said he was thus able to observe the movements of the Plan's leaders, especially as Jacobo Ayala Villarreal, who was Zuazua's cashier, was prominent in the movement as well as being a staunch *carrancista*.

While associated with Zuazua, Forseck was introduced to a Japanese known as "Pablo Nago," which wasn't his real name and who lived at 4a Calle de Frontera 98, Colonia Roma in Mexico City. Nago had been connected with Carranza and Acuña while their headquarters had been in Veracruz in 1914 and 1915.

Carranza apparently decided to control the Plan de San Diego leaders by imprisoning them. There is anecdotal evidence regarding Aniceto Pizaña. He was reportedly taken to Mexico City from Matamoros on April 6 as a prisoner and was freed on April 18.[12] Second, there is an indignant letter in March from Texas by one Marcos Mendoza, presumably a *magonista* militant, demanding the immediate release of Pizaña and threatening Carranza if he kept Pizaña in prison or agreed to his extradition.[13] As for Luis de la Rosa, we have no information.

By contrast, there is a first-person account of Agustín Garza's imprisonment. At this time, presumably March 1916, Zuazua was purchasing arms and ammunition and recruiting men to go north. One day the secret police raided his office and arrested everyone in the place. Zuazua asked Forseck to go immediately with one of the policemen and notify Mario Méndez, the director of federal telegraphs, who was arguably Carranza's closest associate.[14] Méndez ordered the policeman to return to Zuazua's office and release everyone, and in the future to refrain from interfering in any way with that office, and to advise the chief of police that Zuazua's office was not to be molested again, which fact Méndez had neglected to communicate to the police department. From that date, Forseck said, he and Méndez became close friends.[15]

Several days later, Agustín Garza was arrested. His operation was tightly controlled and only a few knew of it, and this landed Garza in serious trouble. He was busily recruiting men for the Texas venture, and he wasn't particularly concerned with their political affiliations. Two of his agents were negotiating with representatives in Mexico City of *huertista* chieftains such as Marcelo Caraveo and Benjamín Argumedo. However, secret agents who reported to General Jacinto B. Treviño, Carranza's chief of staff, had Garza's people under surveillance and arrested them on March 8. Under "enhanced interrogation" they spilled their guts, implicating Agustín Garza and revealing his whereabouts. As luck would have it, that night, March 8–9, Pancho Villa attacked the New Mexico border village of Columbus, plunging the Carranza administration into international complications and resulting in the incursion into Chihuahua on March 15 of General John J. Pershing and the Punitive Expedition. Because Garza had been dealing with dissident elements in his recruiting drive, the authorities thought he was in league with Villa, Carranza's deadly enemy, and they promptly arrested Garza.

Garza was incarcerated incommunicado behind the grim walls of Lecumberri, the penitentiary of the Federal District, cell block number 1, in cells 296 and 298. The irony was that three days earlier, Garza had approached the Carranza administration seeking support for the renewed Texas revolution; instead, he found himself in prison, something that really rankled, for on several occasions he would bitterly refer to his unjustified incarceration.[16]

General Zuazua rescued him. Informed of Garza's predicament, the general began making inquiries; among others, he wired repeatedly to Jesús Acuña, who replied that Garza was being held at the disposal of General Treviño.[17] A frustrated Zuazua then telegraphed to Venustiano Carranza himself on March 29. At the time, Carranza was in Querétaro, where the *carrancistas* were engaged in drafting a new, and radical, constitution for Mexico. Zuazua wired: "I respectfully inform you that Agustín Garza, my commercial partner, was detained some days ago at the disposal of the Secretariat of Interior without the nature being known. I have contacted the Secretary repeatedly without receiving a reply. I implore you if there is no grave reason for his detention that you order that he be freed."[18] Carranza replied the next day saying that through the Secretariat of Interior he would order that Garza be freed.[19]

General Zuazua wasn't the only one lobbying for Garza's release from prison. The Japanese associate of Garza's who went by the alias "Pablo Nago" also wrote to Secretary of Interior Jesús Acuña on Garza's behalf. Reminding Acuña that on a previous occasion he'd spoken with him about Garza, Nago now vouched for Garza's innocence and requested that Acuña grant Garza an interview so that Garza could "explain the real reasons for his detention, whether it is extra-official, as he has been told, and in any case to inform you about a matter that both Garza, like a great number of Mexicans and foreigners (except the North Americans) we believe inspired in the pursuit of patriotic sentiments. Garza hopes, not just for the consolidation of his beloved Fatherland, Mexico, but of all the Latin nations of the new continent, and impelled by those noble sentiments of true patriotism and in accord with a great number of his compatriots for some years, in tenaciously fighting for and has fought for, propagating the ideals that he does not consider contrary to the sublime goals of the Mexican Revolution." Stressing that the matter was of transcendental national importance, Nago asked that Acuña permit Garza to accompany Nago to Querétaro for the interview, pledging his word of honor for Garza's good conduct.[20] When Forseck asked Pablo if he knew why Garza had been arrested, Nago said he was in no danger and would shortly be released.

In less than two weeks Garza was indeed released, in April, and found to his delight that his status had suddenly changed. Heretofore his commitment to the Texas revolution caused uneasiness in Mexico City, for his actions could embroil the Carranza administration in difficulties with the United States. But when the Punitive Expedition crossed into Chihuahua on March 15, the situation changed dramatically. Carranza was in the precarious position of having to expel the thousands of American invaders but doing it without plunging Mexico into a disastrous war. But by reigniting the Texas revolution, raids into Texas could provide the necessary leverage to secure the Punitive Expedition's withdrawal; when it crossed back into the United States, the raids into Texas would cease. Since using Plan de San Diego raids in 1915 in order to obtain diplomatic recognition had succeeded brilliantly, the Carranza administration now backed the *sediciosos* in hopes of repeating the coup.

The crucial elements in this new strategy were, first, to maintain plausible deniability, and second, to ensure that none of the raids was so serious as to provoke massive American retaliation. Agustín S. Garza, as "León Caballo," was to be a key player.

On the day of his release, he and Zuazua went to the residence of General Pablo González at Tacubaya. They returned with ten thousand pesos in Carranza paper money and a thousand dollars in American gold. Forseck remarked to Garza that he didn't care to have the Carranza paper money but he sure would like the American gold. Garza explained that he needed the gold in order to send a black man to the United States who'd been employed to foment a revolt among black soldiers on the border. Forseck said he subsequently saw the black man, who was over six feet tall and had a crippled left leg that made him limp.

The individual referred to was in all probability Dr. Jesse M. Moseley.[21] An accomplished surgeon, he had lived in Denison, Texas, for a number of years and was well thought of by his white colleagues. He moved to Fort Worth, then to Tampico, Mexico, where he practiced his profession until 1915. Moseley claimed to be the personal physician of the governor of Tamaulipas, General Luis Caballero. Allegedly through Caballero's influence, Moseley was commissioned as a captain in the medical corps of the Carranza army and subsequently was assigned to General Emiliano Nafarrate's command at Matamoros. Nafarrate promoted Moseley to the rank of major and assigned him the mission of recruiting blacks in Texas. Moseley, described as "a Negro of light brown complexion, very dignified in his personal appearance," and well spoken, had enjoyed a lucrative medical practice in Tampico for the previous eighteen years, catering to upper-class Mexicans. In 1916 he became the partner of Melvin J. Chisum, a black newspaperman in Oklahoma City, in a scheme to acquire from the Mexican government some ten thousand acres on which to settle black colonists. But he also became involved in the Plan de San Diego, agreeing to be an organizer in Texas. He reportedly recruited blacks in the vicinity of Austin and San Marcos and spent about three months in Texas and Oklahoma.

He then traveled to Laredo; since there were very few blacks living there, Moseley was hardly inconspicuous. His trip proved to be a colossal mistake. Moseley's nemesis was Tom Ross, a former Texas Ranger captain who was now an agent of the federal Bureau of Investigation. Ross experienced no difficulty in locating Moseley in a brothel in Laredo's red-light district located between downtown and Fort McIntosh. When Ross arrested Moseley on June 30, 1916, for soliciting the desertion of American soldiers on behalf of a foreign power, the doctor was found to be carrying seditious propaganda, maps, and his commission as a major in Carranza's army. He was whisked off to the Webb County jail.

On the afternoon of July 11, an army patrol discovered the decomposing corpse of a black man in an arroyo about nine miles southeast of Laredo. There was unmistakable evidence of foul play, for the skull showed considerable blunt-force trauma. The corpse of the man whose skull had been bashed in with a rock was soon identified as that of Dr. Jesse M. Moseley.

Following a coroner's investigation into Moseley's death and an examination of the body, the justice of the peace swore out a complaint against Ross charging him with taking Moseley from his cell and killing him. A constable arrested Ross and placed him in the county jail. Ross claimed that he had released Moseley, who came by Ross's office in the federal building at night to pick up papers seized at his arrest and who left alone, a version corroborated by fellow bureau agent Davis McGowen and by Captain Allen Walker, deputy U.S. marshal. However, a jail guard claimed to have witnessed Ross leaving the jail with Moseley. At Ross's preliminary hearing the judge discounted the jailer's testimony and ruled that the evidence against Ross was negligible. Ross was released under a thousand-dollar bond, which a number of prominent Laredoans vied to post for him. The judge then turned to the matter of two Hispanics charged as accomplices, Félix Carillo, an employee of Ross's, and Carillo's friend Antonio Pérez. They were released on a two-hundred-dollar bond each. And that ended the matter. As far as the law was concerned, Dr. Jesse Moseley had met his end at the hands of persons unknown.[22]

In April, Colonel Maurilio Rodríguez, another of Venustiano Carranza's many nephews, had been jailed for fighting. He was released through the good offices of General Pablo González and came to Zuazua's office, where arms and ammunition were furnished to him for the Texas revolution. Moreover, he received passes to Monterrey on the Constitutionalist Railways[23] for himself and about twenty-five men, including seven or eight Japanese. General Juan Barragán, Carranza's new chief of staff, issued the passes.

Mario Méndez wanted to see Forseck at his office. Forseck asked Méndez why he had sent for him, and Méndez remarked, "See what this fellow Maurilio [Rodríguez] has done; we sent him to fight the Americans (meaning the Texas revolution) and now he is fighting our own people." Méndez showed Forseck a telegram from the town of Bustamanate, Nuevo León, reporting that Maurilio Rodríguez had arrived with twenty-odd men and had gone to the barracks, whose colonel was a friend of his. While giving the colonel a big *abrazo*, Rodríguez grabbed him and held him while his men proceeded to seize the garrison's horses and weapons. A few shots were exchanged. Rodríguez then made his way to the Rio Grande with the force he'd brought from Mexico City.

Méndez got down to business, telling Forseck that General Cándido

Aguilar, the foreign secretary and Carranza's son-in-law, wanted to hire him. But Forseck's repeated attempts to see Aguilar were unsuccessful because Aguilar was too busy to see him. Méndez gave Forseck a thousand pesos for expenses and asked him to accept a commission to return to the United States via Cuba and Key West to recruit anarchists, at good compensation, to dynamite places in the United States. Forseck said he told Méndez he didn't do that kind of work but was willing to help them in any other way. On Méndez's instructions he returned the next day, whereupon Méndez's secretary escorted him to see First Chief Carranza's private secretary, who said he had a position for Forseck. But Forseck never heard anything further.

About this time, Colonel Esteban E. Fierros, superintendent of the Constitutionalist Railways terminal in Tampico, arrived in Mexico City. (On November 10, 1914, Fierros had secured a ten-year government concession for the exploitation of oil seepage into the Buenavista River. However, the concession had lapsed because Fierros hadn't implemented it. In March1915 a company consisting of Juan Guimbarda, customhouse administrator, Carlos Arana, an engineer and government oil inspector, and Colonel Carlos Fierros, Esteban's brother, claimed to have acquired the concession. The petroleum company El Aguila vigorously disputed their claim.)[24] While Fierros was in Mexico City, Forseck arranged to sell him a large tract of land[25] for 1.5 million pesos in bills of the Banco Nacional, 1 million going to the owners of the property and 500,000 being divided between Zuazua, a Spaniard whose name Forseck said he didn't recall, the general manager of the Bank of San Luis Potosí, and Forseck in equal portions. At that time the peso notes of the Banco Nacional were worth about seventeen cents in U.S. currency. Fierros gave Forseck a check for five thousand dollars dated May 25, 1916, on Robert M. Beakie & Co., Bankers, Tampico, as part of Forseck's commission.[26] But when Forseck sent his son Sandor to Tampico to cash the check, payment was refused and the check was endorsed "No Funds." Forseck accompanied Zuazua to meet with the politician Nicéforo Zambrano, who was then residing in Mexico City with his family, to discuss some oil properties.

Fierros was accompanied by Luis de la Rosa and four or five other men who'd been associated with de la Rosa in the Texas revolution.

They went to Zuazua's office. General Zuazua and Colonel Fierros made daily trips to the residence of General Pablo González.

The individual charged with implementing the new strategy—reviving the Plan de San Diego and invading South Texas—was General Pablo González. He was not just another revolutionary general. González was Carranza's favorite and most loyal commander. González, from his headquarters in Cuernavaca, Morelos, was not only combating the agrarian rebels led by Emiliano Zapata but also commanded Carranza's Army Corps of the East, encompassing all of eastern Mexico. González had sent to the border an agent, the turncoat ex-*villista* General Juan Antonio Acosta, who supplied intelligence on U.S. Army dispositions and also served as liaison between *sediciosos* in Texas and González.[27]

General Zuazua left Mexico City on May 24, 1916, for Coahuila on a special train carrying his personal automobile and 150 former *huertista* soldiers. According to Forseck, these men had hidden their arms, but when they learned of the Texas revolution they approached Zuazua and offered their services and weapons. Even before Zuazua left for Coahuila, other men had been recruited and dispatched north, their railroad passes being furnished by General Juan Barragán. Zuazua established his headquarters at Sabinas, Coahuila.

Perhaps hoping to acquire merit with the American authorities, in his affidavit Forseck claimed that when his son Sandor returned from Tampico he sent him to Piedras Negras with instructions to speak with a Mr. Schmidt, manager of the ice plant in Eagle Pass, whose brother, E. H. Schmidt, was president of the Border National Bank and mayor of Eagle Pass.[28] Sandor was to inform Schmidt about the Plan de San Diego conspiracy in hopes that he in turn would inform his brother, but Schmidt refused to listen to Sandor, and thus the American authorities weren't alerted. Forseck had instructed Sandor to remain close to General Zuazua and report on his activities.

Early in June 1916, Forseck spoke with Colonel Esteban Fierros, Luis de la Rosa, and others, who left Mexico City for Monterrey. (The charges from the Constitutionalist Railways for the railroad car provided to Fierros were to be paid by the Secretariat of War, but since Fierros was the superintendent of the Tampico railroad terminal there would be no charge.)[29] When Forseck told de la Rosa that he was running a big risk in going to Texas, he replied that he and fifty men had kept five thousand American soldiers busy for several months and that he had not lost a man. (De la Rosa's claim about his lack of casualties was false, and his boast about pinning down thousands of American soldiers was hardly in keeping with the Plan de San Diego's objectives.) After Fierros and de la Rosa went to Monterrey, Agustín Garza, the military chief of the Plan, also left for Monterrey, and the office at 17 Independencia was closed.

Shortly thereafter, Pablo Nago told Forseck that Mario Méndez had instructed him to go to Monterrey with money to pay the men under Garza. Nago invited Forseck to accompany him on this mission, but Forseck declined. After the Plan de San Diego personages left for Monterrey, Forseck had no further dealings with Mario Méndez.

Mexican preparations for the impending operation included Luis de la Rosa openly recruiting in places such as Ciudad Victoria without interference by the Carranza authorities. Moreover, there was an orchestrated campaign of anti-American propaganda in the government newspapers.[30] Reinforcing the propaganda campaign were demonstrations by mobs who on occasion attacked American consulates. Additionally, fliers were circulated bearing bloodthirsty poems announcing the merciless thrashing the Americans would receive in the event of war.[31]

12 An Improbable Operation

In furtherance of the grand design, León Caballo began expanding his network. Garza dispatched to the city of Puebla one Gerardo Garza González, who began sounding out General Marciano González and his staff regarding recruitment for the Texas enterprise. Gerardo Garza González was a real firebrand—at least on paper. He wrote to Agustín Garza that he was willing to be assigned to the vanguard, "as you know that I'd like to die at the hands of your good friends *los sanabibiches [sic] gringos*," whose hour of reckoning was rapidly approaching. It was "now or never—time to die". He reported on May 4 that the officers in the Puebla garrison were eager to operate along the Rio Grande. He said the enterprise was going well and it had to be implemented immediately regardless of the cost, "and for a lot of gringo blood to flow so that those bastards pay something of what they owe to our beloved Fatherland." He closed with a string of choice anti-gringo expletives, assuring Garza of his thirst for Yankee blood. He closed another of his letters with regards for "the whole Anti-gringo Brigade."[1]

Agustín Garza's old comrade Basilio Ramos wrote to him from Veracruz, where he was employed by El Aguila oil company, in charge of dispatching the company's steamers. Ramos explained that he hadn't answered Garza's recent letters because he feared that anything he put in writing might be used against Garza. And with the latest blow—Garza's incarceration—he feared that their Plan de San Diego enterprise might have suffered a fatal blow. But he urged Garza to persevere.

In mid-May he congratulated Garza on the latter's forthcoming trip to the border. Ramos regretted that his own precarious financial condition precluded his even traveling to Mexico City, but he had every confidence in the enterprise, given its nobility. He urged Garza to keep him informed of developments.[2] Garza wired him five hundred pesos with which to make the trip and promised to wait for Ramos until May 27. However, when Ramos finally received the telegram, on May 28, and went to the telegraph office to collect the money, the personnel refused to deliver it, allegedly because it wasn't a money order, and in any case it would be difficult for Ramos to leave his job on short notice. Ramos said he bitterly regretted not being able to accompany Garza but urged the latter to write him a detailed account of his arrangements and the course they should follow, as well as what resources they could count on for their necessary expenses, since this was of primary importance.[3]

By May 31, Agustín Garza had established his headquarters at the Hotel Independencia in Monterrey; he later moved to room 12, Hotel del Centro. He received a report from one of his subordinates, Colonel José O. Flores, from Mexico City enclosing a list of recruits being sent to Monterrey under a Colonel Villegas and a notation that five thousand pesos had been advanced to them for expenses on the trip. The colonel would give Garza an accounting upon reaching Monterrey. Flores assured Garza that he would send more recruits shortly, for in Mexico City there were many enthusiastic volunteers. What was needed was money to keep sending them north.

Most interestingly, Flores said that the firebrand Gerardo Garza González would deliver to Garza a cipher to be used whenever necessary. And indeed there is a cipher wheel among Garza's personal papers, along with several telegrams in code, all of which were much more sophisticated than anything the *sediciosos* had.[4]

On June 1, Colonel Flores again wrote to Agustín Garza, addressing him as "General," and introducing Major Enrique Porras, who with six officers and six enlisted men was going to the border to join the command of General Fortunato Zuazua, whose headquarters were now in Piedras Negras.[5] And the next day, Flores reported that on tomorrow's train there were leaving for Monterrey forty-six officers to join Zuazua's command. José María Zuazua had advanced them a thousand pesos for traveling expenses, the officers to receive fifty pesos each; Flores asked Garza to be sure they reached their destination. On June 3, Flores advised that Major Ernesto Coronado was going to join Zuazua.[6] And so on. In addition, Garza's friend the Mexico City bank employee Samuel Rendón eagerly volunteered for the Texas enterprise. Garza readily accepted his offer to function as a banker once they were established across the Rio Grande, and said that in any case he would be welcomed.[7]

On June 5, León Caballo sent a crucial note to General Zuazua: "Tomorrow the ready personnel leave for there [Piedras Negras] under Gerardo Garza González. Everything is arranged for the night of the 9th. All personnel are ready. Don Venustiano expects you to order that we receive all elements. Please do so. It is all arranged. Your orders are awaited. [signed] León Caballo."[8]

Some scholars simply refuse to believe that Venustiano Carranza was in any way involved in the Plan de San Diego conspiracy. Allen Gerlach, for example, in referring to the Mexican government's press campaign supporting the Texas revolution, states that although Constitutionalist newspapers in Matamoros and Monterrey carried articles by Luis de la Rosa urging implementation of the Plan, this in no way implicated either the *carrancistas* or Carranza himself "even though they permitted the publication of de la Rosa's pleas." Referring to General Nafarrate's transfer from Matamoros, Gerlach writes that "Carranza's apparent desire to end disorder along the boundary assuredly proves his lack of connection with the Plan de San Diego."[9]

Joseph A. Stout argues that just because de la Rosa moved about freely to recruit, this has made some scholars conclude that at least in 1916, Carranza supported de la Rosa. But, Stout writes, Carranza's control of Mexico during much of 1916 was so tenuous that his authority was doubtful in northern Mexico. Regarding Carranza's involvement in the Plan, "No specific documentation in Mexico supports the theory" and "There is no hard evidence implicating Carranza."[10] Evidently Agustín Garza, aka León Caballo, would disagree.

Among Mexican writers, Carranza apologist Isidro Fabela stoutly denied any *carrancista* involvement with the Plan de San Diego, all the while emphasizing that it was Venustiano Carranza, not his generals such as Alvaro Obregón or Pablo González, who formulated foreign policy.[11] Running a high-stakes covert operation against the United States would seem to fall into the category of foreign policy.

On April 8 a Matamoros newspaper reported that Aniceto Pizaña had been taken to the penitentiary in Mexico City under a guard of twenty soldiers to await a formal trial, by Carranza's order. Pizaña had been incarcerated in Matamoros but had been free on bail. Since Mexican authorities were to try Pizaña on a charge of being a *huertista*, there was no chance that he would be extradited to Texas. However, in May the newspaper reported that Pizaña had returned to Matamoros ostensibly as a prisoner, but General Alfredo Ricaut announced that his prison was the city of Matamoros. Pizaña was free to continue his *sedicioso* intrigues.[12]

While León Caballo was organizing the Texas revolution from Monterrey, another component of the enterprise had taken shape near Nuevo Laredo. General Pablo González assigned Colonel Esteban Fierros to command a brigade of irregulars being formed to invade Texas.

Fierros came from a prominent Laredo family. His father, Andrés Germán Fierros, was a successful customs broker. In 1912 he established the firm of A. G. Fierros Sucs., with offices in both Laredo and Nuevo Laredo. He was a director of the Merchants State Bank and Trust Company in Laredo in 1918 and 1919.[13]

Andrés Germán's three sons became staunch supporters of Venustiano Carranza and the Constitutionalist movement. His middle son, Leocadio, born in December 1883, was engaged in smuggling ammunition to the Constitutionalists as early as May 1913, and he plotted to capture Nuevo Laredo from the *huertistas*. He was vigorously opposed by Amador Sánchez, the sheriff of Webb County, who had been instrumental in a coup by Huerta sympathizers that had seized Nuevo Laredo on February 15 by subverting the garrison. Leocadio became a major in the Constitutionalist Army.[14]

Andrés's youngest son, Carlos, was born in February 1889 in Camargo, Tamaulipas, but had lived in Laredo since he was a baby. In

1910 he was a paymaster in Laredo for the Texas Mexican Railroad. Carlos was a strong supporter of Francisco Madero. During the 1912 Orozco rebellion against President Madero, Carlos recruited men to fight in Mexico for Madero. Arrested for violating the neutrality laws, he pleaded guilty and was fined six hundred dollars. He recruited Constitutionalist fighters in Laredo the summer of 1913.[15] Carlos subsequently crossed into Mexico and joined the Constitutionalist Army. When Huerta fled into exile in 1914, Carlos was made superintendent of the Southern Division of the Constitutionalist Railways, a position he held into 1915. He died in September 1915 in Mexico City of either typhoid fever or pneumonia. At the time of his death he was a colonel in the Constitutionalist Army. His remains were returned to Laredo for burial.[16]

Andrés's eldest son, Esteban, born in August 1880, worked as a yardmaster in Laredo for the Mexican National Railroad as a young man, then became a Constitutionalist officer, rising to the rank of colonel in the Army Corps of the East and holding a succession of staff positions on the Constitutionalist railroads. When chosen for this latest assignment he was superintendent of the railroad terminal at Tampico.[17]

The selection of Esteban Fierros for this mission might seem odd at first glance. But he came from a prominent, and fervently Constitutionalist, Laredo family, was loyal to General Pablo González, and had invaluable administrative background. His job was not to lead men in combat but rather to repair a railroad line to the border and to organize and direct the irregular brigade, whose members would be infiltrated into Texas.

In May, Colonel Fierros was promoted to brevet general and placed in command of the Brigada Fierros, which was quietly being assembled in Monterrey. As was the case with military formations throughout the Mexican Revolution, the brigade was top-heavy. It has been stated that in 1916, on paper the Constitutionalist Army numbered some 200,000, including about 50,000 officers, 500 of them generals—one officer for every three enlisted men. General Jacinto Treviño, commander in Chihuahua, had "forty-four generals, 1,347 field-grade officers, 3,699 other commissioned officers and 11,118 enlisted men."[18]

Fierros had as subordinates three other generals. Two of them were Luis García and Luz Elías de Pérez. Significantly, the third subordinate general was none other than Luis de la Rosa, the man who was supposed to be the leader of the Plan de San Diego in Texas. His subordinate status illustrates the extent to which the Carranza administration, not the Tejanos, controlled the movement. Reinforcing this control, it was Fierros who handled the brigade's finances, and de la Rosa had to approach him for money. It will be noticed that Aniceto Pizaña wasn't even in the picture.

To provide Fierros with the requisite *sedicioso* credentials, on May 30, 1916, the "General in Chief of the Liberating Army of Races and Peoples in America," León Caballo himself, commissioned Fierros as a brigadier general in the revolutionary forces. The commission was purportedly issued at San Diego, Texas, but as with everything else it was actually issued in Monterrey.[19]

Fierros's credentials were much more impressive than the unit he commanded: four generals and a corresponding proportion of subordinate officers down to sub-lieutenant for a brigade numbering 450 men. For instance, Lieutenant Colonel Miguel Partida's command consisted of one lieutenant colonel, three majors, two first captains, five second captains, five lieutenants, five sub-lieutenants—and thirteen enlisted men. The brigade's personnel were a motley aggregation. Some were *sedicioso* refugees from Texas, but most were raw recruits. There was a cadre of *carrancista* regulars, including forty from the Railroad Corps. The latter's assignment was to repair the track to La Jarita, near Nuevo Laredo, which station had been selected as the brigade's headquarters, and to rebuild the branch line to Colombia on the Rio Grande. To facilitate Fierros's operations, a military train was placed at his disposal. Perhaps the most intriguing aspect of the Brigada Fierros was that it contained seven Japanese.[20]

By June 8 the brigade was poised for action, and Fierros conducted a formal review at La Jarita station. The next day he sent a status report to General Pablo González. The brigade currently numbered 310 cavalry and 143 infantry, not all of whom were at La Jarita. Fierros said he had been infiltrating three or four men across the Rio Grande every night to conduct reconnaissance and to act as guides for the rest of the brigade when it crossed the river. This was imminent, just as soon as Fierros settled some last-minute details with General Zuazua.

In a handwritten postscript, Fierros added:

> Most of the cavalry have crossed into Texas to penetrate the interior of the State, disguised as vaqueros, and to date we have had no difficulty in crossing in parties of 25 and 30 men, dividing them into bands of 20 each [deployed] in different directions, designating Kennedy [Kenedy, southeast of San Antonio], Texas, as the assembly point. The Coup should break out tonight after midnight [June 10]. I expect we will soon have very good news to communicate to you. I leave on Monday to put myself at the head of my troops, depending on the orders that Fortunato [Zuazua] gives me. I send you a strong *abrazo.* [I am] expecting you to telegraph me the latest on the International situation. [signed] Esteban E. Fierros. The lady who will deliver this to you is an intimate friend who has my entire confidence, who has just returned from Laredo, Texas, where I sent her on a mission.[21]

These preparations didn't go unnoticed. Bureau agent Barnes reported that it was an open secret in Monterrey that the Carranza government was extending amnesty to all political offenders and ex-soldiers of the old Porfirio Díaz regime in order to enlist them for an invasion of the United States. Furthermore, General Esteban Fierros had arrived from Tampico on a special train bringing five thousand rifles that General Pablo González had furnished him in Mexico City.[22]

The Fierros Brigade's accounts shed some light on the preparations. A selection includes an "Account of the sums delivered to the Chiefs in command of troops, for their maintenance [in pesos]":

	Veracruz issue	***Infalsificables* [Uncounterfitable] issue**
N. Peña		2,500.00
L. de la Rosa	2,500.00	2,300.00
M. M. Arellano		3,030.00
J. I. de los Santos	10,000.00	4,760.00
F. Cabañas		1,610.00
T. Medina	925.00	965.00
M. Zayas		620.00

J. A. Elizondo	5,000.00	
P. Viña		8,000.00
M. Ramírez		980.00
M. Partida Pérez		2535.00
L. E. de Pérez	15,000.00	9,300.00
A. Valdez		1,210.00
M. M. García	3,000.00	100.00
A. B. García	2,000.00	603.00
A. G. Vivero for provisioning the troops		2,200.00
Total	38,425.00	46,211.00

Spent for the purchase of arms and ammunition, provisions, recruiting expenses, expenses for various commissions, and disbursed to the Chiefs and officers for their personal expenses

	6,470.00	19,695.84
Total	44,895.00	65,906.84[23]

I received from the General Treasury of the Fierros Brigade the sum of 800 pesos *Infalsificables*, which was distributed among the individuals listed below. Monterrey, June 2, 1916, General (signed) Luis de la Rosa. [There follow the names of nineteen individuals who received forty pesos each; another forty-peso entry was for miscellaneous expenses, for a total of 800 pesos.]

I received from the General Treasury of the Fierros Brigade the sum of 1,000 *Infalsificable* pesos for my expenses. General [signed] Luis de la Rosa.

Monterrey, June 2, 1916: I received from General Esteban E. Fierros the sum of 15,000 pesos in Veracruz issue or its equivalent in *Infalsificables*, for the expenses of the force under my command. General [signed] Luis de la Rosa.

undated [early June] To: General E. E. Fierros at Monterrey: I confirm our conversation of this afternoon, and I beg you to assist me pecuniarly because I have begun the mobilization of my troops. I also beg you to send me General Ricaut's letter. N. S. Méndez

June 2 Received from the treasury of the Liberating Army: 3,000 pesos for the force leaving [Monterrey] tomorrow under my command. Lt. Col. Manuel M. García.

June 2 Received of General E. E. Fierros: 10,000 pesos for expenses of my regiment. Liberty Equality and Reconquest. Isabel de los Santos. [He was a former captain of *rurales* who had issued a flier on March 14, 1916, from Monterrey stating that newspaper accounts said American troops were invading Mexico. If the accounts were true, everyone should support Venustiano Carranza and his associates.][24]

June 4 Received from the treasury 50 pesos for my personal expenses. Lt. Colonel M. P. Pérez.

June 5 Received from General Esteban E. Fierros 15,000 pesos for the expenses of the forces under my command. General Luis Elías de Pérez.

June 5 Received of General Esteban E. Fierros 100 pesos for ammunition and arms sold to the general. P. Villarreal.

June 6 Received of the treasury 5,000 pesos for the expenses of my forces. Colonel Pedro Viña.[25]

But suddenly the whole operation, which was aimed at Laredo—the town was to be isolated by the Fierros Brigade, then the garrison of Nuevo Laredo would attack across the international bridge—was put on hold. It apparently occurred to somebody that even if Laredo were captured, then what?

On June 6, General Zuazua had telegraphed to Agustín Garza from Piedras Negras that he was "leaving violently" for Mexico City, presumably for urgent consultations.[26] His departure resulted in considerable confusion. On June 7, Garza's subordinate, Guillermo Ortiz, telegraphed to him from Piedras Negras, saying that since Zuazua had left, he didn't know with whom to deal, especially since the planned day, June 10, was so near at hand. Several of the militants had suddenly lost their fervor, and Ortiz was having great difficulty in assembling his men. He anxiously awaited Zuazua's return, and in case this didn't happen he pleaded with León Caballo to send him instructions by wire, for he was completely isolated. Ortiz added that General Francisco Murguía was expected in Piedras Negras, and although he didn't know what Murguía's orders were he hoped the general would support the Texas enterprise. Finally, he stated that if Zuazua chose not to attack across the Rio Grande, he, Ortiz would do so with whatever force he had, although he lacked everything—presumably arms, ammunition, and supplies.[27]

León Caballo's enterprise was disintegrating. Besides the crisis in Piedras Negras, he received a telegram from Lieutenant Colonel A. Sánchez at Monclova urgently requesting two thousand pesos for his men's rations. And on June 10, Colonel Luis Santos received five hundred pesos for general expenses. Lieutenant Colonel Ambrosio Sánchez at Piedras Negras asked for instructions and for six hundred pesos for his men's expenses. León Caballo had to scramble to raise money, among other things wiring to his brother Francisco in Tampico to send him five hundred pesos. Caballo was no doubt heartened when General Zuazua wired from Mexico City on June 8 that he was returning the next day.[28] But Zuazua's arrival on the scene must have been a bitter disappointment, for he promptly shut down the whole operation. Evidently, common sense had prevailed in Mexico City.

13 The Morín Affair

The Hispanic uprising that was to support the planned *sedicioso* offensive collapsed as a result of the Morín affair. The key figure in uncovering this conspiracy was William Martin Hanson. He had been appointed U.S. marshal for the Southern District of Texas in 1902; he was reappointed in 1906 but resigned. In 1911 he was a private detective in San Antonio directing a network of informers and secret agents for the government of Porfirio Díaz. Hanson went to live in Mexico, where he engaged in the oil and land business in the vicinity of Tampico and Veracruz. He also acquired the three-thousand-acre Hacienda de Guadalupe near Ciudad Victoria, Tamaulipas. The Mexican Revolution devastated Hanson's enterprises. In January 1914 the *carrancistas* seized his hacienda, briefly imprisoned him, and then expelled him from Mexico as a *huertista* spy. Hanson returned to San Antonio, where his friend Duval West, who'd been one of President Wilson's emissaries to Mexico, appointed Hanson as chief special agent for the San Antonio, Uvalde, and Gulf Railroad, of which West was the receiver.[1]

Operating out of his office at room 509 Calcasieu Building in San Antonio, Hanson revealed the Morín conspiracy to the Bureau of Investigation by introducing Agent Howard P. Wright to Colonel Viviano Saldívar Cervantes, a former Carranza officer whom Hanson had known in Mexico and for whose veracity he vouched. Saldívar Cervantes's revolutionary career had evidently begun in November 1911 when he was commissioned as a colonel in the rebel forces of Emilio Vázquez Gómez.[2]

Saldívar Cervantes disclosed the plot to Agent Wright and became a bureau informer. The key plotter was José María Morín, who like the colonel was an experienced revolutionist. In 1912 Morín had recruited men in San Antonio for the Vázquez Gómez movement, and he and his brother had left from Karnes City and crossed into Mexico to fight for that faction.[3] Saldívar Cervantes described Morín as being five feet eleven inches tall, weighing two hundred pounds, having a black mustache and dark brown skin, and being about forty-five years old. He was said to be living at 415 Travis Street and using the alias "J. M. Leal." As a security measure Morín never slept more than two nights at a time in any one house. Morín claimed to have been commissioned as a brigadier general by Pancho Villa.

Agent Wright had one of the bureau's informants, "Informant Galed," make discreet inquiries, and Galed reported that Morín had been in San Antonio for about a month; his ostensible business was buying roosters to ship to Mexico for cockfights. Galed also interviewed José Escudero, the man whom Morín had hired to drive him around San Antonio, as well as the man's sister, Domitilia Escudero, who operated a brothel at 505 Durango Street under the professional name of Lucía Padovani and to whom the bureau was prepared to pay a reasonable sum for information. She told Galed that she understood Morín's mission to be to recruit Mexicans for a projected uprising. Morín had been busy in late April and early May organizing Hispanics from San Antonio to the border, trying to enlist followers of Villa and Félix Díaz, among others. He professed to be a *villista* and urged his listeners to participate in the rising scheduled for May 10.[4]

Colonel Saldívar Cervantes gave his reports in Hanson's office each day at 11 a.m. He had met with Morín, who revealed that his subordinate chieftains were Blas de la Garza, who was a saloonkeeper on Matamoros Street in San Antonio; Néstor Bazán at the town of Calaveras;[5] Victoriano Ponce at Kingsville; Ramón Borunda at Saspamco; Santos Amador at Falls City; Gabino Sánchez,[6] Pedro Rosales,[7] and Marcos

Botello[8] at Poth; and Teófilo Vázquez at Brownsville. Morín asked Saldívar Cervantes to write a proclamation based on a memorandum that Morín had drafted.[9] Saldívar Cervantes delivered the memorandum to the bureau to be copied, then took the document back in case Morín wanted to see it. More importantly, Saldívar Cervantes provided the bureau with the code that Morín and his associates were using.[10] And the informer said that Morín was conducting meetings of his supporters in an upstairs room in the market hall. Morín's idea was to have a number of meetings so that the Anglos wouldn't know just when the plan was to be carried out—the plan being to cut the railroads entering San Antonio, seize the arsenal at Fort Sam Houston, then deploy squads in automobiles to set fires and hurl bombs around the city and vicinity. Morín said he was getting arms and ammunition, including five or six boxes of dynamite, and assembling the munitions in the vicinity of Saspamco and Calaveras in Wilson County. He mentioned that his brother, Leandro Morín, was expected in San Antonio shortly.[11]

Morín was issuing commissions to those who would lead the envisioned army of liberation in Texas. He commissioned his loyal friend Colonel Saldívar Cervantes as a brigadier general, impressing on him that he was the first brigadier general to be so commissioned. Morín even had a form for issuing commissions—on one side was the name and rank of the officer and on the reverse an oath to be taken before the officer was appointed. Agent Wright had the form photographed.[12] According to Saldívar Cervantes, General Morín planned to leave for Austin and San Marcos briefly to attend to details; he had already dispatched an assistant, a certain Santiago Longoria, at whose house in San Antonio Morín was staying, to notify militants in Austin and San Marcos to be ready, and another assistant, José Luna from Falfurrias, had been sent to Calaveras, Kingsville, and Falfurrias with the same instructions. Morín himself planned to travel to Saspamco to ensure that everything was in readiness there. At Agent Wright's suggestion, Saldívar Cervantes persuaded Morín as a memento of their friendship to have his picture taken together with him. Saldívar Cervantes of course promptly delivered the photograph, with himself cut out, to the bureau. The informer also revealed that Morín was running short of funds, having to rely on donations of arms and ammunition from sympathizers. Morín "expected to get the majority of his arms and ammunition by robbing and pillage when he started his movement."[13]

Saldívar Cervantes next reported that Morín had decided not to go to Austin and San Marcos after all because he was to meet in San Antonio with one Librado Palacios of Stockdale, Texas, who was coming to receive Morín's orders and be commissioned as a colonel.[14] "Col. Cervantes says that Librado Palacios is a 'war-like' man and that that he did not have very much confidence in Col. Cervantes at first but that Gen. Morín told Palacios that Col. Cervantes was a good man and would make a good officer under Gen. Morín." On April 26 Morín left for Stockdale, where he intended to get two thousand dollars from Librado Palacios; if he succeeded he planned to proceed on to Brownsville. Morín told Saldívar Cervantes that when he came to Texas he had about five thousand dollars but that his funds were now running low.[15]

The bureau assigned Special Employee Manuel Sorola, who had once lived in Toluca, Mexico, to assist Saldívar Cervantes in surveilling Morín and checking independently the veracity of Saldívar Cervantes's information. Sorola was "an American citizen, highly recommended by former United States Marshal Hanson and has impressed me [Agent Barnes] as being entirely reliable."[16] Sorola is an interesting figure. Born in San Antonio on December 4, 1880, he attended business college there and worked as a bookkeeper, insurance agent, and investigator for several railroads before joining the bureau on April 27, 1916, as a special employee. He was hired because of his fluent Spanish and knowledge of Mexican politics. On July 1, 1922, he became the first Hispanic special agent, remaining with the bureau until his retirement on January 31, 1949.[17]

Ironically, Saldívar Cervantes, who of course knew nothing of Sorola's bureau connection, surmised that Sorola "is either a Detective or really entering the Revolution. I do not know whether he is really trying to join the Revolution or trying to get something to give away."[18] Sorola passed himself off as an insurance salesman when he went to Blas de la Garza's saloon to gather information. Sorola soon ingratiated himself with the saloonkeeper, who told him "that Gen. Morín had warned his officers that they had better not carry papers on their person for fear the American authorities would catch them and find out about this movement." Blas de la Garza also told Sorola that when Morín was ready to strike, he would not harm the Mexicans, the blacks, the Italians, or the Jews, but that he would go after the gringos, and he wanted his loyal followers to be ready.[19]

While Agent Wright directed operations in San Antonio against Morín, the U.S. attorney in that city received word that Luis de la Rosa planned to invade Texas between May 10 and 15. The agent in charge, Robert Barnes, promptly notified the chief of the bureau.[20]

Blas de la Garza allowed Sorola to read a letter he'd just received. It was from Victoriano Ponce in Kingsville, proprietor of La Reina bakery in that town and announcing that he was in command there, was getting everything ready, and inquiring just when the movement would start. Ponce believed he should receive a formal commission from Morín, and he urged Blas de la Garza to take the matter up with Morín as soon as possible.[21]

Morín's conspiracy crumbled. At Hanson's suggestion, the army was notified of the plot and General Funston agreed to have his aide, Captain S. Adams, meet at Hanson's office to review the situation with the police commissioner, Hanson, Wright, and Saldívar Cervantes, Hanson acting as interpreter. Not only was Saldívar Cervantes keeping the bureau informed about Morín, but others had also taken an active interest in the Mexican general. Caesar Kleberg became concerned about Morín's effect on the King ranch's numerous Hispanic employees. He called at the bureau office accompanied by Hanson to discuss the matter. Hanson said that he and Kleberg had gone to Austin and had a long conversation about the Morín plot with Governor Ferguson, who not only offered his cooperation but had Hanson write him a report on the case.[22]

Caesar Kleberg also hired his friend D. E."Cap" Hamer, an "old Mexico hand," who had spent several years as a soldier of fortune in that country, as a private investigator to work on the Morín case.[23] Hamer, incidentally, was a brother of Frank Hamer, the most famous Texas Ranger of his generation, and like Frank would become a Ranger captain.

FIG. 1. Venustiano Carranza, president of Mexico during much of the Mexican Revolution. He sponsored the Plan de San Diego during the period 1915–16. George Grantham Bain Collection, Library of Congress.

FIG. 2. General Pablo González, commanding general of the Army of the Northeast and President Carranza's principal operative for the Plan de San Diego. George Grantham Bain Collection, Library of Congress.

FIG. 3. General Emiliano P. Nafarrate, *carrancista* commander in 1915 of the military district along the Rio Grande. He was in charge of Plan de San Diego operations. Photo courtesy of http://mayoremilionafarrate.blogspot.com/.

FIG. 4. Agustín de la Garza, the mysterious leader of the Plan de San Diego militants, is standing on the left. The identity of the other person (*seated*) is unknown. The photo is unique in showing de la Garza armed with a holstered hand gun. A rifle and clip of ammunition are displayed on the table. Photo courtesy of the Museum of South Texas History.

FIG. 5. Luis de la Rosa, Tejano commander of the Plan de San Diego militants. Reproduced by permission of the Huntington Museum Library, San Marino, California.

FIG. 6. Major General Frederick Funston, commanding general of the U.S. Army's Southern Department, was forced to combat a guerrilla insurgency along the Rio Grande in South Texas. Photo courtesy of the Kansas State Historical Society.

FIG. 7. Texas governor James Ferguson gave shoot-to-kill orders to a special Ranger company fighting Plan de San Diego raiders. George Grantham Bain Collection, Library of Congress.

FIG. 8. Texas adjutant general Henry Hutchings had to stamp out a scandal in his office and fight off an invasion of South Texas by Plan de San Diego raiders. Photo courtesy of the Texas State Library and Archives Commission.

FIG. 9. Texas Ranger captain Henry Lee Ransom was perhaps the toughest of all the Ranger captains. During the "Bandit War" he would exhibit his toughness. He is seated in the first row, the last person on the left. Photo courtesy of the Texas Ranger Hall of Fame and Museum.

FIG. 10. (*opposite top*) Texas Ranger captain John J. Sanders commanded a Ranger company that spent most of the "Bandit War" acting as nightwatchmen guarding the King ranch. Photo courtesy of the Texas State Library and Archives Commission.

FIG. 11. (*opposite bottom*) The most famous photograph of the "Bandit War" was taken the day following the Norias raid. *Left to right*: Texas Ranger captain Monroe Fox, E. B. Scarborough, a scout for the Kleberg county home guard, and Tom Tate, a King ranch foreman and former Texas Ranger. The photo was posed for Brownsville photographer Robert Runyon. Fox, Scarborough, and Tate had roped the bodies of four of the dead raiders and were dragging them back to Norias. There was much criticism of the Rangers' disrespect for the dead bandits. It should be noted that not a single Ranger participated in the defense of Norias. Runyon (Robert) Photograph Collection, "Los Norias Bandit Raid" (runo0096), the Dolph Briscoe Center for American History, University of Texas at Austin.

FIG. 12. (*above*) The heroes of the Norias raid of August 8, 1915, were not the Texas Rangers but an eight-man squad from C Troop, Twelfth Cavalry regiment, six of whom are pictured here. Two troopers were wounded and are not in the photo. The unit commander was Corporal Allen Mercer (*back row, third from left*). Runyon (Robert) Photograph Collection, "Los Norias Bandit Raid" (runo0104), the Dolph Briscoe Center for American History, University of Texas at Austin.

FIG. 13. King ranch manager Caesar Kleberg is shown petting one of his favorite bird dogs. Kleberg was a political and financial power not only in the lower Rio Grande valley but throughout Texas. Following the August 1915 Norias raid on one of the King ranches, an entire Texas Ranger company camped out on the King ranch for months. Photo from *Trails and Trials of a Texas Ranger* by William Warren Sterling. Copyright 1959 by William Warren Sterling. Assigned 1968 to the University of Oklahoma Press. Reprinted by permission of the publisher.

FIG. 14. Resplendent in his uniform as a lieutenant colonel in the Texas National Guard, Francisco A. Chapa served three successive governors as a member of their personal military staff. The most powerful Hispanic in Texas, Chapa was also wealthy and was always waist-deep in Mexican revolutionary intrigue throughout the decade. Photo courtesy of the Texas State Library and Archives Commission.

FIG. 15. *Left to right*: James B. McAllen, Rentfro B. Creager, and Dr. Harry Love pose as they prepared to go hunting in the fall of 1914. The men are in front of McAllen's residence on the McAllen ranch near Monte Christo in South Texas. The following year—September 24, 1915—McAllen singlehandedly (with only the help of his housekeeper who loaded his weapons) held off eight Plan de San Diego raiders, killing two and wounding three more. Photo courtesy of the McAllen Ranch Archives.

FIG. 16. (*opposite top*) An unidentified young man looks at four bodies lying in the brush at Ebenezer Crossroad in Hidalgo County in late September 1915. Although only four bodies are visible in the photograph, a total of fourteen bodies were found. The Texas Rangers were suspected of this atrocity. Photo courtesy of the Museum of South Texas History.

FIG. 17. (*opposite bottom*) During September and October 1915, gun battles between U.S. Army troops based along the river in the lower Rio Grande valley and Carranza troops had become so intense that trenches were dug to protect army units. Photo courtesy of the Museum of South Texas History.

FIG. 18. On October 18, 1915, Plan de San Diego raiders carried out their spectacular raid. They derailed a St. Louis, Brownsville, and Mexico Railroad passenger train less than seven miles north of Brownsville. The raiders killed three passengers and wounded three others. Photo courtesy of the Museum of South Texas History.

FIG. 19. Texas state representative José Tomás Canales of Brownsville, in the latter part of October 1915, recruited a group of Hispanics named the Canales Scouts to assist the U.S. Army's efforts to thwart raids from Mexico. Photo courtesy of the State Preservation Board, Austin, Texas.

FIG. 20. This photograph of Juan K. Forseck is reproduced from a Mexican naturalization form. It is the only image of Forseck of which we are aware. Forseck is a mysterious figure in the Plan de San Diego. The form from which the photo is lifted is found in the files of the Office of Counselor, Department of State, Archives II, College Station, Maryland, National Archives and Records Administration.

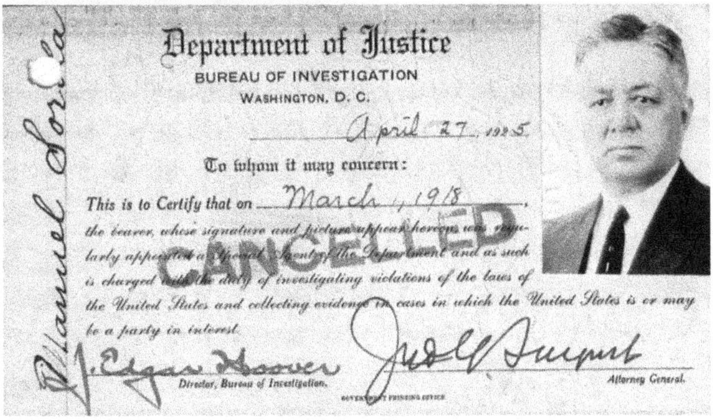

FIG. 21. (*top*) This very poor photograph of General José Morín is the only known image in existence. This photo was found in the Bureau of Investigation's so-called Old Mexican 232-84 file. Photo courtesy of the National Archives and Records Administration.

FIG. 22. (*bottom*) Manuel Sorola was the most important Bureau of Investigation agent used to penetrate the Hispanic community in South Texas during the period 1915–17. He would later become the bureau's first Mexican American special agent. Photo courtesy of the Federal Bureau of Investigation.

FIG. 23. William Martin Hanson, shown seated in the front row on the far left in a 1919 photograph, was deeply involved in the investigation of the Plan de San Diego conspiracy in 1916 in Texas. Aldrich (Roy Wilkinson) Papers, "Lawmen with rifles" (di_04571), the Dolph Briscoe Center for American History, University of Texas at Austin.

Agent Barnes traveled to Kingsville and conferred with Sheriff J. Scarborough, gave him the name of Victoriano Ponce, General Morín's representative in Kingsville, and arranged to have Ponce arrested upon receipt of a telegraphic notice from the bureau's San Antonio office. Agent Barnes noted that Scarborough "will keep a very close watch upon the activities of Mexicans in this vicinity and immediately advise me of any suspicious happenings." Barnes also conferred with D. E. Hamer, whom Caesar Kleberg had sent to San Antonio to secure information about the Morín conspiracy. Hamer furnished Barnes with a list of Hispanics who would probably be active in any uprising against the King ranch.[24] Barnes also gave the sheriff the names of two brothers, Luciano and Juan Marroquín, who had recently arrived in Matamoros and were allegedly heading for Kingsville to blow up the railroad roundhouse. "These Mexicans will be closely watched by the local officers at Kingsville."[25]

Morín's absence from San Antonio made his associates nervous, as they were awaiting his orders. But he returned briefly to that city from his trip to Nixon, Texas, and announced that he was going to make a quick trip to Kingsville. Those working to foil Morín faced the classic counterintelligence dilemma of whether to let Morín continue his intrigues in order to identify more of his contacts or to arrest him before he could cause serious damage. They decided to neutralize him.

On May 10, Morín took the night train from San Antonio for Kingsville to confer with one of his key associates, the baker Victoriano Ponce. Saldívar Cervantes saw Morín off at the station and no doubt gave him a big *abrazo* and wished him well. Morín settled into the smoking car. What Morín didn't know was that Hanson and Agent Wright were also on the train shadowing him. Wright checked with the conductor and learned that Morín had a ticket to Saspamco. Agent Wright described what happened when the train stopped at that way station, five stations down the line from San Antonio: Saspamco "is a Mexican settlement and there is no County officer there. After talking to Mr. Hanson, who is familiar with the case, I decided that quick action should be taken and that by all means, Gen. Morín should not be allowed to get away. I therefore arranged with Mr. Hanson to assist me in getting Morín just before he attempted to get off the train at

Saspamco." Wright and Hanson approached Morín. Wright identified himself and told the general to throw up his hands. Morín offered no resistance. Wright was quite surprised, for Morín had been described to him as a dangerous character. Morín was led to the smoking compartment of the coach in order not to attract attention. Wright searched Morín and took all his papers, which included a list of the officers under his command and commissioned by him. (Again, it's remarkable how many Mexican revolutionary figures in the United States went around with all kinds of incriminating papers on their persons. Thus, literally thousands of documents bearing on the revolution are in U.S. archives because they were seized by American authorities.)

Agent Wright also arranged with the conductor to pay Morín's fare to Kingsville. At Floresville, Sheriff W. L. Wright and a county commissioner boarded the train and accompanied them to Kingsville, where they arrived at 7:30 a.m. Wright had telephoned ahead to Kingsville to have the sheriff meet the train in an automobile. Sheriff Scarborough waited until the passengers had left the train, then unobtrusively transported Morín to jail.[26]

Wright had Scarborough arrest Victoriano Ponce. He and Morín were placed in separate cells, and Wright decided to let them stew in jail for a day before interrogating them. As he put it, "My reason for this was that each knew the other was arrested and it would probably cause each to think the other had told of the plot and thus produce better results in their statements."[27] Agent Barnes in San Antonio mailed Wright a copy of the bureau's file on Morín and photostatic copies of letters that Ponce had written in Kingsville concerning the conspiracy, adding, "I suggest that you endeavor to have Ponce admit that he wrote the letters of which the enclosed are photographic copies."[28]

The next day Wright interrogated the prisoners at his room in the Casa Ricardo Hotel in Kingsville, with Kleberg County attorney Gus L. Kowalski as interpreter. Morín and Ponce of course stoutly proclaimed their innocence. Wright stated that "From the first I realized that Gen. Morín had made up his mind not to give any information whatsoever and to deny positively all material facts. He even went so far as to claim that he did not know why he was arrested." But when Wright had arrested Morín he confiscated several documents. They included two letters addressed to J. M. Leal, and when Morín entered the room, Wright asked Ponce to tell him his name and he unhesitatingly replied "J. M. Leal." Wright questioned Morín about these letters and Morín admitted that he frequently used that name, saying that he didn't want Mexicans across the border to know where he was. The confiscated documents included a red notebook containing the code that Morín used. There was also an envelope that Morín foolishly had on his person and on which were written a number of names.[29]

After prolonged interrogation, the prisoners gave partial confessions. Morín stated that he had worked from Karnes City to San Antonio. What was really significant, however, was that while Morín admitted that he had been a *villista* major, ever since 1914 he had been a general in the Carranza army.

The Mexican general was also asked about his relatives and his mission in Texas, which he maintained was merely to find work. When asked whether he knew anyone in Calaveras, Texas, he replied evasively, "I know the major portion of the Mexicans there." When pressed, he admitted that he knew a Néstor Bazán, a saloonkeeper there. Asked if he knew a Ramón Borunda in Saspamco, he said that he did, and that the individual worked in a factory at night. But when asked how long he'd known Victoriano Ponce, he flatly denied knowing Ponce at all. Wright then asked him whether he knew a series of men: José Angel Muñoz at Poth, Román Borunda, Pedro Rosales, Marcos Botello, Santos Aranda, Teófilo Vázquez, Librado Palacios, and José Luna. Morín stated that he had spent about six months in San Antonio, admitting that he knew the saloonkeeper Blas de la Garza (whom he'd commissioned as a colonel) and Santiago Longoria there. He denied ever being in San Marcos. Wright kept hammering Morín with a list of names of more men in various Texas towns; Morín admitted knowing some of them. Wright then said, "Now, General, did you know that all of these men we have been talking about have been arrested and are telling about this plot?" Morín denied that they were his officers, insisting that they were just working men. And he adamantly denied ever having commissioned anybody.

When asked if he knew a Colonel Viviano Saldívar Cervantes who lived in San Antonio, Morín insisted that he was merely a casual acquaintance, but when informed that he'd had his picture taken with Saldívar Cervantes, Morín said that maybe he knew Saldívar Cervantes after all. Wright asked, "Didn't you meet Col. Saldívar nearly every day when you were in San Antonio?" to which Morín replied, "I would see him, nothing more." As for contacting the men Wright had listed, Morín said, "I visited several places, but I didn't indicate anything to them; had conversation with them, but didn't indicate anything to them." But he grudgingly admitted that the list of names was in his own handwriting. And getting to the meat of the interrogation, Wright said, "As a matter of fact, you are at the head of the expedition to cause an uprising among the Mexicans here, is that correct?" Morín denied it. Wright continued: "Your original idea was to carry out this expedition, first on the 5th and then on the 10th of May?" Wright: "Do you positively deny that for the past few months that you have had anything whatever to do with the organization of a military expedition?" Morín: "Yes sir, I deny it." Wright: "When you came back you told Blas Garza and Col. Saldívar you had seen a good many of your men, and things were ready, isn't that true?" Morín: "No sir." Wright: "Have you anything to say now for yourself?" Morín: "No sir."[30] A despondent Morín was returned to jail, having "denied that he was commissioned by Gen. Villa, but stated that he was working under Carranza."[31]

Wright next turned to interrogating Victoriano Ponce, over a two-day period with Kowalski and Hanson acting as interpreters. Ponce said he was forty-six years old and was born in Santa Catarina, Nuevo León. He'd served in the Mexican Army in 1912 as a first lieutenant and a second captain. He had lived in Kingsville for a year and nine months, being in the bakery business. He first met Blas de la Garza of San Antonio on March 1 at de la Garza's saloon, where he stopped to drink beer, but insisted that he had gone to San Antonio only for medical treatment, remaining there a month. Wright: "What did Blas, what did Blas Garza, as well as you can remember, tell you about the intervention of General Morín?" Ponce: "He told me that there had been a sort of a junta, and in the event of [armed American] intervention, would I be willing to go over there and fight, because I had fought before; I had been a federal." Wright: "Who did he say was the leader of this fight?" Ponce: "That general, I don't know him." Wright: "Did Blas tell you that you would receive a commission?" Ponce: "He says upon going over there I was to be his first captain, because I had been second captain."

Ponce denied knowing Morín or organizing Hispanics in Kingsville: "I have not said anything to anybody here at all." Wright: "Do you recognize this letter (offers letter) as one written by you to Blas Garza? It is a photograph of a letter." Ponce: "To Blas Garza, yes." Wright: "In this letter you say 'All is arranged, I wrote my General to have the kindness to tell me and send me as soon as possible that which will justify myself with these people.'" Wright: "Whom do you mean by 'my General'?" Ponce: "No I have not written, I must be mistaken, I must have written to Blas, I have not written [to] any General. Blas is the only general that I know." Ponce: "I remember seeing him [Morín] in San Antonio, drinking in a saloon in front of the Imparcial, but I was not introduced to him. He was drinking with four or five men, but I did not know any of them." Wright: "Do you wish to tell the truth about this matter, or do you wish to stay in jail?" Ponce: "You can keep me in as long as you want. I told him to write me and tell me when to go." Wright: "General Morín says he knows you, why is it that you do not know him?" Ponce: "He can't say that because he don't know me. I don't know him." Wright: "Are you absolutely positive that Blas did not tell you about the General?" Ponce: "No, he didn't tell, he told me that there was a general, but he didn't tell me who it was. It might be [Benjamín] Hill or [Antonio] Villarreal, I don't know who."

Ponce stated that Blas had invited him as he invited everyone else. Wright pounced on this: "You said a little while ago that you did not know of anybody else, you now say that he invited you as well as many others. What do you mean?" Ponce: "No, I have not invited anybody, nothing like that. I have told them all that in case of intervention it would be necessary for us to go. Matters looked very bad in San Antonio." Wright: "You said a little while ago that you had not said anything about this to anyone." Ponce: "Yes, I have told, I have told two or three times since I came back, there in the bakery shop, I have told them all." Wright: "We know, Mr. Ponce, that you have the Mexicans here organized; we would like to have the names of the officers and the number of meetings that you have had." Ponce: "Not a single one, you can inform yourself and the whole town." Wright: "Now, Mr. Ponce, you have had a great deal of correspondence with Blas de la Garza of San Antonio. I would like to have all the letters you have received from him." Ponce: "I don't think so. I don't think I have any letters from him, you can look and see." Wright: "You state right at the beginning of this letter: 'Replying to your letter under date 15th of this month.' Where is that letter?" Ponce: "I don't know, it was there in the house. It must be there. I read them and I left them there." Wright: "Evidence shows very plainly that you were appointed, among a good many other officers, as commander at this city. General Morín has a man at Calaveras, one at Saspamco. You were a commander here, and there are a number of other cities where they have commanders, you understand, this has been explained to you by Blas Garza?" Ponce: "No." Ponce insisted that he didn't know any general, that he didn't know about any proclamation, and that the expedition to be organized in case of American intervention in Mexico was a *felicista* enterprise.

When Wright asked him the names of Mexicans with whom he talked in Kingsville, Ponce said he didn't know any names. Wright asked sarcastically: "You have lived here 21 months and don't remember the name of one man you spoke to?" Ponce: "I don't know. There are a great many here. I don't remember those that I talked to. Some of them work at the roundhouse. All of those that come in to buy bread. There are a great many." Wright: "Before leaving, have you anything that you want to tell in explaining this matter?" Ponce: "Nothing. I don't know anything."[32] Ponce was returned to the Kingsville jail.

While Morín and Ponce were undergoing interrogation, Sheriff Scarborough and Texas Ranger captain John J. Sanders led a roundup of suspected Hispanics in Kingsville and vicinity. The jail was soon crowded with fifteen prisoners, arrested on information obtained from Morín. They were allegedly involved in a conspiracy to set fire to some houses in Kingsville in order to lure the authorities there while they dynamited the bank and looted stores. Among those arrested was Eulalio Velázquez, editor of the Spanish-language weekly *El Popular*. Three sacks full of his papers were taken to the hotel room of Agent Wright, who painstakingly went through them and found several letters "which would indicate that this man has been corresponding with other Mexicans in 'code.'" Wright interrogated Velázquez, with Kowalski acting as interpreter. Velázquez said he'd been born in Roma, Starr County, Texas, had worked as a schoolteacher, bookkeeper, newspaperman, and for a short time as a merchant. In 1899 and 1900 he'd been the treasurer of Starr County. He'd lived in Kingsville for two years and was both publisher and editor of the weekly *El Popular*. Wright commented that "This man is still in jail and will be kept under surveillance when he is released."[33]

Wright also interrogated the jailed Luciano and Leonardo Marroquín, who had allegedly come to Kingsville to blow up the railroad roundhouse. Luciano said he'd gone from Kingsville to Monterrey in April, armed with a letter of introduction from Robert Kleberg to Daniel Yturos in Brownsville; he left Monterrey on May 1, arriving in Kingsville on May 3. Marroquín adamantly denied being involved in any conspiracy. Wright reported that he had no evidence against the Marroquín brothers.[34]

On the other hand, the district attorney and the sheriff were attempting to arrest one Zacarías Flores, a "well known agitator in and around Mission." He was supposed to be at the Flores ranch up the Rio Grande about sixteen miles from Camargo. "He bears the reputation of being connected with every revolution on the Mexican side for the past five years. Besides he has always been a bad citizen." But as Agent Barnes telegraphed: "Zacarías Flores representative Morín formerly Mission, now Brownsville; receiving mail under name Tomás Rangel; not sufficient evidence make case but in correspondence with conspirator here; states has horses and men ready." In June the bureau was still trying to locate Flores.[35]

Wright wrote that "In conversation with Captain Burnside U.S.A.[at Fort Sam Houston], he suggested that he thought it would be well to have a Mexican informant work under cover at San Diego, Texas, for a while. Capt. Burnside said that he believed that if Gen. Morín's alleged followers in Mexico crossed over and proceeded to San Diego, that they could pick up more recruits there than in any place in this part of the State."[36]

Wright also interrogated one Ignacio Rodríguez, who bought bread from Ponce and sold it to Mexicans who were grubbing trees on the

King ranch. Assisted by D. E. Hamer, William M. Hanson, and Sheriff Scarborough, Agent Wright succeeded in locating Rodríguez and had him brought to Wright's hotel room. Rodríguez had been born in Ciudad Victoria, Tamaulipas, and had been working on the King ranch for the past year. At first Rodríguez positively denied knowing Victoriano Ponce, but then he did admit that he knew Ponce "by sight." He finally admitted that Hispanics on the King ranch had several hundred guns and several hundred men all ready. And he said that another King ranch employee, a certain Lupe López, also bought bread from Ponce. Wright arranged with Scarborough to have López brought to his hotel room. López said he came from Linares, Mexico, about six years ago. Not surprisingly, he said he didn't know anything. After extensive questioning, he did remember that he'd been in Ponce's bakery, "that Ponce asked him how many Mexicans were working on the Kleberg ranch and that he replied that there are about three hundred; that Ponce then asked him who is the 'Jefe' or the chief and that he replied that the Jefe's name is Félix González; that Ponce intimated that they should get together." Wright noted that "This man . . . corroborates in part Victoriano Ponce's statement. I am confident that Lupe López knows more than he has told. Sheriff Scarborough will keep him in jail until he says he will tell the whole truth to me."[37]

In Victoriano Ponce's sworn statement he gave the names of Mexicans living in Kingsville whom he had told about this movement: Baltasar González, Agustín Saldaña, Isidoro Castañeda, and Cástulo Pérez. Isidoro Castañeda was a well-known Hispanic merchant in Kingsville and had never been in any trouble. Wright promptly interviewed him. Castañeda said he'd been born about thirty miles from Kingsville, on Las Motas ranch, and had been in the general merchandise business in Kingsville for the last eight years. He'd known Ponce for about two years, but Ponce had never told him anything about any organization. All he knew was what he'd read in the papers. Wright commented that "This man is very much above the average Mexican but I am convinced that he is not telling the truth."[38]

A tired and frustrated Agent Wright recorded that "I have questioned a great many Mexicans about this plot, in the last day or two, but obtained nothing substantial from them."[39] He left for San Antonio, where Blas de la Garza had already been arrested. Ignacio de la Rosa, Luis's cousin, who was involved with Morín, had also been arrested. De la Garza denied everything, although he admitted corresponding with Victoriano Ponce, and was released on bond. However, informant Sorola said he talked with de la Garza, who told him he had a commission from Morín and that the commission, a map, and the plans were in a book in a dresser in de la Garza's home. But he'd sent his brother Gonzalo there, who spirited the items away just minutes before the officers arrived to search the house. In any case, Blas de la Garza felt that the cause was lost.[40]

Agent Wright planned to prepare the Morín and Ponce cases for presentation to a federal grand jury, and in San Antonio he conferred with the U.S. attorney.[41] At Agent Barnes's suggestion, Morín was kept in the Kingsville jail. But Wright was in for a shock.

On May 23, 24, and 29 the *San Antonio Express* ran articles reporting the deaths of Morín and Ponce, shot while trying to escape; the article on the twenty-fourth included a photograph of Morín. *La Prensa* of San Antonio published a similar article on May 29, alleging that they had been shot while attempting to escape from their Texas Ranger custodians—an application of the Mexican *ley fuga*, or law of flight, in which prisoners were shot while allegedly attempting to escape. Agent Wright was dumbfounded, and he immediately telephoned Sheriff Scarborough, who informed him that the sheriff of Willacy County had taken the two prisoners away for identification: Morín as an alleged murderer and Ponce as a participant in the Brownsville train wreck in 1915. At Norias, Manuel Rincones had identified them.[42]

Wright telephoned Sheriff Clint Atkins of Willacy County, who told him that he'd delivered the prisoners to Texas Rangers for transport to Brownsville. Most improbably, the sheriff claimed he didn't know the names of the Rangers involved. The bureau agent in Brownsville, J. B. Rogers, made inquiries and reported that "The official class here are as close mouthed as those at Kingsville, which leads to the fear that Morín and Ponce are dead." When Wright telegraphed Ranger captain Sanders asking whether the press reports were true, Sanders replied, "I have no knowledge of Morín and Ponce being killed. Do not know their whereabouts."[43]

While the authorities dismantled Morín's revolutionary network the question remained—where were Morín and Ponce? If, as the press had reported, they'd been killed while trying to escape, where were their bodies? No one seemed to know anything. Agent Wright encountered a stone wall. Agent Rogers: "All that is definitely known to me is that Morín and Ponce were delivered to the Rangers of Capt. Sanders's Company. Mr. Scarborough himself told me this last Tuesday night at Kingsville as I was en route to San Antonio. It has been reported that the men were seen tied to a tree at Norias.[44] This is likely true as the men were to be identified at Norias and there is no jail there. It is reported that while the men were being taken to some place in Willacy County to be identified and they were killed while trying to make their escape. I do not believe this because I do not believe they would have tried to escape from Sanders' Rangers. But if the Rangers did kill them while they were trying to escape, I do believe they would object to telling it."[45]

A thoroughly frustrated Wright finally called on Texas adjutant general Henry Hutchings, who said he hadn't received any official report from the Rangers. But Hutchings said he had telephoned the Willacy County sheriff, who said he'd turned the pair over to Ranger (and future Ranger captain) Joe B. Brooks and Special Ranger W. T. Moseley, a brand inspector for the Cattle Raisers' Association of Texas, and that he'd heard that Morín and Ponce had gotten away. Hutchings was also of the opinion that the prisoners were alive and at large. Wright reported that "I formed the impression, while talking to Gen. Hutchings, that this matter has been treated lightly by the State and that Capt. Sanders' report, whatever it may contain, will be accepted; the authority of the rangers appears to be unlimited in matter of this character."[46]

After a month had passed without Captain Sanders's report being sent to the bureau, Wright again went to see Hutchings. The adjutant general happened to be out of his office, and a clerk obligingly allowed Wright to see the report. When Hutchings returned he reprimanded the clerk, but Hutchings later explained to Wright that he was just concerned about the legality of letting Wright have access to the report.

Sanders's report stated that the prisoners had been taken to Norias for identification. That night Brooks and Moseley had taken them in an automobile for further identification in Raymondville. En route the car became stuck in the sand, and while the Rangers were busy digging it out the prisoners dashed into the brush and escaped. A search for them was unsuccessful. This version of events was a variation on the *ley fuga*—the prisoners allegedly did escape, hence no bodies, and the Rangers could profess ignorance as to their whereabouts.[47]

The report led Assistant Attorney General of Texas (and future chief justice of the Texas Supreme Court) C. M. Cureton to remark: "You know, Wright, from this report they killed them." This was certainly not the only instance of the Rangers administering summary justice.[48]

Although most people weren't upset about two Hispanic agitators "evaporating" at the hands of the Rangers, the Morín case became noteworthy. A crusading Kingsville attorney named Thomas Wesley Hook generated considerable publicity about the case. On June 4 he wrote to President Wilson enclosing a petition to Governor Ferguson protesting the treatment of Hispanics in general and Morín and Ponce in particular. Despite the fear of reprisals, the twenty petitioners signed their names.[49] The *Austin American* published the petition in its edition of June 5. Hook also sent the petition to President Wilson.[50] Hook caused the Rangers so much trouble that Captain Sanders tried to pistol-whip him in the courthouse in Falfurrrias, which of course generated even more publicity. And Hook's letter and petition ended up in the hands of Secretary of War Lindley Garrison, who suggested that in the future federal prisoners should be turned over to the army rather than to the civil authorities. The federal government objected to having its prisoners killed before they could be brought to trial.[51]

14 The Bureau Investigates

As these events were unfolding in the spring of 1916, the Mexican situation was deemed so serious that the bureau chief Bruce Bielaski hurried to San Antonio to coordinate the agency's operations. Bielaski met with the special agent in charge in San Antonio, Robert Barnes, and with J. B. Rogers, the agent stationed in Brownsville. Bielaski ordered that arrangements be made to broaden the bureau's intelligence-gathering capabilities and share intelligence with the army's Southern Department headquarters at San Antonio.[1]

Accordingly, Agent Rogers dispatched William C. Chamberlain, who had been an important bureau informant in the 1911 Reyes conspiracy, to work under his direction in Brownsville.[2] Chamberlain was to investigate whether Mexicans were meeting under the pretense of fraternal lodge meetings and to check on conditions in several small valley towns. Rogers also employed Fred E. Marks of Rio Grande City to work undercover at a salary of three dollars per day and five dollars for expenses when away from Rio Grande City. Marks reported in August that "When I first heard of Luis de la Rosa, it was the time that the First Chief Don Venustiano Carranza and his staff came on a special train to Matamoros and De La Rosa was on the same train and returned on the same train with the party."[3]

George R. Head, the captain of the Brownsville National Guard company, made an extended journey in Mexico in April and May 1916.[4] Rogers debriefed him on his return to Brownsville. Besides providing information on the Mexican Army's dispositions, Head said that on March 8 he'd gone to Tampico, where General Emiliano Nafarrate was in command and had the city under very good control. Luis de la Rosa was in Tampico while Head was there. On April 13, Head left Tampico for Mexico City via San Luis Potosí in company with Colonel Esteban Fierros, "who has been appointed General Superintendent of the Constitutionalist Railroads of Mexico. We were traveling by special train." Head painted a dismal picture of conditions in Mexico, not just on the railroads, which were in terrible shape and subject to frequent bandit attacks, but starvation and typhus were ravaging the population. Head was in Mexico City for about two weeks and saw Carranza several times. He was in Veracruz on April 29 and back in Tampico on May 1.[5]

And on May 4, a well-educated German, a certain W. H. Young, arrived in Brownsville from Tampico and immediately went to Colonel H. P. Blocksom with information about the rumored plan to invade Texas. He said that a large number of Carranza officers were in the plot and that they would repudiate Carranza unless the Punitive Expedition were soon withdrawn. According to Young, one of the plotters' objects was to lure American troops away from Brownsville so they could loot and burn the town. In Kingsville there was a secret lodge of Mexicans, and several railroad employees planned to blow up the roundhouse there. Colonel Blocksom stated that "Mr. Rogers, Department of Justice, believes a large part of our informant's statements are true. Mr. Rogers knows a good deal about the Tampico country."[6]

Another bureau informant, José García, the businessman from Monterrey who had been a confidential informant of Agent Rogers, arrived in Brownsville on May 19, having been sent by Randolph Robertson, American vice consul in Monterrey. This was a delicate matter, for as the chief of the bureau noted, "Consul Garrett of Nuevo Laredo is characterized by our agents in Texas as the most indiscreet person imaginable and utterly unfit for this reason for the position which he holds. It is stated that he devotes nearly all of his time to drinking and talking. Recently when arrangements were made for Vice Consul Robertson and one or two men from Mexico to meet agents of the Department at Laredo, Garrett apparently told everybody in the two towns of the proposed meeting."[7] Because of Garrett's indiscretion, Robertson was confidentially directed to report to Consul Johnson in Matamoros, who was to instruct him to telegraph to the State Department any information he had concerning the Mexican situation.[8]

Informant García said he associated with the group planning to invade Texas and had recently talked with Luis de la Rosa himself. De la Rosa claimed the German consul in Monterrey had provided him with considerable money. García said, "De la Rosa is not recruiting men himself but is delegating the authority to others on account of the fact that he has been advised by his superiors to keep himself in the background until the time to take charge of the forces for the invasion is at hand."

The informant also stated that "Stefans [*sic*] Fierros and de la Rosa recently went to Mexico City to confer with General Pablo González," whom he said was a party to the proposed invasion. When pressed for the date of this trip, García could not fix it exactly but said it was three or four weeks earlier. He did not know who composed the party but said they went from Tampico by a special train. It will be recalled that George R. Head said that he and Fierros went to Mexico City about this time. García stated that this trip was to secure González's approval of the plan of invasion and that González consulted Carranza and received word that it was not time yet to begin operations, but to wait until the conference at El Paso between General Alvaro Obregón and Generals Scott and Funston, about to be held, was concluded.[9]

But the bureau soon dispensed with García's services, and he was naturally reluctant to provide further information. Agent Rogers persuaded him to make a written report anyway. García related that on May 16 the governor of Tamaulipas telegraphed the mayor of Matamoros that, in compliance with orders from Carranza, he should arm the citizenry as a precaution against trouble with the United States, which seemed imminent. Accordingly, the municipal council requested weapons from General Ricaut, who replied that arming the citizens at that time was imprudent but that in the event of a real conflict with the United States he had ample weaponry to distribute. The council complained to the governor, who on May 19 again telegraphed reiterating Carranza's order. Informant García was unsure whether arming the population had begun.

Agent Rogers commented that García was genuinely trying to provide accurate information but was unhappy because he didn't receive money more promptly "and is disposed to be resentful. I have been unable to explain away the feeling by telling him that it was necessary to have the approval of his accounts."[10]

Consul Jesse Johnson placed absolute faith in General Ricaut's good intentions. On February 26, 1916, Johnson received a telegram from Secretary of State Lansing: "Department informed that the bandits are getting active again and threaten to invade Texas at some point between Matamoros and Reynosa; inform Commander at Matamoros and request him to use all means in his power to prevent." Johnson forwarded the telegram to Ricaut and added, "I know you will investigate this matter without delay. For my part I do not believe it is true, but it might be."[11]

Ricaut informed Johnson that he knew of no bandits planning to invade Texas, much less because he had a number of suspects in jail in Matamoros.[12] In May, Ricaut informed Johnson that his secret agents had discovered a filibuster plot in Hidalgo County involving Deputy Sheriff Everett Anglin and Deodoro and Fidel Guerra. Anglin allegedly had a contract to hire five hundred men, ostensibly to clear a large tract of land on the Texas side of the Rio Grande, but in reality to join the exiled General Antonio Villarreal's projected invasion of Mexico. Johnson believed everything Ricaut told him, for "He is a strong man physically and mentally and thoroughly reliable. Therefore what he told me about this plot is true. He succeeded in checking this plot in its infancy."[13]

Ricaut did make some effort to round up troublesome bandits. On May 31, Consul Johnson reported that four of the six bandits that Judge S. P. Silver of Mercedes had inquired about were in Matamoros, three of them in jail: Manuel Longoria, Manuel Zamora, and Tomás Guzmán. The fourth, one Rocha, was in the hospital suffering from gunshot wounds in the hips.[14]

Bureau special agent Tom Ross in Laredo sent informant Rafael

Schiaraffa "with instructions to go to Mexico; I told him to go to Monterrey, and from there down the line to Matamoros, with instructions to make a thorough investigation as to the exact number of troops and locations between N/Laredo, Monterrey and Matamoros." Schiaraffa left on July 10 and went by rail from Monterrey to Reynosa. While in Monterrey he saw Luis de la Rosa on the streets but he appeared to be under arrest, as two officers accompanied him everywhere he went. Schiaraffa tried to go to Colombia on the Rio Grande but was turned back at La Laguna de la Leche by Mexican troops, "who advised him to return to N. Laredo as it would not be safe for him to go on to Colombia. They stated to him that they had about six hundred men at La Laguna."[15]

Ross was a competent operative, but he had a serious drinking problem. Chief Bielaski warned him confidentially that it might cost him his job. In September, a Laredo resident, A. Smith, who had known Ross for years, complained to Bielaski about Ross, who "was a disgrace to himself and to the Department he represents; he remains constantly under the influence of liquor, and it is no uncommon thing to see him on the streets of Laredo in a disgraceful intoxicated condition, staggering from one side of the street to the other, and having to be assisted to his room by some bystander, where he usually takes from twelve to eighteen hours to recuperate." As of December 1916, Ross was still on the payroll, but as of January 10, 1917, he was referred to as "Former Informant Tom Ross."[16]

Colonel Viviano Saldívar Cervantes, the bureau's confidential informant in San Antonio, reported to Special Agent Wright and later to Special Agent Beckham with William M. Hanson interpreting. Saldívar Cervantes sent his written reports to "D. L. Roberts," signing himself "José Rodríguez." But he didn't divulge everything he knew; he had "a friend" among the *carrancistas* in San Antonio but declined to reveal the name of this friend, who passed along items of intelligence interest. The bureau subsequently used the colonel as a confidential informant to penetrate the *legalista* and *felicista* movements in San Antonio.[17]

By the end of May, in Matamoros it was generally believed that war with the United States was imminent, but Agent Rogers complained, "It is very difficult to get the Mexicans to talk. There are a great [many]

Secret Service men over there and the people do not know whom they are talking to. They send Secret Service men across the River all the time."[18]

The American authorities collecting intelligence in Mexico oftentimes acted independently, with one agency being unaware of what other agencies were doing. For example, a certain man named Newman who arrived in Tampico on May 13 incurred the suspicion of the captain of the USS *Marietta*, stationed off Tampico, who reported on May 16 that he was suspicious of this Newman, who purported to be a Texan and who'd gone to the American consulate saying he was collecting information about one Luis de la Rosa. The captain had been told that de la Rosa had been in Tampico several months ago as General Nafarrate's guest and no effort was made to apprehend him. Newman claimed to be a secret agent sent by Colonel Blocksom in Brownsville to check on de la Rosa's reported presence in Tampico. When told the *sedicioso* leader hadn't been seen there for the past six weeks, Newman announced that he was going to Ciudad Victoria to make further inquiries. The captain admitted that he'd been unable to see Newman and that perhaps his suspicions were unfounded, but if intelligence about de la Rosa were needed, the consul could readily have provided it; there was no need to send a secret agent.[19]

The mysterious Mr. Newman continued to figure in intelligence circles. On June 6 the American consul in Tampico received a letter written on June 4, presumably from Ciudad Victoria: "Kindly get enclosed off by wireless as quickly as possible. It is urgent. Semi-officially it is mooted that the Carranza forces are going to open the ball not later than the tenth [of June]. At what point have not been able to ascertain. Am advising the few countrymen in my section that I can get to. Yours truly, [signed] Figure Seven." The enclosed message read: "P. A. N., 107 Charles Street, Brownsville. Yellow heads today's train. Red heads later. Nigger referred to should be looked after. Letter confirming tomorrow. [signed] Figure Seven." The message was delivered to the State Department and to Chief Bielaski, who sent it to Agent Rogers in Brownsville.[20]

Rogers wrote to Bielaski explaining the message: "Party referred to [is] Special Agent War Department. Yellow heads means troops moving by rail, red heads hot times for Grego [*sic*] here. Information confirms reports sent agent Barnes today: 'Reliable report Victoria Americans attacked unless troops withdrawn today, general Mexican belief there.' Informant just returned Matamoros reports concentration from surrounding towns and ranches. Information given War Department."[21]

Rogers had recognized the initials P. A. N. as referring to P. A. Newman, who lived at 107 St. Charles Street in Brownsville. The bureau agent was confident that the mysterious message was meant for Newman because the latter had been sent into the interior of Mexico by Colonel Blocksom on a mission for the military, going as far as Ciudad Victoria and Tampico. Rogers called on Newman at his garage on Eighth Street and asked him the meaning of the "Figure Seven" and "red heads" and "yellow heads." Newman at first hesitated but was reassured by Rogers's manner that Rogers was entitled to the information and accordingly gave it to him. Newman then explained, after consulting his code, that "yellow heads" meant "troops are moving by rail" and "red heads" meant "hot times here for the gringos." Newman said that "the 'nigger' referred to was Dr. Moseley who has been under surveillance suspected of anti-American tendencies." But Newman declined to tell Rogers the identity of Figure Seven, assuring him that Seven was one of the most responsible Americans living in Victoria. As there are only about six American residents of Victoria, and since Rogers knew them all, he was convinced that Figure Seven was a Mr. Storms, who was formerly consular agent at Ciudad Victoria. Rogers's assessment was that Storms was the only one there who could or would act in that capacity. "He is a good man, prudent, not excitable, and conservative. He was recently in Brownsville and while here stayed at Newman's house and several times called on Captain McCoy, now Post Adjutant. This is immaterial except that I feel positive Figure Seven is Storms and Storms is reliable. Newman is a very dependable man too. He knows the Mexicans very thoroughly. He used to run automobiles from here to Victoria, Mexico, and was always intimate with the Carrancistas. He is close mouthed and eyed and eared."[22]

On June 9, General Esteban Fierros at Monterrey wrote to General Pablo González informing him of the difficulties Fierros was experiencing at the hands of Generals Ricaut and Carlos Osuna. Fierros had telegraphed to González that he planned to cross into Texas with the remainder of his troops. However, this had proved impossible because Osuna had forced Fierros to return to Monterrey and had tried to disarm his men. Fierros was worried about those soldiers he had already infiltrated into Texas and hated just to abandon them to their fate without providing some assistance. Fierros reported that currently he had 570 men in his brigade and recommended that they be concentrated in Monterrey in reserve. He had already requested from General Pablo de la Garza a barracks in which to house the Fierros Brigade for the next six months. Regarding money for expenses, González had sent Fierros funds through General Zuazua, but the latter had kept the ten thousand pesos and had sent Fierros only the one thousand dollars. Fierros asked González for additional funds. He awaited González's order regarding the disposition of the brigade.[23]

However feasible the Mexicans' plan may have seemed to them, at the last minute it was suddenly halted.[24] Precisely how this decision was reached remains unclear, but presumably a realization that the Americans had uncovered the invasion plan and were taking steps to repel it influenced the Mexican high command. The Americans had learned the planned date of the invasion, the location and strength of the Brigada Fierros, and that the Carranza administration was aiding and abetting Luis de la Rosa.

What occurred on June 10, therefore, was not a combination of invasion and *sedicioso* rising but the frantic shutdown of the planned operation. General Ricaut, who was in command of the region from Piedras Negras to Matamoros, rushed to Nuevo Laredo. At the international bridge he met the American commander of the Laredo District, Brigadier General William A. Mann, at 8 a.m. A conference was held on the spot between Mann and members of his staff; General Ricaut, accompanied by General Reynaldo de la Garza, commander at Nuevo Laredo, and members of his staff; the American consul in Nuevo Laredo, Alonzo Garrett; and Vice Consul Shelby Theriot. Ricaut assured Mann that the force assembled at La Jarita really consisted of bandits, who were rebuilding the railroad line from La Jarita to Colombia on the Rio Grande opposite Palafox, Texas, for their own nefarious purposes. Ricaut promised to deal with them immediately.[25]

Up to that point Ricaut had somehow been unable to locate these miscreants although La Jarita was not some kind of remote mountain hideout—it was a station on the rail line only twenty miles southwest of Nuevo Laredo, and the camp of de la Rosa "was in sight of passengers and even the troops of the de facto government who moved north and south over the National Railroad."[26] This reminds one of the Pakistani military's inability to locate Osama bin Laden, who was dwelling comfortably in their midst.

Ricaut promised to deal with de la Rosa immediately, although he "denied that De la Rosa was an officer of the Carranza army and that he has a commission." The meeting ended with expressions of hearty goodwill and firm handshakes all around.[27] However, the commander at Matamoros, Colonel J. R. Quntanilla, denied that de la Rosa was anywhere near the border, declaring that he was in the interior of Tamaulipas, where he was being closely watched. As a precaution, a squadron of Texas National Guard cavalry was rushed from San Antonio to Laredo to reinforce the Fort McIntosh garrison.[28]

So, with the Mexican operation fatally compromised, what happened on June 10 was not an armed attack but rather the appearance of revolutionary newspapers. What purported to be an extra edition of *The Tribunal: The Revolutionary Organ of the Liberating Army of Races and People in America*, published in San Diego, Texas, carried a headline trumpeting that "The Revolution Scourges the Yankee in Corpus [Christi], San Diego, and San Antonio: The Revolution in the South, Annihilating and Devastating, Proceeds with Its Work of Justice." There was also a different June 10 edition of *The Tribunal* whose headline contained the same kind of triumphalist fantasy: "Overwhelming and Formidable, the Civil War in the United States Explodes: Simultaneous Uprisings Occur along the Border, and in the South and Center of the Country."[29]

Despite the San Diego, Texas, dateline, these newspapers were in fact printed in Monterrey, along with all the rest of the Plan de San Diego propaganda, as proved by the printer's bill, dated June 28, 1916, and sent to León Caballo at Monterrey:[30]

10,000 Manifestos November 1915 and May 1916		150 pesos
5,000 fliers BASTA!!!		50 pesos
5,000 LEVANTEMONOS		50 pesos
500 Commissions		25 pesos
4,000 extra TRIBUNAL		120 pesos
300 Circulars		15 pesos
200 Ribbons for flags		40 pesos
7,000 Brothers of America		75 pesos
Total		525 pesos

And Garza was also billed fifteen pesos for the Plan de San Diego seals used on some of the documents.[31]

On June 11, General Ricaut left Nuevo Laredo aboard a special train to capture Luis de la Rosa, who was reportedly incognito in Monterrey. Ricaut lamely asserted that he had been bamboozled, hoodwinked, and duped by de la Rosa into furnishing the *sedicioso* a special train to transport de la Rosa's men from Monterrey to La Jarita. The press reported that "General Alfredo Ricaut, Carrancista commander at Matamoros, today admitted that he was tricked by a ruse of de la Rosa's into furnishing a special train to bring his precious command of bandits from Monterrey to La Jarita, where they detrained and spread up and down the river. Ricaut was made to believe through fake telegrams a la Villa[32] that 500 or 600 men were waiting to go north from Monterrey for railroad repair work."[33] This explanation was met with considerable skepticism. "It is not believed in military circles that General Ricaut has brought about the arrest of Luis de la Rosa at Monterrey. It is known Ricaut was in conference with De la Rosa at La Jarita two or three days ago, and that he would not arrest the bandit then, but would do so later, seems highly improbable, it is asserted."[34]

The *carrancistas* claimed to have arrested de la Rosa as he was about to board a train for Matamoros and to have seized a quantity of weapons and ammunition that de la Rosa was carrying. On June 15, Consul Johnson reported that he'd had a talk with General Ricaut, who had just returned from Monterrey. Ricaut said he had arrested forty of de la Rosa's men as well as de la Rosa himself, who was now in jail in

Monterrey. Ricaut added that he had left his men on the border with instructions to arrest parties who could not give a good account of themselves.[35] However, Ricaut issued a formal statement from Saltillo that de la Rosa was interned in the penitentiary in Saltillo, along with those who had accompanied him. In addition, he announced that the forces of General Carlos Osuna, recently assigned as the commander in Lampazos, had arrested a number of de la Rosa's partisans between Lampazos and La Jarita; at Lampazos one of de la Rosa's officers and six enlisted men had been arrested. They too were to be sent to prison in Saltillo.

The Americans were dubious about the report that de la Rosa had been arrested at Monterrey. "He has been entering and leaving Monterrey with apparent impunity for some time, and army officers here [at the Southern Department in San Antonio] have taken that as an indication that only feeble efforts were being made to capture him."[36]

Agent Rogers, for one, was unimpressed with these reports of de la Rosa's arrest. In September 1916, Rogers discussed changes of command in the Mexican Army on the border: "Referring to the changes in commandants noted herewith there is some expression of regret among some American admirers of Ricaut that he is gone [temporarily] and the statement is made that he co-operated with officials of the United States. The extent of this co-operation may be measured by this fact, that the bandits known to have been the leaders and the cause of the trouble along the border here are now and have always been in Matamoros and have never been arrested by him or any effort made to turn them over to the United States or to Texas for punishment. Ricaut is a little better diplomat than Nafarrate but less courageous and frank. To secure favors he is conciliatory."[37]

The Mexican shell game continued.

15 New Raids

The ill-considered invasion plan had been shelved, and on June 13 the Mexican Foreign Office formally notified the American representative in Mexico City that de la Rosa had been captured, this news based on a telegram from the military commandant in Tamaulipas.[1] But Carranza fully intended to continue exerting pressure on the United States in hopes of forcing the withdrawal of the Punitive Expedition. Therefore he reverted to the successful 1915 strategy: a wave of raids into Texas, none of which would be serious enough to provoke American retaliation. The Fierros Brigade would mount these raids under the aegis of the Plan de San Diego.

A report from the bureau's informant García stated that Generals Osuna, Garza, de la Rosa, and Fierros had met in Monterrey and agreed they would simultaneously attack along the Texas border, selecting the most vulnerable points. Furthermore, three manifestos were being prepared urging Tejanos to rebel. García promised to secure copies before they were published and mail them to Barnes.[2]

The revised strategy was quickly implemented. On June 10 a large party of Mexicans attacked the Coleman and Johnson San Samuel ranch near La Jarita. They began to round up horses; the two Anglo and one Hispanic cowboys on the scene fled. One Cenobio Méndez said he had been captured by the party and was forced to accompany them to the American side of the river. When the raiders started for Webb Station, twenty miles north of Laredo on the International and Great Northern Railroad, he was given a red flag with the wording diagonally across it "Libertad, Igualdad y Independencia." Nearing Webb, Méndez was able to escape, carrying the flag and a can of kerosene, and galloped to alert the nearest cavalry detachment, at Minera, warning that raiders were heading for Webb Station to loot the place and burn the railroad bridge. A posse of fifteen ranchers and cowboys quickly formed under the leadership of Tom Ross, the ex-Ranger captain and currently Bureau of Investigation agent. They raced to Webb in autos, arriving there about midnight on June ll. They deployed in the brush to await the Mexicans. Shortly after their arrival they spotted and seized two men who proved to be members of the raiding party. Subsequently another raider was captured. Throughout the rest of the night posses and a detachment of the Fourteenth Cavalry searched for the other marauders. Early the next morning a posse encountered them and a firefight ensued.[3]

From Laredo came the following report: "A small party of armed Mexicans invaded Texas last night with a red flag and a can of kerosene oil." The report referred to the commando that had crossed the Rio Grande above Laredo, dispatched by Maurilio Rodríguez to cut the telephone and telegraph wires at Webb Station and burn several bridges, "in order that the Carranza force which had been augmented at Nuevo Laredo could attack Laredo, Texas." As we've seen, the planned attack on Laredo had been hurriedly canceled. The commando's mission failed. In a running fight with a posse and an army detachment the raiders fought desperately but were overwhelmed and three were killed. Deputy Sheriff Dolores Cano killed Lieutenant Colonel Pedro Villarreal in single combat. Villarreal was in full *carrancista* uniform wearing a Stetson and with a Carranza commission in his pocket; three raiders, also wearing Carranza uniforms, were captured, and Tom Ross took them to Laredo. Ross also took charge of the red-and-white flag that the raiders had carried. One of the prisoners was taken back to the battlefield and identified the body of Lieutenant Colonel Villarreal. On June 12 a posse killed Antonio Carbajal, who lived on a ranch near Webb Station. Whether he'd been involved in the raid is unclear. Posses composed of stockmen continued to scour the area, and a company of the Ninth Infantry was rushed by truck to Webb Station. As a further security measure the army converted some freight cars into mobile blockhouses, sandbagged and loopholed, to protect railroad bridges from attacks.[4]

The prisoners confessed to belonging to Luis de la Rosa's command. Simón Solís said he was a Laredo native and had lived there for many years. He had recently gone to Lampazos to visit his father and while there was approached by General Maurilio Rodríguez of the Carranza army and involuntarily impressed into that army. He related that on June 8 he'd met Lieutenant Colonel Villarreal and five men mounted and armed with .30-.30s. On June 10 the party crossed the Rio Grande at the San Samuel crossing above Palafox. There were six of them: "Lieutenant Colonel Villarreal, Alberto who is captain, Antonio, Cenobio, and I and Manuel, Sub-Lieutenant." They had a flag carried by "Cenobio from Encinal." The flag was red with something white in the center. Solís was told to take the group to Palo Blanco. He said he didn't know the road, so a guide named Isidro took them. There they obtained fresh horses. Colonel Villarreal told Solís to accompany him to the Peñoles tank, and a guide, the son of Manuel Flores of Palafox, took them. They obtained fresh horses from a remuda that was in a pasture, then left for Rancho Nuevo at night, arriving there in the morning. At 5 p.m. they left and started toward Cactus, near Webb Station. Villarreal told them they were going to burn the bridge and cut the telegraph wires. Solís and Cenobio left them to go to Laredo, but Cenobio ran away. Solís left his weapons and horse in the brush and started for Laredo on foot but was arrested on the road. "I heard that General Maurilio Rodríguez told Col. Villarreal to come over here, and burn the bridges and cut the wires and to kill me if I abandoned them."[5]

Prisoner Antonio Cuevas said, "General Maurilio Rodríguez told us to go with the Lieutenant Colonel but he did not say what for." They crossed the river on the night of June 10. "I crossed the river only to benefit my condition. I am an artisan and as business is bad in Mexico I came here." Six of them, mounted and armed, crossed at San Samuel. The guide had a red flag. At the last moment when they got near the railroad track the lieutenant colonel told them his mission was to cut the wires and burn bridges.[6]

His fellow prisoner, Captain Norberto Pezzot, also confessed, stating that General Maurilio Rodríguez, "commanding Carranza troops at La Jarita," had given them instructions to cut telephone wires, to burn bridges, and to loot.[7] Lieutenant Colonel Villarreal, Simón Solís, Antonio Cuevas, and three others had crossed the river at San Samuel. At the ranch Villarreal obtained a can of kerosene; when Pezzot asked him why, Villarreal replied that he'd come to burn a bridge. They were guided to the railroad bridge by men who carried the red flag. Pezzot further stated that General Maurilio Rodríguez had conferred on him the rank of captain. He had been in the Carranza army for the last two years, as chauffeur for General Alfredo Flores Alatorre. Villarreal had joined them at Rodríguez Station. When General Rodríguez left to go to La Jarita he told Pezzot to go with Villarreal.[8]

Pezzot demanded that the Mexican consul be present in court; instead a representative of the consul attended. In court Pezzot vehemently denied that he was a bandit: "I am a member of the Constitutionalist Army. I am not a bandit. I came here obeying superior orders. I was under the command of a superior officer. I want the government that furnished me arms to protect me. If the government of my country, for which I did this, will not protect me my conscience will be clear and I will abide by the laws of this state." Pezzot declared that his codefendants were also members of the Carranza army. He asserted that the raiders were assured of covering fire from Carranza troops on the Mexican side of the river if they succeeded in reaching the Rio Grande after carrying out the raid.

Press coverage of the trial stressed that "the testimony given by Pezzot proved conclusively that the so-called de la Rosa bandits, while actually under the direct command of the notorious bandit are in fact nothing more nor less than Carranza soldiers operating secretly against Americans and American property along the Mexican border sections." The account continued: "Pezzot told of how Lieutenant Colonel Villarreal, his superior officer, himself and other so-styled bandits were guests at a banquet given in a [railroad] car of a Mexican general."[9] Pezzot also wrote an indignant letter to the Mexican secretary of war demanding his assistance and asserting that he was not a bandit but a captain in the Carranza army who had just been following orders.[10]

Pezzot told Agent Barnes that he was born in Monterrey in 1880. In 1915 at Tampico he became a lieutenant on the staff of General Flores Alatorre. "I remained in the service of the Carranza army until March of this year when I retired on account of weak eyes and lived in Mexico City. I went to the penitentiary in Mexico City to see a friend of mine," a captain who introduced Pezzot to General Maurilio Rodríguez, who "was also confined in this jail at that time. I do not know what charge was against Rodríguez as he was very soon thereafter released."[11]

Pezzot was told to call on Rodríguez at the Garza Brothers store in Mexico City. Rodríguez recruited Pezzot to go north with him. Pezzot missed several trains to Monterrey, but in the meantime Garza Brothers had turned over several Japanese to Pezzot to escort to Monterrey to join Rodriguez's command. As matters developed, they left on an earlier train, a special train carrying Nicéforo Zambrano, the secretary of the treasury. Pezzot remembered that General Esteban Fierros, Agustín Garza, and "another well-dressed Mexican, who[se] name I did not know" traveled on the train with Zambrano. When Pezzot arrived in Monterrey he saw the Japanese, who were staying in Zambrano's private railroad car waiting to catch the train north. While in Monterrey, Pezzot saw General Zuazua, who traveled in a special train.

Pezzot gave a detailed account of how Maurilio Rodríguez took him and his companions to Lampazos, Nuevo León, where he gave them each twenty pesos and departed. The next day Rodríguez returned accompanied by Lieutenant Colonel Villarreal and a captain who was a telegrapher. "When our party was finally made up as instructed by Maurilio Rodríguez it was composed of Lieutenant Colonel Villarreal in command, two Japanese, Simón Solís, Antonio Cuevas and myself. Ramón Solís acted as guide."

The Japanese and Cuevas were left behind, for they didn't appear fitted for the expedition. The party crossed the Rio Grande and secured fresh mounts. "I began to scheme to get away." He and another man dropped behind. "We then took a different direction and escaped, as we wore uniforms." They were trying to make their way to Laredo when they were captured. Pezzot asserted that "Villarreal is known as a Carranza officer; so is Maurilio Rodríguez. I would say that the Carranza authorities are supporting this movement."

Tom Ross prepared a report on the kerosene, pole-climbers, and other paraphernalia belonging to the expedition as well as a detailed report on the raid itself.[12] The prisoners were charged with theft of horses, conspiracy to destroy telegraph wires, and conspiracy to burn a railroad bridge. District Attorney John Valls, who prosecuted them, testified that "The evidence of these men—four of these men were indicted in Webb County, Tex. I prosecuted those four men, and the jury gave each one of them the death penalty.[13] I also prosecuted the men who were arrested for attempting to burn the bridges and for attempting to cut the telegraph wires at Webb Station. The men who made the attempt to burn the bridges had in their possession all the implements to cut wires; they had coal oil to burn the bridges with."[14] Valls detailed the involvement of Carranza officials in recruiting and planning the affair.

The U.S. Army was skeptical about the wild rumors prevalent in Laredo that Luis de la Rosa at the head of four hundred men planned to attack somewhere near Laredo. Information from Monterrey stated that de la Rosa had been openly recruiting there for an expedition against Texas and that he had left the city in a private railroad car furnished by the Carranza authorities. Moreover, intelligence reports reaching Fort McIntosh were to the effect that de la Rosa and three hundred of his followers were concentrating at La Jarita and had looted an American-owned ranch in the vicinity.[15] As a precaution the army went on alert in Laredo and deployed patrols up and down the Rio Grande.

On June 15 there indeed occurred a serious raid. As early as December 18, 1915, the bureau had reported to General Robert Evans, commander at Laredo, that its information indicated that Plan de San Diego militants planned a raid in the vicinity of San Ignacio, some thirty miles downriver from Laredo. Evans stated that there had been no recent *sedicioso* activity in his territory but that about four hundred feet of the military telephone line between Laredo and San Ignacio had been destroyed.[16]

Yet Tom Ross informed the military of rumors that an attack would occur sometime on June 14 or 15. And on June 15, Colonel Isabel de los Santos, a follower of de la Rosa and a firebrand in the Brigada Fierros, crossed the Rio Grande with seventy men, mostly Carranza soldiers under Major Cruz Ruiz, for a surprise attack against an army detachment encamped near San Ignacio. He reportedly had more than three hundred men initially, but his command had dwindled to about sixty by the time he attacked San Ignacio, due to a lack of armament and because of desertion as the troops became aware of the purpose of their trip north.[17]

A Colonel Frías of the Carranza army had crossed the river that afternoon to reconnoiter and observed that there were ten tents containing four soldiers each, a total of forty soldiers of Troop I, Fourteenth Cavalry. That afternoon the commander at Fort McIntosh notified the sheriff to dispatch immediately a messenger to all ranches near the river advising the ranchers, their families, and the cowboys working for them to evacuate to a place of safety. As a precaution, Troop M of the Fourteenth was dispatched to reinforce the troop at San Ignacio. Both units were under the command of Major Alonso Gray.[18] Thus the Mexicans unknowingly attacked a force twice as large as they'd anticipated.

Guiding the Mexicans raiders across the Rio Grande was Captain Federico Gutiérrez Zapata, chief of the Mexican customs guards at Nuevo Laredo. This contingent also had a red flag, and the men were told they were invading Texas to carry out the Plan de San Diego. The Mexicans struck at 2 a.m., and sentries returned their fire. In the ensuing engagement six of the raiders, including Major Cruz Ruiz, were killed and several were captured (revised figures were that nine raiders were killed, four were wounded, and five were captured). One of those killed was Eduardo Ruiz, a longtime resident of San Antonio who had been a cook most of his life. He reportedly led the charge against the American troops and was shot while attempting to pull up the side of a tent.[19] The rest were pursued as they raced for the safety of the river.[20] The army also recovered two printed revolutionary fliers found on dead Mexicans.[21] The Americans lost three killed and six wounded. Corporal William Oberlies later died of his wounds. Two additional prisoners were captured on the American side of the Rio Grande, and the body of another dead Mexican was found in the brush near the scene of the attack.[22]

Major Gray pursued the fleeing raiders down the Rio Grande as far as Zapata, crossing briefly to the Mexican bank of the river.[23] He communicated with Carranza troops opposite San Ignacio and was told that they were pursuing the raiders on the Mexican side and had killed four of them and had patrols up and down the river. "But little credence is given here [the Southern Department] to report that Mexican troops have killed four of the bandits on the Mexican side."[24]

The *sedicioso* force that raided San Ignacio hardly impressed the American commander on the scene, for he later testified: "I do not wish to convey the idea that this force that crossed the river and attacked my camp was a military organization."[25] For his part, General Ricaut had informed General Parker prior to the San Ignacio raid that "he is making such disposition of his force that raids across the border will be practically impossible."[26] Now a discomfited Ricaut informed Parker that "in case American troops do cross he will be obliged to prevent such incursion into Mexican territory."[27] However, Ricaut took no action.

On the subject of guides for the raiders, Deputy Sheriff Tom Mayfield testified, "these raiding parties that would come over, they would pick up one or two scouts or guides for them, all Mexicans who lived on this side, to help them through the country and show them roads and different localities, different ranches, that way, that they were not familiar with; but the most of the parties consisted of Mexicans from the other side of the river, on the Mexican side," and "That was a saddle machete that was lost by 10 of those raiders that crossed over at Granjeño ranch sometime in October. They used these machetes to cut the wire fences with. In this raid they cut 47 fences on their trip from the river out through the ranches and back, and we were trailing them, and this was lost on the trail."[28]

The *sediciosos* weren't doing very well on the field of battle, but the propaganda mill continued to grind. A newspaper titled *La Semana* and published in Laredo, in its June 16 edition, sent a special report to *El Día* in Monterrey:

> LAREDO, TEXAS IS BURNING IN AN EXPLOSION OF POPULAR DISCONTENT
> To-day in the neighbor [*sic*] American city a great anti-Intervention demonstration took place, the greater part being Texas-Mexicans, negroes, and

> Germans, who ran [through] the streets burning buildings and yelling VIVA the Texas Republic. From the time that the demonstration started the American forces in the city instead of rendering aid started to leave, taking autos, horses, carriages, etc., leaving the town without a garrison. Some of the American soldiers who were forced to open fire against those partaking, before doing each preferred to commit suicide. The International bridge was closed. I will continue furnishing information. The reporter, Rodolfo Cabrera.[29]

General Ricaut had raised the possibility of an armed clash if American troops crossed into Mexico after the raiders, and he announced that an additional one thousand Carranza soldiers were en route to reinforce the border patrol, many of them to be assigned to the sector across the river from San Ignacio. He also stated that three of the San Ignacio raiders had been captured by Carranza troops. Interestingly, ten dead and some twenty wounded raiders were taken to Nuevo Laredo. The press reported: "This would also indicate that the Carrancistas and the De la Rosa bandits are practically one and the same, as the caring for the wounded would not otherwise be undertaken by the Carrancistas of Nuevo Laredo."[30] Plan de San Diego flags were found both at San Ignacio and at the Webb Station after those raids.[31]

A certain Charles Lavallade informed the bureau in San Antonio that he'd been in Monterrey at the time that de la Rosa organized the San Ignacio raid. He said that "The population of Monterrey, Mexico, believes that de la Rosa organized his men with the government's consent." Lavallade "knows this for a fact that the civil authorities know all about De la Rosa's organization and they helped him organize. He also believes that the military authorities know all about it. General Fueras' [Fierros's] residence is near the place where de la Rosa's headquarters were. They were in the Government's barracks on Calzada de [la] Unión. De la Rosa transported all his men to the border in a government train. After the raid they all disbanded. The government is only pretending that they are trying to catch de la Rosa. It is not so; they don't want to prosecute him."[32]

José Antonio Arce, Vicente Lira, Paulino Sánchez, Jesús Cerda, Isabel de los Santos, and Federico Gutiérrez Zapata were charged with killing Corporal William Oberlies. Arce, Lira, Sánchez, and Cerda, all Mexican citizens, were captured on the battlefield on June 15; Paulino Sánchez was seriously wounded with a bullet in the groin. Despite their attorneys' attempts to secure a change of venue, they were tried in Laredo as bandits.[33] Arce voluntarily gave a confession, but the other three entered pleas of "not guilty."

In a surprising development, José María Cerda, a major in the Carranza army, was arrested while nonchalantly strolling down a street in Laredo on June 23. His uniform coat, found on the battlefield at San Ignacio, contained his commission signed by Luis de la Rosa, general in chief, and Isabel de los Santos, commander of the regiment. When shown his coat and commission he confessed his identity. At his trial, Higinio Cantú and Joaquín Flores testified that Cerda had told them he had participated in the San Ignacio raid. Cerda stressed that he'd been threatened with imprisonment if he didn't carry out the orders of his superiors and attack San Ignacio. In his interview with Agent Barnes, Cerda said he'd been born in Salinas Victoria, Mexico, in 1888 "and have resided in Mexico all of my life, with the exception of a period covering seven months terminating in May, 1916." During those seven months he lived in Laredo.

Cerda told a rather convoluted tale. He said he went to Monterrey in search of work. There he met one "Manuel García, a tall Mexican, with one eye, wearing a mustache." While he and García were sitting on a park bench they were arrested and jailed. Interestingly, Manuel García negotiated their release with General Carlos Osuna, commander at Monterrey, on condition that they enlist in the army. Cerda not only enlisted but was commissioned as a major, the commission signed by de la Rosa and de los Santos.

On June 2, along with twenty others under the command of de los Santos, Cerda traveled from Monterrey to La Jarita. During the next few days reinforcements arrived. On June 15, de los Santos received a telegram ordering everyone back to Monterrey. He informed the troops of the message, giving them the option to return or to remain with him. Cerda claimed he was one of those who returned and did not participate in the San Ignacio raid.

In this connection, Cerda was questioned about a uniform coat containing his commission which was found by the American troops in the vicinity of San Ignacio. He claimed that he'd loaned the coat to a certain Pérez, one of the men under de los Santos.[34]

Vicente Lira, one of the officers in the raid, was put on the stand by the defense to explain what he termed extenuating circumstances in his "involuntary" connection with the de la Rosa contingent, a claim that met with derision.[35] Lira gave Agent Barnes a detailed account of his life. He was born in 1859 in Matamoros. He had lived and worked in Texas for years, crossing back and forth along the border. In 1916 he worked for the Pánuco Navigation Company at Tampico but was arrested by the Carranza authorities on suspicion of being a *felicista* spy. He claimed that "the basis of their suspicion was that I spoke English and smoked a pipe." He escaped and reached Monterrey on June 10. While there he was told that de la Rosa was living in room 8 at the National Hotel. From Monterrey he took a train for Laredo, but when the train arrived at La Jarita on June 11 he was detained and questioned by the Carranza commander. Significantly, Lira stated that at 5 p.m. that day Generals Alfredo Ricaut and Esteban Fierros arrived at La Jarita from Nuevo Laredo. "I learned that men were being gathered in the vicinity of La Jarita where a movement was being formed for the purpose of making raids into the United States." After a conference between Ricaut, Fierros, and the local commander, the latter notified the men hidden in the brush that they would all go to Monterrey to be paid. Then Ricaut and Fierros left for Monterrey on a special train.

Lira claimed that later that evening he was taken to join de los Santos's command of about seventy-five, many of whom wore Mexican Army uniforms. Proceeding to the border, the unit sent two spies, names Frías and Quintana, to determine the strength of the American troops at San Ignacio. They reported one hundred soldiers in nine tents. De los Santos assigned nine men each armed with a bomb to blow up the tents. A tenth man, also armed with a bomb, was to detonate it as the signal for a concerted attack by the infantry and cavalry. A Carranza officer named Zapata acted as guide and cut the telephone wires as the raiders crossed into American territory. For this de los Santos chewed him out, saying the action was premature and might alert the Americans.

Lira said he didn't participate in the attack; he was left behind with a boy and a woman to hold the horses. "When the fighting commenced, I ran away and hid in a gulley near the town of San Ignacio. The little boy followed me. The next day I gave myself up to the Sheriff. Ruiz was killed in the attack on San Ignacio. He wore a Carranza uniform. There were eight Mexican and four American soldiers killed in this attack and six Mexicans have been captured."

However, Judge J. T. Griner, a San Antonio attorney, told Agent Barnes that years earlier he had become well acquainted with Vicente Lira and that Lira "was a very rank Socialist, in fact almost an anarchist."[36]

Lira claimed that when the men assembled near La Jarita, General Ricaut arrived on a special train for the specific purpose of breaking up this unlawful gang. Soon after his arrival Ricaut dispatched an army officer to locate the bandits' camp and inform them that the commanding general forbade their planned raid into Texas.

Lira said he accompanied the officer "for solely patriotic purposes and to remonstrate with the leader of the so-called bandits to desist from their purpose of committing depredations on American territory, as this would cause war between the United States and Mexico." Lira asserted that the day before the battle he learned that he was being forcibly detained, and later he was compelled to cross the river with the raiders. Lira stated that all the raiders at one time or another had been Carranza soldiers.[37] He thus concluded explaining his "extenuating circumstances."

José Antonio Arce, another of the San Ignacio raiders, made a voluntary confession to District Attorney Valls. At his trial the newspaper reported that "This forenoon Jose Antonio Arce, the third of the bandits to be put on the stand, testified and told some interesting things in connection with events transpiring before and after the organization of what was practically the 'bandit branch' of the Carranza army, which operated under the direction of Carranza officers, though 'General' Luis de la Rosa was in supreme command of the 'bandit' department." Arce testified that Carranza generals were present at the National Hotel in Monterrey during a meeting where de la Rosa declared his intention of fighting the Americans and reclaiming Texas.

In a statement to Tom Ross, Arce stated that he was sixteen or seventeen years old and a resident of Torreón, Coahuila. He was a musician and belonged to an orchestra in Torreón. On June 5 he was penniless, sitting in the depot at Ciudad Victoria when Luis de la Rosa approached and recruited him. A train arrived from Tampico with General Fierros and another Carranza general whose name Arce didn't know aboard. De la Rosa and Arce boarded the train for Monterrey. There Ernesto Ramírez, who was de la Rosa's aide, took Arce to the International Hotel, where de la Rosa was staying. General Fierros and his paymaster distributed forty pesos in Carranza currency to Arce and the numerous others awaiting payment. Fierros and de la Rosa placed Colonel Morelos Zaragoza in charge of the men, who traveled by train to La Jarita. After remaining there for three days, Fierros and his paymaster distributed an additional thirty pesos to each man. They were assigned to the command of Colonel de los Santos. On the third day Colonel Cruz Ruiz and Vicente Lira joined them. About sixty of the troops followed Colonel de los Santos across the Rio Grande to San Ignacio. De los Santos formed them "in ranks, cavalry in front and the infantry in the rear" to attack the American soldiers' camp. Arce said "I fired one shot when my rifle hung fire and I dropped it and ran away." He was arrested by two soldiers and two civilians as he tried to make his way back to the Rio Grande.[38]

Paulino Sánchez, the fourth captured raider, was in no condition to testify, for he was seriously wounded. Nevertheless, he was brought into court, his stretcher being placed in front of the jury box. The newspaper speculated that although he was pale and emaciated, he might regain his health.[39]

At the trial some of the most damning testimony came from a ten-year-old boy, Francisco de León,[40] who had accompanied the San Ignacio raiders by holding the horses of the officers. He stated that "three other boys the same size as me were given jobs like this, too." (One of them was Benito Rodríguez, age twelve.)[41] De León was arrested at a ranch near San Ignacio by customs inspectors and gave his account of the engagement.

He said that de la Rosa's force recruited in Monterrey numbered three hundred when it reached the Rio Grande opposite San Ignacio but that only seventy were sent across the river to carry out the attack. "The boy further avers that many of the men were recruited into the bandit gang under the belief that they were all 'good Carrancistas,' and that they were equipped and started on their expedition to San Ignacio by Carrancistas who had visited them while concentrating at La Jarita." The newspaper stated that "De León even betrayed the Mexicans to the extent that he related in court their secret signals and passwords. He said when the bandits bivouacked for the night they had passwords. If anybody passed along he was challenged with 'Who goes there?' If he was a member of the bandit gang he would reply, 'Mexico,' and be allowed to pass." The boy readily admitted to hating Americans and eagerly participating in the attack in order to "kill gringos and then rob them. I was going to kill them with bombs, but when the Americans shot at my *compadres* and they rushed to where I was holding their horses and jumped on them and rode away they left me and another boy behind and today the gringos captured me." For the edification of Laredoans the boy was given a gun and a bomb found on the road near San Ignacio and photographed in front of the Hamilton Hotel before a curious crowd.[42]

After deliberating for eleven hours, the jury on July 15 convicted them all and sentenced them to death. They were remanded to the county jail. "The verdict of the jury assessing the death penalty against them appeared to meet with general approbation," the local newspaper reported.[43] The prisoners were closely guarded, for in November there was discovered a plot to break them out of jail.[44]

In a very indirect way, the Carranza regime did admit some very slight involvement in the San Ignacio raid. The Mexican consul formulated an appeal contending that although the four prisoners were indeed Constitutionalist soldiers they had acted as individuals motivated by patriotic zeal in the belief that war with the United States had broken out.[45] The consul's argument was disingenuous, since it was contradicted by the prisoners' own testimony.

The prisoners' court-appointed attorneys announced that they would file a motion for a new trial and that if this were overruled they would appeal to a higher court on the grounds that the Laredo district court had lacked jurisdiction. The motion for a new trial was overruled.[46] In December 1916 the defense attorneys indeed appealed the convictions to the Texas Court of Criminal Appeals,[47] arguing that the prisoners weren't bandits but rather soldiers acting under orders.[48]

16 The War Crisis

Historian Joseph A. Stout Jr. poses the question: "How close did the two countries come to war in 1916?" Contrary to those historians who believe that war was imminent, Stout maintains that there was no war crisis, for Wilson and Carranza were just "sparring for diplomatic and political advantage in their respective countries."[1]

Ever since Villa's Columbus raid on March 9, 1916, the U.S. Army had been increasing its presence on the international boundary. This was in addition to the dispatch into Chihuahua of General John J. Pershing's Punitive Expedition.[2] The army, it should be mentioned, was handicapped by a lack of accurate maps of the Mexican border.[3]

Then, on May 5, Mexican irregulars attacked a squad of American troops stationed at the riverside hamlet of Glenn Springs in the Big Bend, killing several soldiers.[4] It has been alleged that Luis de la Rosa personally led the raid,[5] but there is no credible evidence to support this assertion.

Two companies of the Nineteenth Infantry were rushed by special train from Fort Sill, Oklahoma, to Fort Clark on May 7. And men of Company E, Signal Corps, were transferred from Fort Shafter, Hawaii, to Fort Sam Houston in San Antonio for border duty.[6] But even as troops were being dispatched to the border, General Funston felt that there were simply not enough regulars available to protect the Big Bend from future raids. Almost every regular infantryman in the United States was either on the border or on his way there. To alleviate the critical lack of cavalry, Funston even wanted to mount two thousand infantrymen on Texas ponies.[7] Not a good idea. He renewed his request to the War Department for fifty thousand national guardsmen for border protection. He particularly wanted the National Guard of Pennsylvania and New York, the only two states that boasted a division each.[8]

However, the War Department, reluctant to admit that the army couldn't defend the border by itself, on May 9 called up only the National Guard of Arizona (984 strong), New Mexico (737), and Texas (2,470), a total of only about 4,200 indifferently trained men. These organizations were ordered to recruit immediately up to war strength (e.g., the war strength of the Texas National Guard was 6,118).[9]

In addition, three regular infantry regiments from Plattsburg, Watertown, and Oswego, New York, Vancouver Barracks, and Fort Lawton, Washington, were ordered to the border. The Pacific Coast was virtually stripped of mobile units; there remained only two troops of the First Cavalry and a battalion of the Twenty-First Infantry at Calexico and a battalion of the Fourteenth Infantry in Alaska, plus a company of engineers and a field hospital.[10] The army was figuratively scraping the bottom of its manpower barrel: eleven companies (20th, 41st, 69th, 74th, 77th, 102nd, 103rd, 120th, 127th, 141st, 164th)—some fourteen hundred men—of Coast Artillery, the last available regulars, were likewise ordered from stations such as Pensacola, Florida, Charleston, South Carolina, and Fort Oglethorpe, Georgia, to Texas to be employed as infantry in static defense of railroad bridges and other strategic installations. Funston's command had thus been increased by about eleven thousand regulars, which he still deemed insufficient. To support the infantry, five batteries of the Fifth Field Artillery at Fort Sill and three batteries of the Third Field Artillery at Tobyhanna, Pennsylvania, were placed in readiness for border service. The artillery battalion from Tobyhanna joined the other battalion of the Third Field Artillery, which had been stationed at Fort Sam Houston for the last nine years.

The School of Musketry at Fort Sill was suspended, and the infantrymen attending were sent to Texas. About one hundred regular officers attending the four army service schools at Fort Leavenworth, Kansas, were hurriedly graduated and ordered to join their commands at once. Even those whose regiments were in the Philippines or Hawaii were ordered to the border for special assignment.[11] Serious consideration was given to graduating the senior class at West Point early, commissioning them as second lieutenants, and assigning them to units on the border. Major General Tasker H. Bliss, the assistant chief of staff, spent a week at West Point, whose Academic Board finally persuaded him to abandon the idea.[12]

Further strengthening border defense, Fort Brown in Brownsville, which had been deactivated in 1906 and in 1911 turned over to the Interior Department, was by executive order returned to the War Department and reactivated in May 1916.[13]

The Army War College was also putting the finishing touches on a plan of campaign in the event of war with Mexico. The Mexican border towns would be occupied quickly; pontoons were being stockpiled for crossing the Rio Grande, it being assumed that the Mexican Army would blow up the international bridges. Next, three columns would strike south from El Paso, Laredo, and Brownsville, occupying the area down to the level of Torreón, the major railroad hub in northern Mexico.[14]

Washington viewed Carranza troop movements as a menace—thirty thousand men were rushed into northern Mexico instead of the ten thousand agreed on at the recent El Paso conference between Generals Bliss, Funston, and Alvaro Obregón, appointed on March 13 as Carranza's new secretary of war and marine. Some of these *carrancista* formations potentially threatened General Pershing's lines of communication. Obregón stated that the troops were moved north only to comply with Mexican promises for the protection of the border.[15]

General Funston, for one, didn't buy that explanation. Funston observed that rushing Carranza troops by rail to various parts of northern Mexico couldn't be explained by claiming they were to be used against Pancho Villa. Even less credible was Obregón's recent announcement that they would be employed against the *felicistas*, for Félix Díaz had few followers in the north. Funston said these explanations "should not fool a child."[16]

The speculation was that either Carranza hoped to convince the United States of his ability to protect the border or he was making a show of force to back up his demand for withdrawal of the Punitive Expedition. Particularly troubling was that General Jacinto Treviño had massed his troops along the Mexican Central and Mexico Northwest Railroads, threatening Pershing's lines of communication. Carranza issued a demand on May 22 that American troops be withdrawn from Mexico at once; their presence was intolerable and was a violation of Mexican sovereignty.

The Wilson administration considered Carranza's note of May 22 insulting, and Secretary of State Lansing began working on a suitable reply.[17] Disingenuously, Carranza also declared that Mexico did not want war but that the United States' holding up of munitions shipments to Mexico showed warlike intent. The State Department's special representative in Mexico, James Linn Rodgers, reported: "Know personally that *de facto* Government [is] greatly embarrassed by lack [of] ammunition."[18] Not only was the Carranza administration short of ammunition, but, as had been the case throughout the Mexican Revolution, Mexico was dependent on the United States for most of its munitions—not a favorable situation in the event of war with the United States. Mexico tried to end the dependency by developing a domestic munitions industry, but the results were less than encouraging.[19]

Regarding the possibility of war, Funston stated that the Mexicans would be allowed to strike the first blow, and if a clash resulted from some subordinate Mexican commander attacking Pershing's force, the U.S. Army might learn of the event before the Mexican commanders along the border. If so, the Americans would attack all the way from Brownsville to Yuma. Funston strongly believed that nothing impressed a Mexican like thrashing him, unless it was killing him.[20] The army planned to seize the bridges across the Rio Grande and to seize the great railroad bridge at Sabinas, ninety miles south of Piedras Negras.[21]

Funston requested that the National Guard of Louisiana, Arkansas, and Oklahoma be called into federal service. His request was denied. His request for yet more Coast Artillery companies was also denied, because this would so deplete the organization that there would be insufficient men to care for the equipment.[22] So, Funston decided to protect the Big Bend with the Coast Artillery companies already there, plus the Fourth Texas Infantry regiment and the First Texas Cavalry Squadron, and he recalled the Sixth Cavalry back from the Punitive Expedition to reinforce these formations. The lack of cavalry was one of Funston's greatest concerns, but only three squadrons were not either in the Southern Department or in the Punitive Expedition.[23]

By mid-June, Funston could breathe easier, for he now had some fifty thousand troops in the Southern Department and the Punitive Expedition. The only mobile troops left in the United States were a squadron of the Second Cavalry at Fort Meyer, Virginia, assigned to guard Washington DC. Of the roughly fifteen thousand Coast Artillery, two thousand were on the border or under orders to go there. And additional units were headed for the border, such as an ambulance company and a field hospital from Fort D. A. Russell, Wyoming.[24]

As a counterpoint to the American buildup, the Carranza administration orchestrated a wave of anti-American demonstrations. On June 8 there was a large demonstration in the city of Chihuahua. The leaders didn't confine themselves to oratory—they issued a call to arms; the mob attacked the American consulate and the Foreign Club. General Treviño had to declare martial law to restore order. On June 9, Carranza sent Treviño a telegram of congratulation regarding the anti-American riot. The telegram was widely circulated throughout the state.[25]

On June 8 the American consulate in Durango was burned during an anti-American demonstration. The rioters set fire to the consulate after dragging the American flag through the streets. On June 15 there was a massive anti-American demonstration in Monterrey, with some fifteen thousand persons participating to show their patriotism and their readiness to defend the fatherland if necessary. On June 18 there occurred violent anti-American demonstrations in Sonora, at Naco and Nogales, while in Cananea rioters riddled an American flag flying over the consulate. In Torreón a mob of three thousand led by the mayor stoned the U.S. consulate for several hours on June 18.[26]

In the midst of the American military buildup there occurred yet another raid, this time nine miles west of Brownsville at a place called Ranchito, a ranch opposite the Rancho Tahuachal on the Mexican bank of the Rio Grande. On June 14, Abel Sandoval led eighteen men across the river to strike a blow for the Texas revolution. Their aim was to kill some Tejanos who opposed the Plan de San Diego, to wreck trains north of Brownsville, and to ambush army patrols.[27]

One of the band, Felipe Sandoval, was arrested on the night of June 21 by home guards near San Benito. He stated that "a merchant" in Matamoros told them that when they reached the American bank of the Rio Grande they'd be joined by a large company of *sediciosos*. Sandoval said that "otherwise we would not have come." The promised *sediciosos* failed to materialize. He also related that he'd participated in the Norias raid led by Luis de la Rosa. Sandoval was charged with conspiring to overthrow the U.S. government and was jailed in Brownsville in default of a five-thousand-dollar appearance bond.[28] He pleaded guilty and was sentenced to eleven months in the county jail. Since he'd been in jail since June 20, 1916, he had already served most of his sentence.

Sandoval stated that he was a Mexican citizen, forty-six years old, and a resident of Matamoros. Abel Sandoval had summoned him to a ranch, where men were assembling, according to Abel Sandoval, "to defend the Constitution of Fifty-Seven," although Felipe Sandoval had absolutely no idea what that meant. Abel Sandoval had eighteen men, including Lázaro Guerra, Joaquín Vargas, and Pedro Cavazos, captains. He issued each man a .30-.30 Winchester or a Mauser and 200–300 rounds of Mauser ammunition but only 100 rounds of .30-.30, which was in short supply.[29]

The Americans had learned that the guerrillas planned to assemble at the Cortillo ranch and were waiting for them. On June 16 the raiders tried to ambush an army detachment searching the brush for them about nine miles northeast of San Benito. The guerrillas had kidnapped a Hispanic farmhand as a guide. His nephew led the soldiers to the spot where the kidnapping had occurred, and the raiders opened fire from the brush. The ambush failed. One Mexican was captured, and the rest fled back across the river with the army in hot pursuit. Searching the ground the next day, the army found the body of a raider, well armed with a .30-.30 and 145 cartridges, who had been badly wounded and who had shot himself. The raiders abandoned fifteen rifles, a quantity of ammunition, forty-five pounds of dynamite, and thirty-two bombs. "The bombs were of the small, plunger and cap variety. They were about the size of a man's two fists, pear shaped, and had plungers at the ends. The plungers are struck on the hard ground, or a rifle butt, then the bomb flung into a trench or at men. They are supposed to explode after about eight seconds have elapsed."[30]

This Plan de San Diego raid had consequences on which the Carranza administration hadn't counted. The U.S. Army's rules of engagement had changed since Pancho Villa's Columbus raid. Brigadier General James Parker had taken command of the Brownsville District on May 18, 1916. On June 9 he had issued an order that bandits were to be pursued wherever they went. And he spent money liberally to secure information, stating that "The most valuable spies are those in the ranks of the raiders."[31]

Immediately upon receiving news of the raid Parker dispatched troops in pursuit of the marauders not just to the Rio Grande but across it. He ordered Lieutenant A. D. Newman, with fifty men of Troop H, Third Cavalry, to go after the marauders. At midnight on June 16, Newman and his troop left Brownsville, and at 9 a.m. on the seventeenth the Americans crossed the river by swimming their horses. They followed the tracks of the Mexicans, and at Pedernal ranch, about a mile from the river, had a skirmish with some of them, killing two. No casualties among the Americans.

Also on June 17, at 1:30 p.m., Major Edward A. Anderson, with the Third Cavalry's Troops E, F, and G and machine gun troop left Fort Brown accompanied by twenty men of the Fourth Infantry transporting two small boats and a wireless outfit on trucks. At about 6 p.m. the cavalry and machine gun troop crossed over at the Tahuachal Ranch and marched eastward toward Matamoros, encamping for the night three miles east of the crossing and only seven miles west of Matamoros.

The man on the spot was now General Ricaut, for Carranza had issued inflexible orders to his commanders in northern Mexico. Carranza's commander in Chihuahua, General Jacinto Treviño, had been instructed on June 16 to notify General Pershing that the Punitive Expedition would be attacked if it moved in any direction except north. Pershing stated that if he saw fit to move troops in any direction he would do so and would resist any attack.[32] And Ricaut had received a direct order from Carranza to repel any American incursion.[33]

Through the Mexican consul in Brownsville, Ricaut notified General Parker that his troops were moving to drive out the American units. The press reported that "Stung by criticism that he was partial to the Americans, General Ricaut at a command meeting Thursday night declared he would prove he was a better Mexican than his critics: 'Send your families from Matamoros and report for enlistment for military action. I will issue the necessary weapons. I have ordered my soldiers to shoot the first American soldier crossing the Rio Grande.'"[34] Parker in turn informed the consul that if Ricaut's troops fired on his men he would counterattack with the full force of his command.

Ricaut's mettle was tested, and he failed the test when Parker called his bluff. Ricaut had to explain to Carranza why he had disobeyed a direct order to repel the American incursion on June 17. The best excuse Ricaut could come up with was that the sorry state of his men's horses had prevented him from doing so.[35] Pretty lame.

With American troops less than ten miles away, the citizens of Matamoros were in a state of utter panic. Ricaut built breastworks on the Mexican side of the international bridge and stationed a strong detachment of troops there; he also posted a heavy guard at the Mexican end of the international ferry. Moreover, he distributed weapons to some fifteen hundred citizens and had them patrol the streets.[36]

But then instead of attacking the Americans Ricaut hastily evacuated Matamoros with his entire garrison and ordered every woman and child out of the city. Except for a few pickets and a number of citizens who preferred to risk an American bombardment to the loss of their property at the hands of thieves and looters, the city of Matamoros for the first time in its history was almost completely deserted.

General Parker assured Ricaut that the Americans would under no circumstances bombard the city as long as women and children might remain in it, and that in any event notice would be given in time to allow an evacuation. But he also insisted that the raids must stop immediately. Ricaut assured Parker that not a man would pass to the American side except at regular crossings, and that he would execute anyone caught in the act of banditry. The American consul in Matamoros, Jesse H. Johnson, met with Ricaut and assured him that American troops had no intention of attacking Matamoros.[37] But to put Ricaut's actions in perspective, it should be noted that the Mexican Army also hurriedly evacuated the border cities of Ciudad Juárez, Nuevo Laredo, Piedras Negras, and Agua Prieta.[38]

On the morning of June 18, Colonel Bullard deployed two battalions of his Twenty-Sixth Infantry to protect Major Anderson's crossing. One boatload of the Twenty-Sixth had already reached the Mexican bank when the wireless conveyed Washington's order to withdraw. After the machine gun troop and all but one troop of cavalry had crossed back to the American side, *carrancista* soldiers fired on the Americans' rear guard. The chief of the immigration service in Matamoros, Pelayo Quintana, led a detachment of twenty soldiers who sniped at Anderson's rear guard. In a sharp but brief skirmish, the cavalry wheeled around and chased the *carrancistas* eastward until the dust thrown up by their horses' hoofs hid them. In this encounter two *carrancistas* were killed, one a subaltern officer, and two were wounded. The Americans suffered no casualties. It was reported that Jesús Elizondo at the head of a considerable command had left Matamoros for Las Rusias ranch, about six miles away, to attack Major Anderson's left flank but that Elizondo got cold feet at the critical moment and failed to assist the Quintana detachment.[39]

The story given out in Matamoros was that a small band of heroic Mexican troops had driven some three hundred American invaders back across the Rio Grande. Ricaut on June 19 sent an official dispatch to the governor of Coahuila: "I have the pleasure of announcing to you that yesterday at 8 a.m. my troops advanced under orders to fight the invaders and had a sharp encounter with them, making them recross to American territory, but not followed up, on the instruction of the First Chief." Matamoros ecstatically celebrated this "victory."[40]

Subsequently it was reported from Monterrey that there was posted an official order from Carranza stating that Ricaut had been recalled to Mexico City and was to be replaced by General Emiliano Nafarrate.

The supposed reason for Ricaut's recall was his refusal to fight the American cavalry that had crossed into Mexico on June 17.[41] In the event, however, Ricaut kept his job. In fact, in November he was given command of a district along the Rio Grande border extending for more than six hundred miles, from opposite Glenn Springs, Texas, to Matamoros, and including Monterrey, which city was his headquarters.[42]

General Parker demanded that Ricaut arrest and punish the bandits who attacked San Ignacio on June 15. On June 20 he sent Ricaut a list of those allegedly involved.[43] On June 22, Ricaut answered that he would endeavor at once to arrest them, that he would cooperate with the Americans, and that he would punish any who might be guilty.[44] Ricaut notified Parker that he'd dispatched troops to Las Rucias, where they'd arrested Eliseo Escamilla, and Ricaut already had under arrest a number of other alleged bandits whose names Parker had given him. The Mexican general assured Parker that his troops were patrolling the riverfront and that the militants arrested would be sent to the penitentiary in Monterrey to await trial under Mexican law.[45]

Whereas General Ricaut was falling all over himself professing cooperation with the Americans, General Nafarrate had published and signed as military commander in Tamaulipas a circular dated at Tampico on June 17 and issued on June 18. The circular, distributed throughout Tamaulipas, called on Mexicans to arm themselves against an American invasion and announced that a state of war existed between the two countries. The handbill also warned that armed Americans found in Mexico would receive no quarter, but that all Americans in Tamaulipas not armed and pursuing peaceful occupations would be protected.[46] It was later claimed that the circular was just intended as a contingency in case of hostilities. Nafarrate also threatened to blow up the vital Tampico oilfields if the Americans ever tried to seize them.[47]

Nafarrate, accompanied by Raúl Gárate, governor of Tamaulipas, made a flying one-day visit to Matamoros on June 30, ostensibly to review the troops. He was said to be leaving for Mexico City to confer with Venustiano Carranza.[48] Replacing Nafarrate in July as commander of the Fifth Division of the Northeast, with headquarters at Tampico, was General Luis Caballero. The American consul wrote: "It is not exactly clear why Nafarrate was relieved of this command, though it is surmised to have been by way of convincing our government of the de facto government's sincerity following the recent exchange of notes; and possibly because of his many blunders of administration here including the imposition of the war tax on oil exports and the firing on our marines. He left the city very quietly."[49]

In addition to the massive military buildup on the border, President Wilson on June 18 took the extraordinary step of ordering the call-up of virtually the entire National Guard of the United States, to defend the border and free the regular army to fight a war with Mexico.

National Guard units were ordered to recruit up to war strength immediately, and they were rushed to the border as quickly as rail transportation could be arranged. By mid-July there were some 110,000 guardsmen deployed along the border, with the principal concentrations being at San Antonio, Brownsville, El Paso, and Nogales.

On the night of June 19, a small bridge on the International & Great Northern Railroad thirty miles east of Laredo was burned. Texas Rangers and military authorities investigated to determine whether it was the work of Mexican raiders or their sympathizers. The night train to Laredo was delayed pending reconstruction of the bridge.[50]

On June 19 the decidedly anti-American governor of Coahuila, Gustavo Espinoza Mireles, who had once been Carranza's private secretary, issued a proclamation informing the public that he had ordered Colonel F. Peraldi, commanding the northern district of the state, to communicate to the American commander through the Mexican consul in Eagle Pass that from the moment that the first American soldier crossed into Mexico, Espinoza Mireles would consider hostilities to have begun, and Peraldi was to fight the invader with all the forces at his command.[51]

On June 20, Secretary of State Lansing sent a sternly worded note, approved by President Wilson, to the Carranza administration in reply to Carranza's note of May 22. Lansing recounted American grievances with Carranza, emphasizing the Mexican raids into Texas and Nafarrate's role in them.

> Attention is again invited to the well-known and unrestricted activity of De la Rosa, Aniceto Pizaña, Pedro Vinos [Viña], and others in connection

with border raids and to the fact, as I am advised, up to June 4 De la Rosa was still collecting troops at Monterey [*sic*] for the openly avowed purpose of making attacks on Texan border towns, and that Pedro Vino was recruiting at another place for the same avowed purpose. . . . With the power of censorship of the Mexican press so rigorously exercised by the de facto Government, the responsibility for this activity cannot, it would seem, be avoided by that Government, and the issue of the appeal of Gen. Carranza himself, in the press of March 12, calling upon the Mexican people to be prepared for any emergency which might arise, and intimating that war with the United States was imminent, evidences the attitude of the de facto Government toward these publications.[52]

On June 20, Carranza telegraphed General Reynaldo Garza, commander at Nuevo Laredo, ordering him to do everything possible to prevent border raids and to exercise strict supervision over all Mexicans crossing the Rio Grande. Garza was to use all means in his power to prevent raiders from crossing the river, and if caught they were to be summarily executed.[53]

General Alvaro Obregón, Carranza's secretary of war and marine, weighed in. If his remarks were reported accurately, Obregón made one of the silliest speeches on record. Addressing students, he said: "In all contests of honor the contestants first take the measure of their arms in order that they may be able to fight on equal terms. If the United States desires to defend its honor unquestionably it should take the same number of men as we have and have them equally armed and fight on a field selected by mutual consent. But the United States does not intend to do this. It has designs to crush us with brute force and to defile our soil with the feet of the invader. Before this prospect we are determined to sacrifice the last drop of our blood to avoid it. It gives me the greatest satisfaction to see the attitude of the students far in the north as well as in the south of the republic."[54] Suggesting that Mexico and the United States settle their differences on some medieval field of honor was simply ridiculous. Speaking of Obregón, his role in the events preceding the war crisis remains unclear and merits further research.

By June 20, headlines read: ONLY A MIRACLE CAN AVOID BREAK WITH MEXICO IS BELIEF OF OFFICIALS; U.S. NOT TO FORCE HOSTILI-

TIES BUT ATTACK ON AMERICAN FORCES OR RAID WILL BE SIGNAL FOR INVASION; and WAR SEEMS INEVITABLE; and ARMY HEADS PLAN A COMBINED MOVE BY LAND AND SEA; WAR COLLEGE BELIEVES MATTERS GONE TOO FAR TO STOP SHORT OF INTERVENTION.

Further, "Officers of the Army General Staff and the Navy General Board are thoroughly convinced that Carranza intends to force war on the United States. They believe his course from the first has demonstrated this. They know that with the army of 35,000 to 50,000 men General Trevino has mobilized in Northern Mexico, Carranza could have long ago exterminated the bandits menacing the American frontier. The main Atlantic and Pacific fleets have been ordered to be ready to steam south at a moment's notice at the first sign of the opening of hostilities." The navy was confident that it could quickly blockade Mexican ports with little trouble. And the marines were anxious to revisit the halls of Montezuma.[55]

Then on June 21, there occurred a clash that seemed to mark the opening of hostilities. Two troops, some eighty men, of Pershing's black Tenth Cavalry under Captain Charles Boyd marched eastward to the hamlet of Carrizal, between Ciudad Juárez and the city of Chihuahua. Boyd tried to enter the town, which was defended by some three hundred *carrancista* troops under General Félix U. Gómez. Advancing across open ground, the Americans were raked by machine gun fire and suffered heavy casualties. The survivors who weren't captured retreated. Both Captain Boyd and General Gómez were killed in the engagement.[56]

The *Brownsville Daily Herald* commented editorially on the Carrizal clash: "The fact that the American soldiers engaged in the Carrizal fight were negroes must be an eye-opener to those Mexicans who have been cheating themselves with the dream of a negro-Mexican republic to be carved out of the southern United States. They are learning that the American negroes are not only satisfied to dwell under the American flag, knowing when they are well off, but also are loyal defenders of that flag."[57]

On June 21 President Wilson replied to a "personal and confidential" letter from Secretary of State Lansing. Wilson agreed with Lansing's suggestion not to use the term "intervention" in Mexico. The president "had thought to wait until hostilities were actually forced upon us. As I write this, 'extras' of the evening paper are being cried on the Avenue which, if true, mean that hostilities *have* begun."[58]

Also on June 21, it was reported that Aniceto Pizaña had been commissioned as a *carrancista* colonel.[59] And "information received from [a] Mexican source" was that General Fortunato Zuazua had established his headquarters at Sabinas (116 kilometers from Piedras Negras on the National Lines of Mexico). "Zuazua has 1200 raw recruits under his command scattered over the railroad. Circulars were posted at Piedras Negras signed by Jacinto Treviño, military commander of the northern states, for the Mexican people to arm themselves."[60]

On June 22 the American consul in Piedras Negras reported: "Had frank talk with Governor of Coahuila. Before leaving endeavored to impress upon him concentration of American troops along border did not imply invasion of Mexico; that they would not enter Mexico except upon Mexican initiation. . . . He still remains under the delusion that in the event of a rupture Mexico will receive assistance from many elements in the United States."[61]

On June 22, Major General Hugh Scott, chief of staff of the U.S. Army, was quoted as saying that "War may be declared at any moment."[62] The massive military buildup in the United States in which the National Guard was called up and placed on a war footing was surely more than just some kind of charade by Wilson in order to gain "diplomatic and political advantage."

On June 23, Carranza ordered the detention of de la Rosa and prohibited armed bands from crossing into the United States. General Pablo González was dismayed to learn that Ricaut had de la Rosa in custody in Monterrey. On June 24 he wired to Carranza: "Please tell me if this was Your Excellency's order and if said individual could be liberated so that he can proceed into the interior of the United States to continue carrying out the mission that he has in conjunction with Fierros."[63]

On June 23 the Mexican Foreign Office announced that de la Rosa had indeed been captured, the information based on a telegram from the military commandant of Tamaulipas.[64]

Carranza issued a proclamation calling on rebel chieftains to join in fighting the United States. And for its part, the U.S. Army began raising ten new regiments of regulars.[65]

On June 25 the secretary of war telegraphed the commanding generals of the Eastern, Central, and Western Departments: "Grave necessity for additional troops on border." In Brownsville, General Parker reported that in the event of war he would cross the Rio Grande with his three regiments of regulars, occupying the line from Matamoros to Camargo, dispersing any bandits or guerrillas encountered and establishing a base for an advance on Monterrey.[66]

The United States sent what amounted to an ultimatum to Carranza on June 25 demanding that he repudiate the attack at Carrizal and that he immediately release all the captured American soldiers being held in the Chihuahua penitentiary as well as all U.S. property captured with them.[67]

On June 26, Wilson drafted an address to a joint session of Congress requesting authorization to use the military power of the United States not only to protect the border but if necessary to enter Mexico and force the suspension of all military activities in the northern tier of Mexican states.[68] Mexico probably would have regarded this as a warlike act.

The war crisis was the moment of truth for Carranza and his policy of brinksmanship, and he folded. He agreed to the American demands. War was averted, and the disputes between the United States and Mexico were moved to the realm of diplomacy.

In an ironic footnote to the war crisis, an officer in Mexico City, Lieutenant Colonel Rosendo Maury, jubilantly sent to General Pablo González an "extra" edition of the newspaper *El Tribunal*, ostensibly published in San Diego, Texas, carrying a detailed account of the revolutionary movement and its triumphant progress in Texas.[69] What Maury didn't know of course was that, as we've seen from the printer's bill to Fierros, despite the San Diego dateline, the "extra" had actually been printed in Monterrey, part of the *carrancista* propaganda campaign.

The war crisis having passed, the bureau could get back to investigating the Plan de San Diego. On June 30, Agent Louis Mennet, writing from Rio Grande City, advised that there were Mexicans on both sides of the river who were willing to provide information but feared to do so, "knowing that if it became known that they had given such information they would surely be killed."[70]

Meanwhile, the Hungarian Forseck was still in Mexico City when the Japanese who'd accompanied Colonel Maurilio Rodríguez to the Texas border returned. Pablo Nago told Forseck that they'd returned because they'd received orders from the Japanese minister in Mexico City to do so under penalty of forfeiting their rank should they disobey. Forseck knew them by sight, Pablo Nago having previously pointed them out, "as Nago and Garza had boasted to me about these men being associated with them in the Texas Revolution." According to Forseck they were all Japanese officers. Pablo Nago told Forseck that the Japanese were quite disappointed with the actions and conduct of Maurilio Rodríguez, who, when the raid was made into Texas, remained on the Mexican bank of the Rio Grande. After relating all this, Nago said he'd been summoned to the Japanese legation by the minister for a conference.[71]

During the run-up to the June war crisis, General Pablo González had been coordinating the raids into Texas. He forwarded to Carranza the reports from Generals Juan Antonio Acosta, Fortunato Zuazua, and Esteban Fierros, and he asked the first chief for additional funds to keep the operation going. Acosta, who was a brigade commander under General Reynaldo Garza, the commander in Nuevo Laredo, issued a proclamation on June 20 stating that he intended to carry out General Ricaut's order to suppress bandit raids.[72] In a deliciously cynical development, on August 21, General Acosta, who had been Gonzalez's secret agent in Texas, was dispatched to Austin as the special representative of the Carranza government and had a lengthy conference with Governor Ferguson, assuring him of Venustiano Carranza's most distinguished compliments.[73]

Historian Alan Knight dismisses the Plan de San Diego out of hand. He states that since 1915 there had been sporadic incidents on the border, including Villa's Columbus raid, but "those did not add up to much." It would seem that the presence of the Punitive Expedition (which eventually totaled some 10,500 troops) in Chihuahua from March 15, 1916, to February 5, 1917, would qualify as something "much." Further, Knight discounts American fears of a Mexican invasion coupled with a Hispanic revolt as being "ill-founded and short-lived," adding that it's unclear that the Plan de San Diego and the border turmoil influenced events in Mexico. Knight suggests that Carranza's ability to police the border, not his alleged sponsorship of border raids, secured diplomatic recognition for his regime, and that fragmented authority, "not Machiavellian statecraft," accounts for the "apparently contradictory statements and policies of Carrancismo." In his view any contemplated invasion of the United States was inconceivable except in a war provoked by the United States. He raises the possibility that *carrancista* flirtation with Tejano agitators was just a contingency plan rather than the beginning of an aggressive war "which the Carrancistas would have been crazy to undertake."[74]

Knight seems unaware of the fact that on June 18, in response to the Plan de San Diego raid near Brownsville, President Wilson called up virtually the entire 158,000-strong National Guard of the United States, rushed most of them to the border, and ordered the Guard to recruit up to war strength immediately.

Secretary of War Newton D. Baker stated that "This call for militia is wholly unrelated to General Pershing's expedition and contemplates no additional entry into Mexico, except as may be necessary to pursue bandits who attempt outrages on American soil."[75] Some would consider the National Guard mobilization and deployment in response to a Plan de San Diego raid a significant event.

Knight's contention that the Plan had no effect on the course of the Mexican Revolution can be questioned on the ground that thereafter Carranza abandoned his policy of brinksmanship. When in 1917, Germany in the notorious Zimmermann telegram proposed a military alliance with Mexico by which Mexico would declare war on the United States and Germany would assist Mexico in recovering the American Southwest, Carranza prudently declined the offer.[76]

The proposed invasion appears to be what CIA official Duane R. Claridge uncharitably refers to as the "wog factor"—when, against all reason, a weaker nation decides to attack a stronger one.[77] The Japanese attack on Pearl Harbor and the Argentine seizure of the Falkland Islands come to mind.

There was a footnote to the Brigada Fierros's operations. Whereas most of Fierros's infiltrators had either slipped back across the Rio Grande or had melted into the Hispanic population, one forlorn group was still trying to carry out their mission. On June 20 a band of ten men dragged two Hispanics from their homes sixteen miles west of San Antonio and forced them to act as guides. According to one of their prisoners, the guerrillas were trying "to capture Texas and restore it to the Mexicans." He said the leader of the group told his guides that he was authorized to recruit Mexicans wherever he could get them to "fight for the First Chief Carranza." Sheriff John Tobin organized posses totaling two hundred men and composed of deputy sheriffs, federal Bureau of Investigation agents, city detectives, and citizens who set out from San Antonio in pursuit of the mounted fugitives. For the next three days posses staked out water tanks and scoured the area in automobiles. On June 23 the fugitives fired on two officers from the brush, but neither was hit. The officers returned fire, but the Mexicans, who had dwindled to four, escaped.[78]

The Plan de San Diego had passed into history. In assessing the movement as of July 1916, the army observed that "many times during the year there were reports of raids that had occurred, or were to occur, but which in fact never occurred. These reports were variously attributed to hysteria, and occasionally to a desire to keep troops in, or have more troops sent to, the locality concerned." After careful investigation the military identified thirty-eight cases that could be considered raids, "and it is even possible that some of these were acts of revenge or robbery rather than raids in the sense in which that word is commonly used."[79]

As for whether there had been a war crisis, President Wilson certainly believed there had been, as did the chief of staff of the U.S. Army. And the learned judges of the Texas Court of Criminal Appeals ruled that in 1916 there had existed an undeclared state of war along the Rio Grande. On April 17, 1918, the court reversed the Webb County district court's verdict in the case of the San Ignacio raiders.[80] Thus the prisoners weren't bandits as had been claimed at their trial but were prisoners of war. They were released to the commander at Fort McIntosh, who delivered them to Mexican consul Melquiades García, who escorted them to Nuevo Laredo, where they received a hero's welcome.[81]

17 Aftermath

In the aftermath of the war crisis, General Zuazua moved from Piedras Negras to Monterrey, leaving there on July 20 for Mexico City.[1] Esteban Fierros moved into the Hotel del Centro in Monterrey, occupying room 13, across the hall from Agustín Garza.

Fierros said he was in dire financial straits. He dispatched José María Zuazua, General Zuazua's brother, to Mexico City with a letter to General Pablo González requesting that the latter pay Zuazua's expenses for his trip to Monterrey; Fierros was broke. José María Zuazua, incidentally, was taking General Zuazua's furniture to Monterrey—in two boxcars. González approved the expenditure and gave Zuazua a letter of recommendation to Carranza's chief of staff.[2] A week later, Fierros on June 30 wired a "very urgent" appeal in cipher to General Pablo González at his Cuernavaca headquarters. Fierros informed the general that Juan M. García, "a millionaire of the Revolution," was prepared to advance funds to Agustín Garza but only if General González authorized the move.[3] If González approved, Fierros urged that the funds be dispatched by train immediately. And he added that on that day's southbound train there had left a courier who would personally deliver a letter recounting the difficulties they had experienced.[4]

Fierros was involved in numerous financial transactions, as shown by the accounts of the Fierros Brigade found in General González's papers. Perhaps the most interesting items are:

June 30	Colonel E. E. Fierros in account with E. Hellion y Cia.: June 21–30, meals for Mr. Luis de la Rosa at 4 pesos a day, and on June 30 a bottle of wine—210 pesos.		
July 28	E. E. Fierros in account with E. Hellion y Cia.: for Luis de la Rosa—		
	July 2	1 beer	4 pesos
	July 2	4 meals	40 pesos
	July 2	2 boxes corn-shuck cigarettes	3 pesos
	31 days of meals at		
		4 pesos	620 pesos
		Total	667 pesos
	E. E. Fierros account:		
	July 14 bar		123 pesos
	July 15 bar		37.50 pesos
	July 18 bar		52 pesos
	July 18 6 breakfasts		37.50 pesos
	July 18 20 dinners		200 pesos
	July 19 26 dinners		260 pesos
		Total	710 pesos
July 29	Received of the treasury of the Fierros Brigade 1,000 pesos for my expenses. General Luis de la Rosa.		

Fierros wrote to González from Calzada Unión number 80 in Monterrey explaining that during the time he spent in Mexico City his illnesses and later those of his wife in Monterrey had prevented him from arranging his affairs and talking with Carranza to learn how he could best continue to serve. He therefore asked González to speak with the first chief, as Fierros was jobless and in financial difficulty. If possible, he wanted to return to working on the Constitutionalist Railways. He also asked González to send him an order on the Constitutionalist Lines for two boxcars so he could ship his horses and his two automobiles to Mexico City (which raises the question of just how "broke" he was). Fierros reiterated that he was desperate.[5] González replied that at the earliest opportunity he would talk with Carranza about Fierros's plight, and González enclosed a letter to the governor of Nuevo León authorizing Fierros's boxcars and directing that the fee be charged to González's headquarters.[6] González subsequently suggested that Fierros contact the director of the Constitutionalist Railways regarding employment.[7] On December 28, 1916, González gave Fierros a letter of recommendation to General Francisco Murguía, commander in Chihuahua, explaining that Fierros sought employment on the Constitutionalist Lines.[8]

In September, General González had received a plaintive letter from Captain Pedro Yoshida in Mexico City, writing in the absence of his general, Luis Elías Pérez, commanding the First Brigade of the Division of the East. The general had to leave unexpectedly for the north and told Captain Yoshida that General Esteban E. Fierros would supply their rations. Unfortunately, when Yoshida talked with Fierros, the latter caused a lot of difficulty and refused to provide the rations. Yoshida said he and the troops hadn't eaten for the last two days. He asked for railroad passes to join their general and for rations to save them from starvation.[9]

Meanwhile, Agustín Garza was having financial troubles of his own. Garza ran up substantial bills at the Hotel del Centro in Monterrey through October for the lodging of a number of his associates. Likewise, he paid for three meals a day until July 25 for twenty men at the Restaurante Mexicano in Monterrey. Interestingly enough, ten of these individuals had Japanese names.[10] Garza himself was short of cash, having to wire his brother in Tampico for five hundred pesos.[11]

Some of the less fortunate Plan de San Diego types were now cooling their heels in the Matamoros jail. One Eduardo Leal gave Agent Rogers the names of those who were in jail at the same time as he was: Antonio L. Rocha, Manuel Longoria, Tomás Guzmán, Manuel Zamora, Victor Flores, Victor Ramos, Octaviano Cantú, and Eugenio García. Leal said that Octaviano Cantú owned a house in Mission and that a man living in that house constantly brought Cantú information about developments on the Texas side of the river. Leal also reported that the Mexicans had a very complete espionage system and kept well posted about everything that was going on. According to Leal, Julián García, a brother of Eugenio García, was a spy who frequently came to the American side. He was a small, slender man, about twenty years old, with a little mustache, curly hair, dark complexion, and dressed well. Another spy was Anacleto Ramos, about twenty-three years old, beardless, of Indian appearance, and was short and heavy-set.[12]

An American agent in Monterrey reported on July 16 that it had been eight days since Luis de la Rosa had left the jail in which he'd been imprisoned, that he was now living with Esteban Fierros and his family in Monterrey, and that the German consul had furnished five thousand Mauser rifles and twenty thousand rounds of ammunition being held by General Nafarrate at Tampico for use in the Texas revolution.[13]

Propaganda continued. On July 20, 1916, the newspaper *El Día* in Monterrey published that "general headquarters at San Antonio, Texas [!]," on June 19 reported that the liberating troops, operating in connection with the Mexican soldiers, were advancing toward Falfurrias. They had taken Gloria, and later had taken Falfurrias. That same day there occurred another imaginary feat of arms—the liberating troops wrecked a passenger train near Arlington, between Fort Worth and Dallas, disarming a gringo guard of fifty and executing some of them. These battles of course existed only in some propagandist's fertile imagination. Agent Barnes sent to his chief a translation of an article from *El Día* of June 22, commenting: "In view of the fact that this alleged publication is under the control of the de facto government, the contents of this news item are rather interesting."[14]

There were still some last gasps of the Plan de San Diego, however. Sometime after the clash on June 21 at Carrizal, involving elements of the black Tenth Cavalry, someone purporting to be "Negro Delegate Number 33" and representing the Revolutionary Congress of San Diego, Texas, wrote in longhand a screed titled "Negro Brothers Come to Life and Liberty," urging them not to be used like the "10th Regiment" and never to take up arms against Mexico. The document also called for them to assert their rights against the white man. Although written in English, the document was produced by someone whose native language was Spanish; for instance, instead of "cannon" was written "cañón."[15]

The bureau was assisting in preparing cases against alleged Plan de San Diego militants. Guadalupe Ramos, indicted by a federal grand jury in 1916 on a charge of seditious conspiracy, pleaded guilty in federal court on May 18, 1917, and was sentenced to five months and twenty days in the Cameron County jail. Since his sentence ran from December 28, 1916, he had already served most of his time. Quirino Guajardo, accused of murder, was acquitted of the charge.[16]

Lorenzo López was charged with participation in the Olmito train wreck. His lawyers, the firm of Graham, Jones, and Pierce, attempted to get his bond, recently set by the Court of Criminal Appeals, reduced. It was in fact reduced by half. As it developed, the charges against López were dismissed. In 1913, López had lived in Matamoros and became a captain of volunteers in that city. He killed a captain in the federal army and fled to Brownsville shortly before the Constitutionalist general Lucio Blanco captured Matamoros. In 1915 he was arrested in connection with the Olmito train wreck. After the charges against him were dismissed, he continued to live in Brownsville. In late 1917 he was a lieutenant colonel in the *felicista* movement fighting against the *carrancistas* in Nuevo León and Tamaulipas.[17]

The bonds of some others in the Brownsville jail accused of being *sediciosos* were also reduced: that of Quirino Guajardo to twenty-five hundred dollars (Guajardo was eventually acquitted) and that of Refugio Domínguez to three thousand dollars. If they couldn't post the bonds they remained in jail until the November term of the federal court. Domínguez, however, died before his case came to trial.[18] Jesús Guerra of Raymondville, charged with involvement in the Plan de San Diego, was released on a five-hundred-dollar bond.[19]

Ramón Pizaña, Aniceto's brother, had been arrested in his mother's house after the shootout at Los Tulitos ranch in August 1915. He was hiding beneath blankets under a bed. Pizaña was held to the grand jury without bail in Brownsville, on a charge of helping the *sediciosos* in the Tulitos fight. His case was continued until November 1916. His attorneys, the firm of Canales and Dancey, began habeas corpus proceedings on his behalf and arranged a twenty-five-hundred-dollar bond for Pizaña, but he couldn't raise the money.[20] Pizaña was convicted in district court of the killing of Corporal McGuire, Twelfth Cavalry, in the firefight and was sentenced to fifteen years in the penitentiary.[21] But the Texas Court of Criminal Appeals in March 1917 reversed the verdict on the grounds that there was insufficient evidence to support a conviction. Pizaña was released from the Cameron County jail.[22]

On August 28 and 29, 1916, Agent Rogers went to Matamoros. There he met Vicente Dávila, "one of the worst of the border bandits, wanted on this side in several indictments, who is now an officer of the Carranza army. He said he would be glad for something to start so that he could make some more raids on this side. As he expressed it: 'Now we cannot flap our wings over there, because there are too many Gringo soldiers.'" "I also saw Aniceto Pizaña, who is an officer of the army. I asked him where his men are. He replied they are not far away. . . . I had a conversation with General Ricaut and he told me that General Nafarrate and General Procopio Alesando [Arredondo?] are both prisoners in Mexico City. It is feared that if Nafarrate should be allowed to come to the frontier, he might cause trouble. On the reported imprisonment of Nafarrate I place no credence. I know Nafarrate and know the place he holds in the public opinion of Mexico. There is not a man in Mexico big enough or bold enough to put him in prison. He may be detained in Mexico [City] for diplomatic reasons but he is not a prisoner."[23]

Rogers also reported, through an informant, that on September 10 the informant went to Matamoros and learned that "Abel Sandoval and Ricardo Gómez, owners of a gambling house in Matamoros and both members of Col. Aniceto Pizaña's brigade, also both being Texas Mexicans prominent in the bandit raids of a year ago, last Sunday badly beat an American in their joint because he was too lucky."[24]

And the bureau in October compiled a partial list of those who were known to have participated in the raids around Brownsville and who hadn't been apprehended by the Mexican government.[25] For its part the Cameron County grand jury returned a series of indictments.[26] Although the Plan de San Diego was dead, the authorities remained keenly interested in its participants.

18 Informants

Although the Bureau of Investigation remained interested in the Plan de San Diego players, information was not always easy to come by. Agent W. A. Wiseman wrote from San Antonio in July 1916 that he had arranged to send a Mexican informant to Monclova. Unfortunately, the man had backed out, saying he didn't feel he'd be safe in Mexico. Wiseman couldn't find a reliable replacement, so he offered to make the trip himself, telling his superiors that he'd secured "several good passports" from friends holding responsible positions in the Carranza government and would make the trip under his own responsibility. "I assure you that should anything happen, my mission shall never become known." Wiseman was quite confident of maintaining his cover. Not only had he been working undercover in San Antonio, but he'd entered Mexico several times without being molested. He earnestly requested that he be permitted to show what he could do.[1]

Wiseman's wish was granted. He made a trip to Monterrey seeking the whereabouts of Luis de la Rosa and reporting that "Luis Hellion, a Spaniard proprietor of the Continental Hotel and [the] Iturbide [Hotel] informed me where de la Rosa was, at [the] Cuartel General (Headquarters)." The next day, August 30, Hellion pointed out de la Rosa to Wiseman in the lobby of the Iturbide Hotel The *sedicioso* leader was accompanied by a captain of the garrison and by a certain Alberto Valdés. De la Rosa's left hand was bandaged; according to Hellion, he'd been wounded in one of his border raids. "Luis de la Rosa is under arrest and makes his appearance once a day to the headquarters here; his family is living on Zaragoza Street #243 near the Gulf station."

Wiseman secured further information about de la Rosa from Major Julio Colunga, a member of the governor's staff who was in close touch with Plan de San Diego chieftains. According to Colunga, de la Rosa had been an officer in General Emiliano Nafarrate's brigade in Matamoros. Moreover, "Luis de la Rosa and León Caballo came to Monterrey and drew up the Plan de San Diego, which was published or either printed by *El Día* and afterwards sent to Texas to be distributed." One Jesús Villarreal carried the Plan to Texas and was León Caballo's agent there. During the 1916 crisis, Carranza authorized de la Rosa and Caballo to recruit in order to invade Texas at a point across from Reynosa. De la Rosa assembled two hundred men at the headquarters of the Thirty-Ninth Regiment on Avenida Madero in Monterrey. The city's military commander, General Pablo de la Garza, aided him with equipment. When de la Rosa went to the border, Caballo remained in Monterrey, sending subordinates such as Severo Jiménez to Coahuila and Vicente Lira to Colombia on the Rio Grande.

Wiseman added that in July de la Rosa returned to Monterrey and was arrested by the military commander. Caballo went to Mexico City, while José Miranda took charge of de la Rosa's followers at Reynosa and raided several ranches in that vicinity. At the present time León Caballo, José Miranda, and Alberto Valdés were the active workers in Monterrey. They tried to organize a body of men on August 15, but due to the failure of Caballo's followers to secure financial aid and equipment they disbanded. De la Rosa and Caballo had a disagreement and they seemed to have separated. Wiseman returned to the United States through Eagle Pass on September 2.[2]

Informant José García, whose real name was Juan Cisneros, reported to "F. Ligardi," Agent Barnes's accommodation address in San Antonio. García was back in Monterrey in October 1916. On October 11 he advised that Garza and Basilio Ramos were together in room 12, Central Hotel, and that Aniceto Pizaña wanted to mount another raid in Texas. García then proceeded on to Torreón.[3]

With Agent Breniman as his handler, the bureau arranged for García to make another trip in November, to report on the Mexican Army in northern Mexico and specifically to check on the status of the Plan de San Diego. From Monterrey he would proceed on to Mexico City, "where he will endeavor to obtain information concerning the report that German submarines are operating on the coast of Mexico south of Veracruz."[4]

On this trip, from November 9 to 30, García commented extensively on the Mexican government's aviation efforts. He also wrote that Esteban Fierros was in Mexico City, Nafarrate was in Tampico, Pizaña was in Matamoros, and Agustín Garza, Basilio Ramos, and Maurilio Rodríguez were in Monterrey. De la Rosa was also in Monterrey but was no longer confined to the barracks. "Some of the Chiefs, among them Rodríguez, have been kind enough to give me a very interesting report. Said report is that they have received an order from General Fierros, who received it from Carranza. Fierros said to have all the men ready, as everything depended on the elections in the United States, for if Wilson is not elected, they will again start attacking the border towns. The report was confirmed by one of the officers of Pizaña, when I was in Matamoros."[5]

García arrived in Monterrey on November 12, reporting that "I talked with persons interested in the matter. They tell me that they think there will be no danger during this month. Nevertheless Pizaña ought to be watched as he may try one of his schemes, although he has orders to remain inactive."[6]

In December, García traveled to Mexico City, where he profitably sold a quantity of flour he'd bought in the United States. García reported that de la Rosa was no longer confined to the barracks in Monterrey and that Basilio Ramos had told him that "the revolutionary movement was about to end as all the men were disappointed on account of there being no money."

On December 23, García talked in Monterrey with Joaquín Sada, "former Secretary of de la Rosa," who said General Ricaut had imprisoned de la Rosa in the barracks near the railroad station because they had quarreled. He also learned that Maurilio Rodríguez had been in Nuevo Laredo for some time. "It would be well to watch and see if he should cross the river." On December 26 he reported that the *sediciosos* were anxiously awaiting the exchange of their ammunition. The twenty thousand rounds on which the movement depended were defective, reaching only to a thousand meters, but a general in Saltillo had offered to exchange them. Informant García was a good friend of José Chávez, Agustín Garza's secretary, who kept him informed on a daily basis about *sedicioso* activities.

On December 28, García inquired about Esteban Fierros and learned that he had been in Mexico City for some time and that he had promised his followers that he'd return soon with some money to resume operations. "Very few people believe him." On December 29, García "talked to some of Garza's officers and other leaders, and they seemed to be very disappointed. I think the department [the federal Bureau of Investigation] need not worry about them, for some months at least, for I think that this revolution had gone to nothing. It seems that this [*sic*] men like the Carrancistas are not paying attention to the revolution but to making money, as they see their end coming and wish to be well supplied with money for the future." On December 30, García wrote that Agustín Garza was in Mexico City, Maurilio Rodríguez was in Saltillo, and Luis de la Rosa was in Reynosa. That same day García left for Matamoros, where he spoke with several officers concerning Pizaña. "They told me that these men have completely fallen; that for a long time they have kept up merely through promises, and that the majority of them are now working in different things, as they have lost hopes of making money."[7]

Yet another informant, the Japanese Frank Fukuda, who had a perfume business in Monterrey, was in Monterrey and Linares, Nuevo León, in December 1916. At the time, Agustín S. Garza was living in the Hotel del Centro in Monterrey. "I heard that he is a poor man now, but somebody is helping him." Fukuda said that Esteban Fierros was living in a house, number 80, Calzada Francisco I. Madero, in Monterrey, but he was in Mexico City at present, as was his private secretary, Major Alfonso Gómez M., "a former Villista under Raul Madero." Fukuda knew him well.[8]

Of course the bureau also received intelligence from the Texas side of the Rio Grande. Prominent in South Texas was the Idar family of Laredo, who published *La Crónica* newspaper, "that did more than any other venue to articulate the Progressive viewpoint to south Texas's Tejano community." Nicasio Idar was both editor and publisher. Three of his children, Jovita, Clemente, and Eduardo, were the principal writers for the newspaper. "After the ordeal of the Plan de San Diego, Clemente and Eduardo would help to pioneer Mexican-American politics."[9] Clemente has been described as a "labor organizer, journalist, civil-rights activist, and orator."[10] He became an icon in the Mexican American civil rights movement.

What is perhaps not as well known is that he also became an informant for the federal Bureau of Investigation. The earliest mention of him in this connection was in May 1916. But Idar was not just an informer; he became a "Special Employee" of the bureau, ranking just under "Special Agent." Adeptly utilizing his job as a journalist, Idar worked undercover, and by June 3 he was submitting written reports and translating documents in Laredo for Tom Ross. Idar also explained to his superior, Agent Barnes, that he was denying to suspicious immigration officers that he worked for the government, for "I believe it unnecessary to work in with such officers. I can get information that they cannot possibly obtain. The more you permit me to develop my work without divulging it to anyone but yourself, the better I think I can work for you. However, this is not a suggestion nor an opinion, for I am most absolutely determined to bend my will to your superior knowledge and instructions."[11]

Barnes authorized Idar to pay "a reasonable amount" for information.[12] And Idar passed along the word that his brother had just arrived in Laredo, and on the train it was freely discussed that the raids would begin on June 10.[13] Idar received reports on Mexican troop dispositions from the sheriff of Zapata County. He also discreetly debriefed passengers arriving from Mexico by train.[14] And Idar experienced the frustrations of dealing with bureaucracy. Tom Ross reported that "Mr. Idar and myself are at a loss to know as to what to do in reference to our per diem and expense account, having received no blanks in which to make out our accounts."[15] But Idar's reports kept coming, and he provided useful details about de la Rosa's activities. His June 20 report contains much information on the background of Esteban Fierrros.[16]

Idar said his mother and brother had just returned from Monterrey on July 27, 1916, and told him that Generals Esteban Fierros and Manuel García Vigil were summoned to Mexico City by First Chief Carranza and were on their way there. De la Rosa was still in the penitentiary in Monterrey, according to common gossip. Idar's mother said she knew positively that General Esteban Fierros paid, in a Monterrey restaurant, apparently from his own means, the board of a good many of the men whom he impressed into the service of the raiding bands. "My mother being mentioned in this report, I respectfully request that same be treated with the reserve it merits."[17]

Idar notified his colleague Tom Ross that "the de facto officers have been gradually arresting the San Diego raiders wherever found." Ross speculated that Isabel de los Santos, knowing this, had gone to some other part of Mexico.[18] Idar mentioned on August 10 that his informant stated that General Fierros, who'd gone to Mexico City in response to a telegraphic order from Carranza, had returned to Monterrey with his status intact. At the time of the raids the Fierros Brigade boarded for many days at the restaurant for railroad men situated near the yards in Monterrey. They also camped for several days at Topo Chico, in the northern suburbs of the city. Most of the men were railroad employees from different branches of the service, and Idar's informant characterized them as "one of the toughest crowds he has seen in all his life."[19]

Idar reported from San Antonio in August, explaining that he was not familiar with that city. But he was soon working his way into the Mexican exile community.[20] The bureau even asked him to assist in persuading one Esteban Guerrero, said to be in Monterrey, to return to Laredo, where he'd be served with a subpoena to testify before the grand jury.[21] However, Idar's bureau associate Tom Ross was distressed because Idar appeared to be indiscreet, for example, using the district clerk's phone in the presence of the district clerk's son to discuss sensitive matters.[22] In 1917 the bureau decided that Idar's services weren't satisfactory because of his indiscretions, and he was dismissed. In November 1917 he wrote a confidential letter to James P. Tumulty, President Wilson's secretary, giving his views on revolutionary activity, especially on attacks against the Mexican government by the newspapers *La Prensa* and *Revista Mexicana* in San Antonio.[23] In 1919 the bureau described Idar as a "labor agitator."[24]

The bureau's investigations were also focused directly on the town of San Diego itself. In August, Special Employee Manuel Sorola, using the cover name of "Manuel Rodríguez," went there undercover as an agent provocateur armed with two commissions that the San Antonio office of the bureau had forged for him, so that he could infiltrate any revolutionary cell. One of the documents, ostensibly signed at the headquarters of the revolution by General in Chief Luis de la Rosa and Isabel de los Santos, commander of the "Equity [*sic*] Regiment," commissioned "Manuel Rodríguez" as a major in the "Equitative [*sic*] Reconquering Army." Just in case he came across a *villista* conspiracy, the other document commissioned him as a major in Pancho Villa's Liberating Army. The commission was ostensibly signed by Francisco Villa at Chihuahua on April 12, 1916.[25] However, when the forger signed Villa's name, he signed it as "Francis Villa." The sloppy tradecraft went unnoticed—no one in the bureau caught the misspelling of Villa's name. Fortunately for Sorola he didn't have to use the commission.

Sorola used his cover as an insurance salesman during his stay in San Diego. Evidently he didn't need the forged commissions, for he decided to go by the name of "Manuel Zorola," not much of a cover.[26] He ingratiated himself with the locals, who proved friendly enough, and he uncovered no revolutionary activity. However, Sorola succeeded in locating Agustín Garza's sister, Margarita Garza de Barrera, married to Macario Barrera. She said that her brother Francisco Garza wrote to her from Mexico saying not to worry about their brother Agustín. "She also said that she has another brother by the name of José Garza. Last month he wrote to her from New York City."[27]

Sorola commented that the Texas Rangers were in town enforcing the liquor laws and shutting down the local gambling parlor, but bootlegging flourished in San Diego. Several days later he mentioned that the businessmen and better class of citizens weren't interested in politics of any kind or in revolution. "They are very quiet and good citizens, but when I start to work among the peon class of Mexicans, I discover right away the anti-American feeling."[28]

Sorola hired an automobile and went to the camp where about thirty Mexicans were working on the Texas-Mexican Railroad. Again portraying himself as a revolutionary organizer, Sorola learned that they'd gladly join a revolution "if it was a revolution against the United States but if it was for another revolution in Mexico, against Carranza, they will not do it because they are tired of that." The Mexicans warned Sorola to be very careful, because if an Anglo learned of his activities, in less than twenty-four hours the Texas Rangers would have him in jail or kill him.[29]

The versatile Sorola traveled to Corpus Christi to interview José A. Vázquez and Luciano Villarreal, whom the Rangers had arrested in San Diego on April 4, 1917, on suspicion of being Carranza officers and connected with the Plan de San Diego. Because the Rangers felt that they "did not want to put them in jail at San Diego, because all the County Officers were Mexicans and they would not get any justice or protection," they asked Sheriff Robinson if they could transfer them to Corpus Christi.[30] Sorola introduced himself as their attorney, assuring the prisoners that he would represent them in court, but of course they had to tell their attorney the truth. It turned out that the prisoners had gone to San Diego merely to look for work, and the matter was dropped.[31]

The bureau continued its efforts to investigate the Plan de San Diego. Agent Mennet interviewed a number of people. A certain Charles Coy was implicated by the two Mexicans named by Sam Robertson by numbers (to safeguard their identities) as being involved with the Plan. The U.S. attorney was of the opinion that the state of Texas should prosecute people like Coy rather than the federal government because Texas would impose a harsher punishment.[32] Manuel and Jesús Treviño, Emeregildo Cruz, and Sóstenes Saldaña Jr. were also reportedly connected with the killings of Donaldson and Smith in 1915. One informant stated that Aniceto Pizaña, Eduardo García, Ricardo Gómez Pizaña, Manuel Treviño, Felipe Campos, Jesús Treviño, Margarito Buenrostro, and Aniceto Pizaña's son had fired at the posse in the 1915 fight at Los Tulitos ranch. José González, brother of Bernardo, who worked on Jeff Scribner's ranch, stated that the son of Ramón Pizaña had once asked him to subscribe to *Regeneración*, the *magonista* newspaper, but he had refused. Furthermore, one Faustino García was a compadre of Aniceto Pizaña and could allegedly shed considerable light on Pizaña's organization if he could be made to talk.[33]

The problems that Anglo lawmen such as Agent Mennet faced in trying to obtain information from Hispanics are illustrated in one of his reports. He called on Alfredo Garza, who had been recommended to him by Sam Robertson and others in San Benito as a reliable informant. Mennet had recently approached Garza in hopes that he would introduce Mennet to other informants, but Garza claimed to know nothing in addition to the little that he'd already told Mennet and said he really had no knowledge of Pizaña's efforts to organize in that vicinity. Mennet was convinced that Garza knew more, and he recommended that if Garza's schoolteacher daughter could be approached without Garza's knowledge by someone who could gain her confidence, she would tell the bureau enough to pressure Garza to talk. Mennet believed Garza wanted to provide information but was afraid to do so.[34]

One thing the bureau learned was that the *sediciosos* had gone far afield in their efforts to attract support. Andrés García, the *carrancista* consul and intelligence chief in El Paso, informed the bureau in January 1916 that a messenger bearing dispatches from Pancho Villa had informed García that eight men in an automobile had gone to see Villa at Valle de San Buenaventura, in Chihuahua, entering through the port of Columbus, New Mexico. The men were both Mexicans and Tejanos and were authorized to offer Villa the leadership of the Plan de San Diego. Allegedly Villa sent men to investigate the strength of the movement; he was not impressed and declined the offer.[35]

19 Further Investigation

The bureau continued to rely on a stable of informers, some of whom were less than enthusiastic. Agent Mennet had tried to persuade one Amado Cavazos, who had operated a store in Santa María on the Rio Grande and was now living in Nuevo Laredo, to cross into Laredo and tell what he knew of the San Diego movement, but Cavazos refused, and Mennet felt it was too dangerous for him, Mennet, to cross into Mexico.[1]

On January 1, 1917, Agent Rogers at Brownsville had arranged to send a paid informant in whom he had confidence, Jesús María González, a Mexican merchant, to learn what he could about the current status of Plan de San Diego players Aniceto Pizaña, Luis de la Rosa, Evaristo Ramos, Basilio Ramos, Agustín Garza, Emiliano Nafarrate, Esteban Fierros, and Maurilio Rodríguez. Informant González was of the opinion that a conspiracy had existed in 1915 by the Carranza administration to launch raids into Texas as a ploy to get Carranza diplomatic recognition, and "they boast now that the purpose was actually accomplished." González added that the ignorant class of Mexicans actually believed that the Texas revolution had succeeded and that Texas had been overrun and plundered, a view based on the propaganda they'd been receiving.[2]

The Carranza authorities announced that de la Rosa was arrested in Monterrey on January 11, 1917, for having plotted with disaffected army officers to seize the city. De la Rosa, allegedly the chief conspirator, had planned to arrest Pablo de la Garza, the governor of Nuevo León; General Alfredo Ricaut, the military commandant; the mayor; and other notables on January 16. The conspiracy was discovered and de la Rosa was arrested together with several mutinous officers before the plot could be implemented.[3] Reportedly several of the Carranza officers who had supported de la Rosa at one time "now were ready to overthrow him." The speculation—improbable as it was—was that de la Rosa might have made arrangements to deliver the city to Pancho Villa or to the *felicistas*. General Ricaut announced to reporters that all those arrested were going to be tried by a military court and would be given the penalty they deserved.[4]

On January 25, informant Fukuda visited Agustín S. Garza in Garza's room, number 19, at the Hotel Independencia in Monterrey. He found Garza reading a book. Garza knew Fukuda and received him warmly. After the usual pleasantries in which Garza inquired about Fukuda's perfume business, the Japanese asked him about de la Rosa. Garza bitterly replied that the man was "a fool and a drunkard. I did so much for him until now." Asked if de la Rosa would be executed, Garza replied, "No, he has some very influential political friends," and expressed doubts that de la Rosa had actually planned to revolt. Changing the subject, Fukuda asked when Garza planned to revive his revolutionary movement. Garza answered, "Someday. I have not given up yet, only the First Chief does not want us to make trouble." With regard to the Texas revolution, Fukuda reported that Garza had two Japanese friends in Mexico. "One of them was his right hand man in the Texas revolution. His name is Kuwabara" (aka "Pablo Nago"?).[5]

Informant Fukuda reported on January 28, that he had made inquiries about de la Rosa and was told that he was imprisoned with eight or nine of his comrades and was enjoying much consideration inside the penitentiary although facing court-martial. The *sedicioso* Pedro Viña was brought from Villaldama under arrest and confined in the penitentiary.[6] Fukuda added that the president of the court-martial, Francisco G. Peña, had returned from Querétaro, and the tribunal would soon convene to try Enrique Valle, de la Rosa, and a number of others.[7]

Interestingly, though, Ed Gifford, a Monterrey businessman, told bureau agent Mennet in January that he had personally witnessed de la Rosa having dinner with General Alvaro Obregón, Carranza's secretary of war and marine, in the latter's private railroad car at the Monterrey station. "Informant does not remember the date but says positively that it was after the United States had been officially informed that de la Rosa was detained in the Monterrey penitentiary awaiting trial. Informant also said that de la Rosa used to spend most of his time in the saloon of Rodríguez Hnos. in Monterrey where he made it a point to insult and throw slurs at every American he happened to see."[8]

Rudolph Leopold Panster, formerly chief of the secret police in Yucatán, who claimed to have been until recently "employed in a secret service capacity by the Carrancistas in Monterrey and was assigned to investigate the activities of de la Rosa in which he was charged with having instituted a plot to cause the garrison of Monterrey to revolt," gave a statement to the bureau in Laredo in January. Panster claimed that he'd been placed in a cell adjoining that of de la Rosa in the Monterrey penitentiary and that de la Rosa had given him a note for delivery to a friend in Monterrey "which enabled the Carrancistas to locate guns and ammunition stored by de la Rosa to be used by the revolters. Panster states that when he left Monterrey the latter part of January, 1917, de la Rosa was still confined in jail awaiting sentence." Panster subsequently became a confidential informant of the bureau.

Informant Fukuda, traveling on his perfume business, reported in February that he'd gone to see a lawyer named Espinoza in Monterrey about when de la Rosa's court-martial would be convened. "He said that he had not any notice yet." Fukuda also looked up Agustín S. Garza again at the Hotel Independencia, room number 19. Garza expressed his virulent anti-American views and decried the deaths of innocent Mexicans in Texas. Garza said that de la Rosa would soon be tried by court-martial as a colonel. Garza commented that he had a concession to import about five hundred automobiles without paying a cent of duty, and if he made any money he'd go to South America or elsewhere.

Fukuda observed that "Garza is not so interested in the Texas revolution at present. Seems to me that he is financially broke." Garza also gave Fukuda Basilio Ramos's address: 39 Matamoros Street, in Nuevo Laredo. Fukuda went to see Ramos, "former secretary of Agustín Garza," at his home, reporting that "He keeps a soda factory and is [a] general commission merchant."[9]

A subsequent informant report claimed that de la Rosa had been court-martialed on March 6 in Monterrey for sedition and was sentenced to death.[10] However, the American vice consul in Monterrey reported on March 27, that de la Rosa would be tried by court-martial "next week."[11] De la Rosa and Pedro Viña were supposed to have been sentenced to be executed for sedition at the court-martial, but a bureau informant subsequently saw de la Rosa on the streets with a Carranza officer who was apparently guarding him; he concluded that the *sedicioso* chieftain had as much liberty now as before the court-martial. Some bureau sources in Monterrey believed that the charges against de la Rosa were fake, the plan being to send him to southern Mexico and then report that he'd been executed for sedition.[12]

Significantly, the cloud of obfuscation ended with de la Rosa regaining his liberty instead of being shot for sedition, an offense that the Carranza administration ordinarily took very seriously. As for Pedro Viña, in April 1917 he was reportedly a Carranza colonel stationed at Villaldama, Nuevo León.[13]

In March 1917, State Department agent George Carothers wrote that the border situation was becoming more desperate every day. Mexicans were destitute and were ready to do almost anything. This accounted for the large number of small bands that were continually crossing back and forth across the Rio Grande "with hatred against everybody in their hearts, and ready to commit depredations anywhere, in the United States or Mexico." These groups were fodder for the promoters of the Plan de San Diego. "When Carranza realizes that he is lost, he will countenance these border troubles again. . . . All of the Socialists and I. W. W. are in with the San Diego Plan, and I am of the opinion that the Flores Magón, of Los Angeles are in it. I also have suspicions of [the refugee] General Antonio Villarreal, in San Antonio."[14]

In June 1917, army intelligence reported that the old leaders of the Plan of San Diego were gathering in Monterrey. Maurilio Rodríguez and Pedro Viña were known to be near the city. The headquarters for the rejuvenation of this Plan were supposed to be the offices of Salinas y Garza, "both assumed names, since Garza was formerly known as León Caballo, while the real name of Salinas is Santiago." (Army intelligence was a bit confused about names.) General Ricaut, considered friendly toward the United States, was expected to prevent this movement from gathering much headway. The report also mentioned that the secret police in Monterrey were very numerous, utilizing hack drivers, drayman, and so forth.

In July 1917 it was reported from Brownsville that Aniceto Pizaña, his brother Ramón, and de la Rosa had been arrested by order of Carranza. The Pizañas were arrested at Ciudad Victoria and de la Rosa at Matamoros. De la Rosa was reportedly confined in the penitentiary in Monterrey. A strong guard accompanied them to Mexico City.[15] But it turned out that this story originated with the *Brownsville Daily Herald*, whose editor admitted to Agent Mennet that he'd simply heard the story shortly before going to press, so he published it without verifying the facts. This incident illustrates the difficulty the bureau had in separating fact from rumor and conjecture.

Mennet then inquired of one of the Mexican secret service men in Brownsville, José Alemán, and was told that de la Rosa, the Pizañas, Abel Sandoval, and others of their crowd had been arrested in Matamoros and vicinity and sent to Ciudad Victoria on orders of General Ricaut and that others were being watched. The Mexican agent also told Mennet that he had seen Aniceto Pizaña (or a man he believed to be him) at a house of prostitution in Matamoros, on Sunday, July 15. One of Mennet's confidential informants reported that the smugglers he was infiltrating said that Aniceto Pizaña had been living at a ranch near Matamoros belonging to his brother Ramón.

Judge Frank Pierce, a Brownsville attorney recently returned from Tampico and Ciudad Victoria, advised Mennet that he had seen de la Rosa on the streets of Victoria on Thursday, July 12, that he knew de la Rosa before his *sedicioso* activities, that when he saw him in Victoria he was wearing a pistol, and that they did not speak but de la Rosa smiled at him from across the street.[16] Upon reflection, Judge Pierce stated that he'd first seen de la Rosa on July 6, and the last time was either July 10 or 11. And Mennet's confidential informant Eduardo claimed that he was in Crixell's saloon in Brownsville and heard a Mexican say that he would bet two to one that de la Rosa was not under arrest as reported, for he had talked to de la Rosa in Victoria on July 17.[17]

A report in September stated that de la Rosa was recruiting men near Camargo, presumably for launching raids into Texas.[18] There were the usual rumors that Pizaña and de la Rosa were organizing on the Rio Grande opposite the hamlet of Sam Fordyce, but the Mexican consul in Brownsville stated that Pizaña was with Colonel Tirso González in Matamoros. "He does not know the whereabouts of de la Rosa, but other sources of information state that he is in such bad health that he could not take part in bandit activities."[19]

A. Osterveen Jr., formerly a bureau informant now working for the Mexican consul in Laredo, conducted a confidential investigation for Agent Breniman at Nuevo Laredo in February 1917 and stated that Basilio Ramos was in business at number 39 Matamoros Street in company with his brother J. M. Ramos; that the Ramos brothers get their ice from Laredo but probably did not visit Laredo themselves; and that they sent a boy with a wagon to get their supplies from Laredo.[20] To check Osterveen's story, bureau informant Seman went to the bottling works of José María Ramos and spoke briefly with his brother Basilio.[21]

But the bureau's attention was increasingly focused on the *felicista* movement, whose followers were busily plotting in Brownsville and Laredo. Regarding the Plan de San Diego, Agent Barnes on January 21 telegraphed Agent Mennet at Brownsville: "Please expedite present investigation [as] speedily as possible consistent with efficient service as have other important investigation pending needing your attention."[22] The U.S. attorney objected to Mennet's reassignment, reminding Agent Barnes that he'd promised to have Mennet work on the Plan de San Diego for six months to conduct an exhaustive investigation. The indictments were based largely on hearsay testimony, and unless the government's case was materially strengthened, very few of the defendants could be convicted.[23] In this connection, the bureau was not interested in punishing the Plan de San Diego rank and file, "who had been deceived but wanted to get the leaders who had been responsible for getting them into trouble." The foot soldiers were encouraged to make a clean breast of their participation in return for lenient treatment.[24]

Agent Mennet spent two and a half months in Monterrey observing and reporting on conditions there. He recapitulated the instances in which de la Rosa received help and consideration from prominent Carranza officials, among them Nicéforo Zambrano, General Obregón, and General Nafarrate, despite Carranza's repeated promises to have him arrested. And when General Ricaut allegedly arrested him for his role in the Texas revolution he was observed still running around freely. As for his more recent arrest for allegedly trying to suborn part of the Monterrey garrison, nothing was going to happen because "De la Rosa could tell too much about those 'higher up.'"[25]

An army report in February 1918 stated that "Luis de la Rosa is in Monterrey. He is being watched by Carranza military authorities, and has been warned not to leave Monterrey without consent of the commanding officer. Aniceto Pizaña is in Matamoros reporting to Colonel [Tirso] González every day. He has been warned that he will be shot if he attempts any movement without consent of Colonel González. Mexican Consul Garza claims that it is merely a question of time when some good excuse will arise for having both Luis de la Rosa and Aniceto Pizaña executed."[26]

During the United States' involvement in World War I, Carranza maintained a posture of neutrality, albeit an anti-American and pro-German neutrality. But because of what had occurred with the Plan de San Diego affair, Carranza didn't accept the notorious Zimmermann note from the Germans, proposing a military alliance and Mexico declaring war on the United States, the inducement being the recovery for Mexico of the territory lost to the United States in the nineteenth century.

The dominant Carranza faction wrote a new, and radical, constitution, promulgated on February 5, 1917, one that threatened the property of foreigners. Venustiano Carranza, the de facto president, was duly elected on March 11 as the constitutional president of Mexico.[27]

Senator Albert B. Fall of New Mexico, never an admirer of Carranza and always an advocate of U.S. intervention in Mexico, launched an intensified campaign against the Mexican president in 1919, a campaign designed to show that Carranza was responsible for most of the United States' problems with Mexico. In response to Fall's charges, the Mexican secretary of the interior, Manuel Aguirre Berlanga, declared that "Mexico has never contemplated or condoned adoption of the 'Plan of San Diego' for the purpose of securing portions of the Southwestern territory of the United States."[28] So there.

Fueling Fall's campaign were American outrage against the treatment of American citizens in Mexico and concerns over the radical Mexican Constitution of 1917's threat to foreign-owned property, especially to foreign oil interests, for the Constitution asserted Mexican ownership of the subsoil. Furthermore, Fall reflected Washington's anger at the Carranza authorities' recent arrest of the U.S. consular agent in Puebla.[29] Fall and his allies hoped to bring about U.S. military intervention in Mexico. Not only did Fall introduce a resolution calling for the United States to withdraw diplomatic recognition of Carranza, a move that would have enormously encouraged Carranza's enemies, but Fall also headed a Senate subcommittee created to review conditions in Mexico and U.S.-Mexican relations.[30]

Jack Danciger, incidentally, had drastically changed his tune. From being a fervent admirer of and propagandist for Venustiano Carranza, Danciger in 1916 resigned as Mexican consul in Kansas City, and by 1920 he was vehemently denying published reports that he'd ever been a Carranza propagandist or was in any way connected with the Plan de San Diego for that matter. Senator Fall promptly exonerated Danciger from any such inference. A grateful Danciger wrote to Fall stating, "I take this opportunity to commend the most splendid work being done by the Fall Committee."[31]

Fall used El Paso as his base of operations and quickly assembled a staff that included El Paso attorney and judge Dan M. Jackson, who resigned his wartime commission as a major in the Judge Advocate General's corps to become the committee's secretary; federal Bureau of Investigation special agent in charge of the El Paso office Gus Jones, who received a furlough from the agency to become a committee investigator; William Martin Hanson, senior Texas Ranger captain, who was granted a leave of absence to be the committee's chief investigator; Captain George Hyde, representing Military Intelligence; and Henry O. Flipper, the committee's interpreter and translator. Fall's subcommittee heard testimony in several cities from December 1, 1919, to June 5, 1920, producing the massive *Investigation of Mexican Affairs*.[32]

Texas Ranger captain Hanson, who had figured prominently in the Morín case in 1916, was perhaps the most important member of the staff. He was an experienced lawman who had a flair for intrigue, extensive contacts along the border, and a personal animus against Carranza. As we have seen, in 1914 the *carrancistas* had confiscated Hanson's property in Mexico and expelled him as a *huertista* spy. Hanson returned to San Antonio as a refugee, but through his contacts was soon appointed chief special agent for the San Antonio, Uvalde & Gulf Railroad. Realizing the value of a Texas Ranger commission, which would give him jurisdiction throughout the state, he secured a Special Ranger commission on December 24, 1917, which he parlayed into a Regular Ranger commission on January 31, 1918. He served as a Ranger captain, then senior captain, until he joined the Fall committee.[33]

Hanson was quite effective as the committee's chief investigator. For example, he functioned as agent provocateur, utilizing the alias of "Gus Klumpner," to correspond with one Arthur Thomson, author of a pamphlet titled *The Conspiracy against Mexico*. Hanson established that Thomson was being subsidized by the Carranza administration and that Mexican consuls were distributing this propaganda piece. More importantly, Hanson's contacts along the border, especially in Laredo and Nuevo Laredo, enabled him to secure sensitive information and valuable Mexican documents.[34] He supplied the committee with photostatic copies of two Carranza letters, and he forwarded from Laredo "two TELEGRAMS, that look good to me. This is a connection with the two photostatic letters. . . . I will suggest that Photostatic copies of these telegrams be used and originals filed, for I would not like to have to explain where and how I secured them." A few weeks later he wrote to Fall: "I am herewith enclosing copies of two telegrams that are self-explanatory. I could not get the originals and it was too dangerous for my informer to have photostatic copies made in Laredo, Texas."[35]

As matters developed, Carranza ceased to be a problem because of internal political upheavals. By 1919 many Mexicans were disgusted with the corruption of the Carranza regime. And they were particularly upset by evidence that, although the 1917 Constitution prohibited the reelection of the president, Carranza intended to remain in control by ruling through a puppet. To Carranza's dismay, General Alvaro Obregón, the man who'd been instrumental in elevating Carranza to power and keeping him there, announced his candidacy for president as an independent in the forthcoming 1920 election. Carranza's efforts to neutralize Obregón failed, and in April 1920 Obregón's partisans in his native state of Sonora promulgated the Plan de Agua Prieta, calling for the overthrow of Carranza. What ensued was the collapse of the regime with astounding rapidity. In May, Carranza fled from Mexico City, hoping to reach the port of Veracruz and exile, but on May 25 he was assassinated en route. Obregón was the new strongman of Mexico. Most of Carranza's erstwhile supporters hurried to make their peace with the new regime. The Plan de San Diego was but a memory.

20 Later Careers

After the Plan de San Diego withered away, things did not go well for most of the main protagonists.

The exception seems to have been Basilio Ramos. Unfortunately, we have only isolated glimpses of his later career. In 1917 he was connected with a customs brokerage firm in Nuevo Laredo. In 1919 he again worked for El Aguila petroleum company. Ramos was later elected as an alternate to the Tamaulipas legislature.[1]

General Pablo González, who oversaw Plan de San Diego activities in 1916, had, like a number of others, repeatedly changed his allegiance during his career. Originally a *magonista*, he later became a *maderista* and then a *carrancista*. As Carranza's favorite general his career flourished, and by 1920 González developed presidential ambitions. Declaring his candidacy in January 1920, he aimed to succeed Carranza but faced competition from General Alvaro Obregón, who had also developed presidential ambitions. When Obregón and his associates overthrew Carranza under the banner of the Plan de Agua Prieta, González rebelled in Monterrey. He was captured, tried, and sentenced to death in July 1920. Provisional president Adolfo de la Huerta suspended the execution and González fled into exile in the

United States, where he remained until 1940, when he was allowed to return to Mexico. He died in Monterrey in 1950.[2]

Regarding General Esteban Fierros, as of July 20, 1916, he was in Tampico. In November he was living in Mexico City, at number 191, 9th Mina Street. But he was sick in bed and broke. He complained that his friends, who owed him at least five hundred dollars, hadn't replied to his requests or even come to visit him. He therefore appealed to General Pablo González for a loan of three hundred pesos, which he hoped to repay soon. He evidently recovered, for on November 22 he wrote to González a lengthy account of the problems with the Constitutionalist Railways.[3] As of October 12, 1917, Fierros was under arrest at the Coahuila Hotel in Saltillo awaiting transfer to Mexico City to be tried for treason. He must have been cleared, for in December he was in Tampico.[4] We have no further information about Fierros.

As for General Emiliano Nafarrate, things did go well for him initially. When he was transferred away from Matamoros and replaced by General Alfredo Ricaut in a "bad cop, good cop" kind of proceeding to placate the Americans, Carranza not only promoted Nafarrate to general of brigade but assigned him to command the vital port of Tampico, through which passed most of Mexico's oil exports. This indicates that Carranza rewarded Nafarrate lavishly for a job well done.

Nafarrate was a delegate from Tamaulipas to the convention that produced the 1917 Constitution.[5] On one occasion he resigned in a fit of pique because he'd introduced a proposition that the convention voted down. His resignation was not accepted, and he remained a delegate. On May 24, 1917, he married Luisa Espinoza in Mexico City.[6]

Nafarrate was of necessity deeply embroiled in the politics of Tamaulipas, and these politics were toxic. A bitter struggle for the governorship over a two-year period resulted in armed clashes, numerous deaths, two postponements, recurrent changes in the provisional governorship, an election in which both sides claimed victory and organized a government, the Carranza administration voiding the election, and finally a rebellion.[7]

Carranza faced a difficult choice in 1917—which of two staunch supporters to endorse for constitutional governor of Tamaulipas. Carranza's choice was General César López de Lara, currently governor of the Federal District. His opponent was General Luis Caballero, who had distinguished himself as a Constitutionalist commander and was currently military governor of Tamaulipas. In the course of the campaign in 1917 their partisans engaged in frequent and bloody clashes. Carranza appointed General Alfredo Ricaut as acting governor.[8] Given the murderous political climate, Ricaut postponed the election until February 3, 1918. When the election was held it was marked by violence, with both candidates claiming victory. Caballero appointed Nafarrate as provisional governor.[9] Political passions reached the point that Caballero and López de Lara engaged in a shooting affray at Chapultepec castle, the official residence of the Mexican president; one of Caballero's partisans was killed, and one of López de Lara's was wounded. Eventually charges against both generals were dropped.[10]

Carranza ordered Ricaut to prevent either side from taking control until the federal government could decide the outcome. The situation became ridiculous: "General Ricaut has refused to give over the Governorship to the State; Nafarrate considers himself Governor; and Caballero and de Lara also call themselves Governor, so the State of Tamaulipas has at present four Governors."[11] Nevertheless, Caballero's partisans took over the legislature and proclaimed him governor. Caballero rose in rebellion in April 1918. He finally surrendered to the government on January 4, 1920. As a sop he was appointed ambassador to Guatemala. But in November 1920, with a new regime in power in Mexico City, Caballero tried again. He campaigned against his old antagonist, General César López de Lara. In a much more tranquil election, he lost. López de Lara was inaugurated in February 1921.[12]

General Nafarrate, who had been elected as a senator from Tamaulipas, had been Caballero's strongest supporter, and this allegedly led him to threaten President Carranza in 1918 with making public the letters and telegrams in his possession disclosing Carranza's role in supporting the Plan de San Diego. The U.S. Army's weekly intelligence report for April 13, 1918, stated that "Luis Caballero was liberated because of an ultimatum sent to Carranza by Nafarrate in which he demanded his immediate liberation."[13] The ultimatum proved to be a serious error in judgment on Nafarrate's part.

An American report related:

> General Nafarrate turned the governorship over to General Caballero at Victoria April 9th and came to Tampico April 10th. It was reported that he came to confer with a committee from Pelaez and to get money from oil companies and rich Mexicans that were supposed to be backing the Caballero government and revolution. It was reported that Pelaez was to command rebels in Veracruz State, Cedillo in San Luis Potosí and Nafarrate in Tamaulipas—Nafarrate to be the supreme military commander under Caballero.
>
> At 11:00 [p.m.] on April 11th Nafarrate decided he would go to the Red Light District. His friends tried to dissuade him but he said he feared nothing. He went to a bar and assignation house leaving his machine stand[ing] in front, which was against the city law. The assistant chief of police saw the machine and told the chauffeur to take it to the Police Station. The chauffeur called the General and he came out and roundly abused the assistant chief of police and told him he was not only a general but a senator and was immune from arrest. Nafarrate also reported him to the chief of police.
>
> At about 2:00 a.m. he left this house and went to a road-house of the same character. The Chief of Police was at this road-house. About 2:30 a.m. the assistant chief of police came into this house and told the General he was under arrest. The Chief of Police told the assistant chief of police to get out—that he must respect the exalted position of the Senator. The assistant chief left and in a few minutes someone called the General from outside. He went to the sidewalk, saw no one, and turned to walk back into the house. As he turned a rifle was fired by someone. The ball struck the General between the shoulders and came out through his neck killing him instantly. His death in the early hours of April 12, 1918, had significant political repercussions.
>
> Caballero's followers believe it was a case of assassination. The backers of the revolution feel that his death will cause any local revolution to fail for he was considered the only military leader capable of making it a success.[14]

General Ricaut telegraphed Carranza that "Today at 3 a.m. in a house of ill repute there was a quarrel between General Nafarrate and the police, said general having been killed." Regarding Carranza's involvement, the army's weekly report commented that "innuendo and rumors say the fight staged by López de Lara and Caballero in the Chapultepec yard was connived at by Pres. Carranza who was disappointed Caballero was not killed; as a fact, he went to Police Headquarters to get the would-be assassins out. Nafarrate was next in line for the same treatment."[15] And "It is reported that President Carranza has shown favor to the De Lara faction and that possibly the assassination plan of Nafarrate might have had its origin in Mexico City."[16]

District Attorney John Valls subsequently testified before the Fall Committee: "It was reported to me that he was assassinated by orders of President Carranza. He knew the order that Carranza had given and interviews he had had with Carranza with reference to Americans and what he should do in this matter of the border raids, the Plan of San Diego, and he was about to divulge these things, and he was assassinated by a man sent there from the City of Mexico."

Nafarrate's widow was living in Mexico City, and Valls heard that she claimed to have the original documents that her husband was going to divulge.[17] The Fall Committee had hopes of acquiring Nafarrate's incriminating documents from his widow. Hanson wrote to Judge J. F. Kearful that "I am going to prove that they raided this country, at least twenty times from Laredo to Brownsville, and that it was in furtherance of the Plan of San Diego, and that Carranza was cognizant of it all, and I have some hopes of connecting him directly with it. If your man can work Mrs. Nafarrete in Mexico City, I hope to have the missing link."[18] Evidently the approach was unsuccessful.

Another major figure in the Plan de San Diego affair, Juan Kvake Forseck, remained in Mexico City working on land options until about August 10, 1916, when he left for Kansas City to confer with the Danciger brothers in response to a telegram from them. On August 19, 1916, they made him a proposition in writing to secure some land in Mexico, the Hacienda de Zanatepec in the state of Puebla.[19] Forseck returned to Eagle Pass, then took a Pullman for Mexico City. But on August

26, 1916, the train was blown up and plundered by bandits who killed seventeen passengers and military escort and wounded a like number. Forseck said he lost a number of important documents in the melee.

After Forseck's return to Mexico City, his son Lisandro notified him from Washington that he was coming to Mexico City with Ambassador Eliseo Arredondo. When the latter arrived, Forseck asked Arredondo to use his influence with Cándido Aguilar to get him a position somewhere on the border. To Forseck's relief, Arredondo did so, and Forseck received a commission from the Foreign Office on October 6, 1916.[20]

About October 7 or 8, Forseck left Mexico City aboard Arredondo's private railroad car and arrived at Eagle Pass two days later. He then accompanied Arredondo to San Antonio, where Arredondo instructed the Mexican consul to give Forseck one hundred dollars, with which he went to Naco, Arizona. He remained there until he received a concession from the Mexican government to export five thousand head of cattle, whereupon he moved his headquarters to the Tucsonia Hotel in Tucson.

A federal Bureau of Investigation report stated that while Forseck supervised José Escoboza and one Ronstadt of Tucson crossing the cattle he talked with customs inspector Jack Noonan. Noonan was a colorful border character; he'd been a mercenary working for the Mexican consul in El Paso in 1912, and in 1914 had participated in an expedition against Mexicali funded by Los Angeles newspaper magnate Harry Chandler. Now he was an officer of the federal government.[21]

Noonan reported that Forseck told him that when in Mexico City he had lived with Zubarán, formerly secretary of foreign affairs, and that his son was private secretary to Arredondo, the Mexican ambassador in Washington. Noonan said Forseck was a personal agent of Carranza's, that he had escorted Mrs. Carranza and her party from Mexico City to the border several months previously, that he left her at the border and went to some place on the Texas border where cattle were being exported, that from this exportation of cattle he collected the percentage that was to go to the Mexican government, and that he returned to San Antonio and turned a big bundle of cash over to Mrs. Carranza.

Inspector Noonan also stated that Jacobo Ayala Villarreal, formerly

General Fortunato Zuazua's cashier, now the collector of customs at Naco, Sonora, told him that Forseck and José Escoboza were in Hermosillo in connection with the concession for exporting cattle, under which Escoboza was operating. Noonan was also at the Copper Queen Hotel in Bisbee when Escoboza and Forseck were dividing the proceeds of the cattle deal: about nine thousand dollars for Forseck and two thousand for Escoboza. Forseck remarked that he could skim enough before he sent the funds to Mexico City to pay his expenses to New York. The Bureau of Investigation agent concluded that "It is very evident that this man is a personal Agent of Gen. Carranza operating in the U.S., and in addition to his financial missions acts as a secret agent."[22] Forseck's having escorted Mrs. Carranza to the border indicates that Carranza had confidence in his loyalty and ability.

In January 1917, after exporting the cattle, Forseck went to New York to join his family. In March 1917 he returned to Laredo and purchased a farm near Leyendecker, on the Rio Grande about seventeen miles northwest of Laredo. But he said he remained in touch with developments across the border.[23] He also established a men's furnishing store, John K. Forseck & Sons (Lisandro and Sandor), at the corner of Farragut Street and Convent Avenue in Laredo. In May 1918 he announced that he was selling his "Gents Furnishing Business" in order to concentrate on agriculture for the war effort at his 750-acre farm, Las Islas. Although he reduced the price for a quick sale, he found no buyers for the haberdashery, and in August the store closed and Forseck filed bankruptcy papers.[24] In January 1919 Forseck hoped to remain solvent through the sale of a large tract of land in Mexico, but the sale fell through. Then in March, Forseck sold his home and several lots for a total of $9,250. That same month, he and his sons filed for bankruptcy of their half-interest in Las Islas farm, plus ten mules. As of August 1919, Forseck was manager of Las Islas farms.[25]

In September 1919, Randolph Robertson, the vice consul in Monterrey who was also an agent of the State Department's elite Bureau of Secret Intelligence, met Forseck and learned that the Hungarian could provide crucial evidence regarding the Carranza regime's connection with the Plan de San Diego. Robertson requested, and received, the State Department's permission to take Forseck to Washington to divulge his information. On October 3, Forseck gave his invaluable affidavit.[26]

Jacobo Ayala Villarreal, General Zuazua's onetime cashier, had intimate knowledge of the Plan de San Diego intrigues. The U.S. Army even reported that he'd been the author of the Plan de San Diego.[27] He subsequently held under the Carranza government the lucrative position of collector of customs in Naco, Sonora (any job as collector of customs was lucrative). And as of 1919 he occupied another desirable government post—the office of Bienes Intervenidos (Seized Properties) at Matamoros.[28]

Ayala Villarreal eventually retired to Laredo and decided to expand his educational horizons by obtaining a master's degree at Texas A&I College in Kingsville. In his thesis he presented an interesting perspective on Carranza's recognition,[29] writing that de facto diplomatic recognition enabled Venustiano Carranza to consolidate his government, and that seemingly the United States "was greatly influenced" by the Plan de San Diego movement, which was directed by a revolutionary junta in Monterrey. It was said that the Wilson administration asked Carranza "to obstruct the fomentation of that revolution in the territory under his rule." Carranza demanded in exchange the recognition of his regime. When the United States recognized Carranza the revolution in Texas disappeared "as if by magic," and though the Mexican government conducted the charade of incarcerating some of the Tejano revolutionaries, they were soon freed and were never bothered again.[30]

Luis de la Rosa continued to be of great interest to the American authorities. In December 1917 the army received a report that he was in Monterrey in the employ of the Mexican government.[31] Also in December 1917, the army was informed that he had just been released from prison in Monterrey.[32]

In 1918 de la Rosa was confined to Monterrey and Pizaña to Matamoros, both of them being closely watched by the Carranza military authorities. American military authorities were also watchful. The army's weekly intelligence report of January 18, 1918, mentioned that de la Rosa had completed his nominal sentence in the Monterrey penitentiary and was currently at large in that city. "He claims that he was jailed only to pacify the United States; that he is being paid by the Carranza government as a Federal General; that he contemplates a raid into Texas under Carranza's orders with the object of raising the Ammunition Embargo, and that he has had the assistance of Carranza in his past operations." The report enumerated the *sediciosos* who were now in Carranza's army, holding ranks ranging from sergeant to general and stationed at Matamoros and Monterrey: Aniceto Pizaña, Ramón Pizaña, Luis de la Rosa, Abel Sandoval, Ricardo Gómez, and Antonio Escamilla. Aniceto Pizaña was Colonel Tirzo González's aide.[33]

President Carranza enabled de la Rosa to move up in the world, becoming an hacendado. Carranza carefully monitored the disposition of seized properties, and one of them went to de la Rosa. He was permitted to rent Dr. Aureliano Urrutia's confiscated Hacienda La Luz, located near Xochimilco.[34] This happy state of affairs didn't last long. By 1919 de la Rosa was living in Mexico City and was destitute. He wrote repeatedly to Carranza reminding the president of his services and their friendship and desperately pleading for a government job or financial help. But Carranza had more important matters to worry about. De la Rosa was finally reduced to begging for railroad passes for himself and his family so they could return to Matamoros.[35]

De la Rosa's return to the border immediately got the attention of the Texas authorities, who had placed a thousand-dollar bounty on his head. Of all the Plan de San Diego types, he was the one they really wanted. On January 5, 1920, Fred E. Marks, who had had an interesting career in law enforcement, having been a deputy sheriff and for three years a deputy U.S. marshal and a former special employee of the Bureau of Investigation and whose recent resignation from the Texas Rangers was pending, was currently a druggist in Rio Grande City. He wrote a confidential letter to the Texas adjutant general, W. D. Cope, who had given him a delicate assignment.[36] Marks said that "a friend of mine has made me an offer of $500.00 if I get our man across the river, delivered on this side to me." Marks proposed paying the five hundred dollars if his Mexican contacts could deliver de la Rosa alive on the American side of the Rio Grande.

Two days later, Marks sent the adjutant general a detailed confidential report in which he said de la Rosa was now living with his family in Camargo across the river about five miles south of Rio Grande City. Furthermore, de la Rosa was reportedly making trips up and down the river for some unknown purpose. His fortunes had improved, for he was spending money freely "buying *mescal* and for gambling and claims that he is electioneering on behalf of Carlos Osuna, a candidate for the governorship of Tamaulipas. He is known to carry in his coat pocket several letters from President Carranza, but the contents of these letters is not known to my informant."[37]

Marks stressed that since de la Rosa frequently visited riverside ranches and drank mescal while doing so it would be easy to abduct him, although "He is feared by the natives as he stands in the good graces of President Carranza." Marks mentioned that a friend of his had already agreed to provide the five hundred dollars, and Marks reiterated that "I would not stand for anything else than to have him alive." Having covered himself on paper, Marks also stressed that he wouldn't do anything to embarrass the administration in Texas.

The adjutant general was most interested in the proposition. Although Marks talked of delivering de la Rosa alive, one suspects that Adjutant General Cope wouldn't have been outraged if de la Rosa's corpse, or his head in a sack, were delivered on the Texas bank of the Rio Grande. He wrote to Marks: "Referring to your letter of January 7th, regarding de la Rosa, you are requested to continue the investigation as set forth in this letter, and keep in touch with this office regarding this man's movements. I will advise you later about the matter of going after De la Rosa."[38]

Cope's enthusiasm for the proposed operation grew. He informed Marks that he was on the right track and in a position to render a valuable service to the state and reflect credit on Marks as an officer and the Rangers as a whole. He sincerely hoped Marks would succeed in getting de la Rosa, adding, "I explained to you fully in the phone conversations at the time I detailed you for this particular duty. I feel, with your knowledge of international law, you will be able to handle this situation in a manner becoming a Texas Ranger . . . [Texas Ranger] Captain [William] Wright has three men at Rio Grande City that will assist you if you need them."[39]

Marks advised Cope that he'd made all the arrangements for his informant to deliver de la Rosa to him, but "we encountered certain conditions that I would like very much to discuss with you and our mutual friend Col. Chapa. I consider it very important that you should be aware of certain facts before this delivery takes place."[40] Colonel Francisco Chapa was a wealthy San Antonio druggist whose military rank came from the Texas National Guard because he had been on the personal staff of three Texas governors in succession, including the current governor, William P. Hobby. Chapa was the leading Hispanic politician in the state. And he was politically conservative, thus opposed the likes of de la Rosa. It may be speculated that Chapa was the "friend" who was prepared to furnish the reward that Marks needed.

On January 19, Marks was instructed to report immediately, and upon reaching San Antonio he was to notify Colonel Chapa. On January 23, Marks arrived in Austin and conferred at the capitol with the governor of Texas and the adjutant general, a most unusual kind of meeting, as they ordinarily didn't meet with Ranger privates. Afterward, Marks returned to Rio Grande City to make final arrangements.

But on March 13, the adjutant general notified Marks that his resignation from the Rangers had been accepted and "You will turn over the matter you have in hand to Sergeant Eads [*sic*] of Captain Wright's company stationed at Rio Grande City, giving him the benefit of all information you have in order that he may intelligently proceed with the matter you now have in hand."[41] Colonel Chapa was furious and protested to the governor, to no avail. In the event, the operation aimed at de la Rosa was canceled, for reasons that are still obscure. Perhaps Marks's informant refused to work with anyone but Marks. In any case, de la Rosa got a reprieve.[42]

De la Rosa lived the rest of his life in obscurity in Mexico. He reportedly died between July and December 1939 and was buried in Ochoa, Tamaulipas, a ranch near Comales and Camargo.[43]

Unlike Luis de la Rosa, Aniceto Pizaña didn't even get a taste of the good life. He had steadily been marginalized as a *sedicioso* leader, being a mere colonel while Luis de la Rosa was a general whom the public believed to be the standard-bearer for the Plan de San Diego. As mentioned above, in 1918, Pizaña was an aide to Colonel Tirso González, the Carranza commander in Matamoros. Thereafter Pizaña's role in the Plan de San Diego brought him little reward, for he lived out the rest of his life in obscurity. In 1929 he was police chief and head of the civil registry in the town of Altamira, Tamaulipas. In 1932 he was a mounted policeman in Tampico.[44] In 1946, along with some other landless folks who hadn't participated in the Plan de San Diego, he became a member of an *ejido*, or government collective farm, near the village of Llera, Tamaulipas. Pizaña died destitute on March 1, 1957.[45]

Agustín Garza was the leader of the Plan de San Diego, but aspects of his subsequent career remain obscure. In 1917 he was in Monterrey, a partner in a local mercantile firm known as Salinas y Garza, located at Calle de Morelos number 108.[46] The other partner of the firm was Santiago Salinas, formerly of Camargo, Tamaulipas. The *carrancista* officials of Nuevo León assured the American authorities that they would keep Garza under surveillance.[47]

There was reason to, for Garza and Basilio Ramos, connected with a customs brokerage firm in Nuevo Laredo, remained in contact from 1917 through 1919. In 1919 they were involved in some kind of anarchist intrigue. On January 7, Garza wrote to one Luis García at San Diego, Texas, telling him that Ramos was going there and asking that García aid "our old friend Basilio financially (for of course your testicles are in their proper place) . . . in order that he may carry on the project which he will present to you." Garza assured García that "we will repay you in multiples, thereof, in a few days more," and waxing poetic wrote, "for you will realize that the day is at last breaking; already the cool of the first streaks of the dawn of the morning of the race is felt. Basilio will explain other matters to you verbally."[48]

Then on January 9, Garza wrote to Ignacio R. Rodríguez at Brownsville, that at the suggestion of their friend Jacobo Ayala Villarreal, "my good friend" Basilio Ramos would deliver the letter. Ayala Villarreal had asked Agustín Garza to recommend Ramos to Rodríguez. Ramos would explain the enterprise to Rodríguez.[49]

In February 1919, Ramos wrote to Garza from Veracruz, where he was again working for El Aguila petroleum company. Ramos advised that the papers their comrade Ayala Villarreal had left with him he'd forwarded with sailors on one of the company's vessels to Yucatán, so the Yucatecan contingent could use them, as he understood they were quite militant.

Ramos assured Garza that he was not in the least fearful. He was just sorry that they'd been abandoned "in a matter in which we thought no one would abandon us." Ramos was still hopeful that much could be accomplished if they didn't rely on "cowardly people who at the slightest indication of danger desert."[50]

Garza, meanwhile, was residing at Calzada la Piedad number 52 in Mexico City and was in contact with the Carranza administration. On April 15, 1919, President Carranza telegraphed to Garza in reply to the latter's wire of April 10. Carranza authorized Garza to speak with his private secretary, explaining that the press of work made it impossible for Carranza to receive him personally.[51]

Garza's approach succeeded, for in June, Mario Méndez, the director general of telegraphs, wrote to Garza, who was back in Monterrey, at Calle de Hidalgo number 166, announcing that Garza had been appointed collector of customs at Nuevo Laredo and requesting that he notify Méndez when he arrived there.[52] Significantly, Garza wrote on the back of Méndez's letter: "President Don Venustiano Carranza approves of the above and insists that in recognition of my conduct I accept a commission as a General of Brigade, as a just recompense for the disinterested services I rendered to the Fatherland at the moment when its sovereignty was threatened by the eternal enemy our cousins of the North."[53]

León, or Lino, as he was now calling himself, Caballo replied to Mario Méndez's letter of June 9 in August from Monterrey, explaining that he hadn't answered because he'd been sick in bed for more than two months. He was now feeling better and hoped to be in Nuevo Laredo in a few days and would gladly inform Méndez of his arrival there. Garza stated that during his stay in Mexico City and in the interview he had with Don Venustiano, the latter told him that a grateful fatherland rewarded his efforts and patriotism for having saved its autonomy, by commissioning him as a general of brigade and also by appointing him collector of customs, so that the two salaries would enable Garza to recover at least part of all that he had lost (and, it was hoped, ensure that Garza didn't reveal any secrets to, say, the Fall Committee). Garza answered him, repeating what he had told Carranza "upon accepting to head the new movement," that he didn't serve the fatherland for crowns or out of interest, because he well understood the solemn duty that Mexicans had to defend it. The only thing he wanted was for all his Mexican brothers to learn of the benefits the fatherland had received through the efforts of the humblest of its brothers. According to Garza, Carranza replied: "You ask the impossible . . . most impossible." "Why?" Garza asked. Carranza replied: "Precisely because the Americans have believed that my government has been supporting the Texas matter, as in truth has been the case in this last movement, and no one knows it better than you, who have received money, ammunition, and arms through Mr. Mario Méndez, with the moral and historical responsibility naturally falling on you, and with the movement finally forcing [the Americans] to settle things amicably with our country, as we had hoped, and as you well knew. But the Mexican Government must maintain the greatest secrecy, because otherwise its sovereignty might be in peril."

So, because of this, Carranza appealed to Garza's disinterested patriotism, as he had demonstrated, for all of this to be kept in the greatest secrecy, and "for you to accept what the grateful Fatherland recognizes and offers you." Garza said he told Carranza he'd think it over and would write to him from Monterrey but hadn't done so; but since Carranza insisted, through Méndez, Garza was now ready to accept both the mentioned appointments on the condition that he not be obligated to take up arms against his brothers, regardless of their political affiliation, and he'd only do so against a foreign enemy or against any brothers who try to betray the fatherland.

Garza informed Méndez that he realized that Carranza was anxious for him to accept both commissions, because Carranza feared that Garza might reveal things that should remain in profound silence, and Carranza furthermore believed that if Garza were commissioned in the army and employed in the Carranza administration he would be less likely to reveal anything. Garza told Méndez to assure Carranza that he had nothing to worry about, that Carranza had enough proof of Garza's silence during this long period in which he had endured penury for having lost everything, and further he had remained silent regarding his unjustified imprisonment, unjustified because his crime had been to cross into Mexico seeking support to consolidate the "Separatist Social Movement" known as the Texas revolution because he sincerely believed that if in the United States were formed all the plots to plunder the peoples of Latin America, why couldn't he with his brothers obtain the support that he badly needed and hoped for in those desperate moments in which the future of all Indo-Spanish America was in play, and "especially when we were also trying to save Mexico from the eternal Yankee threat and recover the lands that in an evil hour they stole from the Mexicans."

Garza reiterated his surprise when the reply to his approach was to have him jailed incommunicado in the penitentiary of the Federal District. With that imprisonment the Texas movement was aborted, and because it was aborted the Mexican Revolution obtained de facto recognition, having to thank only Don Venustiano, that Garza wasn't sold for a few dollars to the wolves of the north and burned at the stake in a public plaza. Therefore, he repeated, he would not remain silent about this last movement that he and Carranza knew was a sham, which could have become reality with the Texas phantom, if things had not been settled by diplomacy in 1916. Actions were always better than words, he informed Méndez, and Garza had given ample proof that he knew how to keep silent about causes and to suffer their effects, and especially regarding a matter as delicate as the present one. Because the contents of this letter might hurt the president's feelings, Garza wanted to clarify that it wasn't his desire to injure him but rather to clarify doubtful points for the benefit of posterity which in the future might confuse the true history of these events in which the Mexican Revolution was much involved. Garza closed by assuring Méndez that he could reassure the president of Garza's discretion.[54]

Hanson and the Fall Committee were particularly interested in the activities of "León Caballo." With two other men Caballo had arrived in Nuevo Laredo from Monterrey on December 14, 1919, and stayed at the same hotel as the labor leader Luis Morones, with whom they had reportedly come to confer. According to American military intelligence, León Caballo had been dispatched with the other two to "carry on radical revolutionary propaganda in Texas. His movements should be closely watched and reported to this office with particular reference to establishing his connection with the Mexican government and with leading radicals in this country. . . . Efforts should be made to ascertain the identity and whereabouts of this man." Military intelligence had obtained in Mexico City and had translated several letters involving León Caballo, including the following:

> V. C. Mexico [City], June 14, 1919
> Señor Lic. Manuel Aguirre Berlanga,
> Esteemed Friend:
> Señor Lino [Garza was now using the alias of "Lino," not "León," Caballo] Caballo bearer of this letter, is the person who, in company with two friends, will bring to you the manifestos and the plan which they desire to put into practice in the State of Texas. This plan being very favorable for Mexico, please aid them in every way and give the necessary instructions in the frontier states,
> I remain your affectionate friend
> V. Carrranza[55]

Even as his regime was beginning to totter, Carranza was engaged in making trouble for the United States.

Besides being secretary of interior, Manuel Aguirre Berlanga was one of Carranza's closest associates. Military intelligence had also obtained several other Mexican government telegrams, including one on December 16 from General Juan Barragán, chief of the presidential staff, ordering the commander at Nuevo Laredo to deliver to Agustín Garza and "L. C. Caballo" the sum of one thousand dollars, charged to special service (intelligence), by order of the president. The money was delivered.

A subsequent military intelligence report identified León Caballo as a confidential agent of Carranza's who passed through Laredo en route to New York. "León Caballo's right name is Agustín S. Garza one of the signers of the Plan of San Diego, and now supposed to be in Mexico D. F. acting as an agent for the I.W.W. organization there." On January 22, 1920, District Attorney John Valls testified that León Caballo was a Carranza secret agent.[56]

Senator Fall, for his part, declared that his committee not only had Carranza's June 14, 1919, letter but also an August 1919 Carranza letter directing Aguirre Berlanga, the secretary of interior, to put on the payroll and provide all financial assistance to one Juan M. García and two Americans from Texas, allegedly the same "two friends" referred to in Carranza's June 14 letter. Fall said his committee also had the minutes of "a meeting of Lodge 23, of the City of Mexico, held on October 15, 1919. Lodge 23 appears to be an association of extreme radical anarchist elements." The senator asserted that the "two friends" referred to in Carranza's letters who accompanied Caballo were present at the lodge meeting. Fall expounded on an alleged, and grandiose, anarchist plot to cripple the economy of the United States, establish a rebel capital in Colorado, and reward the Mexicans who had assisted the anarchists by returning the Southwest to Mexico.

The committee planned to introduce a copy of these minutes to connect the original Plan de San Diego, "the resuscitated Plan as announced in the Zimmermann note," and the plan approved by Carranza as shown by his June 14 and August letters.[57]

Furthermore, Senator Fall announced that the committee had a star witness who could connect the Carranza administration to the Plan de San Diego. The mystery witness was, of course, Juan Forseck, and Fall's assertions were based on Forseck's affidavit.[58]

Agustín Garza was never able to capitalize on what Carranza offered him. After Carranza was overthrown and assassinated in 1920, Garza and his patriotic contributions and current problems were of little concern to the Mexican government. It has been said that "in the 1930s Garza and his family moved to Mexico City where he worked for the government"[59] (in an unknown capacity). In July 1936, Garza wrote from Amsterdam number 213-215 in Mexico City to the secretary of war and marine requesting copies of the telegrams that because of the American seizure of Veracruz he'd sent to General Huerta between April 21 and 30, 1914, as well as Huerta's replies. He was told to write to the Military Archive of the Secretariat and provide additional information.[60]

Garza remained in straitened circumstances and by 1938 was becoming desperate in his efforts to persuade the government to recognize his services. Writing from Tonalá number 267 in Mexico City, he applied to the Senate for a pension, enclosing documents that he had kept secret all those years, explaining that he'd done so in order not to damage relations with the United States. He hoped the documents merited "some humble assistance for one who is rather old, rather sick, poor, and with a family." Should the Senate care to verify his claim it could appoint a committee to examine additional documents or to question Garza at its convenience.[61] He was told to address himself to a commission that the president would appoint as a result of Congress having recently passed the Law of Pensions for Civil or Heroic Merit.[62] Garza requested the return of his documents so he could proceed as suggested. They were returned.[63]

A thoroughly frustrated Agustín Garza finally decided to go to the top—he appealed directly to President Lázaro Cárdenas.[64] Recounting his dealings with the Senate, he appealed for the president's help. He enclosed documentation that he'd kept secret for more than a generation. In this connection, there is an undated document in the Garza papers in which six retired generals certify as to Garza's merits:

> We certify that Citizen Agustín S. de la Garza was the General in Chief of the Texas Revolution, having been recognized as such by the Revolutionary Congress of San Diego, Texas, United States of America, many officers of the Constitutionalist Army having fought under his orders, operating both in the State of Texas and in the Republic of Mexico, pursuing the noble proposition of annexing to the Republic of Mexico the territories stolen from her and more, according to the Plan and Manifesto of San Diego, Texas, United States of America. That in the execution of those tasks the aforementioned General Agustín S. de la Garza received money, arms, and ammunition from him who was then President of the Republic Señor Don Venustiano Carranza, who supplied those elements through Mr. Mario Méndez, Director of Telegraphs at that time and who placed at the disposal of said General de la Garza the telegraph lines of his department in order to convey messages from the city of Monterrey, N. L., the aforementioned General using the alias of León Caballo. That the wholesale grocery operating as Garza Hermanos y Cía., located at Independencia 17 in this city of Mexico, that had a capital of more than five million pesos and in which

General Agustín S. de la Garza figured as one of the principal partners and which business was liquidated and absolutely all the proceeds invested in the Texas Revolution which had as its epilogue the de facto recognition of the said Chief Don Venustiano Carranza by the Americans. We likewise certify that in a document dated on June 19, 1919, Mr. de la Garza was offered a commission as General of Brigade as well as Administrator of the Nuevo Laredo customs house, appointments that he did not accept because he was ill. We consider it an act of justice that his rank of General of Brigade be recognized. What is certified will be supported with the appropriate documents.

[signed]: General Maurilio Rodríguez
General Tito Ferrer y Tovar
General Manuel W. González
Licenciate and General Enrique Enríquez
General Régulo Garza
General José E. Santos

In his letter Garza stated that the signatures, both that of León Caballo that he himself used as well as those on the manifesto and Plan de San Diego, were aliases because they were operating in enemy territory, but all were Mexicans. His documents were returned with instructions to resubmit them whenever the appropriate commission was appointed.[65]

After waiting more than two years, Garza, then living at Morena 326, Colonia del Valle in Mexico City, tried again, this time petitioning the Chamber of Deputies and again enclosing supporting documentation. But he was informed that it was a matter for the president to resolve.[66]

Undaunted by the bureaucratic runaround he received, Garza continued his battle to obtain a pension. As late as July 1952 he requested that the government certify that Mario Méndez's signature on his letter was genuine. He was notified that the technical equipment to make a definitive study was lacking, but that a superficial examination indicated that the signature could well be that of Méndez.[67]

Nothing more is known about Garza, who died on January 10, 1970, an idealist who had given his all for the cause.

21 A Question of Numbers

Frank Cushman Pierce, a Brownsville native and attorney, wrote a history of the lower Rio Grande valley in which he stated that "The author cannot let pass this opportunity to say that during the bandit raids of 1915 many evil influences were brought to bear to clear the country of the Mexicans. To his knowledge more than one was forced to flee and to convey his chattels before going."[1] A number of Hispanics were forced to flee leaving not only their fields and crops but their homes and personal possessions. "Consul [José] Garza also reported that some Mexicans had complained that they had been threatened by citizens and rangers and told that if they did not sell their property and leave the community that they would be killed."[2]

The plight of many Tejanos was illustrated by that of C. C. Yznaga, who lived near Sebastian:

> I am moving my family to Brownsville and shall remain there until this trouble is over. If I stay on my ranch the bandits may kill me unless I give them everything they want. If I do this the Rangers or the soldiers may think that I am harboring them and they may kill me. Besides, if this thing continues much longer it will become a race war and as the soldiers and the Rangers do not know me I might be taken as a bad Mexican and killed.

> Everybody in Brownsville knows me and I feel safe here. I do not know anything about the "Plan of San Diego." Of course I have heard that there was such a thing but I have had nothing to do with it. I have not seen any Carrancista soldiers on this side [of] the river since this trouble began. It is very bad. I have sold my cattle, horses, corn and am just leaving my ranch.[3]

It would be most interesting to examine the property tax records of Cameron, Hidalgo, and Starr Counties in particular for the period August–December 1915, to determine who—whether Anglos or Hispanics—acquired the property thus abandoned.

Rodolfo Rocha has written that as many as half of the Tejano population of South Texas, amounting to thousands of people, left for Mexico.[4] Picking up on this statement, Paul J. Vanderwood and Frank N. Samponaro in their book *Border Fury* assert that they migrated to Mexico "never to return."[5] And herein lies the problem—writers have sometimes bandied numbers about without adducing any supporting evidence.

A press dispatch from Brownsville on September 11, 1915, read: "About 2,000 Mexicans have gone into Mexico from this section since the border trouble started, according to today's figures. Many families, known as 'good Mexicans,' left standing crops and everything to seek what they believed was safety in their native country. Dual reasons for their fears were found in the rigid clean-up campaign of the peace officers and the danger from bandits of their own race who in the past two days have killed two. There is little traffic across the border from either side."[6] A Brownsville newspaper estimated that by November 1915 some seven thousand had fled across the Rio Grande.[7]

While there was undoubtedly a "push" factor—Hispanics being forced to abandon their homes and flee across the river—there was also a "pull" factor, which writers have tended to ignore: Mexicans were being encouraged to return to Mexico. Carranza decreed amnesty for all who returned and resumed their previous vocations. Thousands of refugees returned.[8]

What complicates numbers estimates is the wholesale movement back and forth across the Rio Grande by Mexicans, determined by the course of the Mexican Revolution. There were no restrictions on Mexicans entering the United States. Only Chinese were excluded. Not until the United States entered World War I were regulations enacted requiring passports and registration upon entering this country. Moreover, although people were supposed to cross at ports of entry, there were literally dozens of crossing points, including illegal ferries. And when the Rio Grande was low, crossing was especially easy. With every turn of the revolutionary wheel, a multitude crossed into Texas to avoid warfare, poverty, and disease. And with every turn of the wheel, hordes of triumphant exiles returned to Mexico and were replaced by a new wave of losers. There is simply no way of estimating precisely how many thousands were involved.

With the exception of James Sandos, who carefully examined population figures, changing ethnic composition, and the amount and location of irrigated land in the border counties, writers generally haven't used such a basic source as the U.S. Census to determine whether in fact South Texas was partly depopulated during the "Bandit War." For the three counties most heavily affected by that conflict, the census figures are:

	1910	**1920**
Cameron	27,158	36,662
Hidalgo	13,728	38,110
Starr	13,151	11,089

Thus there was an overall increase in population rather than depopulation during the decade.

A much more important numbers controversy involves how many Hispanics (Tejanos and Mexicans) were killed during the "Bandit War." Among the most controversial aspects of the Plan de San Diego affair is the role of the Texas Rangers, who were not only conducting counterinsurgency operations but also combating repeated incursions by Mexican soldiers. The Rangers unquestionably killed Hispanics out of hand, but the number is still in dispute. Frank Pierce, for example, alleged that "During the bandit troubles between August 4, 1915, and June 17, 1916, 100 Mexicans have been executed by the Texas Rangers and deputy sheriffs without process of law. Some place the figures at 300. Most of these executions, it has been asserted, were by reason of data furnished the Rangers, implicating the particular Mexicans in the raids which were occurring."[9]

The problem is that numbers are readily asserted without any supporting evidence. There are, however, available some lists of the dead. The most detailed is that compiled by Frank Pierce. He delivered a list of 102 names, in some cases with the circumstances of their deaths, to the U.S. consul in Matamoros, Jesse H. Johnson, who forwarded it to the Department of State.[10] Johnson noted in his letter to the secretary of state, which is titled "List of Names of Dead Mexicans," that Pierce "is an old settler in Brownsville, Tex . . . speaks the Spanish language fluently." Consul Johnson endorsed the list, explaining that "This statement is thought to be practically correct." Johnson added that Pierce "will be able to get many more [names] soon" but that "There are many more killed whose names will never be known."[11] It should be pointed out, though, that some of those in Pierce's list lost their lives while participating in raids and thus were not innocent victims. In 1917, Pierce published the best available history of the lower Rio Grande valley, in which he increased the number killed from one hundred to three hundred for the entire 1915–16 period.[12]

There exists another list, with sixty-two names, compiled by Jesse Pérez Sr.[13] Pérez had a rather extraordinary law enforcement career as a Hispanic undercover agent for the U.S. Secret Service penetrating *magonista* cells in Texas during 1906–10, then as a Texas Ranger and as a deputy sheriff in Hidalgo County during the "Bandit War."[14] There is some duplication between the Pierce and Pérez lists.

There are two contemporaneous estimates by U.S. government officials. The first is by a Secret Service agent based in San Antonio, Edward Tyrell. He made a swing through the lower valley in November 1915 and reported that "300 or more" Hispanics had been "shot down in cold blood."[15]

The second—and best—estimate of the Hispanic death toll was prepared by General Funston, commanding the Southern Department. In June 1916, Funston reported that state and local peace officers "did execute by hanging or shooting approximately three hundred suspected Mexicans on [the] American side of the river."[16] Funston had no reason to undercount the number of Hispanics killed in the lower valley.

Quite the contrary. Funston needed as many troops as could be rushed to the border, and the larger the death toll the more troops he might receive. Furthermore, he was keenly aware that two members of President Woodrow Wilson's cabinet, Attorney General T. W. Gregory and Postmaster General Albert Burleson, were Texans, and that Wilson's principal diplomatic adviser, Colonel Edward M. House, was a Texan who maintained very close ties to his native state. So if Funston had played numbers games with casualty figures that fact would have been quickly known in Washington. In addition, Funston by the early fall of 1915 had dozens (ultimately forty-one) of small detachments stationed on ranches up and down the Texas border, principally in the lower valley. A number of wealthy and powerful investors located outside Texas owned most of these ranches and were able to bring influence to bear on their senators, who successfully appealed to the secretary of war and army commanders in Washington to station small units on their properties to provide protection against *sediciosos*. These detachments coupled with thousands of cavalry and infantry based up and down the Rio Grande ensured that Funston had a unique reporting system providing daily coverage of casualties.

Among the witnesses who testified before the Fall Committee in 1919 were two who had a particularly detailed knowledge of what had occurred in 1915–16. The Democratic political boss of the lower valley, attorney James B. "Jim" Wells, stated that some 250–300 Hispanics had been killed and that this number was "perhaps exaggerated."[17] Republican leader R. B. Creager of Brownsville said that "conservatively, 100, maybe 200, Mexicans were killed due to bandit troubles. In my judgment 90 percent of those killed were as innocent as you or I of complicity in these Bandit outrages. They had a practice of making 'blood lists.' I have seen a list. No one will deny that they had them. Any Mexican suspected by any man of standing in the Valley or even halfway standing who said 'bad Mexican' would be put on a list. It was commonly reported that those Mexicans would disappear."[18]

Regarding the contentious issue of the Texas Rangers' role, unquestionably the Rangers committed atrocities during the "Bandit War." As we've seen, Captain Ransom summarily executed four Tejano suspects after the Olmito train wreck, and in all probability the Rangers did execute the fourteen Hispanics near Donna. But it is necessary to go beyond sweeping generalizations about the Rangers' conduct. One way of attempting to determine the Rangers' responsibility is to examine just how many of them were actually in the valley during which time periods.

T. R. Fehrenbach is mistaken in stating that Governor Ferguson sent approximately a thousand Rangers, most of them recruited especially for the "Bandit War."[19] The Texas State Ranger Force was not increased to a thousand men until 1918, as a wartime measure.[20] When the fighting broke out in July 1915 the Rangers numbered thirty-nine men. Captain John Sanders and his twelve men of Company A had responsibility for some 16,500 square miles of South Texas. But only Privates Reneau and Aldrich were immediately available for action, although Privates Felps and Edwards were stationed in San Benito and could assist.[21] To reinforce Sanders, Captain Monroe Fox and part of his twelve-man Company B were dispatched from West Texas. As of July 17, half of the Rangers were in the lower valley.[22]

On July 20, Captain Henry Ransom was commissioned to command a new company, Company D. Sanders was transferred out of the valley, and Ransom and his fourteen men were given responsibility for Jim Hogg, Brooks, Cameron, Hidalgo, Starr, and Zapata Counties. On August 9, Sanders returned to Brownsville with eight men; the rest of Fox's Company B, seven men, left from Marfa for Brownsville. So, in August virtually the entire Ranger force was now in the lower valley. However, on August 28, Fox's Company B was ordered back to West Texas, and on August 31 the governor ordered four Rangers from Ransom's Company D to be in attendance in court at Rio Grande City beginning on September 6. And Sanders's Company A was stationed for the better part of two months guarding Norias after the raid.[23] Thus it would appear that Ransom and his Company D did most of the killing. But Ransom never had more than sixteen men, and most of the time only twelve effectives.[24] It is most improbable that they could have killed all the Hispanics that have been claimed.

Furthermore, a complicating factor is that the term "Ranger" was very loosely employed. Rancher E. A. Sterling, testifying before the Fall Committee, stated that "The problem in assessing the Rangers' responsibility is that to the common Mexican class, everybody that wears a six-shooter is a Ranger, it may be an Immigration Officer, Customs, or a Deputy Sheriff or a cowman with a six-shooter."[25]

Folklorist Américo Paredes expounds on this view, writing that the term *rinche*, from "ranger," is important in border folklore, for it covers not just the Rangers but any other Anglos "armed and mounted and looking for Mexicans to kill." According to Paredes, members of posses and border patrolmen were also *rinches*. Even Pershing's cavalry are called *rinches* in some lower border ballads about the pursuit of Pancho Villa. Tejanos referred to the official Texas Rangers as *rinches de la Kinena*, or King Ranch Rangers, believing them to be the personal strong-arm men of Texas cattle barons.[26]

Evidently most Hispanics were killed by county officers and vigilantes, but the army also killed a number. For instance, Captain Frank McCoy reported in November 1915 that his two troops of cavalry had killed twenty-seven raiders since September 1.[27]

Regarding the Rangers, Paredes observed that Hispanics in the valley reassured each other in the belief that if it weren't for the soldiers, the Rangers wouldn't dare appear on the border; the Rangers always run and hide behind the soldiers when there is real trouble.[28] This would appear to be a case of self-delusion. There was a great deal of bombast concerning what the *revoltosos* were going to do to the hated Rangers, but not only did the general Hispanic population fear the Rangers, but the *sediciosos* also declined to take them on—they never attacked a Ranger company, or even an individual Ranger. The fact is that the Rangers killed more Rangers (two) than did the *sediciosos* and their *carrancista* allies (none).[29]

Fear of the Rangers extended to Representative J. T. Canales, who in 1919 launched a legislative investigation of the force. Canales was so terrified of the Rangers, especially Frank Hamer, that he sent his wife to inform the Speaker of the House that Canales was too afraid to go to the capitol.[30]

The numbers of Hispanics killed range from 102 to 10,000, but here again documentation is often lacking. The controversy over the number killed intensified in 1935. The key figure in this regard was the distinguished historian Walter Prescott Webb, who that year published his classic *The Texas Rangers* and asserted that the number killed in the valley was estimated at five hundred to five thousand.[31] Since Webb provided absolutely no evidence to support this statement, he could just as credibly have asserted that the number killed was estimated at five thousand to fifty thousand. In any case, for the last seventy-five years Webb's estimate has been parroted by some writers who haven't bothered to investigate the subject for themselves.

The first scholarly article to appear on the Plan de San Diego was in 1954 by Charles C. Cumberland.[32] He was able to obtain for the first time army documents dealing with the "Bandit War." On the casualty figures, he noted that approximately twenty Anglos, both soldiers and civilians, were killed. Cumberland also quoted General Funston as reporting that more than 150 Hispanics were "summarily executed."

In our 1978 article on the Plan de San Diego we cited General Funston's estimate of approximately three hundred Hispanic deaths. We also cited the official Anglo casualty toll—eleven soldiers killed and seventeen wounded, and six civilians killed and eight wounded.[33]

In 1979, Julian Samora, Joe Bernal, and Albert Peña published *Gunpowder Justice: A Reassessment of the Texas Rangers*,[34] which purported to be a scholarly reexamination. In it they too repeated Webb's estimate.

In his 1981 PhD dissertation Rodolfo Rocha compiled casualties based on army records, newspaper accounts, Ranger records, and so forth. He cites the killing of 222 Hispanics and the wounding of 65 others which "probably falls well below the actual numbers" but adds that historians reported that between three hundred and five thousand Mexicans were killed.[35]

Also in 1981, Robert J. Rosenbaum published *Mexicano Resistance in the Southwest: The Sacred Right of Self-Preservation*,[36] a first-rate study of the topic. But he too subscribed to the assertion that the estimates of Hispanics summarily shot or hanged range from three hundred to five thousand.[37]

In 1988, Vanderwood and Samponaro, in *Border Fury*, wrote that 150 Mexicans and Mexican Americans and 25 Anglos died in 1915 in seventy-three raids. And they added that "Ranger violence" resulted in the death of "hundreds more (some say thousands) of Mexican-Americans."[38]

In 1991, Ben Procter in *Just One Riot* asserted that the "reign of terror" between 1915 and 1919 claimed as many as five thousand Hispanic lives, and that despite this bloodbath Anglos along the border understandably condoned these excesses.[39]

A few years later, there appeared two works that focused increased attention on the matter of numbers. Kirby Warnock produced a television documentary titled *Border Bandits*. In the documentary three scholars commented on the number of Hispanics killed during the "Bandit War." Rodolfo Rocha, in the first portion of the documentary, stated that five thousand died. In a later segment he reduced the number, saying that three to five thousand were killed. Rolando Hinojosa asserted the usual Webb number, that five thousand were killed. Finally, Richard Ribb alleged that "thousands of Tejanos were killed." All this with no evidence whatsoever.

Then in 2003, Benjamin Johnson published *Revolution in Texas*, characterized by sweeping and unsupported generalizations such as "hundreds of names of murdered Tejanos have been documented." It would be interesting to see Johnson's documentation for this statement, or for his assertion that the *sediciosos* "killed dozens of Anglo farmers and drove countless more from their homes."[40]

Robert Utley in 2007 stated in *Lone Star Lawmen* that estimates of those killed by Rangers, local lawmen, and vigilantes usually range between one hundred and three hundred, "although an improbable five thousand also crept into the record."[41]

Following the appearance of Warnock's documentary and Johnson's book, the alleged death toll among Hispanics increased dramatically. Ruben Navarrette Jr., arguably the country's most prominent Hispanic newspaper columnist, wrote to the authors of the present work that according to his sources, seven thousand was a conservative figure, and the actual number could have been as high as ten thousand. His sources were SMU history professor Benjamin Johnson, the author of *Revolution in Texas*, and Kirby Warnock, producer and director of the documentary *Border Bandits*.[42] This grossly exaggerated number was repeated by Tejano historian Dan Arrellano, who stated that as many as fifteen thousand were killed between 1900 and the Plan de San Diego "simply because the Plan itself was not the beginning of the lynchings and murders, it was simply an escalation of a process that had started after the second Texas Invasion." However, "if you isolate the period of the Plan de San Diego, Navarrette's estimate would be more correct."[43]

Here is the most recent case of an unsubstantiated number being repeated. Although the exact number of Hispanic deaths during the "Bandit War" will never be known, it was certainly considerably less than ten thousand, which is a preposterous figure. Where was this mountain of corpses? The most accurate estimate appears to be General Funston's roughly three hundred.

For whatever reason, the Hispanic death toll has been significantly inflated. Perhaps this has been done for political reasons; a larger death toll means that the victimization factor is increased, and the "Bandit War" can be portrayed as some kind of mini-Holocaust.

22 Some Interesting Interpretations

A great deal of attention has been devoted to analyzing the Plan de San Diego itself. These exercises in textual criticism have produced some notable examples of innovative interpretation.

James T. Bratcher has the distinction of producing the most imaginative interpretation. He examines the religious, historic, cultural, and patriotic resonances of the phrase "Plan de San Diego," attempting to clarify a potential meaning of the phrase. Bratcher suggests that historians have perhaps misinterpreted the phrase, which had few ties to the South Texas village of San Diego. He suggests a second possibility—the words "San Diego" refer to San Diego the Moorslayer, the patron saint of Spain. True, there is a coincidence of names and a manifesto titled "Plan de San Diego" confiscated from Basilio Ramos, but Bratcher feels that his thesis deserves mention at least.[1]

A Mexican writer, Ciro R. de la Garza Treviño, published a forty-five-page monograph titled *Plan de San Diego*. Unaccountably, though, the first twenty pages have nothing to do with the Plan de San Diego, treating the activities of the Nazi fifth column in Mexico during World War II. He then discusses Venustiano Carranza's foreign policy, and on page thirty-three finally gets into the Plan de San Diego, which he mistakenly asserts was known among the initiated on October 13, 1915, but not known publicly until January 1916.[2]

Historian Benjamin Heber Johnson writes that the origins of the Plan and its authors' influence were so obscure that some have speculated that the Plan was really a forgery, altered or even entirely fabricated by the Texas Rangers or South Texas Anglos to justify their racism against Tejanos. According to Johnson, the Spanish original of the initial version of the Plan didn't survive. This gave Basilio Ramos's captors the opportunity to alter it. Johnson suggests that the provision calling for killing all Anglo males over the age of sixteen was especially suited to creating mass hysteria; beginning the Plan with a call for black uprising would have had much the same effect.[3]

Some would consider this not only judgmental but also perpetuating a negative stereotype. The problem with Johnson's politically correct scenario is that it is factually incorrect. Johnson ascribes the Plan to some vast racist conspiracy, but his whole speculative edifice crashes because there is a copy of the Plan—in Spanish and with exactly the same wording as the copy translated by the Immigration Service—in the personal papers of Agustín S. Garza, the leader, no less, of the Plan de San Diego movement.[4] Of course it could be argued that the Immigration Service or the Texas Rangers employed their skilled forgers to alter the Plan, as Johnson suggests, and then somehow they craftily planted the doctored Spanish version among Agustín Garza's personal papers, but this would be even more improbable than Johnson's weakly conceived conjecture.

Johnson may have gotten his idea of Texas Ranger involvement from the historian Walter Prescott Webb, who wrote that although the Plan's authorship was never revealed it didn't appear to be a Mexican composition. According to Webb, some said the Germans wrote it in order to cause trouble in Mexico. Others said that a well-known border figure who later held an important position in Texas produced it in order to topple the Carranza regime and regain a ranch that Mexican revolutionists had seized from him.[5]

The unnamed individual was William Martin Hanson, the future Texas Ranger captain who was involved in investigating the Plan. William Warren Sterling, a Ranger captain and later adjutant general of

Texas, in his memoirs repeats the insinuation regarding Hanson, writing that knowledgeable border residents alleged that a politician who later held an important position in a state agency was involved in the Plan's composition. This individual, whom Sterling characterized as a "schemer," had been harmed by Mexicans while living in Mexico and eagerly sought revenge. Sterling, who knew him more than casually, said he brought no credit to his agency and was quite capable of having been involved in the Plan.[6] Nevertheless, Hanson's involvement remains pure speculation.

Another approach to discussing the Plan de San Diego has been to keep changing the interpretation, best illustrated by the works of James Sandos. He initially stated that the Plan began with *huertistas*, then was taken over by the Germans, who subsequently shared their control with Carranza.[7] Sandos later dropped the German connection, continued to ascribe the Plan to Huerta's followers, and absolved Carranza of any involvement.[8] Sandos's third interpretation was that General Pablo González, Carranza's most loyal general, was orchestrating some kind of rogue operation much against Carranza's wishes.[9] Most recently, Sandos argues that the Plan was really an attempt to implement the principles of the anarchist Ricardo Flores Magón, who "did not comprehend the situation" and who "failed to recognize his intellectual progeny."[10] (Flores Magón wrote that the rebellion in Texas resulted not from the Plan de San Diego but rather from a struggle for social justice by Hispanics.)[11]

David Montejano has a simplistic view of what he terms "the armed insurrection of Texas Mexicans and its brutal suppression by Texas Rangers." He argues that the troubles in South Texas were essentially the armed conflict between an established ranch society and an aggressive farm society. The *sediciosos* and the Texas Rangers were the opposed military forces.[12] As has been shown, it was considerably more complicated than that.

One of the most recent writers on the Plan, Robert Utley, tries to cover the waterfront, stating that the "Bandit War" was more a patriotic rebellion against Anglo oppression than raids from Mexico, adding that most Mexicans whom Anglos called "bandits" in 1915 were militants fighting under the Plan de San Diego. Some took the Plan's objectives seriously; others sought revenge against Anglos while obtaining plunder. Some were Mexican nationals, even from Carranza's army, but some were Tejanos, U.S. citizens living and working in South Texas.[13]

And in any case, Utley, like some other writers on the Plan de San Diego, cites no Mexican sources. Thus his treatment not only of the Plan de San Diego but of the whole decade of the Mexican Revolution is completely one-sided.

Several writers arguing for a Tejano rebellion reflect the heated revolutionary rhetoric of the Chicano movement in the 1970s, when militants were cranking out manifestos such as the Plan de la Raza Unida, the Plan de Delano, the Plan de Aztlán, and the Plan de Santa Bárbara.[14] They naturally looked to the Plan de San Diego for inspiration.

Rodolfo Acuña, for instance, wrote a book titled *Occupied America: The Chicano's Struggle toward Liberation*[15] in which he didn't discuss the Plan de San Diego, apparently being unaware of it. In a subsequent work, *Occupied America: A History of Chicanos*,[16] he not only treats the Plan but asserts that genocide is quite acceptable as long as it is for a good cause and is carried out by third-world people. He states that clearly the most controversial aspect of the Plan called for killing all Anglo males over sixteen, but the sensationalism surrounding this provision has obscured a discussion of the necessity for an uprising. "Extremism must be understood in the prevailing conditions," and allowances must be made for the violence endured by Tejanos. Acuña argues that few would have called it extremism had Europeans produced a similar plan against Germany in World War II. "But a different standard seems to exist for Third World people."[17]

In a similar vein, Juan Gómez Quiñones also champions the liberation theme. In a curious exercise in logic he denounces not the Plan's call for a genocidal war without quarter but rather those who would use the Plan's call for a genocidal war without quarter as rationalization for racial persecution, adding that there has been insufficient study concerning the larger social and economic context surrounding the Plan or the concepts underlying "this liberation movement" and the consequences of its implementation.[18]

Another historian who reflects this approach is Dirk Raat. Commenting on the Plan and the later "Manifesto to the Oppressed Peoples of America" that purportedly appeared on February 20, 1915, he notes that because the Plan incited racial warfare, many observers failed to grasp that ten of the twenty-eight provisions dealt with economic subjects, calling for the proposed Social Republic of Texas to be a socialist state, with communal ownership of all rural properties and transportation systems and the abolition of exploitation of the proletariat.[19]

These writers apparently find it odd that Anglos would focus on the Plan's provisions calling for their massacre in a war without quarter and didn't ponder the deeper questions of the conditions producing the Plan. Imagine that.

Most recently, Trinidad Gonzales has challenged our interpretation of Venustiano Carranza's de facto recognition in 1915: "The Harris-Sadler thesis does not appear to hold up against the complexity of the events that surrounded the *revolución de Texas* and the Mexican Revolution."[20] Gonzales's argument rests on three points. First, the United States had already accorded Carranza what amounted to de facto recognition based not on his militarily superior position but because of his policy of protecting property rights, domestic and foreign. Carranza wanted official U.S. recognition but didn't need to foment an insurgency on U.S. soil to achieve that end. However, a complexity of which Gonzales is unaware is that President Woodrow Wilson inquired of Secretary of State Robert Lansing on August 7, 1915, why "you think it wise to put [Pancho] Villa in the way of getting money [through cattle exports] just at the moment when he is apparently weakened and on the verge of collapse?" Lansing replied: "The reason for furnishing Villa with an opportunity to obtain funds is this: We do not wish the Carranza faction to be the only one to deal with in Mexico. Carranza seems so impossible that an appearance, at least, of opposition to him will give us an opportunity to invite a compromise of factions."[21] Sure sounds as though the United States was considerably less supportive of Carranza than Gonzales believes.

Second, Gonzales states that we assume that Carranza could have ended the raids at any time, whereas it was the arrival of more American troops in early October 1915 that ended the raids into Texas, an assertion for which he produces no evidence. He adds that "Certainly

Carranza wanted to end the attacks to facilitate official recognition, but to portray that effort without acknowledging that the United States was already strongly supporting the Constitutional forces is problematic." As we've seen, what's problematic is the assertion that the United States was strongly supporting Carranza. The indisputable fact is that the raids ended within a week after Carranza's de facto recognition. As Jacobo Ayala Villarreal, who had some considerable knowledge of these events, slyly put it, as soon as Carranza was recognized the raids ended "as if by magic."

Third, Gonzales writes that we "operate from the assumption that Carranza had a command and control structure of his military forces that the current U.S. military enjoys."[22] Actually we don't, but what we do maintain is that Carranza had a command and control structure that functioned well enough to enable him to dominate the Mexican Revolution from 1913 to 1920.

Conclusion

As the prophet Hosea warned, "For they have sown the wind, and they shall reap the whirlwind." What were they thinking? Were the *sediciosos* too naive to realize that proclaiming—and trying to implement—a genocidal war without quarter wouldn't have serious—and unpleasant—consequences? You didn't have to be a college graduate to figure this out. A contemporary *corrido*, or ballad, titled "Los Sediciosos" lamented that the fuse had been lit by real Mexicans but it would be Tejanos who'd have to pay the price.[1]

Brownsville attorney and state representative J. T. Canales attributed the Plan to German propagandists and stated that "I don't believe the effect of it, that is the execution of it had any serious consequences."[2] On the other hand, prominent South Texas political boss James B. Wells testified that "Innocent men were killed in Hidalgo and Cameron Counties in 1915–16. I want to add that there were a lot more that should have been killed."[3]

With regard to Canales it should be mentioned that despite his rather odd statement quoted above he did take the Plan seriously, organizing the "Canales Scouts" to assist the army in combating raiders. The Scouts, though, were organized just as the raids ended. And Deodoro Guerra, the political boss of Hidalgo County, also opposed the *sedi-*

ciosos, on occasion leading posses against marauders. In Guerra's case of course his opposition stemmed at least in part from his *villista* sympathies. But what both Canales and Guerra illustrate is that the Hispanic establishment not only brought the Plan de San Diego to light but stood shoulder to shoulder with the Anglos against the militants, who drew their support largely from the lower Hispanic socioeconomic class.

As the Old West saying goes, a man's got to back his play. The *sediciosos*, having proclaimed a war without quarter, proved singularly unable to back their play. Not only didn't they generate much support in the rest of the Southwest, but even in Texas their rebellion was confined essentially to four counties—Cameron, Hidalgo, Starr, and Kenedy—(out of the 254 counties in the state). What the *sediciosos* did produce was a massive Anglo backlash—it became open season on "bad Meskins." In this connection, those who maintain that the Plan was essentially a Tejano rebellion stress the element of Anglo racism as directed at Hispanics. However, the Plan itself embodied a fair amount of Hispanic racism toward Anglos, something that is rarely mentioned. It would be like the Japanese complaining about having atom bombs dropped on them but neglecting to mention Pearl Harbor.

The Plan de San Diego affair unfolded in three distinct phases. The first lasted from January to June 1915 and was characterized by the arrest of Basilio Ramos, the discovery of the Plan, and Ramos's account of the Plan's alleged *huertista* origins. The Plan was really written by *magonistas*, although precisely by whom remains unclear. There appeared an expanded version of the Plan—the "Manifesto to the Oppressed Peoples of America," but since no violence occurred, people generally dismissed the Plan as ridiculous.

The second phase erupted in July 1915 and lasted through October. Luis de la Rosa and Aniceto Pizaña were perceived as the leaders of a Tejano rebellion, but the evidence indicates that it was the *carrancistas* who were manipulating them in a covert operation. A wave of raids into South Texas from Mexico convulsed the region. Despite the turmoil they caused, the *sediciosos* made little headway militarily, their offensive consisting largely of hit-and-run raids. A scorecard listing the principal engagements would read:

Los Tulitos	1915	victory
Galveston Ranch	1915	defeat
Las Norias	1915	defeat
Ojo de Agua	1915	defeat
Progreso	1915	defeat
Olmitos train wreck	1915	victory
Webb Station	1916	defeat
San Ignacio	1916	defeat
Cortillo Ranch	1916	defeat

So, their principal military accomplishment was wrecking a train. The one area where they excelled was propaganda. The *sediciosos* were a lot better at writing than at fighting.

And for all the turmoil they caused, the insurgents inflicted remarkably few Anglo casualties, but they managed to get hundreds of Hispanics killed. This would fit with the *magonistas*' track record of ineptitude, even in this case with substantial assistance and direction by the *carrancistas*. The weight of evidence indicates that Venustiano Carranza, fighting for the survival of his regime, used the *sediciosos* as pawns to achieve his own ends, which revolved around securing diplomatic recognition from the Unites States, which he gained on October 19, 1915. He promptly shut down the *sedicioso* movement, and it collapsed like a punctured balloon. Carranza also imprisoned some of the *sedicioso* leaders, to avoid problems with the United States. The Plan de San Diego passed into history. There it would have remained but for an unexpected development—Pancho Villa's raid on Columbus, New Mexico, and the resulting dispatch into Chihuahua of General John J. Pershing's Punitive Expedition.

This led to the third phase of the Plan—from March through July 1916. Carranza had kept the Plan's Tejano leadership on a short leash. Now, faced with the crisis caused by thousands of American troops in Chihuahua, he resurrected the Plan. The strategy was to be a repetition of that used successfully in 1915—raids into Texas as leverage to achieve foreign-policy goals, in this case to force the recall of the Punitive Expedition. But this time elements in the Mexican military, notably General Pablo González, also planned an invasion of Texas by

Carranza troops. In 1916 the United States was not a military superpower, and evidently some in the Mexican Army believed they stood a reasonable chance in a war.

The strategy backfired badly. The proposed invasion was shelved, and a *sedicioso* raid provoked the crossing of American forces into Tamaulipas. This crisis in June 1916 almost plunged the two countries into war; as the Texas Court of Criminal Appeals ruled, an undeclared state of war existed along the Rio Grande. President Woodrow Wilson prepared a message to Congress requesting authority to suppress military activity in the northern tier of Mexican states. And the United States called up the 158,000-strong National Guard and rushed 110,000 of them to the border. Carranza backed down, abandoned his policy of brinksmanship, and agreed to seek a diplomatic solution. He once again shut down the *sedicioso* movement, and this time the Plan de San Diego did indeed pass into history.

Interestingly enough, Mexican historians haven't conducted serious research on the Plan de San Diego, perhaps to avoid raking up old controversies with the United States, although what the affair reveals is that Venustiano Carranza, the president of a country wracked by revolution, played Woodrow Wilson like a violin in 1915. Even though some scholars argue that Carranza's control of Mexico was tenuous, Carranza dominated the Mexican Revolution from 1913 to 1920. Convincing proof of the Carranza regime's involvement in the Plan has come to light, mainly through the papers of Agustín S. Garza. Carranza's cover story for his covert operation had essentially held up for almost a century. Not bad.

The Plan de San Diego affair has been viewed as a Tejano rebellion led by Luis de la Rosa and Aniceto Pizaña. However, de la Rosa and Pizaña represented neither the brains nor the brawn of the movement, which was organized and directed in Mexico. Mexicans wrote the Plan de San Diego, provided the indispensable rebel sanctuary and base of operations, supplied much of the military manpower, conducted an intensive propaganda campaign, and from Matamoros, Monterrey, and Mexico City directed the rebels' movements. The only times the Plan mattered were when it received support from Mexico, and such support came only when it suited Carranza. Viewing Tejanos as a useful fifth column, Carranza skillfully played on their hopes and fears as a means of exerting pressure on the United States. When his policies changed, they were cynically abandoned to their fate. Unfortunately, the Anglos also viewed Tejanos as a fifth column, with the result that we have seen. The Plan left a legacy of racial tension in South Texas that has endured to the present.[4]

But viewing the Plan in terms of South Texas, ethnic relations, and law enforcement, especially the Texas Rangers, is too narrow a focus. If the Plan is viewed from another perspective—within the context of the Mexican Revolution—a different picture emerges. The Plan was written by Mexicans and was used by the Mexican government for its own purposes. Thus the Plan had significance far beyond just South Texas. It had an impact on U.S.-Mexican relations, as with the mobilization of the National Guard to protect the border. And in an indirect way, the Plan affected the preparedness of the United States for World War I. The training the National Guard received between June 1916 and April 6, 1917, when the United States entered the war, was invaluable. For this the *sediciosos* could claim some credit.

Notes

Abbreviations

AGC	Agustín S. Garza Collection
ABF	Albert B. Fall Collection
ABFFP	Albert Bacon Fall Family Papers
BI	Bureau of Investigation
DHRM	Documentos Históricos de la Revolución Mexicana
Exp. BF	*Expediente* Brigada Fierros
Exp. EF	*Expediente* Esteban Fierros
FA	Forseck affidavit
FRC-FW	Federal Records Center, Fort Worth
MID	Military Intelligence Division
NARS	National Archives and Records Service
PGA	Pablo González Archive
RDS	Records of the Department of State
RG	Record Group

Preface

1. Additional light on the Plan may be shed if and when the estimated fourteen thousand coded telegrams in the Carranza archive are decoded. See Ruiz, "Centro de Estudios," 95.
2. See, for example, Sandos, *Rebellion in the Borderlands*; Johnson, *Revolution in Texas*; Warburton, "The Plan of San Diego."
3. Harris and Sadler, *Texas Rangers*, 212, 213.
4. Microcopy, Investigative Records, 1908–22, Records of the Federal Bureau of Investigation, RG 65, NARS. Years after we began using these twenty-four rolls of microfilm, the National Archives numbered the rolls as 851–74. We use the original FBI roll numbers (1–24) using BI preceded by the roll number.

1. The Plan de San Diego

1. U.S. v. Basilio Ramos, Jr. et al., no. 2152, District Court, Brownsville, FRC-FW.
2. J. R. Harold, Immigrant Inspector, translated the Plan and certified that this was a correct translation. The document was typewritten in Spanish and signed with pen and ink. E. P. Reynolds to Supervising Inspector, January 30, 1915, roll 13, ABF. The Plan was also published in: United States, *Investigation of Mexican Affairs,* 1205–7 (hereinafter cited as *Investigation*); the Plan and various propaganda pieces are quoted in General Funston's Annual Report for the Southern Department, 1916, Records of the Adjutant General's Office, RG 94, NARS.
3. Harris and Sadler, *Texas Rangers*, 212.

2. The Plan Surfaces

1. Ramos Immigration file, ABF; F. J. McDevitt reports, January 26, 27, 1915, 8BI.
2. U.S. Army, "Report of general conditions along the Mexican border . . . ," December 19, 1914, 812.00/14078, RDS, hereinafter cited as "Weekly Report;" Marks report, December 18, 1916, 6BI.
3. Breniman reports, January 31, 1915, 8BI, and April 27, 29, 1915, 7BI; Barnes reports, January 30, March 3, April 19, 22, 1915, 7BI; Barnes to Camp, April 23, 1915, 6BI.
4. McDevitt report, January 22, 1915, 8BI; see also Breniman report, February 3, 1915, 8BI.
5. McDevitt reports, January 22–27, 1915, 8BI; see also Barnes report, January 30, 1915, 7BI.
6. McDevitt report, January 27, 1915, 8BI.
7. Weekly Report, March 31, 1915, 812.00/14791, RDS.
8. McDevitt reports, January 21, 23, 1915, 8BI.
9. Breniman report, February 3, 1915, 8BI.
10. Deodoro Guerra's brother Jacobo was the sheriff of adjoining Starr County.
11. Everett Anglin testimony, *Investigation*, 1302–3; Tom Mayfield testimony, *Investigation*, 1295–96; Breniman report, January 30, 1915, 8BI.
12. Transcripts of Ramos's examining trial, February 4, 1915, and his immigration hearing, March 20, 1915, ABF; *Investigation*, 1785.
13. He was said to be a former lawyer from Nuevo Laredo who died in Monterrey in mid-1916. Customs inspector Robert Rumsey claimed that González was a signer of the Plan de San Diego. Ross reports, December 6, 1916, 6BI.

14. Exhibits 1, 3, 6, 7, 8, ABF; Breniman report, January 28, 1915, 8BI.
15. McDevitt reports, January 24–27, 1915, 8BI.
16. McDevitt finally filed a complaint under Section Six of the Federal Criminal Code. Breniman report, February 3, 1915, 8BI; U.S. v Basilio Ramos et al., no. 249, U.S. Commissioner, Brownsville, FRC-FW.
17. McDevitt report, January 31, 1915, 8BI.
18. AGC.
19. See Montejano, *Anglos and Mexicans,* 117; Stout, *Border Conflict,* 81; Clendenen, *Blood on the Border,* 181.
20. Barnes to Ross, June 20, 1916, 6BI.
21. Barnes to Green, November 5 [?], 1916, 6BI.
22. Mennet report, January 6, 1917, 6BI.
23. "Casa Blanca, San Diego, Texas," 4.
24. Tyler et al., *New Handbook of Texas,* 5:69–70; Lynch, *Duke of Duval.*
25. *Brownsville Daily Herald,* August 11, 1914, December 13, 1915.
26. Tyler et al., *New Handbook of Texas,* 5:69–70; Harris and Sadler, *Texas Rangers,* 311–12; *Brownsville Daily Herald,* August 11, 1914.
27. Harris and Sadler, *Texas Rangers,* 276.
28. See the contract (Exhibit D) dated on June 12, 1915 and the agreement dated on June 19, 1915, between the Royal Brewing Company and J. K. Forseck & Co., and John Kvake Forseck's signed and notarized affidavit, October 3, 1919, Office of the Counselor, Department of State, RG 59, NARS. Hereinafter cited as FA.
29. *Laredo Weekly Times,* July 25, 1915.
30. Richkarday, *Jack Danciger,* 126–35, 137, 150; Ann Marie Swenson translated this work as *Jack Danciger: His Life and Work* (N.p.: self-published, 1963).
31. Smith, "Mexican Immigrant Press."
32. See Smith, "Gringo Propagandist"; see also Smith's "Carrancista Propaganda."
33. Richkarday, *Jack Danciger,* 119–22, 132–36, 141–43, 155, 158–66.
34. Richkarday, *Jack Danciger,* 186.
35. See Smith, "Mexican Revolution in Kansas City."
36. Trial transcript, February 4, 1915, ABF.
37. Breniman report, February 6, 1915, 8BI.
38. One Ignacio Risa was recruiting men for the *carrancistas* in Del Rio in July, but it is unknown whether this was the same man. Barnes report, July 30, 1915, 9BI.
39. Breniman report, January 31, 1915, 8BI.
40. Breniman report, April 30, 1915, 8BI; Barnes report, March 3, 1915, 8BI.
41. Mennet report, February 28, 1917, 10BI; E. P. Reynolds to Supervising Inspector,

January 30, 1915, transcript of Ramos's immigration hearing, March 20, 1915, and Reynolds to Supervising Inspector, February 8, 1915, ABF.

42. Katz, *Pancho Villa,* 483–84; Garrett to Secretary of State, January 7, 1915, 812.00/14159, and January 9, 1915, 812.00/14172, RDS; Hanna to Secretary of State, January 15, 1915, 812.00/14222, RDS.
43. Hanna to Secretary of State, January 16, 1915, 812.00/14228, RDS; Blocker to Secretary of State, May 21, 1915, 812.00/15059, RDS; Garrett to Secretary of State, May 22, 1915, 812.00/15060, RDS.
44. Trial transcript, February 4, 1915, ABF.
45. Allen Gerlach stated that Ramos's father and three brothers were gathering arms in Lajitas, Texas, for the Huerta faction and that one of the brothers was arrested near Alpine. However, this was a different Ramos family. "Conditions along the Border," 198–99.
46. F.H.U. to Ramos, February 2, 1915, ABF; Barnes report, March 3, 1915, 8BI.
47. Barnes to Ross, December 2, 1916, 232-84BI; Ross report, December 3, 1916, 6BI.
48. Garza to Ramos, January 15, 1915; this is a typed English translation from the files of the Immigration Service, ABF.
49. Caballo to Ramos, January 16, 1915, ABF.
50. Interestingly, an undated cryptic notation in a memorandum in Agustín Garza's papers refers to León Caballo's journey from San Diego to Mexico in search of adherents to advance the Plan. This handwritten memorandum also has lists of those who attended three meetings: (1) Francisco González, José López Benavides, one Ayala, Basilio Ramos, and Agustín Garza; (2) Amado González, Luis Ferrigno, Arturo P. Saenz, Domingo A. Peña, Porfirio Santos, Basilio Ramos, one Cisneros, and Agustín S. Garza; (3) "J. F. Walcher" = León Cárdenas Martínez (muerto) [a known *magonista*], "J. R. Becker" = Francisco Múzquiz Garza, "J. N. Nagraqui" = Rafael Ochoa, "F. F. Lippi," "P. Beeni," "Juan Bub," "W. Cárcega," "Juctlaca Ubaqui," and "León Caballo" = Agustín S. Garza. On February 20, 1915, the "Manifesto to the Oppressed Peoples of America" was promulgated. Ramos indeed used aliases for some of the signatories: "J. F. Walcher" was really León Cárdenas Martínez, "J. R. Becker" was Francisco Múzquiz Garza, "J. N. Nagraqui" was Rafael Ochoa, and "León Caballo" was of course Agustín S. Garza. See 2009.0060112f, AGC.
51. Barnes to Postmaster, April 23, 1915, 8BI; Breniman report, April 30, 1915, 8BI; Barnes report, March 3, 1915, 8BI.
52. Breniman reports, February 6, April 30, 1915, 8BI; Barnes to Herring, March 3, 1915, 8BI; Barnes to Breniman, May 7, 1915, 8BI.

53. *Brownsville Daily Herald*, February 4, 5, 1915.
54. "To Whom It May Concern," February 7, 1915, U.S. Consulate Matamoros, Mexico, 1915–1917, Foreign Service Post Records, RG 84, NARS; hereinafter cited as Matamoros Post Records; *Brownsville Daily Herald*, February 6, 8, 1915.
55. Breniman report, February 11, 1915, 8BI; *Brownsville Daily Herald*, February 11, 1915.
56. Breniman report, February 19, 1915, 8BI; *Brownsville Daily Herald*, February 11, 16, 1915.
57. Breniman report, March 4, 1915, 8BI; *Brownsville Daily Herald*, February 20, 27, March 1, 1915.

3. The Magonistas

1. Ramos Immigration file, ABF.
2. Harris and Sadler, *Secret War*, 17–20.
3. Barnes to Bielaski, February 12, 1915, 5BI; Barnes to Welles, February 16, 1915, 5BI.
4. Chief to Barnes, February 20, 1915, 5BI.
5. Breniman report, February 21, 1915, 8BI.
6. *Brownsville Daily Herald*, February 20, 1915.
7. "León Caballo's" commission, February 21, 1915, AGC.
8. "Genealogy Map. Agustín de la Garza Solís, Father Branch," and "Genealogy Map, Agustín de la Garza Solís, Mother Branch," AGC.
9. "Fact Sheet on Agustín de la Garza Solís," Museum of South Texas History, Edinburg, Texas; Valls testimony, *Investigation*, 1210.
10. 1910 U.S. Federal Census; unsigned to Garza, October 23, 1910, AGC.
11. A. S. Garza et al. to Jefe Político, August 30, September 5, 1913, AGC.
12. Undated note: 92009.006b (ii), AGC.

4. The Mexican Connection

1. Crile, *Charlie Wilson's War*, 102.
2. Mendoza, "Perspectives," 2–3.
3. Furman, "Vida Nueva," 183.
4. Hopkins to McCoy, September 5, 1915, Frank R. McCoy Papers, Library of Congress, Washington DC.
5. De la Huerta, *Memorias*, 99–100. We thank Friedrich Schuler, a historian at Portland State University, for bringing this to our attention.

6. The proclamation in quoted in Barnes report, May 20, 1916, 4BI; See Meyer, *Huerta,* 215.
7. Johnson, *Revolution in Texas*, 82.
8. Meyer, "Mexican-German Conspiracy of 1915," and *Huerta*, 215, 218.
9. Gerlach, "Conditions along the Border," 198.
10. Sandos, "The Plan of San Diego."
11. Longoria, "Revolution, Visionary Plan, and Marketplace."
12. Bruscino, "A Troubled Past," 33.
13. Rausch, "Exile and Death of Victoriano Huerta"; Grieb, *The United States and Huerta,* 178–82.
14. Harris and Sadler, *Texas Rangers*, 220–21.
15. Weekly Report, February 9, 1918, 10014-44, Army War College, MID.
16. http://www.mexico-tenoch.com/diputadosconstituyentes.htm; Naranjo, *Diccionario,* 143; *Investigation*, 1554.
17. Exhibits 10 and 11, January 12, 1915, ABF.
18. Garza to Ramos, January 15, 1915, Exhibit 6, ABF.
19. It was also alleged that "Francisco B. Guerra, one of Nafarrates's lieutenants, in the garrison at Matamoros with him, was the man who went on Ramos' bond after his arrest that time." Stone report, October 31, 1915, 8BI.
20. *La Prensa* (San Antonio), May 18, 1915; Sandos, "Plan of San Diego," 10–11; John Valls testimony, *Investigation*, 1205; *Brownsville Daily Herald*, May 9, 1916. The Ramos case was continued through 1917. Judge's Bench Dockets, Criminal Cases, U.S. District Court, Brownsville, vols. 6 and 7, FRC-FW.
21. Cumberland, *Mexican Revolution,* 190–93; Vasconcelos to Bryan, March 24, 1915, 812.00/15106, RDS.
22. Weekly Report, March 20, 1915, 812.00/14737, RDS; Vasconcelos, *La Tormenta*, 312; *Brownsville Daily Herald*, March 8, 1915.
23. *Brownsville Daily Herald*, March 31, 1915.
24. See *Brownsville Daily Herald*, July 12, 13, 23, 26, 1915.
25. De la Garza Treviño, *Historia de Tamaulipas,* 222–23; Garrett to Secretary of State, March 27, 1915, 812.00/14714, RDS; Harrison to Secretary of State, March 27, 1915, 812.00/14710, March 28, 1915, 812.00/14672, RDS; Funston to Agwar, March 28, 1915, 812.00/14724, RDS.
26. Breckinridge to Funston, March 29, 1915, 812.00/14735, RDS.
27. Weekly Report, February 27, 1915, 812.00/14526, RDS.
28. *Investigation*, 1201; Valls's source about the Plan was allegedly Mrs. Adolfo Magnón, a kinswoman of Carranza's. She and her husband had been in Car-

ranza's employ "from the first . . . She must be handled very carefully." W. M. Hanson to J. F. Kearful, November 7, 1919, William Buckley Papers, Nettie Lee Benson Latin American Collection, University of Texas at Austin.

29. *Investigation*, 1201.
30. Robert L. Barnes testimony, *Investigation*, 1231–32.
31. Barnes to Green, November 28, 1916, 232-84BI.

5. The "Bandit War" Begins

1. See, for example, Harris and Sadler, *Secret War*, 64–65.
2. *Brownsville Daily Herald*, July 20, 1915.
3. Vann testimony, *Investigation*, 1297.
4. Hill's testimony, *Investigation*, 1253–54.
5. *Brownsville Daily Herald*, August 6, 1915.
6. *Brownsville Daily Herald*, July 6–9, 13, August 3, 1915; Lon Hill testimony, *Investigation*, 1254.
7. *Brownsville Daily Herald*, July 13, 1915.
8. *Brownsville Daily Herald*, July 9, 1915.
9. *Brownsville Daily Herald*, July 20, 1915.
10. *Brownsville Daily Herald*, July 21, 1915.
11. Lon Hill testimony, *Investigation*, 1254; *Brownsville Daily Herald*, July 19, 20, 1915.
12. *Brownsville Daily Herald*, July 24, 1915.
13. Lon Hill testimony, *Investigation*, 1254–55; *Brownsville Daily Herald*, July 26, 1915.
14. *Brownsville Daily Herald*, July 29, 1915.
15. *Brownsville Daily Herald*, August 2, 4, 1915.
16. Webb report, March 17, 1916, 6BI.
17. Joe Taylor testimony, *Investigation*, 1317.
18. Robert Barnes testimony, *Investigation*, 1233.
19. One of his poems is in Barnes's report, November 13, 1915, 232-84BI.
20. "Pizaña, Aniceto," Tyler et al., *New Handbook of Texas*, 5:223–24; Lon Hill testimony, *Investigation*, 1262–63.
21. Barnes report, October 30, 1915, 8BI.
22. Mennet report, January 17, 1917, 6BI.
23. Figueroa to Pizaña, May 18, 1915, 232-84 BI; Flores Magón to Pizaña, February 11, 1915, 6BI.
24. The Spanish and English versions are in Rogers report, November 16, 1915, 6BI.

25. Harris and Sadler, "Plan of San Diego, 387–88; Barnes to Bielaski, including extracts from the above newspapers, September 2, 1915, 7BI; *Laredo Weekly Times*, August 29, September 5, 1915.
26. Barnes to Barkey, April 19, 1916, 12BI.
27. *La Prensa*, May 18, 1916.
28. *La Prensa*, June 17, 1916; *Laredo Weekly Times*, June 9, 1918.
29. AGC.
30. See the testimony of Captain Harry Wheeler, *Investigation*, 1887.
31. *Laredo Weekly Times*, August 15, 1915.
32. Craft report, May 9, 1917, 232-84 and 6BI; Samson to Craft, May 7, 1917, 232-84 and 6BI.
33. In Arizona: Roberto Dickson—Tucson, Juan Montalvo—Benson, Anatolio Pérez—Florence, Juan López—Nogales, Patricio Mazo—Bisbee, Lucio Garza—Tombstone, Avelino Zertuche—Mineral Park, Antonio M. Sabino—Campo Verde.

    In Colorado: Valentín Lazo—Silverton, Anastacio Sifuentes—Durango, Ildefonso Risa—Rico, Juan Silva—Denver, Ernesto González—Leadville, Francisco Borrego—Bessemer, José Landín—Las Animas, Pedro Garatuza—Trinidad.

    In California: Máximo Saucedo—San Diego, Teodoro Gálvez—Pomona, Domingo Góngora—Los Angeles, Jesús Fernández—San Bernardino, Santiago Ramírez—National City, Fidencio Hinojosa—Sacramento, Teófilo Renegado—San Jose, Juan José de la Cruz—Vallejo.

    In New Mexico: Felipe Santibañes—Las Cruces, Fidencio Samaniego—Albuquerque, Guadalupe García—San Pedro, Hipólito Sandoval—Deming, Juan Antonio Recio—Mescalero, Adalberto Castillo—Springer, AGC.
34. Stone report, July 13 [?], 1916, 232-84BI; Mennet report, December 3, 1916, 6BI and 232-84BI.
35. Barnes reports, August 28, 31, 1915, 6BI; Barkey report, August 30, 1915, 6BI.
36. See Barnes report, December 5, 1915, 6BI, for a translation of Hernández's article of August 26, 1915.
37. Barnes reports, September 1, 2, 3, 1916, 6BI; Barkey report, September 6, 1915, 6BI; Rogers report, October 24, 1915, 6BI; Wright report, April 27, 1916, 12BI; Longoria, "Revolution, Visionary Plan, and Marketplace," 218–20; Beckham report, October 10, 1915, 8BI, contains a copy of another inflammatory circular, titled "Mexicans to Arms!" *Regeneración*, Nos. 110, 221; Barnes report, January 14, 1916, 6BI; Barnes to Braun, April 29, 1916, 12BI; Webster report, June 12, 1916, 12BI.

38. Wright report, September 26, 1915, 6BI; Barnes report, September 25, 1915, January 22, 1916, 6BI.
39. *Brownsville Daily Herald*, August 3, 4, 9, 1915.
40. Barnes report, November 13, 1915, 232-84BI; *Brownsville Daily Herald*, November 24, 1915.
41. Lon Hill testimony, *Investigation*, 1255–56; Mike Monahan testimony, *Investigation*, 1265–66; Mennet report, January 18, 1917, 6BI; Rogers reports, September 29, 1915, 6BI and November 5, 1915, 6BI; Barnes reports, November 18, 24, 1915, 8BI; Aniceto Pizaña's wife and wounded son moved to Brownsville. *Brownsville Daily Herald*, September 27, 1915.
42. *Brownsville Daily Herald*, August 3, 1915.
43. *Brownsville Daily Herald*, August 5, 6, 1915.
44. *Brownsville Daily Herald*, August 4, 1915.
45. *Brownsville Daily Herald*, August 4, 5, 1915.
46. *Brownsville Daily Herald* August 7, 1915.
47. Testimony of W. B. Hinkley, *Investigation*, 1244, 1181–84; testimony of Sheriff Vann, "Proceedings of the Joint Committee of the Senate and the House in the Investigation of the Texas State Ranger Force," 3 vols., 1919, 1:560–62, Archives Division, Texas State Library, Austin; Sterling, *Trails and Trials*, 32–33.
48. Creager testimony, "Proceedings," 1:355.
49. *Brownsville Daily Herald*, August 7, 1915.
50. He stated in 1917 that in November 1914 he was going to start a revolution in Cuero, Texas, but this revolution was postponed until further notice. "The reason for this, he said, was that the heavy rains prevented and that conditions were not favorally [*sic*] to their plans. Máximo Castillo was with Tostado at Cuero and Victoria working for this same cause in 1914." Sorola report, March 19, 1917, 232-84BI.
51. *Brownsville Daily Herald*, July 25, 1916.
52. Barnes report, May 27, 1916, 4BI.
53. Barnes reports, May 20, 27, 1916, 4BI; Barnes to Green, November 28, 1916, 232-84BI; Sorola report, April 4, 1917, 4BI.
54. Wright report, May 30, 1916, 4BI.
55. Barkey report, May 30, 1916, 4BI; Wright report, May 30, 1916, 4BI; Beckham reports, June 2, 1916, 4BI; U.S. v. Francisco Alvarez Tostado, U.S. Commissioner, Brownsville, no number; U.S. v. Francisco Alvarez Tostado, U.S. Commissioner, San Antonio, no. 419, FRC-FW; Barnes to Green, July 5 [?], 1916, 4BI.

56. Barnes reports, July 24, November 7, 1916, 4BI, December 15, 1916, 6BI; Spencer reports, July 30, August 4, 12, 28, 1916, 4BI; Breniman to Walker, November 12 [?], 1916, 4BI; Breniman to Rogers, November 25, 1916, 4BI; Green to Barnes, December 1, 1916, 4BI; Ross reports, December 3, 1916 and December 9, 1916, 4BI; Mennet report, December 14, 1916, 11BI.
57. Mennet report, December 21, 1916, 6BI.
58. Sorola reports, February 13, 14, 18, 20, 22, 1917, 6BI, March 20, 1917, 232-84BI; Beckham report, May 24, 1916, 12BI.
59. Sorola reports, February 23, March 19, 20, 26, 1917, 232-84BI.
60. Sorola report, March 20, 1917, 232-84BI.
61. Sorola report, April [?], 1917, 6BI; However, Catarino Garza's biographer states that Garza was killed in March 1895 in an attack on Bocas del Toro, a town on an island off northern Panama. Young, *Catarino Garza's Revolution,* 295–99.
62. Mennet report, May 11, 1917, 232-84 and 6BI; Sorola report, April 28 [?], May 3, 4, 11, 1917, 6BI; Sorola and Alvarez Tostado to González, March 20, 1917, 232-84BI.
63. Sorola reports, March 5, 13, 23, 1917, 4BI, March 19, 20, 23, 26, 27, 30, 31, April 8, 24, 26, 29, 1917, 6BI; Breniman report, March 28, 1917, 6BI.
64. Sorola reports, May 5, 18, 1917, 6BI; see also Sorola reports, February 4, 14, 1917, 232-84BI.

6. The "Bandit War" Intensifies

1. Lon Hill testimony, *Investigation*, 1256; Nellie F. Austin testimony, *Investigation*, 1312–15; Barnes report, August 19, 1915, 6BI; *Brownsville Daily Herald,* August 6, 1915.
2. *Brownsville Daily Herald,* August 6, 1915.
3. *Brownsville Daily Herald*, August 6, 1915.
4. *Brownsville Daily Herald*, August 7, 11, 1915.
5. Gerlach, "Conditions along the Border," 200.
6. Manuel Rincones's statement is in Barnes report, November 29, 1915, 232-84BI.
7. Mennet report, May 24, 1917, 6BI.
8. Martin became a peace officer and was killed at Raymondville in November, 1917, while trying to quell a disturbance at a *baile*. *Brownsville Daily Herald,* December 1, 1917.
9. Joe Taylor testimony, *Investigation*, 1315–18.
10. Marcus Hines testimony, *Investigation*, 1309–12.
11. *Kingsville Record,* August 13, 1915.

12. Kleiber testimony, *Investigation*, 1287.
13. Sheriff W. E. Vann identified Pedro Paz, Antonio Rocha, and José Benavides as *sediciosos*. Vann testimony, *Investigation*, 1296.
14. Harris and Sadler, *Texas Rangers*, 263–66; Lon Hill testimony, *Investigation*, 1257; Marcus Hines testimony, *Investigation*, 1310; Vann testimony, *Investigation*, 1300–1302; Barnes to Green, November 26, 1916, 232-84BI.
15. *Brownsville Daily Herald*, August 9, 1915.
16. Manuel Rincones statement, *Investigation*, 1284–85; Kleiber testimony, *Investigation*, 1286–87; Barnes report, November 29, 1915, 8BI.
17. Everett Anglin testimony, *Investigation*, 1306.
18. Ricaut to González, September 2, 1915; González to Ricaut, September 13, 1915, roll 26B, PGA; W. L. Gibson to W. K. Adams, December 1, 1915, 5761-1053, MID (Army War College). "W. L. Gibson" was the cover name for Captain W. E. W. MacKinley, a Military Intelligence operative on the border. See "W. E. W. M." to "Dear Friend," November 8, 1915, 5761-1040, MID (Army War College).
19. *Kingsville Record*, August 27, 1915; *Laredo Weekly Times*, August 15, September 5, 1915.
20. *Brownsville Daily Herald*, August 9, 10, 12, 1915.
21. Frank Hamer interview with J. Evetts Haley, February 1, 1947, JEH II, J-4, Haley Memorial Library & History Center, Midland, Texas.
22. E. A. Sterling testimony, "Proceedings," 2:1501–4.
23. Harris and Sadler, *Texas Rangers*, 256–60; For a sympathetic treatment of Ransom, by his granddaughter, see Goodrich, *Captain Ransom, Texas Ranger*.
24. "Proceedings," 2:1329.
25. *Brownsville Daily Herald*, November 27, 1915.
26. See, for instance, "Fighting on the Mexican Border"; George Patullo, "Once a Mexican, Always?" *Saturday Evening Post*, August 12, 1916, 3–4 ff.; Marvin, "Bandits and the Borderland"; Marvin, "The Quick and the Dead."
27. Gerald Scarborough to Louis R. Sadler, e-mail, March 14, 2011; Utley, *Lone Star Lawmen*, 34, 35; Johnson, *Revolution in Texas*, 113–14; and especially Ribb, "José Tomás Canales and the Texas Rangers," 9, 314–32.
28. *Brownsville Daily Herald*, August 9, 1915.
29. Barnes report, November 24, 1915, 8BI; *Brownsville Daily Herald*, August 11, 1915.
30. Barnes report, November 22 [?], 1915, 8BI.
31. *Brownsville Daily Herald*, August 9, 1915.
32. *Brownsville Daily Herald*, August 10, 1915.

33. *Brownsville Daily Herald*, August 10, 1915.
34. *Laredo Weekly Times*, August 15, 1915; *Kingsville Record*, August 13, 1915; *Brownsville Daily Herald*, August 9, 1915.
35. Barnes report, November 24, 1915, 8BI; *Brownsville Daily Herald*, August 17, 1915.
36. *Brownsville Daily Herald*, August 16, 1916.
37. With the arrival of the Fort Sill forces, two troops of the Third Cavalry guarded Rio Grande City; one troop of the Twelfth Cavalry was at Mission; one troop of the Twelfth Cavalry and a company of the Twenty-Sixth Infantry were at Mercedes; a troop of the Twelfth Cavalry and two companies and a half of the Twenty-Sixth Infantry were at Harlingen; one troop of the Twelfth Cavalry was at San Benito; one troop of the Twelfth Cavalry was at Donna, and one and a half companies of the Twenty-Sixth Infantry were at Kingsville. At Fort Brown in Brownsville were stationed a squadron and the machine gun platoon of the Third Cavalry; eight companies, the machine gun company, the band, and regimental headquarters of the Twenty-Sixth Infantry; two batteries of the Fifth Field Artillery; and an airplane. *Kingsville Record* August 20, 1915.
38. *Laredo Weekly Times*, August 22, 1915.
39. *Laredo Weekly Times*, August 15, 22, September 19, 1915.
40. U.S. v. Miguel Saiz, no. 268, U.S. Commissioner, Brownsville, and U.S. v. Miguel Saiz, no. 2178, U.S. District Court, Brownsville, FRC-FW.
41. *Brownsville Daily Herald*, August 19, 28, 1915.
42. *Brownsville Daily Herald*, August 28, 1915.
43. *Laredo Weekly Times*, August 15, 1915.
44. *Brownsville Daily Herald*, August 12, 1915; *Kingsville Record* August 13, 1915.
45. *Laredo Weekly Times*, September 5, 1915.
46. *Kingsville Record*, August 20, September 3, 1915.
47. *Brownsville Daily Herald*, June 26, 1916.
48. *Kingsville Record*, August 20, 1915.
49. *Kingsville Record*, August 27, September 3, 1915.
50. See Lynch, *Duke of Duval*, 20–21.
51. *Brownsville Daily Herald*, August 26, 1915.
52. *Brownsville Daily Herald*, August 16, 20, 23, 1915.
53. *Brownsville Daily Herald*, August 16, 1915; See also A. G. Cranford testimony, "Proceedings," 1:47–48.
54. *Brownsville Daily Herald*, August 17, 27, 1915.
55. *Brownsville Daily Herald*, August 21, 23, 24, 27, 1915.

56. Barnes report, November 24, 1915, 8BI; *Brownsville Daily Herald*, August 26, 1915.
57. "Report on Mexican Situation," August 18, 1915, Matamoros Post Records.
58. *Brownsville Daily Herald*, August 19, 1915; *Laredo Weekly Times*, August 22, 1915.
59. Mike Monahan testimony, *Investigation*, 1268.
60. Bullard to Puig, August 26, 1915, Matamoros Post Records.
61. *Brownsville Daily Herald*, August 30, 31, September 1, 1915.
62. *Brownsville Daily Herald*, September 2, 1915.
63. Mennet report, January 17, 1917, 6BI; Rogers report, December 12, 1915, 6BI.
64. *Brownsville Daily Herald*, September 3, 1915, April 3, 1917.
65. Dodds testimony, *Investigation*, 1250–53; Lon Hill testimony, *Investigation*, 1258; *Brownsville Daily Herald* September 3, 1915.
66. *Brownsville Daily Herald*, September 3, 1915.
67. *Brownsville Daily Herald*, September 3, 4, 1915.
68. Barnes report, February 1, 1916, 232-84BI.
69. *Kingsville Record*, September 3, 1915.
70. Blocksom to Garza, October 22, 1915, Matamoros Post Records; *Brownsville Daily Herald*, September 4, 1915.
71. Baldridge to McCoy, September 14, 20, 23, October 5, 15, 28, 30, November 7, 25 [?], 1915; See also Baldridge to Bullard, September 11, 1915; Plummer to McCoy, December 7, 1915; Baldridge to Sheppard, December 27, 1916, all in the McCoy Papers.
72. Statement of Capt. McCoy, September 7, 1916; see also Kirkes reports, January 30, 1915, and two undated reports, all in the McCoy Papers.
73. *Brownsville Daily Herald*, September 6, 7, 1915; *Laredo Weekly Times*, September 12, 1915; Everett Anglin testimony, *Investigation*, 1305–6; Barnes report, November 22 [?], 1915, 8BI; the citizens of Hidalgo County presented Sheriff Baker with a Studebaker touring car in appreciation of his role in combating banditry. *Brownsville Daily Herald*, December 4, 1915.
74. *Brownsville Daily Herald*, September 25, 1915.
75. *Brownsville Daily Herald*, September 8, 13, 14, 1915; *Laredo Weekly Times*, September 12, 19, 1915.
76. *Brownsville Daily Herald*, September 10, 1915.
77. *Brownsville Daily Herald*, September 8, 9, 1915.
78. *Brownsville Daily Herald*, September 11, December 2, 1915; *Laredo Weekly Times*, September 12, 1915.

79. Johnson to Nafarrate, September 13, 1915; Nafarrate to Johnson, September 13, 1915, Matamoros Post Records; *Brownsville Daily Herald*, September 14, 1915; *Laredo Weekly Times*, September 19, October 10, 1915.
80. Barnes report, November 20, 1915, 6BI.
81. See *Brownsville Daily Herald*, September 24, October 5, 6, 11, 1915.
82. *Brownsville Daily Herald*, September 16, 1915.
83. *Brownsville Daily Herald*, September 13, 14, 15, 1915.
84. *Brownsville Daily Herald*, September 15, 24, 1915.
85. *Laredo Weekly Times*, September 19, 1915.
86. *Brownsville Daily Herald*, September 17, 18, 1915; *Laredo Weekly Times*, September 19, 1915.
87. *Brownsville Daily Herald*, September 17, 18, 1915.
88. *Brownsville Daily Herald*, September 22, 23, 1915.

7. The "Bandit War" Peaks

1. *Brownsville Daily Herald*, September 24, 1915.
2. *Brownsville Daily Herald*, September 25, 27, 28, 1915.
3. *Brownsville Daily Herald*, September 24, 25, 1915; *Laredo Weekly Times*, September 26, October 3, 1915.
4. Mayfield testimony, including Guadalupe Cuéllar's statement, *Investigation*, 1288–89; Rogers reports, November 26, December 6, 1915, 6BI; Burwell to Commanding Officer, October 17, 1915, Johnson to Blocksom, October 27, 1915, Johnson to López, October 26, 1915, and López to Johnson, October 26, 1915, all in Matamoros Post Records; *Brownsville Daily Herald*, September 27, 29, October 1, 1915.
5. Cumberland, "Border Raids," 304–5.
6. *Brownsville Daily Herald*, September 27–29, October 1, 4, 1915, March 22, 1916.
7. *Brownsville Daily Herald*, October 1, 1915; *Laredo Weekly Times*, October 3, 1915.
8. *Brownsville Daily Herald*, September 23, October 1, 1915.
9. Rogers report, September 24, 1915, 6BI; *Brownsville Daily Herald*, October 1, 1915.
10. *Investigation*, 1554; in 1917, Chapa was elected congressman from Matamoros. *Brownsville Daily Herald*, March 15, 23, 1917.
11. The marauders allegedly were José García, Rafael Ríos, Juan Guerra, Jesús Pérez, Juan Garza, Pedro de Luna, Rodolfo Villarreal, Félix Saucedo, and Guillermo Saucedo. Stone report, October 31, 1915, 8BI.
12. Harris and Sadler, *Texas Rangers*, 287; Sterling, *Trails and Trials*, 38–42;

Brownsville Daily Herald, September 25, 27, 30, 1915; *Laredo Weekly Times*, September 26, 1915. Sadly, the trauma of the gun battle affected McAllen's nervous system, and he died on November 18, 1916. *Brownsville Daily Herald*, October 3, December 6, 1917.

13. *Brownsville Daily Herald*, September 28, 1915.
14. *Brownsville Daily Herald*, September 28, 1915.
15. "Report on Red Cross Work, August 25, 1915, to September 25, 1915," *Investigation*, 569.
16. United States, *Eleventh Annual Report of the American National Red Cross*, 6.
17. *Brownsville Daily Herald*, October 2, 5, 1915.
18. *Brownsville Daily Herald*, October 2, 4, 11, 1915; *Laredo Weekly Times*, October 3, 10, 1915; Johnson to Secretary of State, October 12, 1915, Matamoros Post Records; *Brownsville Daily Herald*, September 27, October 1, 1915.
19. Stone report, October 31, 1915, 8BI.
20. *Brownsville Daily Herald*, October 2, 1915.
21. James Wells testimony, "Proceedings," 2:676–77; R. B. Creager testimony, "Proceedings," 1:356.
22. *Brownsville Daily Herald*, October 4, 1915.
23. *Brownsville Daily Herald*, October 19, 20, 1915.
24. See *Brownsville Daily Herald*, October 19, 23, 1915.
25. H. J. Wallis testimony, *Investigation*, 1342; *Brownsville Daily Herald*, October 19, 1915.
26. Sterling, *Trails and Trials*, 43.
27. Vann testimony, "Proceedings," 1:574–77.
28. *Brownsville Daily Herald*, October 20, 21, 22, 1915; five Mexicans were being held in the Cameron County jail on suspicion of murder because one of them was found with army shoes inscribed with the name of a soldier recently killed at Fort Brown: Francisco Cortés, Florentín Cortés, Pedro Cortés, Carlos Cortés, and on an unrelated charge, Guadalupe Sosa. The four Cortéses were subsequently found innocent and were released. *Brownsville Daily Herald*, October 20, 22, 1915.
29. *Brownsville Daily Herald*, October 20, 21, November 27, 1915.
30. Lon Hill testimony, *Investigation*, 1259–60; John Kleiber testimony, *Investigation*, 1269–82, 1098–99, 1246; W. E. Vann testimony, *Investigation*, 1297; Barnes reports October 30, 1915, 232-84, and November 18, 1915, 8BI; *Brownsville Daily Herald*, December 2, 3, 14, 15, 18, 27, 1915; *Laredo Weekly Times*, October 31, 1915.

31. Aniceto Pizaña, Alberto Mejía, Jesús Sánchez, Toribio Ramos, Pedro González, Evaristo Ambrís, Quirino Guajardo, Luis Muñoz, Refugio Domínguez, Luis de la Rosa, Aniceto Rodríguez, Santiago Solís, Pedro Mireles, Pedro Martínez, José María Rodríguez, Lalo "Soldado" [*sic*], Daniel Mejía, Evaristo Ramos, José Benavides, Toribio Hernández, Francisco Fernández, Refugio Escamilla, Chano Flores, Juan Mejía, and Carlos Hernández.
32. Barnes report, November 18, 1915, 232-84BI; *Brownsville Daily Herald*, November 17–19, 1915.
33. *Brownsville Daily Herald*, April 3, 1917.
34. *Brownsville Daily Herald*, May 26, 1917.
35. Johnson to López, October 19, 1915, Matamoros Post Records.
36. López to Johnson, October 20, 21, 1915, Matamoros Post Records.
37. Johnson to López, October 21, 1915, Matamoros Post Records; *Brownsville Daily Herald*, October 21, 1915.
38. Blocksom to Johnson, November 1, 1915, Matamoros Post Records.
39. López to Johnson, November 6, 1915, Matamoros Post Records.
40. Blocksom to Johnson, November 11, 1915, Matamoros Post Records.
41. López to Johnson, November 12, 1915, Matamoros Post Records.
42. López to Johnson, November 18, 1915, Matamoros Post Records.
43. Ricaut to Johnson, December 4, 1915, Matamoros Post Records; *Brownsville Daily Herald*, October 8, 1915.
44. Johnson, *Revolution in Texas*, 97–98.
45. Harris and Sadler, "Plan of San Diego," 390, 392.

8. The "Bandit War" Winds Down

1. General Funston's Annual Report For the Southern Department, 1916, 24, Records of the Adjutant General's Office, RG 94, NARS.
2. Wilson to Secretary, October 19, 1915, 5BI; Blanford report, October 21, 1915, 5BI; Consul J. H. Johnson sent the Secretary of State a list of the clashes with *sediciosos*. Johnson to Secretary of State, January 22, 1916, 812.00/17136, RDS.
3. Memorandum by Canova, April 13, 1918, 812.00/21907, RDS.
4. Funston to Scott, February 23, 1916, Frederick Funston Collection, Kansas State Historical Society, Topeka, Kansas.
5. Rocha, "Tejano Revolt of 1915," 103–19; Harris and Sadler, *Texas Rangers*, 642.
6. Richmond, "La Guerra de Texas Se Renova," 19–20.
7. Richmond, *Venustiano Carranza's Nationalist Struggle*, 201.
8. Cumberland, "Border Raids," 308.

9. Hager, "The Plan of San Diego," 336.
10. Hanson to Kearful, November 7, 1919, Buckley Papers.
11. Citizens were also organizing at a different level. For example, the Edinburg Rifle Club was organized with fifty-seven charter members, and the organization expected to have at least one hundred by the end of the year. *Brownsville Daily Herald*, October 22, 23, 25, 26, 30, 1915.
12. *Brownsville Daily Herald*, October 29, November 1, 1915.
13. *Brownsville Daily Herald*, October 4, 1915.
14. *Brownsville Daily Herald*, October 21, 1915.
15. *Brownsville Daily Herald*, October 22, 1915.
16. *Brownsville Daily Herald*, October 22, 23, 1915.
17. *Brownsville Daily Herald*, October 21, 1915, May 23, 1917.
18. *Brownsville Daily Herald*, October 29, 1915.
19. Everett Anglin testimony, *Investigation*, 1303–4; *Investigation*, 1246–47; *Brownsville Daily Herald*, October 21, 1915; *Laredo Weekly Times*, October 24, 1915; the Twenty-Eighth U.S. Infantry was ordered to Harlingen, from where detachments would be deployed to protect small outposts such as Ojo de Agua. *Laredo Weekly Times*, October 24, 1915.
20. Barnes report, November 22 [?], 1915, 8BI.
21. Tom Mayfield testimony, *Investigation*, 1290, 1293–94.
22. Johnson to Secretary of State, October 25, 1915, Matamoros Post Records; Lon Hill testimony, *Investigation*, 1260; *Brownsville Daily Herald*, October 25, 27, 1915; *Laredo Weekly Times*, October 31, 1915.
23. *Brownsville Daily Herald*, October 26, 1915.
24. *Brownsville Daily Herald*, August 20, 1917; see also *Brownsville Daily Herald*, October 28, 29, 1915.
25. Rogers report, December 7, 1915, 232-84BI and December 20, 1915, 6BI.
26. Those known to have been involved in raids in the vicinity of Mission were Vicente Cantú, Guadalupe Cantú, Santos Cantú, Pancho Hernández, Avelino Garza (an escaped convict from the Corpus Christi jail "said to have participated in every attack on this side"), Pancho de León, José de León. Bandits staying in Corrales, Mexico: Evaristo Ramos, Chief, Juan Villarreal, José María Ramírez. Bandits with Pizaña at Ansualdos, Mexico, opposite Cavazos Crossing: Pizaña, Luis de la Rosa, Teodoro Hernández (killed by our soldiers in Ojo de Agua fight), Teodoro Olivares, Florencio Gandaris [*sic*], Romualdo Cantú, León Zúñiga, Lucas Zúñiga, Mercedes Aréchiga, Macario Cavazos. There was also a list of names taken from a notebook containing considerable other data

and found on the ground where Antonio Pérez was seen to fall badly wounded in the Ojo de Agua fight. Pérez subsequently died of his wounds. The notebook was badly spotted with his blood. (Pérez scratched through the names of those killed by the military): Alberto Gallegos, Francisco Hernández, Vicente Cantú, José Flores, Pablo Garza, Alberto Gallego, Guadalupe Cantú, José de León, Carlos Parra, Nieves Garza, Gerónimo Vela, Guadalupe Zamora, José María Ramírez, Juan Moreno, Jesús Gallegos, Feliciano Hernández (dead), Nicolás Cantú (dead), Manuel Oviedo, José de León, Jesús Gallego, José Flores, Luis Oviedo, Simón Guerra, Nasario Ochoa, Feliciano Hernández, Mercedes Aréchiga, Guadalupe Z. Garza, Amador Sánchez, Avelino Garza (the escaped convict), Gerónimo Garza (dead), Teodoro Hernández, Pablo Garza, Leandro Martínez, Daniel Ochoa, Santos Cantú, José Vela, Manuel Ramírez, Ventura Arce. Stone report, October 31, 1915, 8BI.

27. Stone report, October 31, 1915, 8BI.
28. Stone report, October 31, 1915, 8BI.
29. Stone report, October 31, 1915, 8BI.
30. Barnes report, November 23, 1915, 232-84BI.
31. Stone reports, October 27, 28, 1915, 8BI.
32. Rogers report, September 26, 1915, 6BI.
33. Rogers report and memorandum, September 26, 1915, 6BI.
34. Rogers reports, October 7, 13, 1915, 6BI.
35. Barnes report, October 28, 1915, 8BI.
36. Stone report, October 30, 1915, 8BI; *Brownsville Daily Herald*, November 25, 27, 1915.
37. Barnes report, November 4, 1915, 8BI.
38. *Laredo Weekly Times*, October 31, 1915.
39. Barnes reports, November 16, 1916, 232-84BI.
40. List, ca. November 25, 1915, 9BI.
41. Breniman reports, November 5, 17, 1915, 8BI.
42. Barnes reports, December 1, 1915, 8BI, December 24, 1915, 6BI, March 6, 1916, 9BI, and December 5, 1915, 232-84BI; Breniman report, January 12, 1916, 6BI; Barnes to Rogers, January 22, 1916, 6BI.
43. Beckham report, November 19, 1915, 6BI; Barnes to Bielaski, November 8, 1915, 6BI; Rogers report, November 29, 1915, 6BI.
44. Blanford reports, November 9, 13, 15, 18, 19, 23, 24, 1915, 8BI, and November 19, 22, 27, 30, December 2, 3, 4, 7, 9, 13, 16, 20, 1915, 6BI; Barnes reports, November 9, 26, 1915, 6BI.

45. Barkey report, November 18, 1915, 232-84BI.
46. Gómez to Juanita L., January 26, 1916, 6BI; Juanita L to Gómez, February 1, 1916, 232-84BI; Barnes to Laulom, February 3, 1916, 232-84BI; Barnes to Bielaski, February 1, 1916, 232-84BI.
47. Rogers report, May 15, 1916, 13BI.
48. Barnes reports, November 26, December 2, 1915, February 3, 1916, 6BI; Barnes to Rogers, December 1, 1915, 6BI; Barnes to Gómez, February 1, 1916, 6BI; Juanita L. to Gómez, February 1, 1916, 6BI; Barnes to Bielaski, February 1, 1916, 6BI; Rogers to Barnes, April 12 [?], 1916, 6BI.
49. Barnes to Breniman, December 6, 1915, 232-84BI; Rogers report, December 9, 1915, 232-84BI.
50. Barnes report, November 6, 1915, 232-84BI.
51. Barnes report, November 18, 1915, 8BI; Barnes to Breniman, December 6, 1915, 6BI; Barnes to Green, November 28, 1916, 232-84BI.
52. Barnes report, November 24, 1915, 8BI.
53. Barkey report, November 26, 1915; Barnes to Cisneros, March 17, 1917, 232-84BI.
54. Barnes report, December 16, 1915, 232-84BI.
55. Barnes report, December 16, 1915, 232-84BI.
56. Weiskopf report, December 19, 1916, 11BI.
57. Sandos, "German Involvement in Northern Mexico"; Munch, "Villa's Columbus Raid"; Katz, "Alemania y Francisco Villa."
58. Sandos, "Plan of San Diego," 11 n. 11, 20 n. 35; U.S. War Department Record of the Court Martial of Lothar Witzke, vol. 8, exhibit 321 and vol. 2, exhibit 24, Mixed Claims Commission, United States and Germany, Federal Records Center, East Point, Georgia; Major General Ralph H. Van Deman, "Memoirs," unpublished manuscript, Library, U.S. Army Intelligence Center and School, Fort Huachuca, Arizona, 62–63.
59. *Laredo Weekly Times*, September 7, 1919, August 23, 1920; Harris and Sadler, "The Witzke Affair."
60. Paul Altendorf testimony, *Investigation*, 1229–30.
61. Rodgers to Secretary of State, May 15, 1916, 812.00/18164, RDS.
62. Mayfield testimony, *Investigation*, 1290–93; Gerlach, "Conditions along the Border," 201; Sandos "Plan of San Diego," 5.
63. Rogers report, May 13, 1916, 13BI.
64. Barnes to Rogers, December 11, 1915, 6BI; Barnes reports, December 13, 15, 1915, 6BI; Barnes to Bielaski, December 17, 1915, 8BI; Rogers report, December 17, 1915,

6BI; Breniman report, December 19, 1915, 6BI; Barnes to Bielaski, January 13, February 8, 1916, 6BI; Barnes to Robertson, January 17, 1916, 6BI.

65. R. E. H. Memorandum, December 17, 1915, 232-84BI; Bielaski to Barnes, December 13, 1915, 232-84BI.
66. In 1951, Antonio Escamilla was the police chief in Matamoros. De la Garza Treviño, *Plan de San Diego*, 42.
67. Barnes report, November 17, 1915, 8BI.
68. Rogers report, November 29, 1915, 6BI.

9. The Plan de San Diego Collapses

1. Johnson, *Revolution in Texas*, 106.
2. *Laredo Weekly Times*, October 31, 1915.
3. Silliman to Secretary of State, February 12, 1916, 6BI; Barnes report, February 16, 1916, 6BI.
4. Weekly Report, January 26, 1917, 812.00/20454, RDS.
5. Rogers report, December 4, 1915, 232-84BI; *Brownsville Daily Herald*, December 3, 1915.
6. Johnson to Secretary of State, December 7, 1915, Matamoros Post Records; *Brownsville Daily Herald*, November 23, 24, 26, 1915; *Laredo Weekly Times*, November 28, 1915.
7. Rogers report, November 30, 1915, 6BI; *Brownsville Daily Herald*, November 27, 1915.
8. Rogers reports, December 5, 8, 1915, 6BI.
9. Dawson to Secretary of State, March 18, 1916, 812.00/17679, RDS.
10. Rogers reports, December 22, 23, 1915, January 1, February 2, 1916, 6BI, and January 27, 1916, 8BI; Barnes report, January 4, 1916, 6BI.
11. Rogers report, January 18, 1916, 6BI.
12. Rogers reports, January 19, 22, February 6, 1916, 6BI.
13. Barnes to Rogers, May 8, 1916, 11BI.
14. Luis de la Rosa, Aniceto Pizaña, Ricardo Gómez, José Benavides, Alberto Mejía, Ricardo López, Nicardio Flores, Gaspar Cantú, Pablo Saenz, Pedro Cavazos, Darío Morado, Sóstenes Saldaña Jr., Marcelino Hinojosa, Catarino Soto, Gerónimo Cruz, Trinidad Tovar, Felipe Tovar, Evaristo Ramos, Santiago Santillana, Felipe Campos, Jesús Treviño, Eduardo García, and Pablo Pérez.
15. Rogers report, October 16, 1915, 232-84BI; *Brownsville Daily Herald*, March 18, 1916.
16. Gen. E. P. Nafarrete, Arturo A. Saenz, Ignacio Risa, E. Ceniceros, Porfirio San-

tos, A. G. Almares or Alvarez, Manuel Flores, and A. González. Barnes to Bielaski, November 4, 1916, 6BI.

17. Breniman reports, December 9, 11, 12, 1915, 6BI; Barnes report, December 11, 1915, 6BI; Rogers report, December 12, 1915, 6BI.
18. Barnes to Green, November 5 [?], 1916, 6BI; Barnes to Green November 26, 1916, 232-84BI; Breniman report, December 2, 1916, 232-84BI; Green to Barnes, December 2, 1916, 6BI.
19. Barnes to Anderson, December 17, 1915, 232-84BI; Mennet report, May 11, 1917, 232-84BI.
20. Indicted were Ernesto Ramos, Alberto Mejía, Pablo Pérez, Darío Morado, José Benavides, Juan Guerrero, José de León, Pablo de León, Jesús Pérez, Crispín Luna, Gregorio Dávila, Rodolfo Villarreal, Santos Cantú, Félix Saucedo, Juan Garza, and Teófilo Regalado.
21. Against Guadalupe Ramos, Quirino Guajardo, Evaristo Ramos, Luis de la Rosa, Alberto Mejía, José Benavides, Aniceto Pizaña, Toribio Ramos, Evaristo Ambrio [*sic*], Pablo Pérez, Darío Morado, Pedro Cavazos, Pedro Cepeda, Pablo Saiz, Juan de los Santos, Pedro Tovar, Refugio Domínguez, Luciano Chapa, Mayin [Martin] Castorena, and Rogerio Caballero. See *Brownsville Daily Herald*, December 23, 1915.
22. Against Manuel García, Francisco Caballero, Aniceto Pizaña, Anastacio Robles, Rogerio Caballero, Manuel Longoria, Charles Coy, Félix Bea [*sic*], Encarnación Domínguez, Eusebio Porras, Secundino González, Fernando Rangel, Pedro Rangel, Encarnación Rendón, Julio Sánchez, Juan Guerrero, Jesús Guerrero, Vicente Dávila , Pizaña Flores [*sic*], Teodoro de la Fuente, Ricardo Gómez Pizaña, Juan Romero, Antonio Rocha, Alberto Gallegos, Jesús Gallegos, Francisco Hernández, Guadalupe Cantú, José [Santiago?] Flores, Manuel Olivares, Luis Olivares, Pablo Garza, José de León, Leandro Martínez, Amador Sánchez, Carlos Peña, Luciano Ochoa, Santiago Ochoa, Nieves García, Feliciano Hernández, Mercedes Archinigo [*sic*], Guadalupe Cámara, Guadalupe Garza, Abelino Garza, José Moro Ramírez, Mario Ramírez, José Vela, Ventura Avila, Francisco Guerra, and Gerónimo Vela. The charges against Santiago Flores were dismissed, *Brownsville Daily Herald*, April 15, 1916. Rogers report, December 14, 1916, 6BI; *Brownsville Daily Herald*, March 22, 28, 30, April 3, 1916.
23. *Brownsville Daily Herald*, April 4–7, 1916, April 3, 1917.
24. Rogers report, December 12, 1916, 6BI.
25. *Brownsville Daily Herald*, March 21, 31, April 2–5, 1917.
26. *Brownsville Daily Herald*, December 1–4, 1915, April 14, 1916.

27. See *Brownsville Daily Herald*, October 18, November 22, 23, 24, 25, 27, 29, 30, December 1, 6, 15, 1915.
28. See *Brownsville Daily Herald*, April 10–15, May 8 [April 8], 1916.
29. See *Brownsville Daily Herald*, December 6, 9, 12–14, 16–18, 24, 27–29, 30, 31, 1915, February 2, 9, 1916.
30. Rogers report, December 12, 1916, 6BI; *Brownsville Daily Herald*, December 17, 21, 22, 1915.
31. Barnes to Goodrich, February 15, 1916, 232-84BI.
32. *Brownsville Daily Herald*, December 14, 1915.
33. *Brownsville Daily Herald*, February 11, 12, 15, 25, March 9, 10, April 11, 1916; Pizaña's seventy-year-old mother, Adela García de Pizaña, lived on Madison Street in Brownsville. On March 7, 1916, while on her way to visit Pizaña in jail, she was seriously injured when a switch engine hit her buggy, demolishing the vehicle. She died of her injuries on March 10. *Brownsville Daily Herald*, March 8, 10, 11, 1916.
34. Rogers reports, April 24, 28, May 2, 12, 17, 1916, 13BI.
35. *San Antonio Express*, May 19, 1916.
36. Rogers report, May 21, 1916, 13BI; See also Rogers report, May 29 [?], 1916, 13BI.

10. Intelligence Gathering

1. Barnes to Green January 12, 1917, 232-84BI.
2. Mennet report, January 28, 1917, 10BI.
3. Harris and Sadler, "The 1911 Reyes Conspiracy," 337–39.
4. Memorandum for the Attorney General, February 12, 1917, 10BI.
5. Mennet report, December 15, 1916, 12BI.
6. Barnes to Walker, December 16, 1916, 6BI.
7. Breckinridge to Secretary of State, December 22, 1915, 812.00/16999, RDS.
8. Bielaski to Harrison, December 1, 1916, 11BI.
9. Seman report, December 11, 1916, 6BI.
10. Rogers reports, December 6, 9, 1915, 6BI; *Laredo Weekly Times*, December 19, 1915.
11. Hanna to Secretary of State, December 8, 1915, 812.00/16946, RDS.
12. Weekly Report, December 4, 1915, 812.00/16951, RDS.
13. McCain to Bielaski, February 5, 1916, 6BI.

11. The Plan de San Diego, Phase Two

1. Garrison to Secretary of State, January 6, 1916, 812.00/17070, RDS; Lansing to Secretary of War, January 12, 1916, 812.00/17070, RDS.

2. Weekly Report, January 12, 1916, 812.00/17112, RDS.
3. Polk to Secretary of War, January 20, 1916, 812.00/17042, RDS.
4. Naranjo, *Diccionario,* 235.
5. Notarized articles of incorporation, January 28, 1916, AGC; for a listing of Garza Hermanos y Compañía's activities, see its letterhead, in J. O. Flores to Garza, May 31, 1916, AGC.
6. Prospectus, March 16, 1916, AGC.
7. World War I draft registration for John Forseck Jr.; John Kvake Forseck affidavit, Exhibit J, Office of the State Department Counselor RG 59, NARS, hereinafter cited as FA. Surprisingly, although Forseck's affidavit has been available to scholars for decades it has been ignored by those writing about the Plan de San Diego.
8. Exhibit A, FA.
9. Acuña resigned on November 29, 1916 and was succeeded by Manuel Aguirre Berlanga, his deputy. Seman report, December 11, 1916, 12BI.
10. Bureau of Investigation Agent A. A. Hopkins report, Warren, Arizona, February 17, 1917, found together with the Forseck affidavit; Naranjo, *Diccionario*, 235–36.
11. During the 1916 war crisis, Ochoa Senior wrote to Carranza that one of his sons was in General Fortunato Zuazua's command, and he asked Carranza's permission to go to Texas to fight against the Americans and plant the Mexican flag in Texas. Ochoa to Carranza, June 21, 1916, Venustiano Carranza Archive, Centro de Estudios Históricos Carso (formerly Condumex), México, D. F. See Richmond, "The Venustiano Carranza Archive."
12. De la Garza Treviño, *Plan de San Diego*, 43.
13. Mendoza to Carranza, March 1, 1916, Carranza Archive.
14. In May 1918, Méndez was elected vice president of the Constitutionalist Railways. *Laredo Weekly Times*, May 19, 1918.
15. FA.
16. Acuña to Zuazua, March 29, 1916, AGC.
17. Zuazua to Acuña, March 27, 1916, and Acuña to Zuazua, March 28, 29, 1916, AGC; Naranjo, *Diccionario*, 213.
18. Zuazua to Carranza, March 29, 1916, AGC.
19. Carranza to Zuazua, March 30, 1916, AGC.
20. Nago to Acuña, April 6, 1916, AGC.
21. The bureau's twenty-seven-page file on Moseley is in 14BI.
22. Mendoza, "Lonesome Death," 1–2; Horne, *Black and Brown,* 164–65; *Laredo Weekly Times*, May 28, July 2, 16, 1916; *El Paso Morning Times*, July 14, 1916. For

additional details of attempts to recruit blacks in the vicinity of Austin for the Texas revolution see Wright reports, September 14, 15, 17, 1915, 6BI and October 24, 25, 26, 1915, 8BI; Barnes report, October 23, 1915, 6BI.

23. Carranza had seized the railroads, saying it was for military purposes. *Investigation*, 1796.
24. Pulford to Spring-Rice, March 12, 1915, FO 115, 1927, X/M00519, British National Archives, formerly the Public Record Office, Kew, England.
25. Forseck cites Exhibit G, which isn't with the affidavit.
26. Unnumbered Exhibit, FA.
27. For Acosta see Military Headquarters to Quiñones, October 22, 1914, roll 3, PGA; González to Carranza, May 30, 1916, roll 3, PGA; Acosta to Martínez, November 10, 1915; González to Carranza, November 10, 1915, roll 3, PGA; Carranza to González, December 7, 1915, roll 3, PGA; Alcázar to González, December 15, 1915, roll 5, PGA; González to Acosta, January 5, 1916, roll 3, PGA; Acosta to González, April 5, 1916, roll 3, PGA; González to Acosta, April 11, 1916, roll 31, PGA; García to González, April 12, 1916, roll 28, PGA; González to Carranza, April 12, 1916, roll 31, PGA; Acosta to González, April 13, 27, May 2, 8, 1916, roll 3, PGA; González to Acosta, April 18, May 15, 1916, roll 3, PGA; Acosta to González, April 22, 1916, roll 3, Villarreal to Acosta, April 23, 1916, roll 3, PGA; González to Carranza, May 8, 15, 18, 20, 1916, roll 3, PGA; Carranza to González, May 15, 28, 1916, roll 3, PGA.
28. Ever since March 18, Mayor Schmidt had two plainclothes men patrolling Eagle Pass under cover from 8 p.m. through the night and reporting daily on the movements of all Mexicans whose actions were in any manner out of the ordinary. Wright report, March 28, 1916, 9BI.
29. González to Valdés, December 30, 1915, roll 11, PGA.
30. See, for instance, *La Prensa*, April 20, 1916.
31. See, for example, "Contra los Invasores del Frailesito Wilson" in Headly to Lansing, June 27, 1916, 812.00/18672, RDS.

12. An Improbable Operation

1. Garza González to Garza, April 29, May 4, 23, 1916; same to same, undated (2009.006), AGC.
2. Ramos to Garza, April 30, May 14, 22, 1916, AGC.
3. Ramos to Garza, May 28, 1916, AGC.
4. Flores to Garza, three letters on May 31, 1916; Same to same, June 4, 1916, enclosing lists, AGC.

5. Flores to Garza, June 1, 1916, AGC.
6. Flores to Garza, June 2, 3, 1916, AGC.
7. Rendón [?] to Garza, June 4, 1916, AGC.
8. Caballo to Zuazua, June 5, 1916, AGC.
9. Gerlach, "Conditions along the Border—1915," 201, 202.
10. Stout, *Border Conflict*, 82, 146, 165, n. 19.
11. DHRM, 12:294–95, 298–99, 301, 308–9, 321, 338, 373–74, 381, 13: part 2, 150–51, 176.
12. *La Prensa,* April 12, May 9, 1916.
13. Andrés Germán Fierros was born in Camargo, Tamaulipas, on May 26, 1856. In 1873 he went to Corpus Christi and became a bookkeeper for a large mercantile establishment, until 1878, when he went to Rio Grande City and opened a general merchandise business. There in 1879 he married María Teresa Saenz. He subsequently engaged in ranching in Starr County. In 1894 his wife died and he moved with his five small children (Valentina, Herminia, Leocadio, Carlos, and Esteban) to Laredo. From 1894 to 1906 he worked for the Texas Mexican Railroad in Laredo and for a time was a Webb County commissioner. In 1910 he was a clerk for the Texas Mexican Railroad. That same year he went to Mexico to engage in mining, returning to Laredo in 1912. He died in June 1920 in Philadelphia, where he'd gone for treatment for stomach cancer. His body was returned to Laredo for burial. *Laredo Weekly Times*, March 17, 1918, January 12, February 22, July 7, 1919, June 13, 20, 1920. J. L. Fierros was the half brother of Andrés Germán Fierros. Ad: "I buy and sell anything from a pin to a locomotive; this includes farms and ranches. J. L. Fierros, 202 Farragut Street [Laredo]."
14. Thompson report, May 23, 1913, 3BI; Spates reports, August 3, 1913, 3BI; Harris and Sadler, "The 1911 Reyes Conspiracy," 325–48; Idar report, June 20, 1916, 13BI.
15. Hebert report, April 17, 1912, 1BI; Spates reports, August 5, 6, 1913, 3BI.
16. González to Galbreath, August 31, 1915, roll 11, PGA; Platas to González, September 3, 1915, roll 25, PGA.
17. *Laredo Weekly Times*, September 5, 19, 1915; 1900 and 1910 U.S. Federal Census; Ancestry.com; Bevan to Lansing, March 24, 1915, 812.00/14761 RDS; González to A. Valdés, December 30, 1915, roll 11, PGA; Fierros to González, November 23, 1916, Exp. EF, roll 10, PGA; J. N. Galbraith to González, August 30, 1915, roll 11, PGA.
18. Stout, *Border Conflict*, 22, 30.

19. Exp. EF, PGA.
20. They were Francisco M. Nakamura, P. Yoshida, J. Yamaguel, Luis Sakaguchi, Luis Nakamaya, Isidro Yoshida, and Francisco F. Takesita. Exp. BF, roll 7, PGA.
21. Harris and Sadler, "Plan of San Diego," 397.
22. Barnes report, June 7, 1916, 11BI.
23. Exp. BF, PGA.
24. AGC.
25. Exp. BF, PGA.
26. Zuazua to Garza, June 6, 1916, AGC.
27. Ortiz to Caballo, June 7, 1916, AGC; see also Villarreal to Garza, June 7, 1916, AGC.
28. Sánchez to Garza, June 8, 1916, receipt by Santos, June 10, 1916, Zuazua to Garza, June 8, 1916, Sánchez to Garza, June 13, 1916, and Garza to Garza, June 14, 1916, all in AGC.

13. The Morín Affair

1. Harris and Sadler, *Texas Rangers*, 383–84; *Brownsville Daily Herald*, July 22, 1915.
2. Guzmán to Saldívar Cervantes, February 18, 1912, J. Y. to Saldívar Cervantes, February 13, 23, 1912, and Lancaster report, April 10, 1912, 1BI.
3. Thompson report, March 30, 1912, 1BI; Barnes report, May 17, 18, 1912, 2BI.
4. Wright reports, April 12, 14, 15, 17, 19, 1916, May 8, 1916, 12BI; Barnes report, June 2, 1916, 12BI; Weakley report, June 8, 1916, 12BI; Harris report, July 1, 1916, 12BI.
5. Bazán, fifty-one years old and born in Roma, Texas, was a saloonkeeper and landowner in Calaveras, where he'd lived for the last seventeen years. He said he knew nothing about any uprising. Beckham report, May 19, 1916, 12BI.
6. Sánchez was a farmer who had come to Texas from Monterrey forty-two years earlier. He served in the army during Porfirio Díaz's regime and worked on a ranch near San Diego, where he still had a ranch. All he knew was what he'd read in the papers. Beckham report, May 19, 1916, 12BI.
7. Sheriff Will Wright of Wilson County believed that Pedro Rosales had been listed by mistake and that his name was really Pedro Servín. Wright report, May 2, 1916, 12BI.
8. Botello, forty-five, was born in San Antonio and had lived around Floresville all his life. He'd worked in Poth at a lumberyard and as a barber. Botello said that Morín had been in his barbershop the previous February. Beckham report, May 19, 1916, 12BI.

9. There is a proclamation titled, in translation, "Countrymen" issued by the Patriotic Club of Karnes City, Texas, with Morín listed as secretary. Barnes report, May 20, 1916, 12BI.
10. Barnes to Bielaski, June 23, 1916, 12BI.
11. Wright reports: April 20, 1916, 12BI, including Morín's memorandum; and April 21, 1916, 12BI, including a photograph of General Morín; Beckham report, May 19, 1916, 12BI.
12. Wright report, April 21, 1916, 12BI.
13. Wright reports, April 24, 25, 1916, 12BI.
14. Palacios, by the way, was the son of Baldomero Palacios, a follower of Catarino Garza, who had attempted to launch an invasion of Mexico from South Texas in the 1890s.
15. Wright report, April 27, 1916, 12BI.
16. Barnes to Bielaski, August 15, 1916, 232-84BI.
17. Sorola died on November 19, 1957. Theoharis et al., *The FBI*, 354.
18. Wright report, May 6, 1916, 12BI; Sorola report, April 12, 1917, 6BI.
19. Wright reports, April 29, May 2, 1916, 12BI.
20. Barnes to Bielaski, May 4, 1916, 11BI and 12BI.
21. Wright report, May 4, 1916, 12BI.
22. Wright report, including Ponce's letter to Blas de la Garza and Hanson's letter to Ferguson, May 6, 1916, 12BI.
23. Berliner reports, May 6, 7, 1916, 12BI; Rogers report, May 28, 1916, 12BI.
24. Juan Mendiola, Pedro Vega, Francisco Bansra [*sic*], Manuel Castañeda, Antonio Falcón, Ismael Vega, Basario Saldaña, Crecerio [*sic*] Vela, Norberto Vela, Felipe García, E. Ortega, Mike Truan, Juan Treviño, Sisiaso [*sic*] Ramírez, José María Montalvo [?].
25. Barnes report, May 11, 1916, 12BI.
26. Wright report, May 11, 1916, 12BI; *La Prensa*, May 12, 1916.
27. Wright report, May 11, 1916, 12BI.
28. Barnes to Wright, May 11, 1916, 12BI.
29. Ramón Borunda, Saspamco; Pedro Rosales, Poth; Néstor Bazán, Calaveras; José Pérez, Quinbel [Kimball?]; Pedro Díaz, Karnes City; A. Liro, San Marcos; Cresencio Palina, Kenedy; Tomás Mata, Cuero; Reyes Amador, Falls City; Librado Palacios, Stockdale; Jesús Morín, Esmaraleke [*sic*]; Francisco Conde, Helena; Rafael Castañeda, Seguin; Bisconte Sánchez, Nornam [*sic*]; Emilio Muñoz, Favershan. ("These names are written with copying pencil very indistinctly.")

30. Wright report, May 13, 1916, 12BI; statement of José Morín, May 12, 1916, 12BI.
31. Wright to Barnes, May 12, 14, 1916, 12BI.
32. Statement of Victoriano Ponce, May 12, 1916, 12BI; statement of Victoriano Ponce, May 13, 1916, 12BI.
33. Wright report, May 13, 1916, 12BI.
34. Wright report, May 14, 1916, 11BI.
35. Wright to Closner, May 16, 1916, 12BI; Closner to Wright, Barkey report, May 24, 1916, 12BI; Barnes reports, June 26, 29, 1916, 12BI.
36. Wright report, May 15, 1916, 12BI.
37. Wright reports, May 16, 17, 1916, 12BI; statement of Ignacio Rodríguez, May 16, 1916, 12BI.
38. Wright reports, May 16, 18, 19, 1916, 12BI; statement of Isidoro Castañeda, May 16, 1916, 12BI.
39. Wright report, May 18, 1916, 12BI.
40. Berliner reports, May 13, 14, 1916, 12BI; Wright report, May 16, 1916, 12BI; Barnes report, May 18, 1916, 12BI; Beckham reports, May 19, 20, 1916, 12BI; Wright report, May 25, 1916, 12BI; *La Prensa*, May 13, 16, 1916.
41. Wright reports, May 22, 23, 1916, 12BI.
42. Scarborough's testimony, "Proceedings," 1:253–67; *La Prensa*, May 29, 1916; see also *Laredo Weekly Times*, May 28, 1916.
43. Rogers report, May 28, 1916, 12BI; Barnes report, May 29, 1916, 12BI; Wright report, May 30, 1916, 12BI.
44. At locations where there was no jail, the "tree and chain" method for securing prisoners was commonly used. *Brownsville Daily Herald*, September 16, 1915.
45. Rogers report, May 28, 1916, 12BI.
46. Wright report, June 5, 1916, 12BI.
47. See *La Prensa*, June 1, 1916.
48. Captain Sanders's incriminating report, in Harris and Sadler, *Texas Rangers*, 306–7, is not found in the Adjutant General's Correspondence in the Texas State Library. The only copy is in the microfilmed records of the Federal Bureau of Investigation.
49. "Proceedings," 1:238–52, 2:1396–98, 1408–10; *La Prensa*, June 8, 1916.
50. Attorney General to the President, June 23, 1916, 12BI.
51. Garrison to Attorney General, June 19, 1916, 12BI; Harris and Sadler, *Texas Rangers*, 303–8; Hook to Wilson, June 4, 1916, Wright report, June 5, 1916, 12BI; Hanson to Kearful, November 7, 1919, Buckley Papers.

14. The Bureau Investigates

1. Barnes to Barnum, June 7, 1916, 11BI; Barnes to Special Agents, Local Officers, Special Employees, Informants, June 9, 1916, 12BI.
2. Harris and Sadler, "The 1911 Reyes Conspiracy," 332.
3. Marks report, August 6, 1916, 11BI; Rogers reports, May 24, 1916, 13BI, and May 30 [?], 1916, 6BI; Memorandum by Chief, June 6, 1916, 6BI; Barnes to Rogers, June 7, 1916, 11BI; Chief to Koons, June 28, 1916, 8BI; see Marks's reports, June 6, 1916, 13BI, June 7, 8, 9, 1916, 12BI, June 15, 12BI, June 20, 21, 1916, 12BI, July 4, 1916, 12BI, August 6, 9, 15, 18, 22, 31, September 16, 18 [?], 19, 21, 30, October 5, 7, 13, 15, 21, 31, 1916, 11BI, November 10, 16, 20, 26, 30, 1916, 11BI, December 5, 1916, 11BI, December 11, 1916, 11BI, December 16, 1916, 11BI, December 18, 1916, 6BI, December 27, 1916, 11BI, December 29, 1916, 11BI, January 7, 1917, 11BI, January 10, 1917, 10BI, January 12, 1917, 10BI, January 31, 1917, 11BI, February 10, 1917, 11BI, February 16, 1917, 10BI, February 18, 1917, 10BI, February 23, 1917, 10BI, February 28, 1917, 11BI, March 4, 1917, 11BI, March 10, 1917, 11BI, March 18, 1917, 11BI, March 25, 1917, 11BI, April 3, 1917, 12BI, April 13, 1917, 5BI, April 28, 1917, 10BI, May 2, 1917, 11BI, May 11, 1917, 11BI, May 16, 1917, 11BI, May 19, 1917, 232-84 BI, May 23, 1917, 11BI, May 26, 1917, 10BI, May 27, 1917, 11BI, May 30, 1917, 6BI, July 31, 1917, 11BI, September 22, 1917, 4BI, October 26, 1917, 11BI, November 16, 1917, 9BI. See Chamberlain's reports, June 7, 13, 1916, 13BI, June 19, 1916, 11BI, June 22, 1916, 12BI, June 29, 1916, 11BI, July 3, 1916, 12BI, July 5, 1916, 2BI, July 6, 1916, 11BI, July 8, 1916, 12BI, July 10, 1916, 12BI.
4. Captain George Head and Lieutenant Colonel Emmett Walker were involved in a National Guard scandal, faking paperwork and selling equipment, sometimes to Mexican revolutionists. They were convicted and sent to federal prison. Harris and Sadler, *Texas Rangers*, 205–8.
5. Rogers report, May 9, 1916, 11BI.
6. Wright report, May 10, 1916, 12BI.
7. Memorandum by Chief, June 6, 1916, 13BI.
8. Lansing to American Consul, May 1, 1916, Matamoros Post Records.
9. Rogers report, May 14, 1916, 13BI.
10. Rogers report, May 20, 1916, 13BI.
11. Johnson to Ricaut, February 26, 1916, Matamoros Post Records.
12. Ricaut to Johnson, February 28, 1916, Matamoros Post Records.
13. "Report on General Conditions," May 1, 1916, Matamoros Post Records.
14. Johnson to Silver, May 31, 1916, Matamoros Post Records.

15. Ross reports, June 10, 1916, 12BI, June 28, 1916, 13BI, August 2, 1916, 13BI.
16. Ross to Bielaski, August 3, 1916, 13BI; Smith to Chief, September 26, 1916, 13BI; Ross report, December 3, 1916, 6BI; Breniman report, January 10, 1917, 10BI.
17. Beckham reports, June 14, 1916, 6BI, June 15, 1916, 12BI; Barnes to Bielaski, June 14, 1916, 13BI, and June 21, 1916, 11BI; Saldívar Cervantes reports, June 23, 1916, 6BI and 10BI, June 30, 1916, 8BI and 12BI, July 1, 1916, 12BI, July 10, 1916, 11BI and 12BI, July 11, 1916, 12BI; Sorola reports, January 2, 3, 1917, 4BI; Guzmán reports, January 31, 1917, 7BI, February 3, 1917, 7BI.
18. Rogers report, May 3, 1916, 6BI.
19. Commanding Officer, USS *Marietta* to Commanding Officer, USS *Kentucky*, May 16, 1916, 812.00/18271, RDS.
20. Dawson to Secretary of State, June 9, 1916, 12BI.
21. Rogers report, June 10, 1916, 12BI.
22. Rogers report, June 12, 1916, 13BI.
23. Fierros to González, June 9, 1916, Exp. EF, PGA.
24. Coerver and Hall, *Texas and the Mexican Revolution*, 101–2.
25. Harris and Sadler, "Plan of San Diego," 88.
26. *San Antonio Express*, June 16, 1916; *Laredo Weekly Times*, March 2, 1919; Ross report, June 7, 1916.
27. *Laredo Weekly Times*, June 11, 18, 1916; *San Antonio Express*, June 10, 1916.
28. *Laredo Weekly Times*, June 4, 11, 1916; *San Antonio Express*, June 10, 11, 1916.
29. *El Tribunal*, June 10, 1916, AGC.
30. Invoice, June 28, 1916, AGC; see also Barnes to Green, February 29, 1916, 6BI.
31. Cruz to Garza, June 19, 1919, AGC.
32. In November 1913, Pancho Villa captured Ciudad Juárez by using the ruse of having fake telegrams clear the way for a captured train containing fifteen hundred of his troops.
33. *San Antonio Express*, June 12, 1916.
34. *San Antonio Express*, June 14, 1916.
35. Johnson to Secretary of State, June 15, 1916, Matamoros Post Records.
36. *San Antonio Express*, June 14, 1916.
37. Rogers report, September 2 [?], 1916, 232-84BI.

15. New Raids

1. *San Antonio Express*, June 14, 1916.
2. Barnes report, June 7, 1916, 11BI.

3. *La Prensa*, June 13, 1916; *San Antonio Express*, June 12, 1916; *Laredo Weekly Times*, June 18, July 9, 1916.
4. *La Prensa*, June 13, 14, 1916; *Laredo Weekly Times*, June 18, 1916; *San Antonio Express*, June 13, 15, 17, 1916; Valls testimony, *Investigation*, 1208; W. M. Hanson to J. F. Kearful, November 7, 1919, Buckley Papers.
5. *Laredo Weekly Times*, June 18, July 9, 16, 1916.
6. *Laredo Weekly Times*, June 18, 1916.
7. Barnes to Bielaski, June 12, 1916, 7BI; Pezzot statement in Barnes report, July 1, 1916, 8BI.
8. *Laredo Weekly Times*, June 18, 1916.
9. *Laredo Weekly Times*, July 9, 1916.
10. State of Texas v. Norberto Pezzar [*sic*] et al., no. 5204, District Court, Laredo; Garrett to Lansing, June 12, 1916, 812.00/18399 and July 9, 1916, 812.00/18683, RDS; Weekly Report, June 15, 1916, 812.00/16505, RDS; *San Antonio Express*, June 14, 1916; *Laredo Weekly Times*, June 25, 1916.
11. Evidently Rodríguez had also been caught up in the wave of jailings of the leaders of the Texas Revolution.
12. Barnes report, July 1, 1916, 8BI; Ross report, July 7, 1916, 13BI.
13. Valls was mistaken; he was evidently referring to the raiders convicted in the San Ignacio raid. See *Laredo Weekly Times*, July 9, 1916, which states that the Webb Station raiders got five years in the penitentiary. In September they were transferred to the state penitentiary in Huntsville. *Laredo Weekly Times*, September 10, 1916.
14. John Valls testimony, *Investigation*, 1203; *Laredo Weekly Times*, June 18, 25, 1916.
15. *Laredo Weekly Times*, June 11, 1916.
16. Breniman report, December 19, 1915, 6BI.
17. Idar report, June 20, 1916, 13BI.
18. John Valls testimony, *Investigation*, 1204–5; Osterveen report, June 15, 1916, 13BI; *Laredo Weekly Times*, June 11, 18, 1916.
19. *El Paso Morning Times*, June 21, 1916.
20. José Antonio Arce et al. v. State of Texas, no.4314, Texas Court of Criminal Appeals; Funston to Adjutant General, June 15, 1916, 812.00/18443, 812.00/19402, and 812.00/18553, RDS; Johnson to Lansing, June 15, 1916, 812.00/18437, and Garrett to Lansing, June 17, 1916, 812.00/18456, RDS.
21. For a translation of the Plan de San Diego propaganda found on the dead raiders, see Commanding General, Laredo District, to Funston, June 21, 1916, Chief, War College Division, to Chief of Staff, Eastern Department, July 25,

1916, and Major R. H. Van Deman to Bielaski, July 25, 1916, all in MID 8528-38; *San Antonio Express*, June 15, 1916.

22. Funston to Adjutant General, June 13, 1916, 812.00/18443, RDS; Funston to Parker, June 15, 1916, and Parker to Funston, June 15, 1916, Matamoros Post Records; *San Antonio Express*, June 18, 1916.
23. *San Antonio Express*, June 18, 1916.
24. Funston to Adjutant General, June 15, 1916, 812.00/18443, RDS.
25. Harris and Sadler, "Plan of San Diego," 94.
26. Parker to Commanding General, June 15, 1916, Matamoros Post Records.
27. Parker to Funston, June 15, 1916, Matamoros Post Records.
28. Mayfield testimony, *Investigation*, 1288, 1293.
29. June 22, 1916, 13BI.
30. *San Antonio Express*, June 15, 16, 18, 1916; *Laredo Weekly Times*, June 18, 25, July 16, 1916.
31. Valls testimony, *Investigation*, 1207; *San Antonio Express*, June 17, 1916, has a picture of the *sedicioso* flag and the cowboy who gave the warning about the Webb Station raid.
32. Harris report, August 10, 1916, 12BI.
33. *El Paso Morning Times*, July 12, 16, 1916.
34. Barnes report, July 1, 1916, 13BI; *San Antonio Express*, June 18, 1916; *Laredo Weekly Times*, June 25, July 2, 16, 1916; *Brownsville Daily Herald*, June 24, 1916.
35. Lawrence report, June 16 [?], 1916, 9BI.
36. Barnes report, July 1, 1916, 13BI.
37. *Laredo Weekly Times*, July 16, 1916; *San Antonio Express*, June 18, 1916; Barkey report, July 31, 1915, 9BI; see also Harris report, July 7, 1916, 6BI.
38. Statement of José Antonio Arce, in Ross report, July 7, 1916, 13BI.
39. *Laredo Weekly Times*, July 16, 1916.
40. See his statement, in Ross report, July 7, 1916, 13BI.
41. See his statement, in Ross report, July 7, 1916, 13BI.
42. *Laredo Weekly Times*, June 25, 28, July 16, 1916.
43. *Laredo Weekly Times*, December 24, 1916.
44. *Laredo Weekly Times*, November 18, 1916.
45. DHRM, 13: part 2, 149–152.
46. *Laredo Weekly Times*, July 16, 23, August 6, 1916.
47. *Laredo Weekly Times*, December 24, 1916.
48. *Laredo Weekly Times*, July 16, December 24, 1916.

16. The War Crisis

1. Stout, *Border Conflict*, xi.
2. Regarding the controversy over just what Pershing's orders were, on March 10, 1916, Secretary of State Lansing sent a communication "To All American Consular Officers in Mexico: The following statement has just been given to the press by the President: 'An adequate force will be sent at once in pursuit of Villa with the single object of *capturing him* [Italics added] and putting a stop to his forays. This can and will be done in entirely friendly aid of the constituted authorities in Mexico and with scrupulous respect for the sovereignty of that Republic.'" Lansing to All, March 10, 1916, 812.00/19517, RDS.
3. *San Antonio Express*, May 13, 1916.
4. Breniman to Bielaski, October 3, 1916, 812.00/19417, RDS; DHRM, 12:290–293.
5. Sandos, "Plan of San Diego," 21.
6. *San Antonio Express*, May 8, 9, 1916.
7. *San Antonio Express*, May 12, 1916.
8. *San Antonio Express*, May 9, 10, 1916.
9. *San Antonio Express*, May 11, 1916; Bruscino, "A Troubled Past,"40.
10. *San Antonio Express*, May 11, 1916.
11. *San Antonio Express*, May 10, 11, 1916.
12. Bliss to Chief of Staff, June 6, 22, December 5, 1916, and Bliss to Finley, June 24, 1916, Tasker H. Bliss Papers, Library of Congress, Washington DC.
13. *San Antonio Express*, May 13, 1916.
14. *San Antonio Express*, May 14, June 18, 23, 1916; the army's general staff estimated that it would take 450,000 men and three years to complete intervention in Mexico. *Laredo Weekly Times*, November 23, 1919.
15. Rodgers to Secretary of State, May 19, 1916, 812.00/18201; see also Hanna to Secretary of State, May 22, 1916, 812.00/18213, Silliman to Secretary of State, May 22, 1916, 812.00/18215, and Garrett to Secretary of State, May 24, 1916, 812.00/18238, all in RDS; *Brownsville Daily Herald*, March 14, 1916.
16. Funston to Scott, April 5, 1916, Funston Collection.
17. *San Antonio Express*, May 27, 29, June 1, 2, 17, 1916.
18. Rodgers to Secretary of State, June 28, 1916, 812.00/18607, RDS.
19. The army's weekly intelligence report of June 8, 1918, stated: "On the 27th of May the Carrancistas in Chihuahua tried the 75 and 80 mm shells which were received from Mexico City. Out of the 20 shells shot from Santa Rosa Hill to Cerro Grande only 7 burst, but none of them had the usual range. For this reason the 1,000 shells which were received in Chihuahua were returned to Mex-

ico City with the remark that they were useless. In regard to the ammunition for the 7 mm Mauser rifles, it is also of very poor quality and not less than 40% of it is useless." Weekly Report, June 8, 1918, 10014-74, MID.

20. Funston to Parker, May 27, 1916, Funston Collection.
21. Funston to Scott, May 30, 1916, Funston Collection.
22. *San Antonio Express*, May 24, 25, 1916.
23. *San Antonio Express*, May 20, 22, 1916.
24. *San Antonio Express*, May 25, June 14, 18, 1916.
25. *San Antonio Express*, June 16, 1916; Pershing to Adjutant General, June 16, 1916, 812.00/18493, RDS.
26. Lege report, June 25, 1916, 12BI; *La Prensa*, June 9, 16, 1916; *Laredo Weekly Times*, June 11, 1916; *San Antonio Express*, June 11, 13, 19, 21, 1916; *El Paso Morning Times*, June 27, 1916.
27. U.S. v. Abel Sandoval et al., no. 309, U.S. Commissioner, Brownsville, FRC-FW.
28. Felipe Sandoval interrogation in Berliner report, July 1, 1916, 8BI; *Brownsville Daily Herald*, July 1, 4, 1916; U.S. v. Felipe Sandoval et al., no. 2208, U.S. District Court, Brownsville, FRC-FW.
29. Statement of Felipe Sandoval, n.d., 8BI; Mennet report, May 24, 1917, 6BI.
30. *San Antonio Express*, June 18, 21, 1916; Lon Hill testimony, *Investigation*, 1261–62; *Brownsville Daily Herald*, January 27, 1917.
31. *San Antonio Express*, June 10, 1916.
32. DHRM, 12:369–72; *San Antonio Express*, June 17, 18, 1916.
33. DHRM, 12:375.
34. *San Antonio Express*, June 18, 1916; *Brownsville Daily Herald*, June 19, 1916.
35. DHRM, 12:381–82, 388–89.
36. *San Antonio Express*, June 18, 1916.
37. *San Antonio Express*, June 16, 18–20, 1916; *Brownsville Daily Herald*, June 19, 1916.
38. *San Antonio Express*, June 16, 18, 20, 1916; Blocker to Secretary of State, June 18, 1916, 812.00/18452, RDS.
39. *Brownsville Daily Herald*, June 26, 1916; *San Antonio Express*, June 18, 19, 21, 1916.
40. *San Antonio Express*, June 20, 1916; *El Paso Morning Times*, June 21, 26, 1916.
41. *Laredo Weekly Times*, July 2, 1916.
42. *Laredo Weekly Times*, November 26, 1916.
43. *San Antonio Express*, June 21, 1916.
44. *San Antonio Express*, June 21, 1916.

45. *Brownsville Daily Herald*, June 23, 1916.
46. A translation of the circular is in Rogers report, July 4, 1916, 232-84BI; Dawson to Secretary of State, June 17, 1916, 812.00/18458, RDS.
47. Dawson to Secretary of State, July 8, 1916, 812.00/18770, RDS; see also Dawson to Secretary of State, July 22 [?], 1916, 812.00/18771, RDS.
48. *Brownsville Daily Herald*, June 26, 28, July 1, 1916.
49. Dawson to Secretary of State, July 24, 1916, 812.00/18832, RDS.
50. *San Antonio Express*, June 20, 1916.
51. *Al Pueblo*, June 19, 1916, 6BI; see also Wiseman report, June 23, 1916, 6BI.
52. Lansing's note is in *Investigation*, 1215–23.
53. *San Antonio Express*, June 21, 22, 25, 1916; *El Paso Morning Times*, June 22, 25, 1916; *Brownsville Daily Herald*, June 26, 1916.
54. *San Antonio Express*, June 20, 1916.
55. *San Antonio Express*, June 20–23, 1916.
56. *San Antonio Express*, June 22, 1916; for an account by an American participant see Morey, "The Cavalry Fight at Carrizal"; for an account by a Mexican participant see DHRM, 13:15–27. See also DHRM, 13:52–120.
57. *Brownsville Daily Herald*, June 27, 1916.
58. Wilson to Lansing, June 21, 1916, 812.00/18533-1/2, RDS; Lansing to Wilson, June 21, 1916, 812.00/18533A, RDS.
59. *San Antonio Express*, June 21, 1916.
60. Wiseman report, June 23, 1916, 232-84BI.
61. Silliman to Secretary of State, June 22, 1916, 812.00/18540, RDS.
62. *San Antonio Express*, June 22, 1916.
63. González to Carranza, June 24, 1916, Telegrams, State of Morelos, 1916, Carranza Archive.
64. *La Prensa*, June 13, 14, 1916; *San Antonio Express*, June 12, 13, 14, 1916.
65. *San Antonio Express*, June 24, 1916.
66. Memorandum for the Adjutant General, June 25, 1916, and Parker to Bliss, June 25, 1916, Tasker Bliss Papers.
67. *San Antonio Express*, June 25, 26, 1916.
68. Link, *Papers of Woodrow Wilson*, 37:297–98, 304.
69. Maury to González, June 26, 1916, roll 10, PGA.
70. Mennet report, June 30 [?], 1916, 11BI.
71. FA.
72. *Laredo Weekly Times*, June 25, 1916.
73. *El Paso Morning Times*, August 22, 1916.

74. Knight, *The Mexican Revolution*, 2:344.
75. *San Antonio Express*, June 19, 1916.
76. See Tuchman, *The Zimmermann Telegram*.
77. Claridge, *A Spy for All Seasons*, 104–5, 147, 151, 221.
78. Harris report, July 3, 1916, 7BI; Webster report, June 23, 1916, 12BI; *La Prensa*, June 23–25, 1916; *Laredo Weekly Times*, June 25, 1916; *El Paso Morning Times*, June 22, 1916.
79. General Funston's Annual Report For the Southern Department, 1916, 15, Records of the Adjutant General's Office, RG 94, NARS.
80. José Antonio Arce et al., Appellants, v. State of Texas, no. 4314, Texas Court of Criminal Appeals, Austin, Texas; See also *Investigation*, 3279–82; John Valls testimony, *Investigation*, 1203–4.
81. *Laredo Weekly Times*, April 21, May 5, 26, 1918.

17. Aftermath

1. Zuazua to Garza, July 20, 1916, AGC.
2. Fierros to González, June 23, 1916, Barragán to González, June 23, 1916, and González to Fierros, July 10, 1916, roll 26B, PGA.
3. Fukuda report, January 30, 1917, 232-84BI.
4. Fierros to González, June 30, 1916, AGC. Professor Joe Chance of the math department at Pan American University, Edinburg, Texas, and Colonel John Smith (Ret.) of Las Cruces, New Mexico, decrypted the telegram, for which the authors are most appreciative.
5. Fierros to González, September 30, 1916, roll 11, PGA.
6. González to Fierros, October 14, 1916, roll 11, PGA; González to Flores, October 14, 1916, roll 11, PGA.
7. González to Fierros, November 28, 1916, roll 10, PGA.
8. González to Murguía, December 28, 1916, roll 10, PGA.
9. Yoshida to González, September 5, 1916, roll 26B, PGA.
10. Hotel bills, June–October 5, 1916, and restaurant bills through July 25, 1916, AGC.
11. Garza to Garza, July 13, 14, 15, 1916, AGC.
12. Rogers report, July 3, 1916, 6BI.
13. "Extracts from '*El Día*' a newspaper published in Monterrey," July 20, 1916, found together with the Forseck affidavit.
14. Barnes to Bielaski, July 15, 1916, 11BI.
15. AGC.
16. *Brownsville Daily Herald*, May 18, September 5, 1917.

17. *Brownsville Daily Herald*, December 7, 1917, January 2, 1918.
18. *La Prensa*, April 11, 18, 1916; *Brownsville Daily Herald*, September 5, 1917.
19. *Brownsville Daily Herald*, May 1, September 5, 1917.
20. *Laredo Weekly Times*, December 5, 1915.
21. Mennet report, December 7, 1916, 6BI.
22. *Brownsville Daily Herald*, March 21, 31, 1917.
23. Rogers report, September 10 [?], 1916, 6BI.
24. Rogers report, October 4, 1916, 11BI.
25. Aniceto Pizaña, Tomás Pizaña, Luis de la Rosa, Ricardo Gómez, Abel Sandoval, Vicente [?] Sandoval, Guadalupe Sandoval, Isidro Sandoval#, Santiago Arismendis [?], Elijio Arismendis, Miguel Reyes, Luis Baymo, Concepción Avalos#, Antonio Arismendis, Manuel Arismendis#, Romualdo Gamboa, Juan Gamboa#, Vicente Dávila Sr., Vicente Dávila Jr., Felipe Dávila, Guadalupe Ramos, Juan Ramos, Pedro Reyes, José Reyes, Juan Villarreal, five Mejía brothers. (Those whose names are followed by # were on the Texas side of the Rio Grande.) Breniman to Bielaski, October 5, 1916, 6BI.
26. Against Luis de la Rosa, Aniceto Pizaña, Ricardo Gómez, José Benavides, Alberto Mejía, Ricardo López, Nicardio Flores, Gaspar Cantú, Pablo Saenz, Pedro Cavazos, Darío Morado, Sóstenes Saldaña Jr., Marcelino Hinojosa, Catarino Soto, Gerónimo Cruz, Trinidad Tovar, Felipe Tovar, Evaristo Ramos, Santiago Santillana, Felipe Ramos, Jesús Treviño, Eduardo García, and Pablo Pérez. Agent Rogers wrote that to this list should be added Antonio Rocha, Cástulo Ramírez and Pilar Rostro. Rogers report, October 15, 1916, 6BI.

18. Informants

1. Wiseman report, July 17, 1916, 11BI.
2. Wiseman to Barnes, September 4, 1916, 7BI.
3. García to Ligardi, October 11, 20, 1916, 12BI.
4. Breniman to Bielaski, November 9, 1916, 11BI.
5. García reports, August 5, November 9–30, 1916, December 9, 1916, 12BI, January 2, 4, 1917, 11BI, and January 5, 1917, 6BI; see also Chief of Staff Southern Department to Adjutant General of the Army, January 10, 1917, 812.00/20395, RDS.
6. García report, November 12, 1916, 6BI.
7. García reports, December 2, 1916, 11BI, January 2, 1917, 11BI, January 5, 1917, 6BI; see also Chief of Staff Southern Department to Adjutant General of the Army, January 10, 1917, 812.00/20395, RDS; Barnes report, January 5, 1916, 8BI.

8. Fukuda report, December 22, 1916, 232-84BI.
9. Johnson, *Revolution in Texas*, 43.
10. "Idar, Clemente Nicasio," Tyler et al., *New Handbook of Texas*, 3:813–14; Orozco, *No Mexicans, Women, or Dogs*, 101–3.
11. Barnes reports, May 20, 27, 1916, 4BI; Idar reports, June 3, 1916, 13BI.
12. Barnes to Idar, June 7, 1916, 11BI.
13. Idar to Barnes, June 9, 1916, 13BI.
14. Idar reports, June 9, 1916, 7BI, June 9, 1916, 12BI, June 12, 1916, 13BI.
15. Ross report, June 13, 1916, 13BI.
16. Idar reports, June 19, 20, 1916, 13BI.
17. Idar report, July 8, 1916, 11BI.
18. Ross report, August 10, 1916, 6BI.
19. Idar report, August 10, 1916, 11BI.
20. Idar reports, August 12, 14, 1916, 12BI, August 15, 1916, 11BI, August 24, 1916, 12BI, September 17, 1916, 11BI.
21. Breniman to Idar, November 10, 1916, 4BI; Barnes report, February 21, 1917, 12BI.
22. Ross report, July 3, 1916, 13BI.
23. Idar to Tumulty, November 19, 1917, 812.00/21501, RDS.
24. Breniman to Allen, March 20, 1919, 232-84BI.
25. Barnes to Bielaski, August 5, 1916, 6BI.
26. Sorola report, August 7, 1916, 6BI.
27. Sorola report, August 25, 1916, 7BI.
28. Sorola reports, August 10, 12, 13 [?], 1916, 6BI.
29. Sorola reports, August 14, 1916, 6BI. See also his August 16 report, 6BI.
30. Sorola reports, April 7, 12, 1917, 232-84 and 6BI.
31. Sorola reports, April 7, 11, 12, 14, 16, 1917, 232-84, April 8, 1917, 6BI; Barnes report, April 9, 1917, 232-84BI.
32. Green to Barnes, January 13, 1917, 6BI.
33. Mennet report, January 17, 1917, 6BI.
34. Mennet report, January 17, 1917, 6BI.
35. Stone report, January 7, 1916, 7BI; *Brownsville Daily Herald* April 18, 1916.

19. Further Investigation

1. Mennet reports, December 31, 1916, January 1, 17, 1917, 6BI; Barnes report, January 13, 1917, 6BI.
2. Rogers report, February 2, 1917, 6BI.
3. Those arrested were de la Rosa, Jesús Martínez, José Aguilar, Juan González,

Ignacio Muñoz Mora, Joaquín Isais, Lieutenant Colonel Pedro Viña, Lieutenant Andrés Moreno, Lieutenant Aurelio Morales, Agustín Morales, Refugio de León, Andrés Vargas, Apolonio Vargas, and several others, totaling some twenty alleged plotters. Barnes report, January 30, 1917, 6BI and 232-84BI.

4. Sorola report, January 22, 1917, 6BI; Fukuda report, February 5, 1917, 13BI; *Brownsville Daily Herald*, January 18, 1917.
5. Fukuda report, January 27, 1917, 232-84BI.
6. Fukuda report, January 24, 1917, 232-84BI.
7. Fukuda report, February 7, 1917, 13BI.
8. Mennet reports, January 23, 1917, 6BI, and January 25, 1917, 232-84BI.
9. Fukuda reports, February 14, 17, 1917, 13BI.
10. Barnes report, January 30, 1917, 6BI; Mennet report, April 30, 1917, 232-84BI; Breniman report, March 8, 1917, 232-84; Seman report, March 7, 1917, 232-84; Ibs report, May 16, 1916, 9BI.
11. Robertson to Secretary of State, March 27, 1917, 812.00/20747, RDS.
12. Seman report, March 31, 1917, 232-84BI.
13. Seman report, April 25, 1917, 232-84BI.
14. Carothers to Canova, March 7, 1917, 812.00/20668, RDS.
15. *El Paso Morning Times*, July 18, 1917; L. H. Memorandum, July 13, 1917, 232-84BI; L. H. [Harrison] memorandum, July 13, 1917, 6BI.
16. Mennet report, July 19, 1917, 6BI.
17. Mennet report, July 20, 1917, 6BI.
18. Barnes to Parker, September 6, 1917, 232-84BI.
19. Weekly Report, November 24, 1917, 812.00/21534, RDS.
20. Breniman report, February 27, 1917, 6BI.
21. Seman report, March 9, 1917, 6BI.
22. Barnes report, January 21, 1917, 6BI.
23. Barnes report, January 13, 1917, 232-84BI.
24. Mennet report, May 24, 1917, 232-84BI.
25. Mennet report, April 30, 1917, 6BI and 12BI.
26. Weekly Report, February 2, 1918, 10014-43, MID.
27. Fletcher to Secretary of State, March 12, 1917, 812.00/20636, RDS.
28. *Laredo Weekly Times*, December 14, 1919.
29. Machado and Judge, "Tempest in a Teapot?"
30. *Laredo Weekly Times*, December 7, 1919.
31. Danciger to Hanson, February 19, 1920, Jackson to Danciger, March 4, 1920, Danciger to Fall, June 8, 1920, and *Kansas City Star*, May 21, 1920, ABFFP.

32. Harris and Sadler, *Secret War*, 373–74.
33. Harris and Sadler, *Texas Rangers*, 383–85, 532.
34. *Laredo Weekly Times*, October 12, November 23, December 7, 1919, January 11, 1920.
35. Harris and Sadler, *Texas Rangers*, 481–82; Hanson to Buckley, November 24, 1919, Buckley Papers.

20. Later Careers

1. Harris and Sadler, *Texas Rangers*, 484.
2. *Diccionario Porrúa,* 666.
3. Fierros to González, November 3, 22, 1916; González to Fierros, November 28, 1916; González to Murguía, December 28, 1916, Exp. EF, PGA; Cobb to Polk, May 22, 1917, Records of the Department of State Relating to the Internal Affairs of Germany, 1910–1929, National Archives Microfilm Publication, Microcopy no. 336, file no. 862.20212: Military Affairs of Germany in Mexico, 862.20212/351, NARS.
4. Lege report, October 16, 1917, 12BI; Harris and Sadler, *Texas Rangers*, 322.
5. *El Paso Morning Times*, August 1, 1916; Naranjo, *Diccionario*, 237.
6. *Brownsville Daily Herald*, January 25, May 30, 1917.
7. Cumberland, *Mexican Revolution*, 368.
8. De la Garza Treviño, *Historia de Tamaulipas*, 240–43, 245; *Laredo Weekly Times*, September 23, 1917.
9. Williams to Secretary of State, 812.00/21880, RDS.
10. Fletcher to Secretary of State, March 29, 1918, 812.00/21832, RDS.
11. Weekly Report, March 27, 1918, 812.00/21862, RDS.
12. De la Garza Treviño, *Historia de Tamaulipas,* 245; *Laredo Weekly Times*, January 11, November 14, 1920, February 20, 1921.
13. Weekly Report, April 13, 1918, 812.00/21921, RDS.
14. Commander Mexican Patrol Detachment to Navy Department (Operations), April 25, 1918, 812.00/21983, RDS; see also Dawson to Secretary of State, April 12, 1918, 812.00/21877, RDS; Williams to Secretary of State, April 12, 1918, 812.00/21880, RDS; Cumberland, *Mexican Revolution,* 368–70; Harris and Sadler, *Texas Rangers*, 393–94; de la Garza Treviño, *Historia de Tamaulipas,* 241; *Laredo Weekly Times*, March 4, May 27, July 22, 1917, February 10, March 10, 17, 31, April 14, 21, 1918; *Brownsville Daily Herald*, February 19, 1917.
15. Moguel Flores, *75 Aniversario,* 66; Weekly Report, April 20, 1918, 812.00/21936, RDS.

16. Weekly Report, April 27, 1918, 812.00/21965, RDS.
17. Valls testimony, *Investigation*, 1211.
18. Hanson to Kearful, November 7, 1919, Buckley Papers.
19. The contract is in FA, Exhibit I.
20. The commission stated that "Juan K. Forseck has been designated by the Mexican Government to carry out a commission of a public nature, and thus it is recommended to civil and military authorities as well as Mexican diplomatic and consular agents abroad, to provide Forseck with all facilities to help him discharge his mission." FA, Exhibit M.
21. In May 1917, Noonan went to New York "to join Roosevelt's proposed Army." Mock report, May 26, 1917, 7BI.
22. Hopkins report, February 17, 1917, found together with Forseck affidavit; Hopkins report, February 11, 1917, 13BI; Blanford report, February 9, 1916, 7BI.
23. FA.
24. *Laredo Weekly Times*, May 12, August 25, September 8, October 6, November 10, December 1, 15, 29, 1918.
25. *Laredo Weekly Times*, January 5, March 16, 23, 30, May 4, August 3, 1919.
26. Robertson to Secretary of State, September 23, 1919, 812.00/23091, RDS; Phillips to American Consul, September 23, 1919, 812.00/23091, RDS; ACT [?] to Fletcher, November 25, 1919, 812.00/23315, RDS; Robertson to Secretary of State, January 7, 1920, 812.00/23314, RDS.
27. Harris and Sadler, *Texas Rangers*, 482–83.
28. Ayala Villarreal, "Maderist and Constitutionalist Revolutions," 194–95, 196 n. 4, 291; see also Valls testimony, *Investigation*, 1212.
29. Ayala Villarreal, "The Maderist and Constitutionalist Revolutions," 196 n. 4.
30. Ayala Villarreal, "The Maderist and Constitutionalist Revolutions," 194–95.
31. Weekly Report, December 29, 1917, 10014-25, MID.
32. *Brownsville Daily Herald*, December 6, 1917.
33. Weekly Report, January 5, 1918, 812.00/21673, RDS.
34. Ayala Villareal, "The Maderist and Constitutionalist Revolutions," 196 n. 4.
35. Johnson, *Revolution in Texas*, 195.
36. Harris and Sadler, *Texas Rangers*, 470.
37. Marks to Cope, January 5, 7, 1920, Adjutant General's Correspondence, Texas State Archives, Austin.
38. Cope to Marks, January 10, 1920, Adjutant General's Correspondence.
39. Cope to Marks, January 13, 1920, Adjutant General's Correspondence.
40. Marks to Cope, January 15, 1920, Adjutant General's Correspondence.

41. Cope to Marks, March 13, 1920, Adjutant General's Correspondence.
42. Harris and Sadler, *Texas Rangers*, 484–88.
43. Information kindly supplied by de la Rosa's great-granddaughter Violeta H. Salinas de la Rosa of Mission, Texas.
44. De la Garza Treviño, *Plan de San Diego*, 44–45.
45. Tyler et al., *New Handbook of Texas*, 5:224; Johnson, *Revolution in Texas*, 196–97.
46. Ramos to Garza, January 12, 1917, AGC; Sorola report, April 14, 1917, 6BI.
47. Chief to Barnes, July 16, 1917, 232-84BI; Harrison to Bielaski, July 13, 1917, 232-84 and 6BI.
48. J. R. Harold, immigrant inspector, certified that this was a correct translation of the letter, which is Exhibit 5 accompanying the Forseck affidavit.
49. "I hereby certify that the above is a correct translation of the letter hereto attached—J. R. Harold, Immigrant Inspector." This is Exhibit 4 accompanying the Forseck affidavit.
50. Ramos to Garza, February 29, 1919, AGC.
51. Carranza to Garza, April 15, 1919, AGC.
52. The collector of customs for the last three years, Domingo González, who happened to be General Pablo González's brother, was being transferred to Tampico. *Laredo Weekly Times*, February 2, 9, 1919.
53. Méndez to Garza, June 9, 1919, AGC.
54. Caballo to Méndez, August 16, 1919, AGC.
55. Valls testimony, *Investigation*, 1224–25.
56. Valls testimony, *Investigation*, 1210; Valls claimed that he'd received anonymous letters threatening his life because of his testimony. *Laredo Weekly Times*, February 1, 1920.
57. Fall statement, *Investigation*, 1228–29.
58. Fall statement, *Investigation*, 1226–28.
59. "Fact Sheet on Agustín de la Garza Solís," Museum of South Texas History.
60. Garza to Secretary of War and Marine, July 2, 1936, and Corral to Garza, July 16, 1936, AGC.
61. Garza to Senate, December 1, 1938, AGC.
62. García and Castélum to Garza, December 7, 1938, AGC. Incidentally, Garza now signed himself "Agustín S. de la Garza."
63. Garza to Senate, December 14, 1938, and García and Marín to Garza, December 19, 1938, AGC.
64. Garza to Cárdenas, December 31, 1938, AGC.
65. Rivas López to Garza, February 9, 1939, AGC.

66. Garza to Chamber of Deputies, April 21, May 20, 1941, and Navarrete to Garza, June 17, 1941, AGC.
67. Garza to Chief of the Office of Personnel of Telecomunications, July 13, 1952, and Secretariat of Communications and Public Works to Garza, July 13, 1952, AGC.

21. A Question of Numbers

1. Pierce, *Brief History*, 115.
2. Barnes report, November 1, 1915, 232-84BI.
3. Rogers report, September 28, 1915, 9BI.
4. Rocha, "Influence of the Mexican Revolution," 333.
5. Vanderwood and Samponaro, *Border Fury*.
6. *Laredo Weekly Times*, September 12, 1915.
7. *Brownsville Daily Herald*, August 19, 24, September 11, 16, December 5, 1915.
8. *Laredo Weekly Times*, October 3, 1915.
9. *Investigation*, 1248–49.
10. "Partial List of Mexicans and of Mexican Americans Killed During the First Period of the Bandit War from July 1, 1915," Attachment to Report No. 234, January 26, 1916, by Consul Jesse H. Johnson, U.S. Consulate, Matamoros, 812.00/17186, RDS. This list is also found in Matamoros Post Records RG 84, National Archives II, College Park, Maryland.
11. Pierce, however, was evidently unable to provide additional names, or if he did they do not appear either in the Matamoros Post Records or in the Mexican Decimal Files in the National Archives II. Consul Johnson reported that "It would be impossible to ascertain the number of Mexicans killed by the American soldiers, Rangers and citizens during the bandit raids on the Texas border. There was no record kept by any one, no one could. Some say 150, some say 200 and some say more." Johnson to Secretary of State, January 21, 1916, 812.00/17129, RDS.
12. Pierce, *Brief History*, 103.
13. See the "Memoirs of Jesse Pérez, 1870–1934," dictated to J. Frank Dobie. The name list is on pages 57–58 of his 63-page memoir, located in the Dolph Briscoe Center for American History, University of Texas at Austin.
14. For Pérez's career see Harris, Harris, and Sadler, *Texas Ranger Biographies*, 304–5.
15. Tyrell to Chief, U.S. Secret Service, November 25, 1915, Records of the U.S. Secret Service, Daily Reports from San Antonio, Texas, vol. 12, Daily Reports of Agents, 1875–1936, Microcopy no. 3.158, RG 87, NARS.

16. Funston to Adjutant General, June 7, 1916, Records of the Office of the Adjutant General: Correspondence Relating to the Mexican Border, file no. 237762-2378529, microcopy no. 1557, Benson Latin American Collection, University of Texas at Austin.
17. "Proceedings," 2:679.
18. "Proceedings," 1:355.
19. Fehrenback, *Lone Star*, 690.
20. Harris and Sadler, *Texas Rangers*, 325.
21. Private Willis was on permanent assignment to the sheriff of Dimmit County, Privates Sanders and Craighead were stationed at Hebbronville, Brooks and Price at Alice, Cardwell and Davenport at Rio Grande City, and Sergeant Grimes at Del Rio, the company's headquarters.
22. Harris and Sadler, *Texas Rangers*, 248–51.
23. Harris and Sadler, *Texas Rangers*, 255–58, 267, 274, 277; Adjutant General to Ransom, August 31, 1915, Adjutant General's Correspondence, Texas State Archives.
24. Harris and Sadler, *Texas Rangers*, 289.
25. W. W. Sterling testimony, "Proceedings," 2:1410.
26. Paredes, *With His Pistol*, 24.
27. Bacevich, *Diplomat in Khaki*, 64.
28. Paredes, *With His Pistol*, 24.
29. Harris and Sadler, *Texas Rangers*, 505.
30. Harris and Sadler, *Texas Rangers*, 433.
31. Harris and Sadler, *Texas Rangers*, 478. Based on Webb's acknowledgments, his source probably was the Brownsville attorney Harbert Davenport, who "was never too busy to answer any questions about the Lower Rio Grande." *Texas Rangers*, xiii.
32. Cumberland, "Border Raids."
33. Harris and Sadler, "Plan of San Diego," 390, 392.
34. Samora, Bernal, and Peña, *Gunpowder Justice*, 65.
35. Rocha, "Influence of the Mexican Revolution," 312, 313.
36. Rosenbaum, *Mexicano Resistance*.
37. Rosenbaum, *Mexicano Resistance*, 51.
38. Vanderwood and Samponaro, *Border Fury*, 122.
39. Procter, *Just One Riot*, 4.
40. Johnson, *Revolution in Texas*, 2; Johnson repeats his unsubstantiated claim that "rebels killed dozens of Anglo farmers" in "Unearthing the Hidden Histories," 6.

41. Utley, *Lone Star Lawmen*, 38 n. 25.
42. E-mail, Navarrette to Sadler, November 16, 2010.
43. E-mail, Dan Arellano to Louis R. Sadler, November 16, 2010.

22. Some Interesting Interpretations

1. Bratcher, "Plan de San Diego."
2. De la Garza Treviño, *Plan de San Diego.*
3. Johnson, *Revolution in Texas*, 220.
4. There is also a Spanish copy in the Espinoza de los Monteros archive in Mexico City. See Raat, *Revoltosos*, 262, 263 n. 20.
5. Webb, *Texas Rangers*, 486.
6. Sterling, *Trails and Trials*, 28.
7. Sandos, "The Plan of San Diego," 10.
8. Sandos, "The Mexican Revolution and the United States," 179, 211–15, 223.
9. Sandos, "Pancho Villa and American Security."
10. Sandos, *Rebellion in the Borderlands*, 100.
11. Bartra, *Regeneración 1900–1918*, 436–39; "The Uprisings in Texas," *Regeneración*, No. 210.
12. Montejano, *Anglos and Mexicans*, 117, 118.
13. Utley, *Lone Star Lawmen*, 26, 334.
14. Gómez Quiñones, "Plan de San Diego Reviewed," 131 n. 1.
15. Acuña, *Occupied America: The Chicano's Struggle Toward Liberation.*
16. Acuña, *Occupied America: A History of Chicanos.*
17. Acuña, *Occupied America: A History of Chicanos*, 176.
18. Gómez Quiñones, "Plan de San Diego Reviewed," 124.
19. Raat, *Revoltosos*, 262–63.
20. Gonzales, "Mexican Revolution," 121.
21. Wilson to Lansing, August 7, 1915, and Lansing to Wilson, August 9, 1915, State Department Decimal Files, Internal Affairs of Mexico, 1910–29, file no. 812.00/15751½.
22. Gonzales, "Mexican Revolution," 120–21.

Conclusion

1. *Los Sediciosos* is published in Paredes, *A Texas-Mexican Cancionero*, 71–72. The Spanish-language text follows. The English version of *Los Sediciosos* is on pp. 72–73.

   En mil novecientos quince,
   Que días tan calurosos!

Voy a cantar estos versos,
versos de los sediciosos.
Ya con esta van tres veces
Que sucede lo bonito,
La primera fue en Mercedes,
en Bronsvil y en San Benito.
En ese punto de Norias
ya merito les ardía,
a esos rinches desgraciados
muchas balas les llovía.
Ya la mecha está encendida
por los puros mexicanos,
y los que van a pagarla
son los mexicotejanos.
Ya la mecha está encendida
con azul y colorado,
y los que van a pagarla
van a ser los de este lado.
Ya la mecha está encendida,
muy bonita y colorada,
y la vamos a pagar
los que no debemos nada.
Decía Aniceto Pizaña,
En su caballo cantando:
Donde están por ahi los rinches?
que los vengo visitando.
Esos rinches de la Kineña,
dicen que son muy valientes,
hacen llorar las mujeres,
hacen correr a las gentes.
Decía Teodoro Fuentes,
abrochandose un zapato:
A esos rinches de la Kineña
les daremos un mal rato.
Decía Vicente el Giro
en su chico caballazgo:
Echenme ese gringo grande,

pa' llevármelo de brazo.
Contesta el americano,
con su sombrero en las manos:
Yo sí me voy con ustedes,
son muy buenos maxacanos.
Decía Miguel Salinas
en su yegüita almendrada:
Ay, qué gringos tan ingratos!
que no nos hagan parada.
En ese punto de Norias
se oía la pelotería,
del señor Luis de la Rosa
nomás el llanto se oía.
El señor Luis de la Rosa
se tenía por hombrecito,
a la hora de los balazos
lloraba como un chiquito.
Decía Teodoro Fuentes,
decía con su risita:
Echen balazos, muchachos,
qué trifulca tan bonita.
Tiren, tiren, muchachitos,
tiren, tiren de a montón,
que el señor Luis de la Rosa
ha manchado el pabellón.
Gritaba Teodoro Fuentes:
Hay que pasar por Mercedes,
para enseñarles a los rinches
que con nosotros no pueden.
Les dice Luis de la Rosa:
Muchachos, que van a hacer?
Por Mercedes no pasamos,
y si no lo van a ver.
Contesta Teodoro Fuentes
con su voz muy natural:
Vale mas que usted no vaya
porque nomás va a llorar.

Pues pasaron por Mercedes,
y también por San Benito,
iban a tumbar el tren
a ese dipo de Olmito.
Ya se van los sediciosos,
ya se van de retirada,
de recuerdos nos dejaron
una veta colorada.
Ya se van los sediciosos
y quedaron de volver,
pero no dijeron cuando
porque no podían saber.
Despedida no la doy
porque no la traigo aquí,
se la llevó Luis de la Rosa
para San Luis Potosí.

2. "Proceedings," 2:954.
3. "Proceedings," 1:703.
4. Harris and Sadler, "Plan of San Diego," 95–96.

Bibliography

Archival Sources

Archives and Special Collections, New Mexico State University, Las Cruces

Albert B. Fall Collection (microfilm)

Albert Bacon Fall Family Papers

Archives Division, Texas State Library, Austin

Adjutant General's Correspondence

José Antonio Arce et al., Appelants, v. State of Texas, no. 4314, Texas Court of Criminal Appeals

"Proceedings of the Joint Committee of the Senate and House in the Investigation of the Texas State Ranger Force," 3 vols., 1919

State of Texas v. José Antonio Arce et al., no. 5209, District Court, Laredo, Texas

State of Texas v. Norberto Pezzar [*sic*] et al., no 5204, District Court, Laredo, Texas

British National Archives (formerly the Public Record Office), Kew, England

Foreign Office

Centro de Estudios Históricos Carso (formerly Condumex), México, D.F.

Venustiano Carranza Archive

Federal Records Center, East Point, Georgia

Mixed Claims Commission, United States and Germany: War Department Record of the Court Martial of Lothar Witzke

Federal Records Center, Fort Worth, Texas

Judge's Bench Docket, Criminal Cases, vols. 6 and 7, U.S. District Court, Brownsville, Texas

U.S. v. Abel Sandoval et al., no. 309, U.S. Commissioner, Brownsville, Texas

U.S. v. Basilio Ramos et al., no. 249, U.S. Commissioner, Brownsville, Texas

U.S. v. Basilio Ramos, Jr., et al, no. 2152, District Court, Brownsville, Texas

U.S. v. Felipe Sandoval et al., no. 2208, U.S. District Court, Brownsville, Texas

U.S. v. Francisco Alvarez Tostado, no. 419, U.S. Commissioner, San Antonio, Texas

U.S. v. Miguel Saiz, no. 2178, U.S. District Court, Brownsville, Texas
U.S. v. Miguel Saiz, no. 268, U.S. Commissioner, Brownsville, Texas
Library of Congress, Washington DC
Tasker H. Bliss Papers
Frank R. McCoy Papers
National Archives and Records Service, Washington DC, and College Park, Maryland
Department of State, Foreign Service Post Records, U.S. Consulate, Matamoros, Mexico, 1915–1917, RG 84
Department of State, Office of the Counselor, RG 59
Records of the Adjutant General's Office, RG 94
Records of the Department of State, Decimal Files, Internal Affairs of Mexico, 1910–1929. National Archives Microfilm Publication, Microcopy no. 274, RG 59
Records of the Department of State Relating to the Internal Affairs of Germany, 1910–1929. National Archives Microfilm Publication, Microcopy no. 336, file no. 862.20212—Military Affairs of Germany in Mexico
Records of the Federal Bureau of Investigation: Investigative Case Files of the Bureau of Investigation, 1908–1922 (microfilm), RG 65
Records of the Military Intelligence Division, RG 165
Records of the U.S. Secret Service, Daily Reports of Agents, 1875–1936, vol. 12, Daily Reports from San Antonio, Texas, microcopy no. 3.158, RG 87
Nettie Lee Benson Latin American Collection, University of Texas at Austin
William Buckley Papers
Pablo González Archive (microfilm)
Records of the Office of the Adjutant General. Correspondence Relating to the Mexican Border, file no. 237762-2378529, microcopy no. 1557
Haley Memorial Library and History Center, Midland, Texas
J. Evetts Haley interview with Frank Hamer
Kansas State Historical Society, Topeka
Frederick Funston Collection (microfilm)
Museum of South Texas History, Edinburg
Agustín S. Garza Collection
U.S. Army Intelligence Center and School, Fort Huachuca, Arizona
"Memoirs" of Major General Ralph H. Van Deman

Published Sources

Acuña, Rodolfo. *Occupied America: A History of Chicanos*. New York: Longman, 2000.

———. *Occupied America: The Chicano's Struggle toward Liberation*. San Francisco: Canfield Press, 1972.

Ayala Villarreal, Jacobo. "The Maderist and Constitutionalist Revolutions in Mexico (1910–1915)." Master's thesis, Texas A&I College, 1943.

Bacevich, A. J. *Diplomat in Khaki: Major General Frank Ross McCoy and American Foreign Policy, 1898–1949*. Lawrence: University Press of Kansas, 1989.

Bartra, Armando, ed. *Regeneración 1900–1918: La corriente más radical de la revolución de 1910 a través de su periódico de combate*. México, D.F.: Hadise, 1972.

Bratcher, James T. "Plan de San Diego as the Name of Border Raids in South Texas in 1915–1916: A Possible Second Meaning." *Journal of South Texas* 21, no. 1 (Spring 2008): 1–9.

Bruscino, Thomas, Jr. "A Troubled Past: The Army and Security on the Mexican Border, 1915–1917." *Military Review* 88, no. 4 (July–August 2008): 31–44.

"Casa Blanca, San Diego, Texas." *El Mesteño* 2, no. 23 (August 1999): 4.

Claridge, Duane R. *A Spy for All Seasons: My Life in the CIA*. New York: Scribners, 1997.

Clendenen, Clarence C. *Blood on the Border: The United States Army and the Mexican Irregulars*. New York: Macmillan, 1969.

Coerver, Don M., and Linda B. Hall. *Texas and the Mexican Revolution: A Study in State and National Border Policy, 1910–1920*. San Antonio: Trinity University Press, 1984.

Crile, George. *Charlie Wilson's War*. New York: Grove Press, 2003.

Cumberland, Charles C. "Border Raids in the Lower Rio Grande Valley—1915." *Southwestern Historical Quarterly* 57, no. 3 (January 1954): 285–311.

———. *Mexican Revolution: The Constitutionalist Years*. Austin: University of Texas Press, 1972.

de la Garza Treviño, Ciro. *Historia de Tamaulipas (anales y efemérides)*. 2nd ed. N.p., 1956.

———. *Plan de San Diego*. Ciudad Victoria: Universidad Autónoma de Tamaulipas, 1960.

de la Huerta, Adolfo. *Memorias de Don Adolfo de la Huerta según su propio dictado*. México, D.F.: Ediciones Guzmán, 1957.

Diccionario Porrúa: Historia, Biografía y Geografía de México. 2nd ed. México, D.F.: Editorial Porrúa, 1964.

Fabela, Isidro, et al., eds. *Documentos Históricos de la Revolución Mexicana*. 28 vols. México, D.F.: Editorial Jus, 1964–76.

Fehrenbach, T. R. *Lone Star: A History of Texas and Texans*. New York: Macmillan, 1968.

"Fighting on the Mexican Border." *Outlook*, September 15, 1915: 105–6.

Furman, Necah S. "Vida Nueva: A Reflection of Villista Diplomacy, 1914–1915." *New Mexico Historical Review* 53, no. 2 (April 1978): 171–92.

General Emiliano Nafarrate. http://www.mexico-tenoch.com/diputadosconstituyentes.htm.

Gerlach, Allen, "Conditions along the Border—1915: The Plan de San Diego." *New Mexico Historical Review* 43, no. 2 (July 1968): 195–212.

Gómez Quiñones, Juan. "Plan de San Diego Reviewed." *Aztlán* 1 (Spring 1970): 124–32.

Gonzales, Trinidad. "The Mexican Revolution, *Revolución de Texas* and *Matanza de 1915*." In *War along the Border: The Mexican Revolution and Tejano Communities*, ed. Arnaldo de León, 105–33. College Station: Texas A&M University Press, 2012.

Goodrich, Pat Hill. *Captain Ransom, Texas Ranger: An American Hero (1894–1918)*. Nappanee IN: Evangel Publishing House, 2007.

Grieb, Kenneth J. *The United States and Huerta*. Lincoln: University of Nebraska Press, 1969.

Hager, William M. "The Plan of San Diego: Unrest on the Texas Border in 1915." *Arizona and the West* 5, no. 4 (Winter 1963): 327–36.

Harris, Charles H., III, and Louis R. Sadler. "The 1911 Reyes Conspiracy: The Texas Side." *Southwestern Historical Quarterly* 83, no. 4 (April 1980): 325–48.

———. "The Plan of San Diego and the Mexican–United States War Crisis of 1916: A Reexamination." *Hispanic American Historical Review* 58, no. 3 (August 1978): 381–408.

———. *The Secret War in El Paso: Mexican Revolutionary Intrigue, 1906–1920*. Albuquerque: University of New Mexico Press, 2009.

———. *The Texas Rangers and the Mexican Revolution: The Bloodiest Decade, 1910–1920*. Albuquerque: University of New Mexico Press, 2004.

———. "The Witzke Affair: German Intrigue on the Mexican Border, 1917–18." *Military Review* 59, no. 2 (February 1979): 36–50.

Harris, Charles H., III, Frances E. Harris, and Louis R. Sadler. *Texas Ranger Biographies: Those Who Served, 1910–1921*. Albuquerque: University of New Mexico Press, 2009.

Horne, Gerald. *Black and Brown: African Americans and the Mexican Revolution, 1910–1920*. New York and London: New York University Press, 2005.

Johnson, Benjamin Heber. *Revolution in Texas: How a Forgotten Rebellion and Its Bloody Suppression Turned Mexicans into Americans*. New Haven: Yale University Press, 2003.

———. "Unearthing the Hidden Histories of a Borderlands Rebellion." *Journal of South Texas* 24, no. 1 (Spring 2011): 6–19.

Katz, Friedrich, "Alemania y Francisco Villa." *Historia Mexicana* 12 (July–September 1962): 88–103.

———. *The Life and Times of Pancho Villa*. Stanford: Stanford University Press, 1998.

Knight, Alan. *The Mexican Revolution*. 2 vols. Lincoln: University of Nebraska Press, 1990.

Link, Arthur S., ed. *The Papers of Woodrow Wilson*. Vol. 37. Princeton: Princeton University Press, 1981.

Longoria, Mario D. "Revolution, Visionary Plan, and Marketplace: A San Antonio Incident." *Aztlán* 12, no. 2 (1982): 211–26.

Lynch, Dudley. *The Duke of Duval: The Life and Times of George B. Parr*. Waco: Texian Press, 1976.

Machado, Manuel A., and James T. Judge. "Tempest in a Teapot? The Mexican–United States Intervention Crisis of 1919." *Southwestern Historical Quarterly* 74 (July 1970): 1–23.

Marvin, George. "Bandits and the Borderland." *World's Work* 32 (October 1916): 656–63.

———. "The Quick and the Dead on the Border." *World's Work* 33 (January 1917): 295–302.

Mendoza, Robert. "The Lonesome Death of Jesse Moseley, Laredo 1916." *LareDos*, February 5, 2008, 1–2.

———. "Perspectives." *LareDos*, February 5, 2008, 2–3.

Meyer, Michael C. *Huerta: A Political Portrait*. Lincoln: University of Nebraska Press, 1972.

———. "The Mexican-German Conspiracy of 1915." *The Americas* 23, no. 1 (July 1966): 76–89.

Moguel Flores, Josefina. *75 Aniversario Luctuoso de Don Venustiano Carranza.* Saltillo: Gobierno del Estado de Coahuila, 1995.

Montejano, David. *Anglos and Mexicans in the Making of Texas, 1836–1986*. Austin: University of Texas Press, 1987.

Morey, Lewis. "The Cavalry Fight at Carrizal." *Cavalry Journal* 32 (January 1917): 449–56.

Munch, Francis J. "Villa's Columbus Raid: Practical Politics or German Design?" *New Mexico Historical Review* 44 (July 1969): 189–214.

Naranjo, Francisco. *Diccionario Biográfico Revolucionario*. 2nd ed. México, D.F.: Instituto Nacional de Estudios Históricos de la Revolución Mexicana, 1985.

Navarrette, Ruben, Jr. E-mail to Louis R. Sadler. November 16, 2010.

Orozco, Cynthia E. *No Mexicans, Women, or Dogs Allowed: The Rise of the Mexican American Civil Rights Movement*. Austin: University of Texas Press, 2009.

Paredes, Américo. *With His Pistol in His Hand: A Border Ballad and Its Hero.* Austin: University of Texas Press, 1958.

———. *A Texas-Mexican Cancionero: Folksongs of the Lower Border*. Urbana: University of Illinois Press, 1976.

Pierce, Frank Cushman. *A Brief History of the Lower Rio Grande Valley.* Menasha WI: George Banta Publishing Co., 1917.

Procter, Ben. *Just One Riot: Episodes of Texas Rangers in the 20th Century*. Austin: Eakin Press, 1991.

Raat, Dirk. *Revoltosos: Mexico's Rebels in the United States, 1903–1923*. College Station: Texas A&M University Press, 1981.

Rausch, George, Jr. "The Exile and Death of Victoriano Huerta." *Hispanic American Historical Review* 42, no. 2 (May 1962): 133–51.

Ribb, Richard Henry. "José Tomás Canales and the Texas Rangers: Myth, Identity, and Power in South Texas, 1900–1920." PhD diss., University of Texas at Austin, 2001.

Richkarday, Ignacio A. *Jack Danciger: Su vida y su obra*. México, D.F.: Imp. M. León Sánchez, 1961.

Richmond, Douglas W. "La Guerra de Texas se renova: Mexican Insurrection and Carrancista Ambitions, 1900-1920." *Aztlán* 2, no. 1 (Spring 1980): 1–32.

———. *Venustiano Carranza's Nationalist Struggle, 1893–1920*. Lincoln: University of Nebraska Press, 1983.

———. "The Venustiano Carranza Archive." *Hispanic American Historical Review* 56, no. 2 (May 1976): 290–94.

Rocha, Rodolfo. "The Influence of the Mexican Revolution on the Mexico-Texas Border, 1910–1916." PhD diss., Texas Tech University, 1981.

———. "The Tejano Revolt of 1915." In *Mexican Americans in Texas History: Selected Essays*, ed. Emilio Zamora, Cynthia Orozco, and Rodolfo Rocha, 103–19. Austin: Texas State Historical Association, 2000.

Rosenbaum, Robert J. *Mexicano Resistance in the Southwest: The Sacred Right of Self-Preservation*. Austin: University of Texas Press, 1981.

Ruiz, Ramon Eduardo. "The Centro de Estudios de la Historia de México, Condumex." In *Research in Mexican History: Topics, Methodology, Sources, and a Practical Guide to Field Research*, ed. Richard E. Greenleaf and Michael C. Meyer, 95–96. Lincoln: University of Nebraska Press, 1973.

Salinas de la Rosa, Violeta H. E-mail to Louis R. Sadler. October 1, 2010.

Samora, Julián, Joe Bernal, and Albert Peña. *Gunpowder Justice: A Reassessment of the Texas Rangers*. Notre Dame: University of Notre Dame Press, 1979.

Sandos, James A. "German Involvement in Northern Mexico, 1915–1916: A New Look at the Columbus Raid." *Hispanic American Historical Review* 50 (February 1970): 70–88.

———. "The Mexican Revolution and the United States, 1915–1917: The Impact of Conflict in the Tamaulipas-Texas Frontier Upon the Emergence of Revolutionary Government in Mexico." PhD diss., University of California at Berkeley, 1978.

———. "Pancho Villa and American Security: Woodrow Wilson's Mexican Diplomacy Reconsidered." *Journal of Latin American Studies* 13, no. 2 (November 1981): 304–11.

———. "The Plan of San Diego: War and Diplomacy on the Texas Border, 1915–1916." *Arizona and the West* 14 (Spring 1972): 5–24.

———. *Rebellion in the Borderlands: Anarchism and the Plan of San Diego, 1904–1923*. Norman: University of Oklahoma Press, 1992.

Scarborough, Gerald. E-mail to Louis R. Sadler. March 14, 2011.

Smith, Michael M. "Carrancista Propaganda and the Print Media in the United States: An Overview of Institutions." *The Americas* 52, no. 2 (October 1995): 155–74.

———. "Gringo Propagandist: George F. Weeks and the Mexican Revolution." *Journalism History* 29, no. 1 (Spring 2003): 2–11.

———. "The Mexican Immigrant Press beyond the Borderlands: The Case of *El Cosmopolita*, 1914–1919." *Great Plains Quarterly* 10 (Spring 1990): 71–85.

———. "The Mexican Revolution in Kansas City: Jack Danciger versus the Colonia

Elite." *Kansas History* 14, no. 3 (Autumn 1991): 206–26.

Sterling, William Warren. *Trails and Trials of a Texas Ranger*. Norman: University of Oklahoma Press, 1959.

Stout, Joseph A., Jr. *Border Conflict: Villistas, Carrancistas and the Punitive Expedition, 1915–1920*. Fort Worth: Texas Christian University Press, 1999.

Swenson, Ann Marie, trans. *Jack Danciger: His Life and Work*. N.p.: self-published, 1963.

Theoharis, Athan G., with Tony G. Poveda, Susan Rosenfeld, and Richard Gid Powers, eds. *The FBI: A Comprehensive Reference Guide*. New York: Checkmark Books, 2000.

Tuchman, Barbara. *The Zimmermann Telegram*. New York: Viking, 1958.

Tyler, Ron, et al., eds. *The New Handbook of Texas*. 6 vols. Austin: Texas State Historical Association, 1996.

United States. *Eleventh Annual Report of the American Red Cross for the Year 1915*. 64th Cong., 1st sess., Document no. 1307, Washington DC: Government Printing Office, 1916.

———. *Investigation of Mexican Affairs, Report and Hearing before a Subcommittee on Foreign Relations*. Senate Document 285, 66th Cong, 2nd sess., Serial 7665, 2 vols. Washington DC: Government Printing Office, 1920.

U.S. Federal Census, 1910 and 1920. http://www.ancestry.com/.

Utley, Robert. *Lone Star Lawmen: The Second Century of the Texas Rangers*. New York: Oxford University Press, 2007.

Vanderwood, Paul J., and Frank N. Samponaro. *Border Fury: A Picture Postcard Record of Mexico's Revolution and U.S. War Preparedness, 1910–1917*. Albuquerque: University of New Mexico Press, 1988.

Vasconcelos, José. *La Tormenta*. 7th ed. México, D.F.: A. Mijares y Hno., 1948.

Warburton, L. H. "The Plan of San Diego: Background and Selected Documents." *Journal of South Texas* 12, no. 1 (1999): 125–55.

Webb, Walter Prescott. *The Texas Rangers: A Century of Frontier Defense*. 2nd ed. Austin: University of Texas Press, 1965.

Young, Elliott. *Catarino Garza's Revolution on the Texas-Mexico Border*. Durham: Duke University Press, 2004.

Index

In The Mexican Experience series

Mexicans in Revolution, 1910–1946: An Introduction
William H. Beezley and Colin M. MacLachlan

Celebrating Insurrection: The Commemoration and Representation of the Nineteenth-Century Mexican "Pronunciamiento"
Edited and with an introduction by Will Fowler

Forceful Negotiations: The Origins of the "Pronunciamiento" in Nineteenth-Century Mexico
Edited and with an introduction by Will Fowler

Malcontents, Rebels, and "Pronunciados": The Politics of Insurrection in Nineteenth-Century Mexico
Edited and with an introduction by Will Fowler

Working Women, Entrepreneurs, and the Mexican Revolution: The Coffee Culture of Córdoba, Veracruz
Heather Fowler-Salamini

"Muy buenas noches": Mexico, Television, and the Cold War
Celeste González de Bustamante
Foreword by Richard Cole

The Plan de San Diego: Tejano Rebellion, Mexican Intrigue
Charles H. Harris III and Louis R. Sadler

Gender and the Negotiation of Daily Life in Mexico, 1750–1856
Sonya Lipsett-Rivera

Mexico's Crucial Century, 1810–1910: An Introduction
Colin M. MacLachlan and William H. Beezley

¡México, la patria! Propaganda and Production during World War II
Monica A. Rankin

Pistoleros and Popular Movements: The Politics of State Formation in Postrevolutionary Oaxaca
Benjamin T. Smith

To order or obtain more information on these or other University of Nebraska Press titles, visit www.nebraskapress.unl.edu.

www.ingramcontent.com/pod-product-compliance
Lightning Source LLC
Chambersburg PA
CBHW021807270326
41932CB00007B/89
9780803264779